30 West Monroe Suite 400 Chicago IL 60603 T 312 920 1888 F 312 920 1775 smithgill.com

ORO Editions
Publishers of Architecture, Art, and Design
Gordon Goff: Publisher

www.oroeditions.com
info@oroeditions.com

Published by ORO Editions

FOLLOW ONLINE
smithgill.com
smithgill.blog
Facebook @smithgillarch
Instagram @asggarch
Twitter @smithgillarch
WeChat: ASGG_Architecture

10 9 8 7 6 5 4 3 2 1 First Edition

ISBN: 978-1-954081-37-6

Color Separations and Printing: ORO Group Ltd.

Printed in China.

ORO Editions makes a continuous effort to minimize the overall carbon footprint of its publications. As part of this goal, ORO Editions, in association with Global ReLeaf, arranges to plant trees to replace those used in the manufacturing of the paper produced for its books. Global ReLeaf is an international campaign run by American Forests, one of the world's oldest nonprofit conservation organizations. Global ReLeaf is American Forests' education and action program that helps individuals, organizations, agencies, and corporations improve the local and global environment by planting and caring for trees.

Table of Contents

Philosophy

Adrian Smith + Gordon Gill Architecture is dedicated to the design of high-performance, energy-efficient, and sustainable architecture on an international scale. The firm approaches each project, regardless of size or scale, with an understanding that architecture has a unique power to influence civic life. We strive to create designs that aid society, advance modern technology, sustain the environment and inspire those around us to improve our world.

Our office is dedicated to the creation of new paradigms for sustainable development. We use a holistic, integrated design approach that emphasizes symbiotic relationship with the natural environment—a philosophy we've termed "global environmental contextualism." We also specialize in the design of high-performance supertall towers.

This approach, which takes into consideration building orientation, daylighting, generation of wind power, solar absorption and a site's geothermal properties, represents a fundamental change in the design process, in which form follows performance. It is predicated on the understanding that everything within the built and natural environment is connected, and that a building's design should stem from an understanding of its role within that context—locally, regionally, and globally.

Such a pluralistic approach acknowledges the interaction among building systems as well as between those systems and the natural environment, and seeks to improve each individual system's performance. By using this principle in the design of buildings, we can create structures that significantly reduce their environmental impact.

AS+GG's practice includes designers with extensive experience in multiple disciplines, including technical architecture, interior design, urban planning and sustainable design. Architects also have expertise in a range of building types, including supertall towers, large-scale mixed-use complexes, corporate offices, exhibition facilities, cultural facilities and museums, civic and public spaces, hotels and residential complexes, institutional projects and high-tech laboratory facilities.

The firm was founded in 2006 by partners Adrian Smith, Gordon Gill, and Robert Forest. For more information, please visit smithgill.com. AS+GG is currently working on projects in the United States, Canada, the United Arab Emirates, Saudi Arabia, and China.

Vision

We believe that architecture has the unique power to influence our world. As architects, we recognize and respect our role in shaping civic life.

We strive to create designs that aid society, advance modern technology, sustain the environment, and inspire those around us to improve our world.

We are dedicated to the creation of intelligent, high-performance, forward-thinking designs that exhibit timeless and enduring qualities.

We believe that the future of architecture relies not on a changing aesthetic but on an integrated design process that gives equal consideration to each discipline.

We support our clients in the realization of their visions while delivering the highest standard of design in the international practice of architecture.

We are not limited by known solutions. We utilize our experience and knowledge to move forward and develop new methods and technologies.

We foster a challenging and rewarding workspace. We understand that the encouragement and development of each member of our staff will advance the practice of architecture.

We seek out collaborations with the world's leading experts: scientists, artists, sociologists, philosophers, and thinkers.

We strive to expand our perspective and generate new discoveries and insights into the world of design.

We believe that the future lies in an integrated relationship between nature and technology in order to improve our built environments.

Select Projects

Jeddah Tower

Jeddah, Saudi Arabia

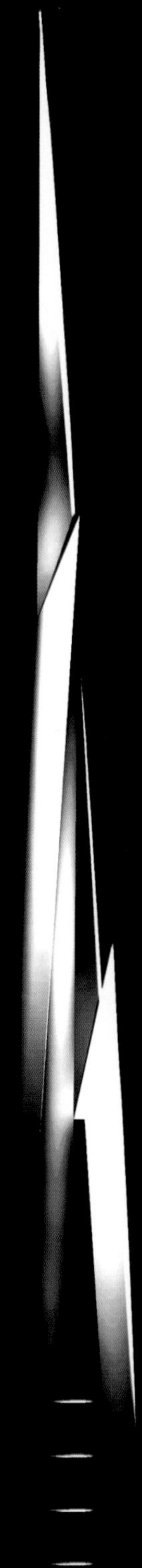

Jeddah Tower

Jeddah, Saudi Arabia

At over 1,000 meters and a total construction area of 530,000 sm, Jeddah Tower will be the centerpiece and first construction phase of the $20 billion Kingdom City development in Jeddah, Saudi Arabia, near the Red Sea.

SERVICES
Architecture
Interior Design
Master Planning

CLIENT
Jeddah Economic Company

FUNCTION
Mixed-use

FACTS
1000+ m height
530,000 sm area

AWARDS
Middle East AIA, Merit Award, Non-Built Projects, 2014

AS+GG's design for Jeddah Tower is both highly technological and distinctly organic. With its slender, subtly asymmetrical massing, the tower evokes a bundle of leaves shooting up from the ground—a burst of new life that heralds growth around it. The tower is a symbol of and a catalyst for the increased surrounding development.

The tower's sleek, streamlined form can also be interpreted as a reference to the folded fronds of young desert plants. The way the stalks sprout upward from the ground as a single form, then start separating from each other at the top, is an analogy of new growth fused with technology.

While the design is contextual to Saudi Arabia, it also represents an evolution and a refinement of an architectural continuum of skyscraper design. The three-petal footprint is ideal for residential units, and the tapering wings produce an aerodynamic shape that helps reduce structural loading due to wind vortex shedding. Jeddah Tower's design embraces its architectural pedigree, taking full advantage of the proven design strategies and technological strategies of its lineage, refining and advancing them to achieve new heights.

The result is an elegant, cost-efficient and highly constructible design that is at once grounded in built tradition and aggressively forward-looking, taking advantage of new and innovative thinking about technology, building materials, life-cycle considerations, and energy conservation. For example, the project will feature a high-performance exterior wall system that will minimize energy consumption by reducing thermal loads. In addition, each of Jeddah Tower's three sides features a series of notches that create pockets of shadow that shield areas of the building from the sun and provide outdoor terraces with stunning views of Jeddah and the Red Sea.

The great height of Jeddah Tower necessitates one of the world's most sophisticated elevator systems. The Jeddah Tower complex will contain 59 elevators, including 54 single-deck and five double-deck elevators, along with 12 escalators. Elevators serving the observatory will travel at a rate of 10 meters per second in both directions. Another unique feature of the design is a sky terrace, roughly 30 meters in diameter, at level 157, which when completed will be the highest observatory in the world.

ADRIAN SMITH + GORDON GILL
ARCHITECTURE

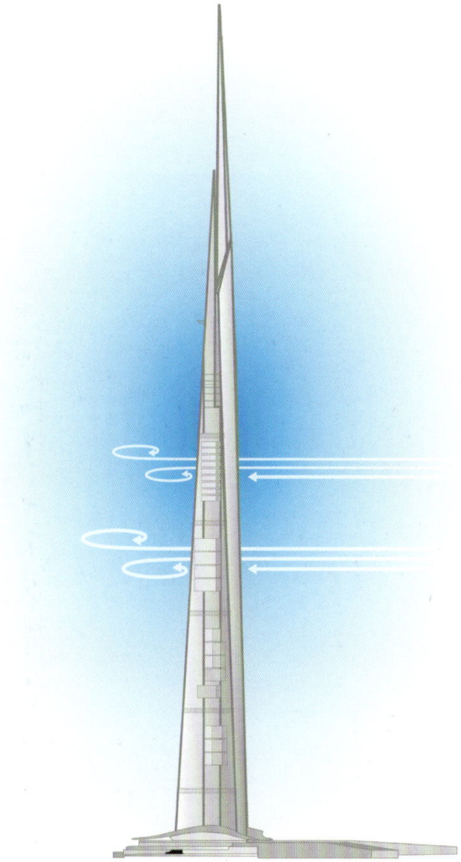

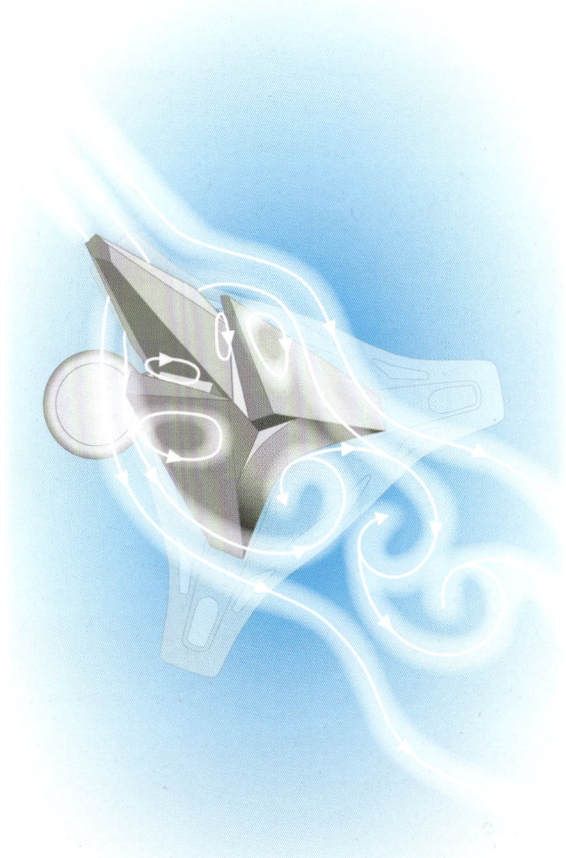

AERODYNAMIC STRATEGIES

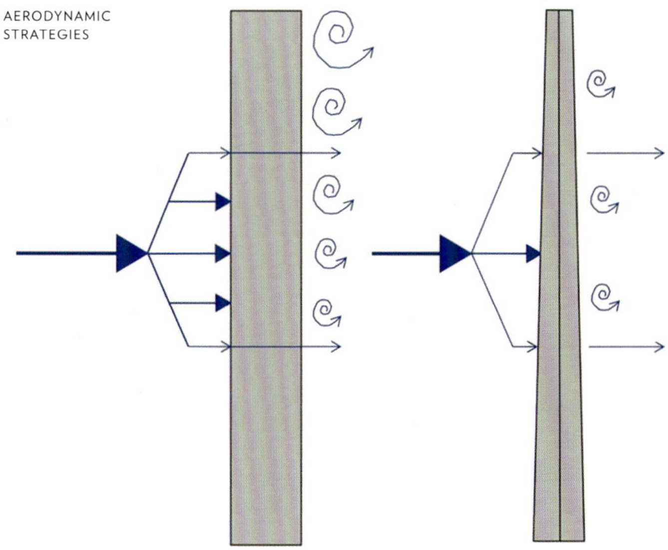

PRISMATIC RECTANGULAR BUILDING

TOWER EXTERIOR TAPERING

As wind loads are generally proportional to a square of the wind speed, a significant increase in wind loads was required to meet the intent of the local Standard Building Code (SBC) and all structural designs for strength of the tower were conservatively carried out for wind loads derived from this higher wind speed.

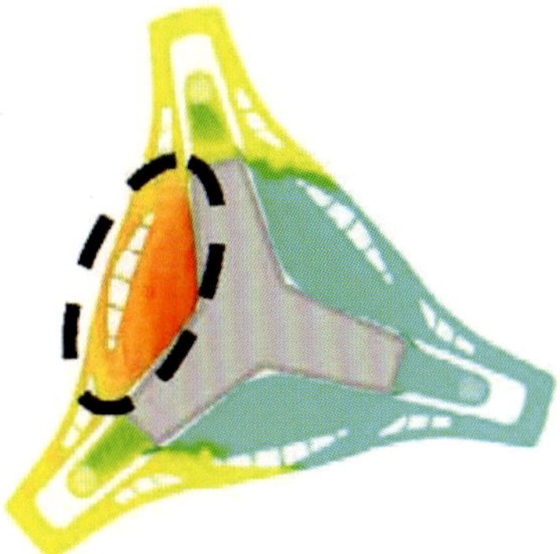

NORTHWEST CANOPY
132°C
MAY 28: 17:00

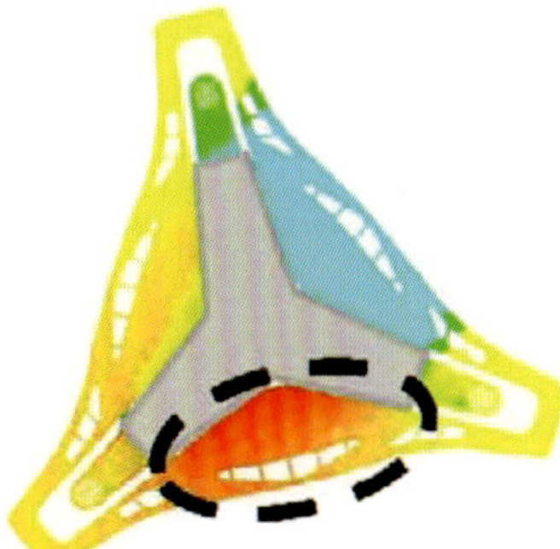

SOUTH CANOPY
134°C
MAY 15: 15:00

NORTHEAST CANOPY
117°C
MAY 28: 11:00

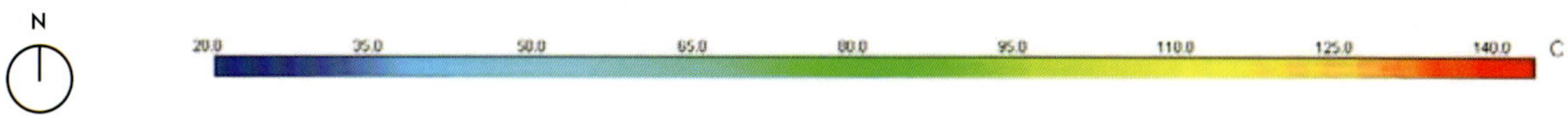

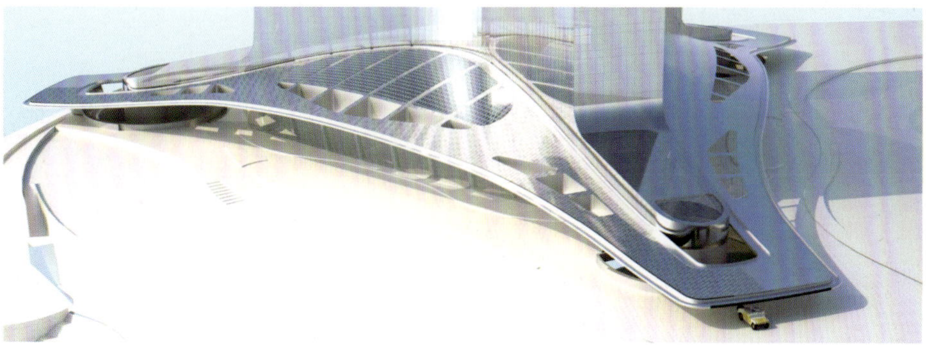

Studies and analysis of the entrance canopy determined the cumulative effects of dynamic transitory solar radiation to anticipate the thermal loading effects. The investigation suggested impact on the south canopy at the base of the tower. We then factored this information into the final detailing of the lower canopies, to protect the temperature-sensitive roofing materials, gaskets, and sealants. We also assessed potential solutions to utilize concentrated solar energy utilizing renewable energy technologies, like solar hot water and solar photovoltaic electricity generation.

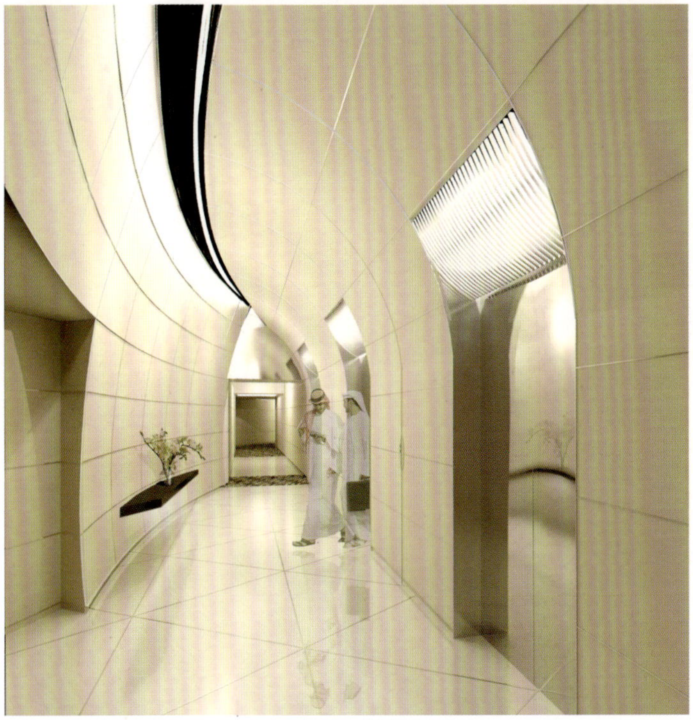

Central Park Tower

New York, New York

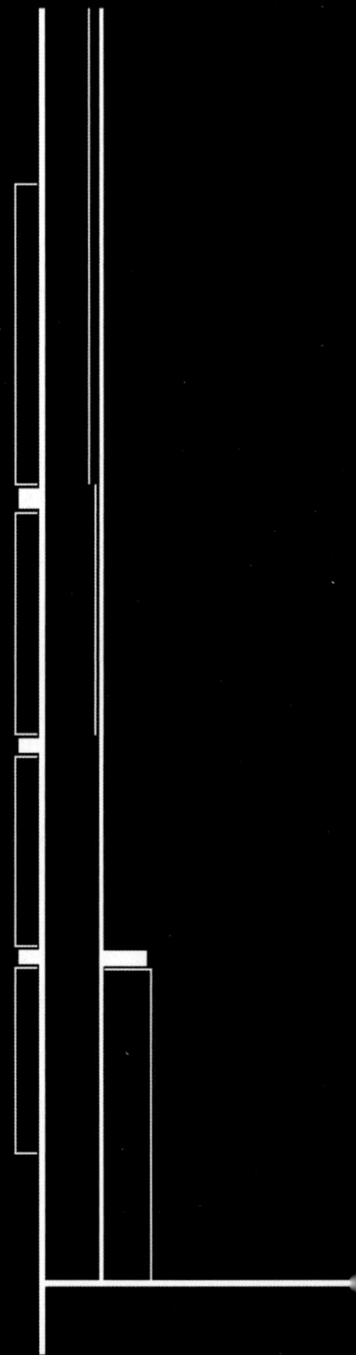

Central Park Tower

New York, New York

A beacon of glass and steel rising 1,550 feet on famed Billionaire's Row in New York City, Central Park Tower is one of the most prestigious addresses in the world. Completed in 2021, the tower offers endless views, exquisite architecture, gracious layouts, and an unprecedented level of service. Central Park Tower is the definitive New York skyscraper.

SERVICES
Architecture
Interior Design

CLIENT
Extell Development Company

FUNCTION
Mixed-use

FACTS
1,550 ft height

AWARDS
The Chicago Athenaeum, American Architecture Award, 2021

CTBUH Awards, Best Tall Building 400 meters and above Award of Excellence, 2021

Located on West 57th Street, New York City's most prestigious corridor, Central Park has exceptional views and floor plans. The grand living and entertaining spaces are strategically positioned in the corners of the residences to maximize multiple panoramas and citywide views. Structural elements are discreetly located between the residential units, resulting in floor-to-ceiling windows with unencumbered views and gracious layouts.

The interiors of the residences are designed by Rottet Studio, whose credits include The James Royal Palm in Miami Beach, and The Surrey Hotel in Manhattan. Starting 300 feet above the ground, the 179 ultra-luxury residences range from one-to-four bedrooms and consist of studio suites, and full floor, duplex, and triplex units.

The tower, which has been designated by the CTUBH as the tallest residential tower ever built, is home to one of the world's most exclusive private clubs. Central Park Club has approximately 50,000 square feet of thoroughly curated luxury accommodations spread across three floors, each location providing a unique experience complemented by five-star service. The first club level, located on the 14th floor, features a residents' lounge with billiards, screening, and function rooms. The centerpiece is 15,000-square-foot outdoor terrace with a 60-foot swimming pool, cabanas, bar, screening wall, food and beverage service, and an outdoor children's playground.

The health and wellness center on the 16th floor has a 63-foot indoor swimming pool, state-of-the art fitness center, half-court basketball court, squash court, sauna, steam and treatment rooms. The Club culminate on the 100th floor at an elevation of over 1,000 feet.

At the base of the tower is a new 300,000-square-foot, seven-story Nordstrom department store. After a 30-year search for the optimum site, the Seattle-based fashion retailer selected Central Park Tower as the location for its premier flagship story in New York City, the first in its over 100-year history.

ADRIAN SMITH + GORDON GILL
ARCHITECTURE

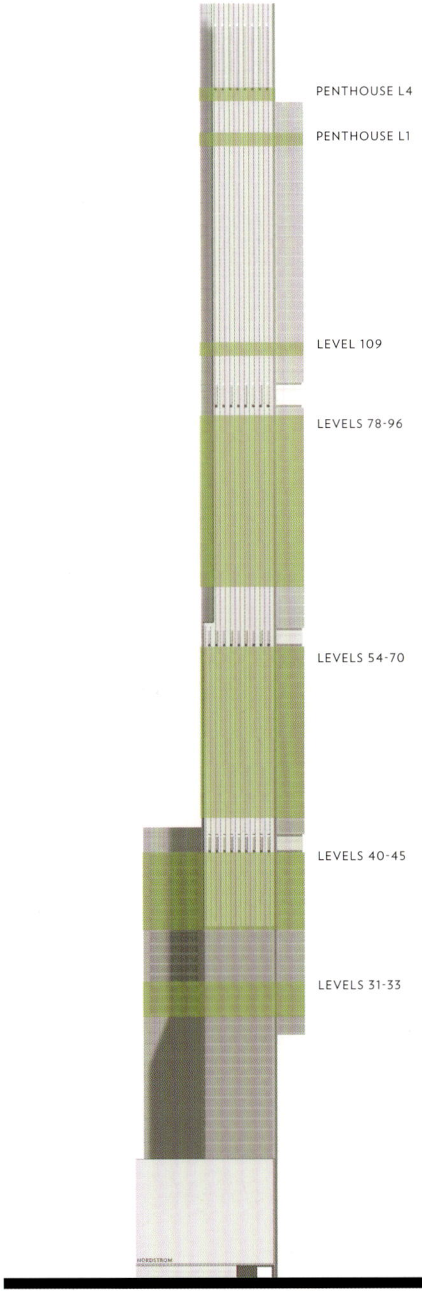

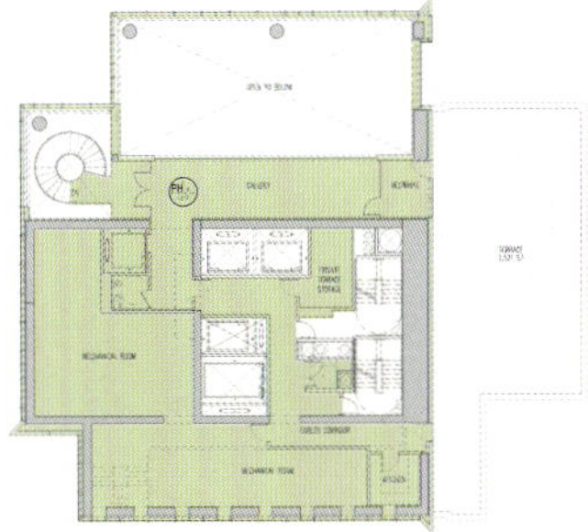

PENTHOUSE L4

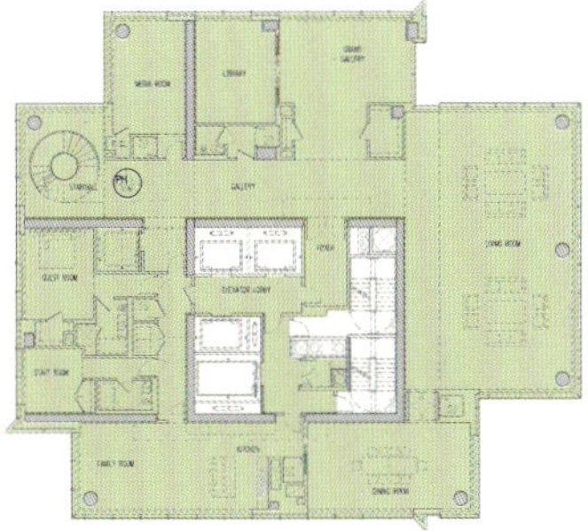

PENTHOUSE L1

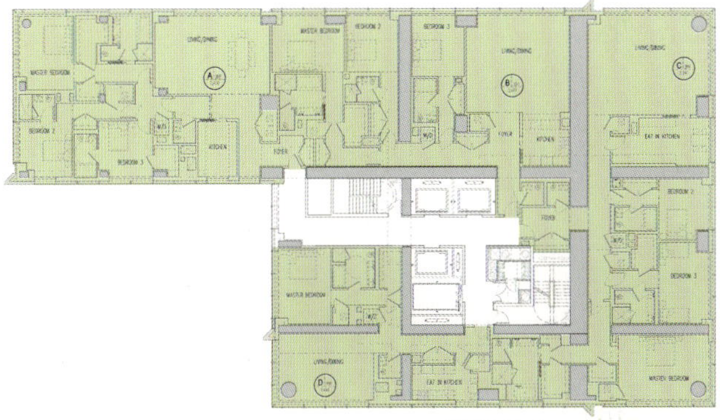

LEVELS 40-45

LEVELS 31-33

Snow and ice studies were performed to determine the best design for the super mullions. Snow build up in the winter was a major concern for this tall structure with regards to the protruding stainless-steel mullion fins and many shapes and sizes were explored to develop the best solution for minimum snow build up.

RWDI was engaged to do simulations in which the conditions of the site were simulated on a piece of the facade. This informed the design of the mullions, changing them from the original elongated oval to the ultimate design which was a rotated oval that was better able to shed ice and snow.

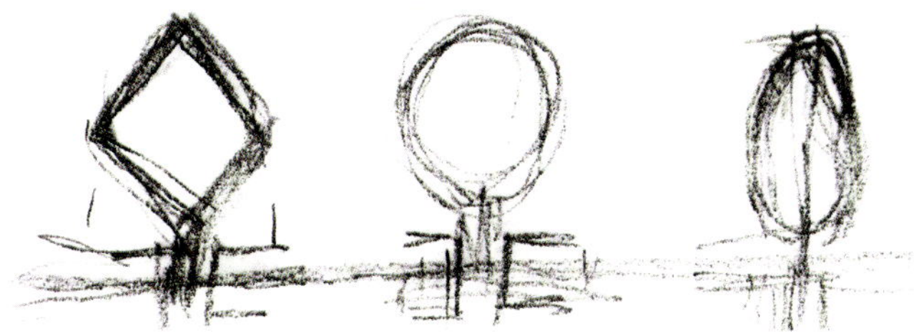

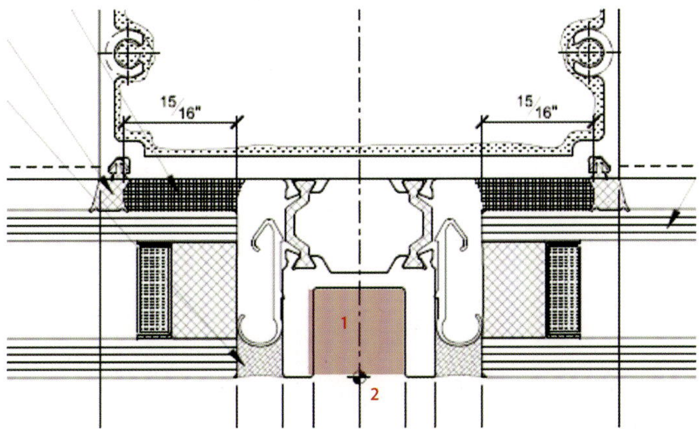

VERTICAL MULLION AT SPANDREL

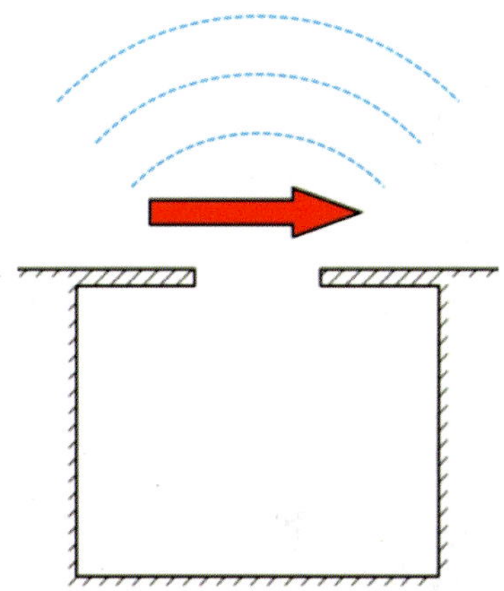

CAVITY RESONANCE DUE TO GRAZING FLOW

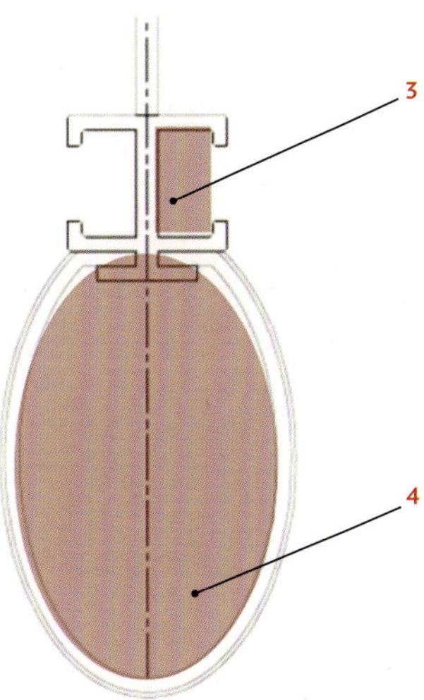

1. Facade Cavity
2. WP
3. Channel Slot
4. Hollow Tube Cavity

POTENTIAL CAVITIES IN SUPER-MULLIO

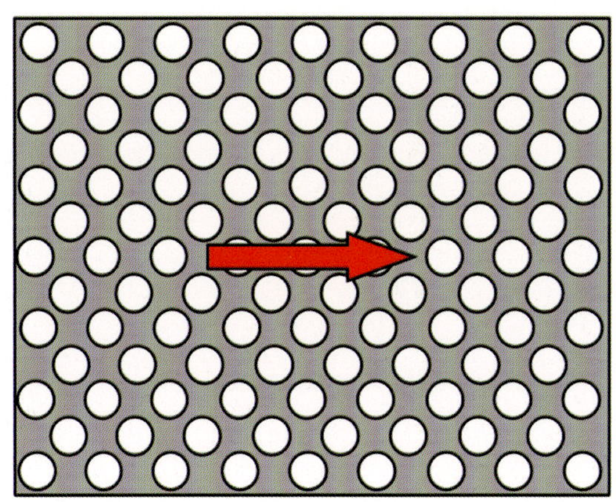

PERFORATED PLATE

Greenland Tower

Chengdu, China

Chengdu Greenland Tower

Chengdu, China

At 468 meters tall, AS+GG's design for Chengdu Greenland Tower is the southwestern China region's tallest building and the fourth-tallest in the nation.

SERVICES
Architecture

CLIENT
Greenland Group

FUNCTION
Mixed-Use

FACTS
468 m height

AWARDS
Architizer A+ Award, Unbuilt Category, Architecture + Technology, Finalist, 2014

Located at the center of Chengdu's booming Dongcun district, the design is inspired by the unique ice mountain topography around Chengdu, which symbolizes the city's growth and promising future. Like the mountain ridges that reflect the light of the sky and the valleys that reflect the light from the earth, the iconic tower performs as a light sculpture; diffuse light from 360 degrees and creating a connection between the sky and the earth.

The design for the complex—including the main tower, two small towers, and six-story podium, with a total building area of 395,305 sm—interprets and integrates Chengdu's urban structure, local culture, and Chinese traditional Feng Shui theory in a modern form. Its goal is to create a comfortable garden-city environment with convenient traffic patterns for vehicular, pedestrian, and metro transportation.

The architecture and structure marry perfectly. The design fully considers the structural requirements of supertall buildings in a high seismic zone by using a geometrical plan, a tapered form, and a high-performance damper bracing system to ensure the structure's stability and efficiency. The building facade, MEP and other systems are designed with high-efficiency sustainability features, creating a new generation of the high-performance supertall building.

The main tower consists of a 120,000 sm Class A office space in the lower zone, a 51,000 sm luxury hotel in the middle zone, and 42,000 sm of CEO suites in the high zone. Two small towers, at 116 m and 147 m, respectively, accommodate high-end SOHO apartments. The podium includes 14,000 sm of retail, a 16,000 sm conference center with bridge connection to the main tower, and an 8,000 sm exhibition center. There is also a roof garden with 360-degree views of the city.

SITE PLAN

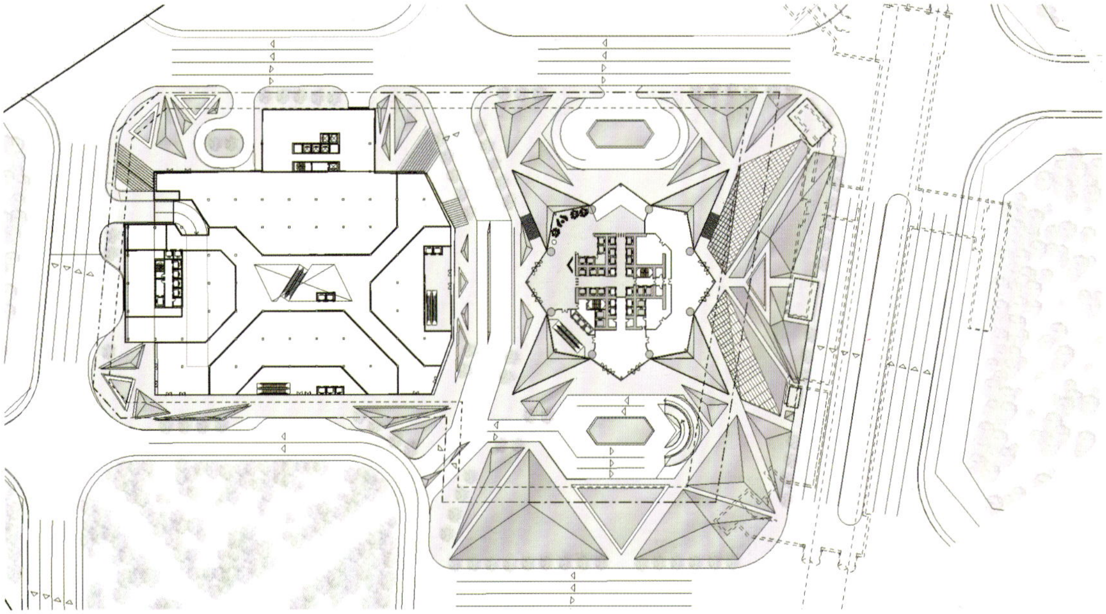

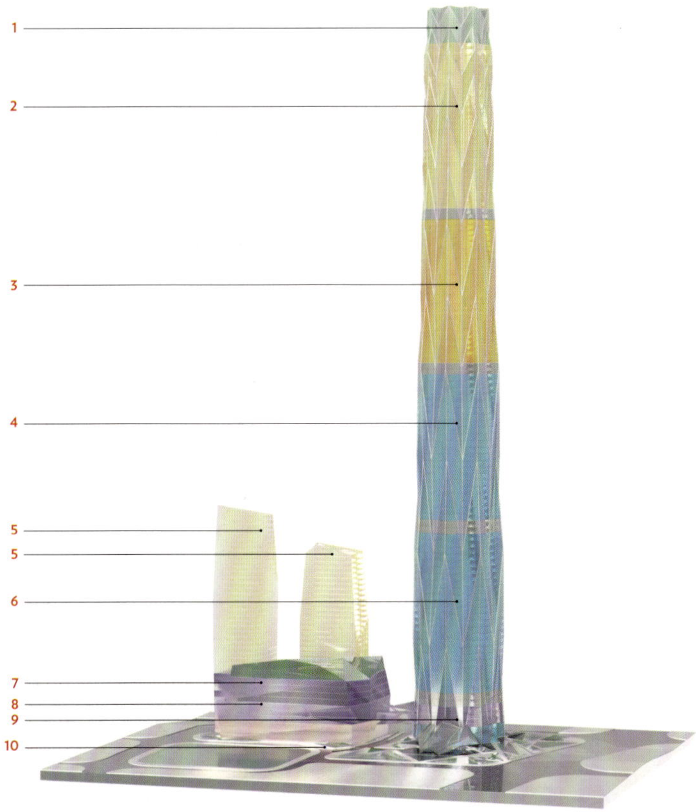

PROGRAM DIAGRAM

1. Roof Garden
2. CEO Residential (41,875 sm)
3. Hotel (51,166 sm)
4. Office (59,996 sm)
5. SOHO Apartments (58,708 sm)
6. Office (59,996 sm)
7. Exhibition (8,300 sm)
8. Conference (15,870 sm)
9. Retail (14,803 sm)

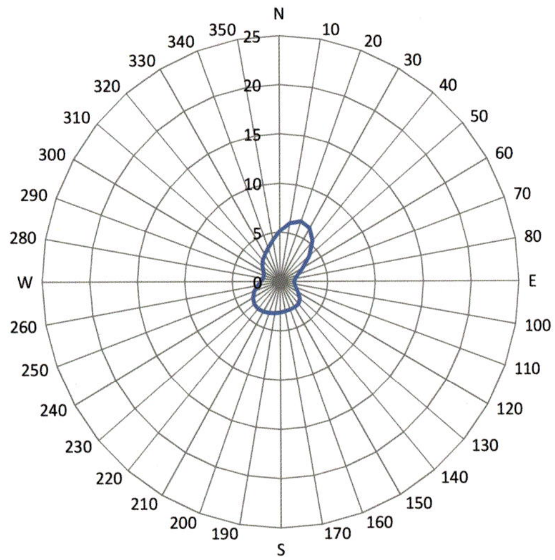

COMMON WINDS

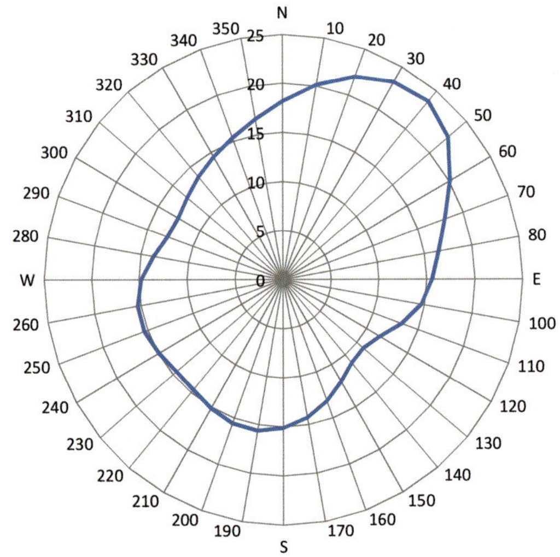

DESIGN WINDS

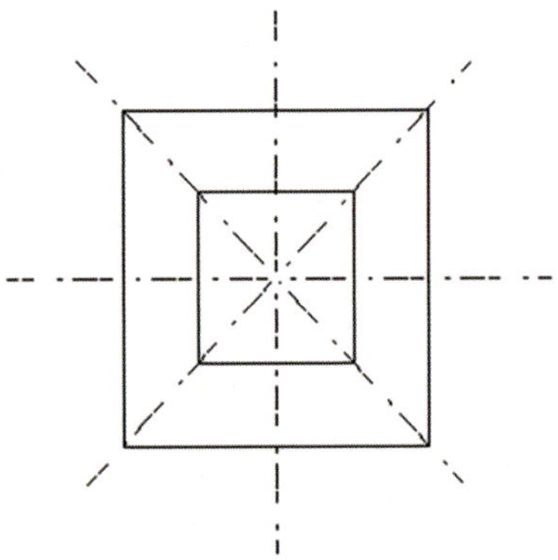

SQUARE PLAN

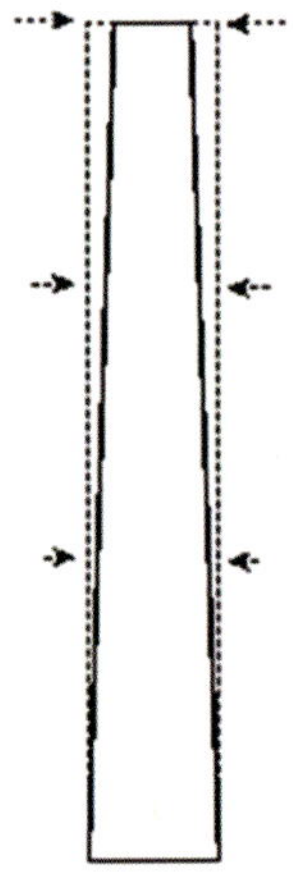

ELEVATION

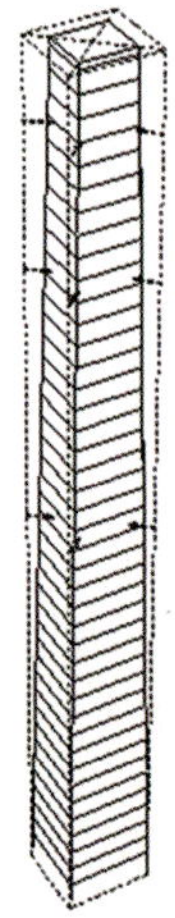

TAPERED FORM

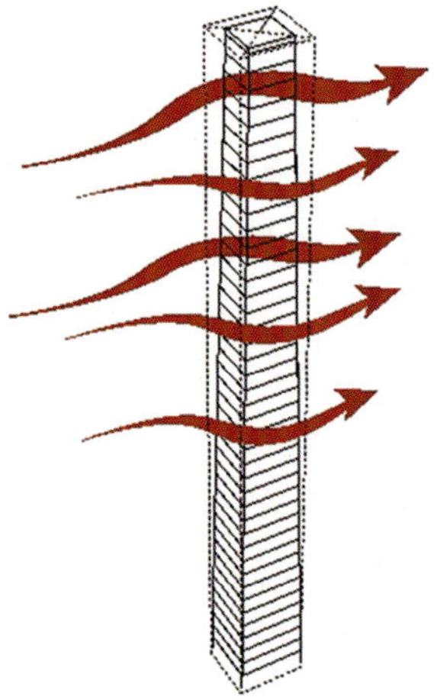

REDUCE WIND LOAD

WIND TUNNEL TESTING

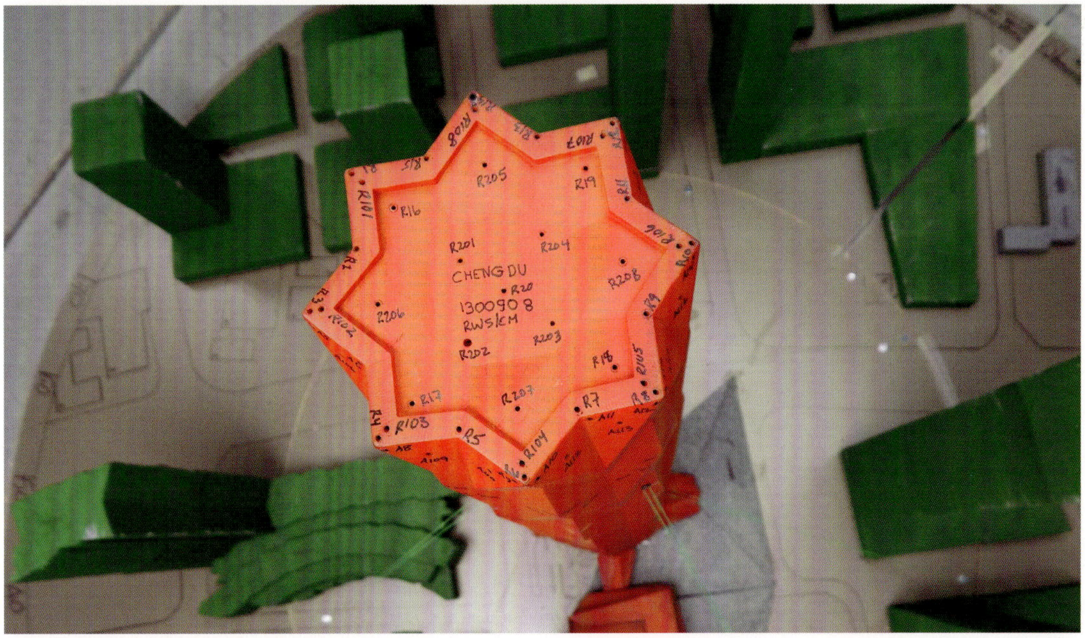

11
22
11
22

CONSTRUCTION, 2019

Wuhan Greenland Center

Wuhan, China

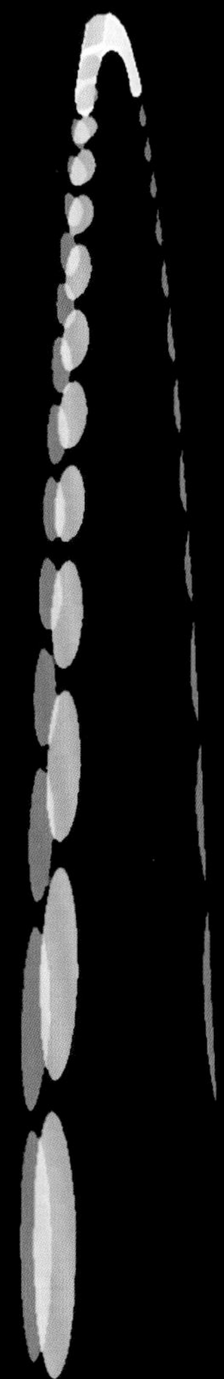

Wuhan Greenland Center

Wuhan, China

SERVICES
Architecture
Interior Design

CLIENT
Greenland Group

FUNCTION
Mixed-use

FACTS
119 stories
636 m height
300,000 sm area

AWARDS
The Chicago Athenaeum, Green Good Design Award, Green Architecture, 2017

Re-Thinking the Future, Sustainability Award, First Award, Mixed-Use, 2016

Wuhan Greenland Center, at 636 meters, was designed to be China's third-tallest building, and the fourth tallest in the world, when completed.

The 119-level tower in Wuhan, China is comprised of about 300,000 sm of floor area, including 200,000 sm of offices, 50,000 sm of luxury apartments and condominiums, a 45,000 sm five-star hotel, and a 5,000 sm 27-meter-tall private club with spectacular views at the tower's penthouse level.

The tower features a uniquely streamlined form that combines three key shaping concepts—a tapered body, softly rounded corners and a domed top—to reduce wind resistance and vortex action that builds up around supertall towers. The building's efficient aerodynamic performance allows for less structural material—and the associated embodied carbon—needed for construction.

The tower's three corners rise from its tripod-shaped base and taper upward, culminating in an arched tip above the dome at the top. The corners are smooth curved glass, contrasting markedly with the more textured curtain wall cladding the body of the tower. The curtain wall encloses a composite concrete core with steel framing. Apertures in the curtain wall at regular intervals assist in venting wind pressure against the tower; the apertures also house window-washing systems and air intake and exhaust systems on mechanical floors.

Other planned sustainable elements of the project include:

- Energy recovery using an enthalpy wheel integrated into the ventilation system; this captures energy from the building's exhaust systems and uses it to pre-heat or pre-cool air entering the building.
- A graywater recovery system, which takes waste water from the hotel laundry, sinks, and showers, and reuses it in the building's evaporative cooling system.
- A high-efficiency lighting system, which uses low-energy-consuming ballasts and lamps to reduce required power consumption.
- A daylight-responsive control system, which automatically turns off electric lights when sufficient daylight is available.
- Water-conserving low-flow plumbing fixtures, which reduce the total amount of potable water required as well as the associated pumping energy.

ADRIAN SMITH + GORDON GILL
ARCHITECTURE

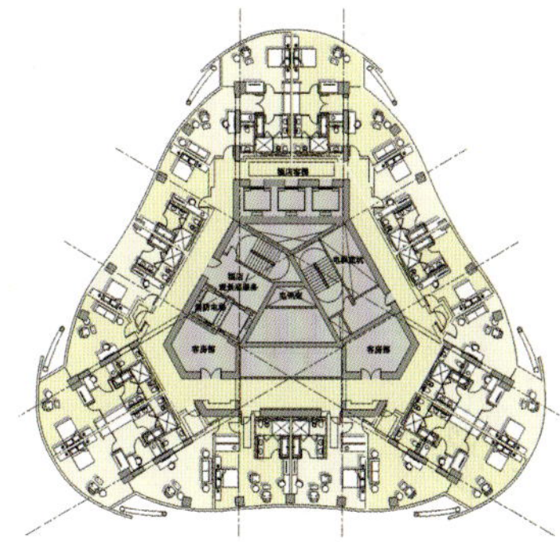

TYPICAL HOTEL

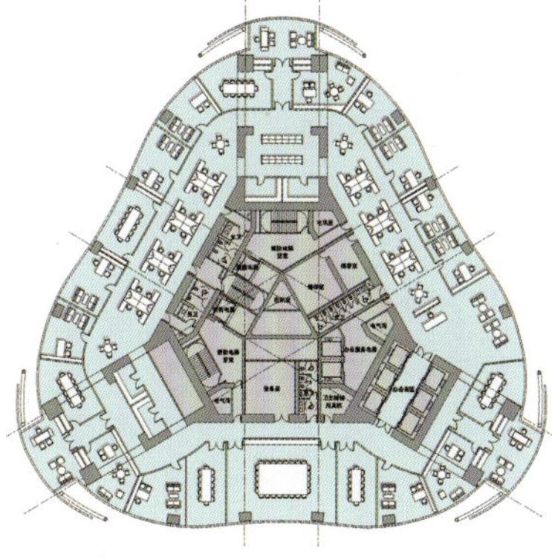

TYPICAL OFFICE

SOFT CORNERS

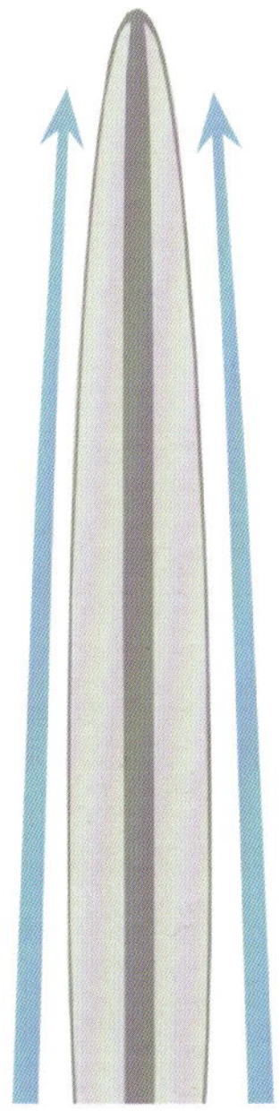

TAPERING

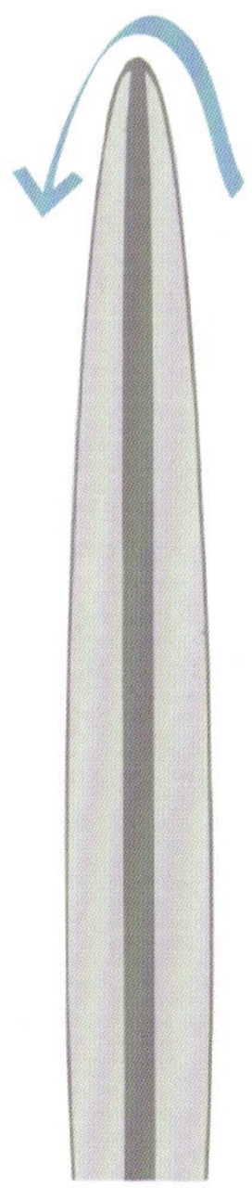

ROUND TOP

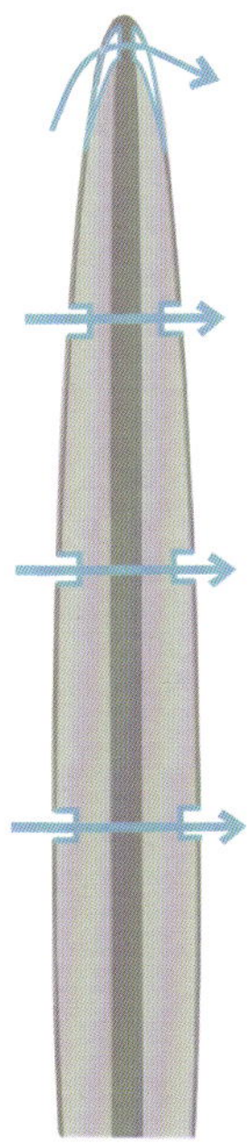

WIND RELIEF

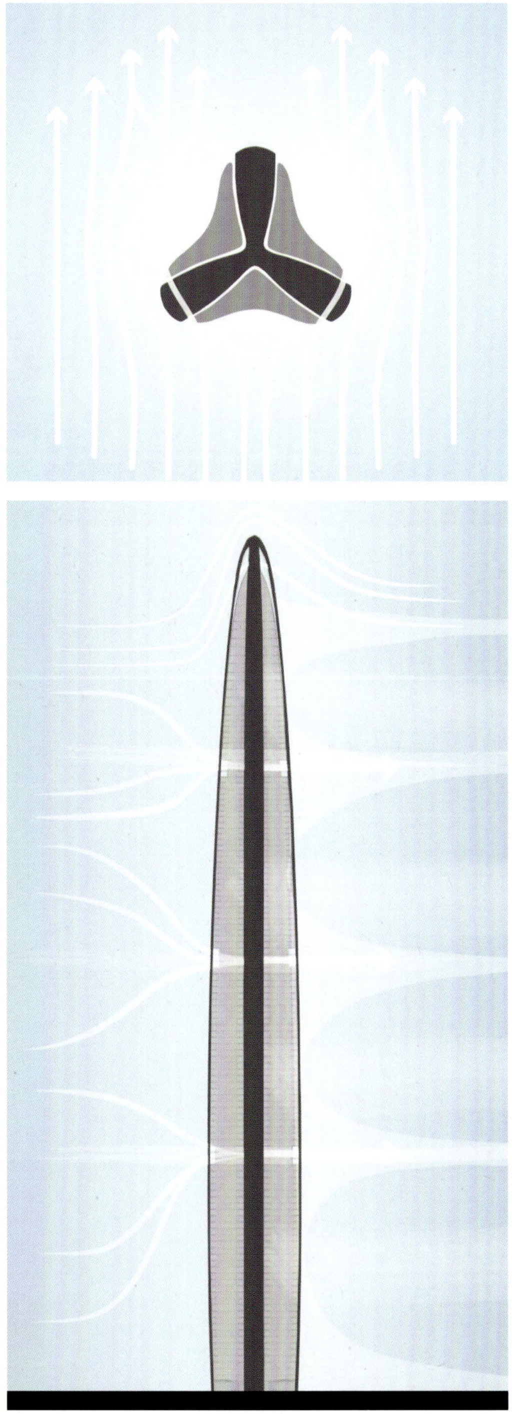

WIND VORTEX NOTCH

FACADE

The tower is comprised of two main exterior wall types, which accentuate the tower's formal expression: a shaded, textured main body and a reflective, smooth, curved shield. The main body of the tower's exterior wall is made up of both vertical polished stainless-steel fins and perforated aluminum horizontal sun shading devices that will protect the interior from both strong mid-day and afternoon solar conditions.

Glare is controlled by an exterior metal sunshade that also filters and diffuses sunlight. Integrated smart shading systems are incorporated into each unit, giving the users and building owners control of the shades. Floor-to-ceiling glass windows also provide unobstructed views to the surrounding city. By reducing incident solar radiation and therefore building cooling loads, daytime energy consumption is greatly reduced.

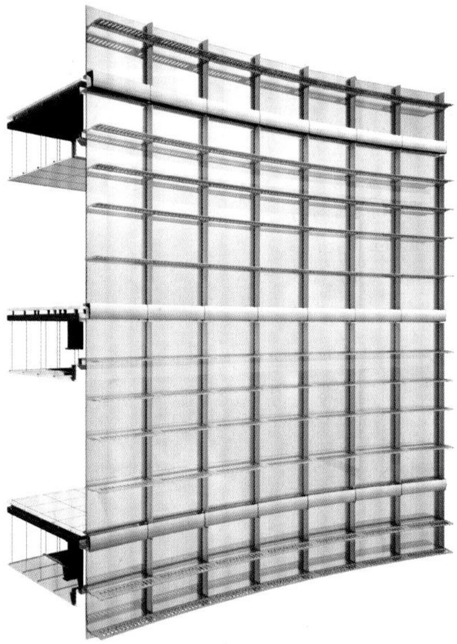

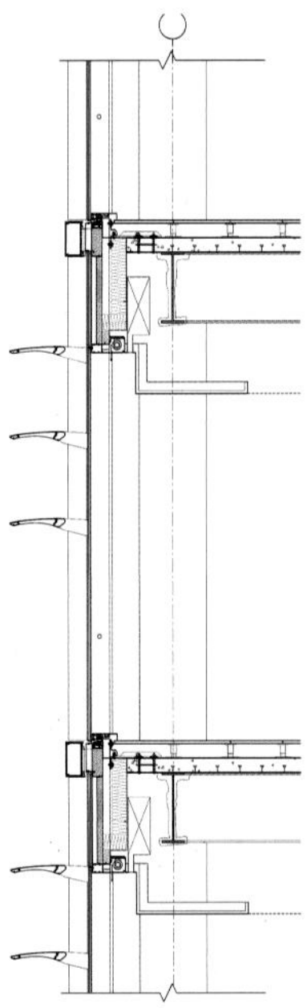

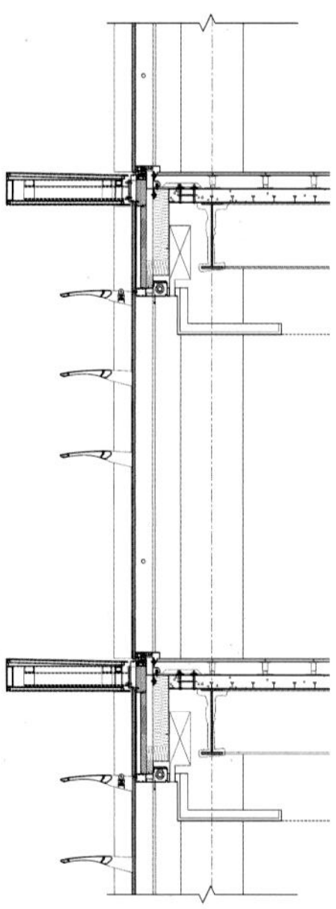

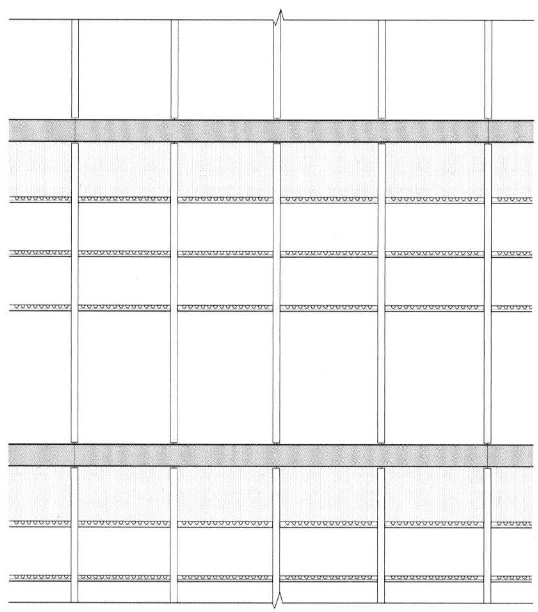

CONSTRUCTION, 2018

Shenzhen-Hong Kong International Center

Shenzhen, China

Shenzhen-Hong Kong International Center

Shenzhen, China

Set between the foothills of Longcheng Park and the Dayun National Park, the tower is adjacent to several major sporting venues. The graceful tower references anthropomorphic characteristics, offering a new sculptural icon for northwest Shenzhen's skyline.

SERVICES
Architecture

CLIENT
Shimao Group

FUNCTION
Mixed-use

FACTS
700 m height

The new tower is located at the center of AS+GG's Shimao Shenzhen Longgang Master Plan and is the main focal point for every office and apartment building within the development. It is envisioned as one of the tallest towers in the world, at approximately 700 meters, and will serve as a symbolic icon for the new district. In the evenings, the tower itself will be a visual, sound, and light show, reinforcing the district's athletic and entertainment purposes. The tower's top has one of the world's highest observation experiences and additional club facilities that include a restaurant, a night club, spa services, and a grand swimming pool, all with views of Shenzhen and beyond.

The mixed-use district that surrounds and connects with the tower contains a five-star hotel, offices, and conference facilities. A major retail facility defines the northeast corner of the site, while a community of apartment towers occupies the northwest section. The master plan integrates a dynamic new public realm that combines cultural and retail programs anchored by a cultural center and a main library. Programed venues have open and enclosed spaces for recreation, leisure, tourism, art, dining, and social gatherings. Beautifully landscaped promenades connect patrons and visitors to every aspect of the activity.

The environmental goal for the Shenzhen-Hong Kong International Center and the surrounding landscape is to obtain LEED Platinum certification, therefore sustainability is considered in a holistic way: High-performance glass will be used to reduced heat gain; Buildings are oriented to respond to existing environmental solar conditions for enhanced passive solar control; Strategic natural lighting for the interior spaces increases human comfort levels; The development was designed so that winds predominantly from the east and northeast are funneled into the open spaces to provide natural ventilation throughout the site and improve outdoor thermal comfort; The complex also will have a major public transportation center and bus terminal to move large groups of people to and from the site efficiently.

Water management was particularly important when designing the site. Shenzhen is known for heavy rains and flooding during the summer months, so it was crucial that the site can manage 100 percent of a 100-year storm event. Landscape features are designed to manage heavy rainfalls using engineered soils, retention ponds, native plants, and foliage as a network of systems that will recycle the rain water for irrigation and other uses.

MASTER PLAN

PEDESTRIAN CIRCULATION

GREEN BELT

ADRIAN SMITH+GORDON GILL
ARCHITECTURE

Shenzhen's wind climate presents a significant design and engineering challenge for the Shenzhen-Hong Kong International Center. Due to the high typhoon-driven wind speeds of the region, a tower of this height is subjected to extremely high wind forces and demands a process of architectural and structural design that maximizes efficiency and occupant comfort, while minimizing construction costs.

Tapering: Design optimization begins with a primary tapering of the form to reduce the "sail area" as the tower increases in height.

Smooth Geometry: Optimization for aerodynamics includes refinement of the tower's geometry to further smooth and allow better wind movement off the faces and around the corners to reduce interactions with the wind.

Surface Sculpting: The tower's form is further sculpted to present varied and articulated surfaces that work with the tapered form to "confuse" the wind by varying the vortex shedding action and reducing the dynamic effect on the tower. The form's slight asymmetry balances the wind forces around the tower, limiting harmonic interactions and reducing the peak lateral/cross wind forces on the tower.

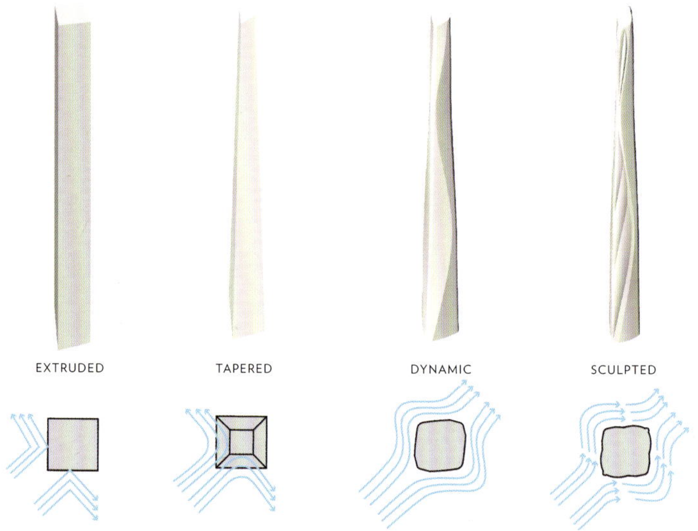

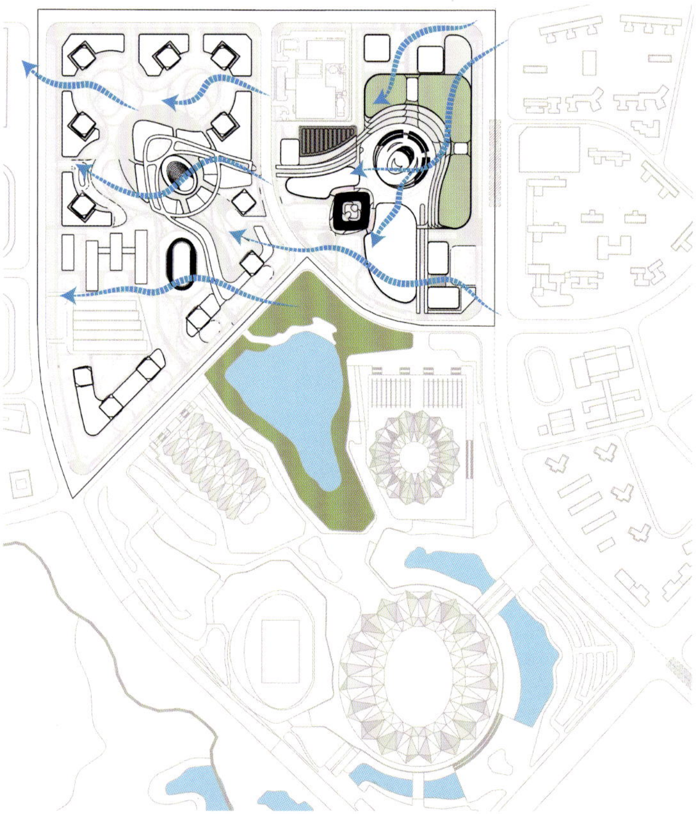

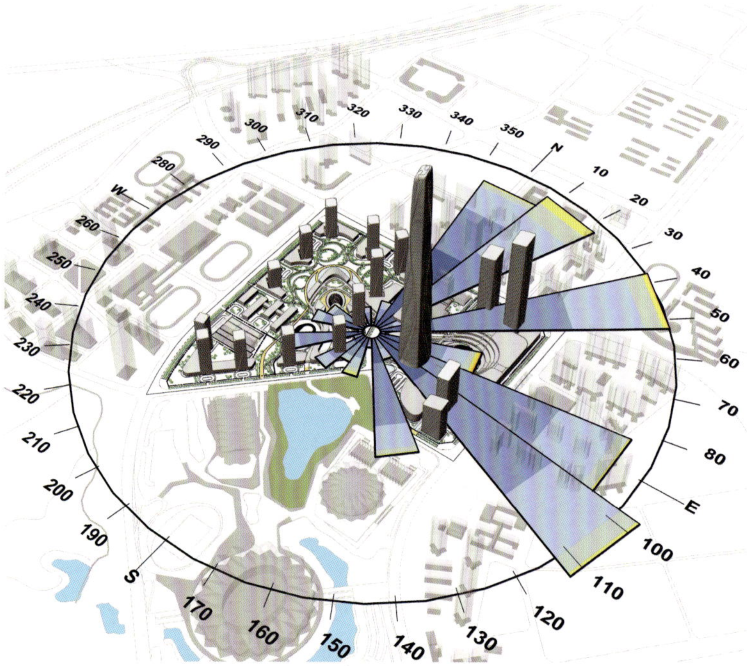

South Hexi Yuzui

Nanjing, China

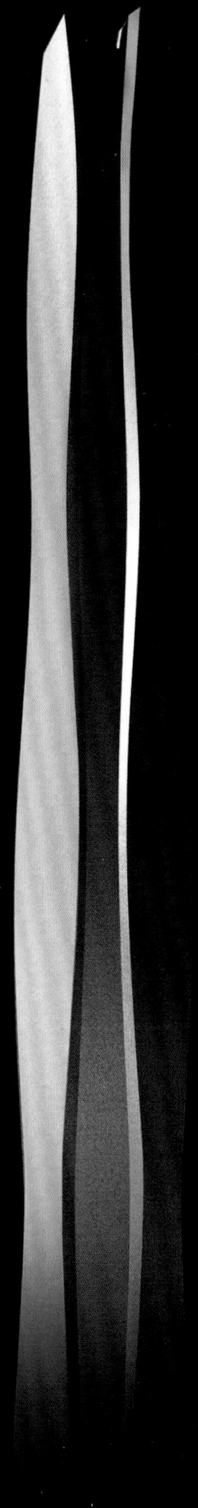

South Hexi Yuzui Financial District Tower

Nanjing, China

AS+GG won an international design competition in 2018 to design the new South Hexi Yuzui Financial District and Tower. The new 860,000 sm development includes a new 500-meter-tall tower that will anchor the district and enhance Nanjing's already iconic skyline.

SERVICES
Architecture

CLIENT
China Jinmao Holdings Group Limited

FUNCTION
Mixed-use

FACTS
580 m height

The tower will be one of the tallest in Nanjing and features a magnificent 360-degree, open-air observatory at the tower's top that will be one of the highest in the world. It will also be one of the tallest buildings to achieve LEED-Gold certification when completed.

The mixed-use development increases the value of the location with networks to access the riverfront, multiple public transportation options, and many new cultural, natural, and technological opportunities. Encouraging increased interaction, the user is invited to experience the district as either a live-work environment or as a visitor to one of the many public parks and art centers.

In addition to the 500-meter tower, the district's master plan includes a 100-meter office tower, a 155-meter office tower, a 220-meter office tower, a 350-meter office tower, and an 86-meter-tall residential tower.

At the heart of the new CBD, the architectural design of the new supertall takes its inspiration from the Yangtze River. The river reflects light, throwing out textures and dimensions, much like the tower's exterior, which is shaped to mitigate wind vortices, optimize views, and enhance both the structure and the program. Its mixed-use office program also features a unique observatory amenity with a stunning viewing platform.

The LEED-Gold design incorporates multiple green spaces that enhance the tower and the surrounding development, allowing users to experience the tactile sensations of the landscaping elements that are shown to promote a sense of well-being and improve air quality and the local micro-climate.

The tower integrates rainwater harvesting into the sky gardens to target onsite water management at greater than 100 percent of rainfall. Rainwater is collected using sponge city concepts including sub-soil collection, permeable paving, and recessed green space. Collected water is drained into tanks below ground level where it is treated and stored for reuse. A 55-percent reduction in total indoor water use is predicted.

The tower is designed to reach LEED-Gold certification. It seeks an overall energy reduction through a combination of energy strategies including reducing the cooling load, installation of a high-performance facade, reducing heating loads, reducing lighting loads, and reducing plug loads. A high-performance, Low-E insulated curtain-wall system has carefully designed fins that work with the building's geometry to efficiently reduce solar heat gain and provide the effective protection to the indoor environment, while maintaining access to daylighting and controlling glare.

ADRIAN SMITH+GORDON GILL
ARCHITECTURE

ADRIAN SMITH + GORDON GILL
ARCHITECTURE

The tower is tapered symmetrically to produce a rational structure that provides multiple, dynamic viewing surfaces, improves wind dynamics, and creates a distinctive landmark icon. Composed of seven typical office zones including one sky lobby, a special trading floor, and two executive office zones. The office program is capped by a unique observatory amenity with a special roof courtyard and viewing platform. Refuge floors are provided as needed for code requirements.

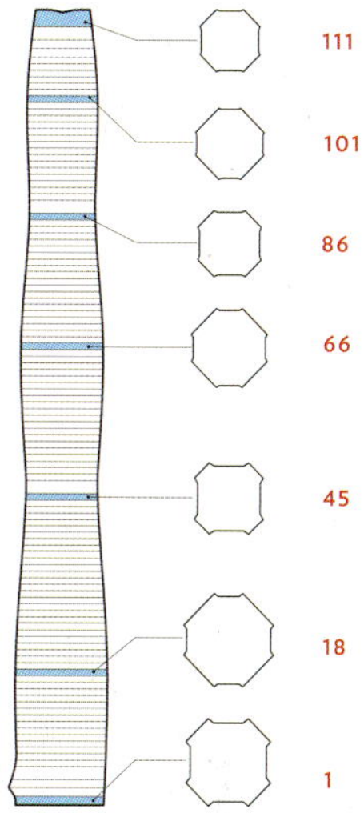

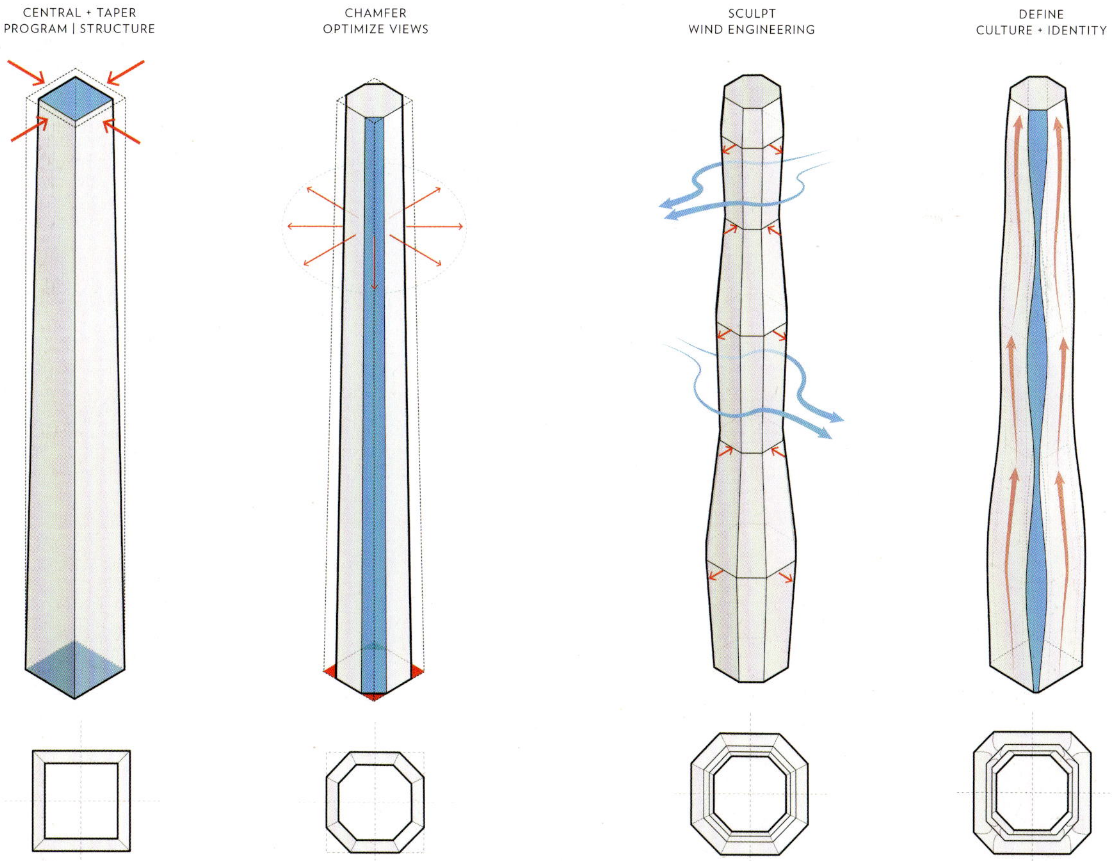

Dancing Dragons

Seoul, Korea

Dancing Dragons

Seoul, Korea

Dancing Dragons was designed as a pair of supertall mixed-use towers for the new Yongsan International Business District in Seoul, Korea. The buildings, which include residential, officetel and retail elements, consist of two slender, sharply angled mini-towers cantilevered around a central core.

SERVICES
Architecture
Interior Design

CLIENT
Yongsan International
Business District

FUNCTION
Mixed-use

FACTS
450 m height
390 m height
23,000 sm site

AWARDS
The Chicago Athenaeum,
International Architecture
Award, 2014

The Chicago Athenaeum,
American Architecture
Award, Scheme 1, 2013

The design aesthetic is highly contemporary yet informed by aspects of traditional Korean culture. The towers feature a dramatic series of diagonal massing cuts that create living spaces that float beyond the structure. This recalls the eaves of traditional Korean pagodas—a design theme echoed both in the geometry of the building skin and the jutting canopies at the towers' base.

The theme is extended in the building's skin, reminiscent of the scales of a mythical Korean dragon, which dance around the core—hence the project's name. Further inspiring the name of the towers is "Yongsan," the name of the overall development, which means "Dragon Hill" in Korean.

Dancing Dragons' scale-like skin is also a performative element. Gaps between its overlapping panels feature operable 600 mm vents through which air can circulate, making the skin "breathable" like that of certain animals.

Towers 1 and 2—about 450 m and 390 m tall, respectively—share an architectural language and, therefore, a close family resemblance, but are not identical. In the taller structure, the 88-level Tower 1, the massing cuts at the top and bottom of the mini-towers are V-shaped. In the 77-level Tower 2, the cuts move diagonally in a single unbroken line; they are also arranged in a radial pattern around the core that is perceptible as viewers move around the tower.

In both buildings, the mini-tower cuts are clad in glass at the top and bottom, making for dramatic skylights above the units at the highest levels and a transparent floor beneath the units at the lowest levels. This offers the opportunity for special high-value penthouse duplex units with spectacular 360-degree views of downtown Seoul and the adjacent Han River, along with an abundance of natural light.

The design of the 23,000 sm site—part of the larger Yongsan master plan—reinforces the angular geometry of the building massing and skin. Landscape features include sloped berms that echo that geometry. The site also includes a retail podium with a crystalline sculptural form and sunken garden that provide access to a large below-grade retail complex.

ADRIAN SMITH + GORDON GILL
ARCHITECTURE

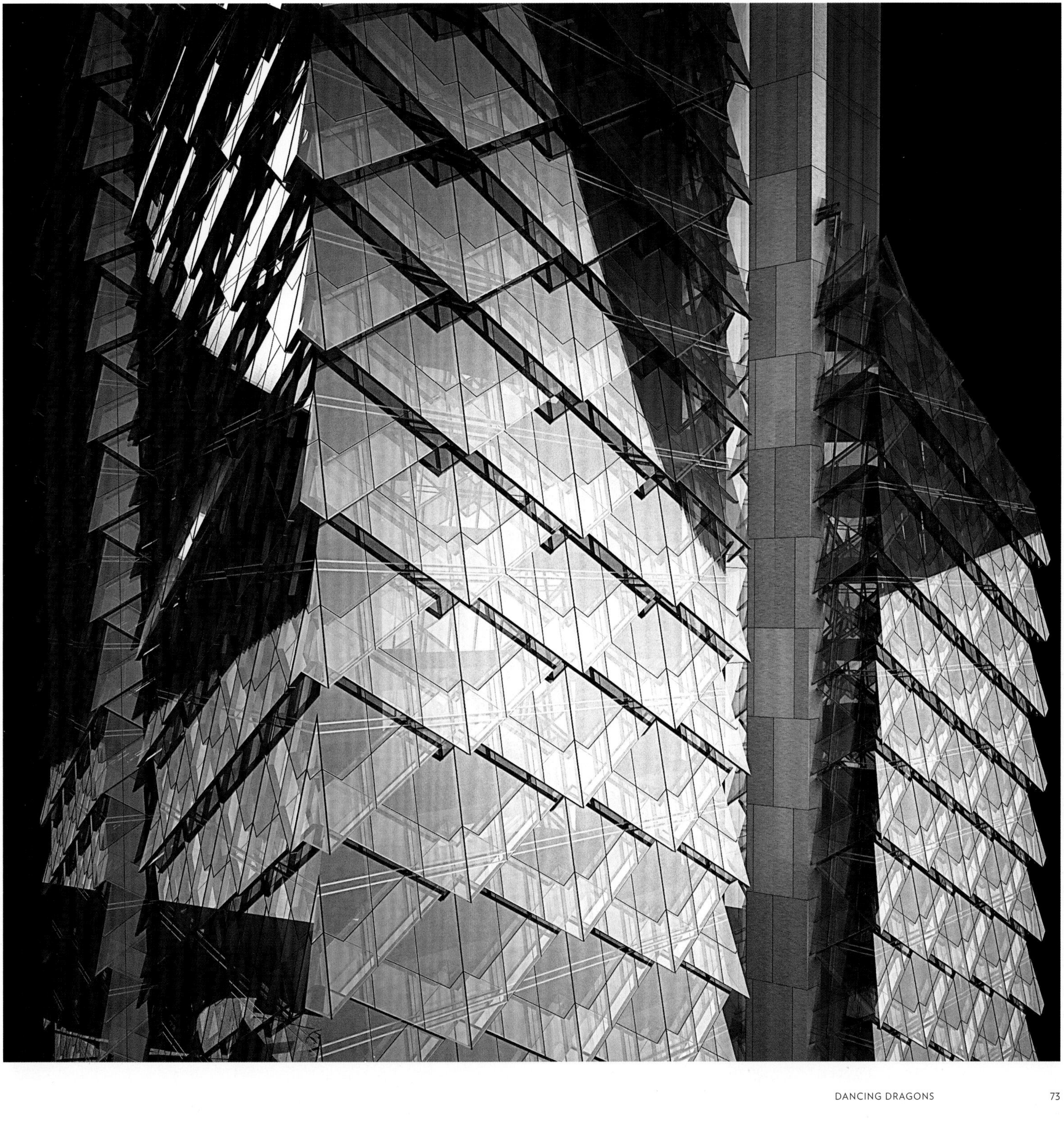

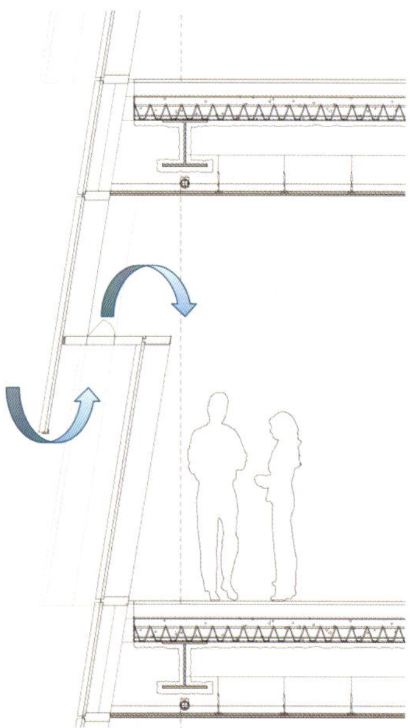

OPERABLE WINDOWS

The Biophilic Tower

Suzhou, China

The Biophilic Tower

Suzhou, China

The Biophilic Tower represents the next-generation of skyscrapers: a self-sustaining, intelligent structure that combines optimal performance with aesthetic beauty focused on people's innate, emotional attraction to nature.

SERVICES
Architecture

CLIENT
Jiangsu Jiangnan Construction Group Co., Ltd.

FUNCTION
Mixed-Use

FACTS
119 stories

AWARDS
Architectural Review, MIPIM Future Project Award, Tall Buildings, Commendation, 2015

The Chicago Athenaeum, American Architecture Award, 2013

The Biophilic Tower's design has three main concepts:

- **Nature in the Space**: Integrating water element, courtyard gardens, and views of nature from inside
- **Nature of the Space**: Adapting to human psychological and physiological responses to different spatial configurations, improving concentration and productivity
- **Natural Analogues**: Using materials and patterns that evoke nature, including building elements that mimic shells and leaves, furniture with organic rather than geometric shapes, and visible wood grain

One of the tower's main features is a continuous vertical garden environment that wraps around the building from grade to the top. Each of the 119 floors will have access to this lush atrium space, giving occupants a direct multi-sensory connection to nature. The garden will be a naturally ventilated space that will create a vertical representation of traditional Suzhou gardens.

The tower design also makes use of fractal patterns, which appear the same from near as from far, and which can positively affect human neural activity, increasing work productivity and physical and mental health. The design uses a common fractal pattern, the Voronoi diagram, as a way to add another layer to the natural environment that has been created within the tower. The Voronoi pattern is incorporated into the curtain wall design, primarily as a solar shading strategy to help reduce heat gain in the internal occupied space, as well as the naturally ventilated gardens.

The Biophilic Tower is shaped to take full advantage of the natural light available on the site. By carving the atrium space deep into the massing of the building, natural light is allowed to enter the building beyond the perimeter envelope and penetrate deep into the floor plates. At the same time, the tower offers stunning views, east to Jinji Lake and west to the Old City. The design intent is to increase the availability of east and west views to occupants on the north and south sides of the building.

ADRIAN SMITH + GORDON GILL
ARCHITECTURE

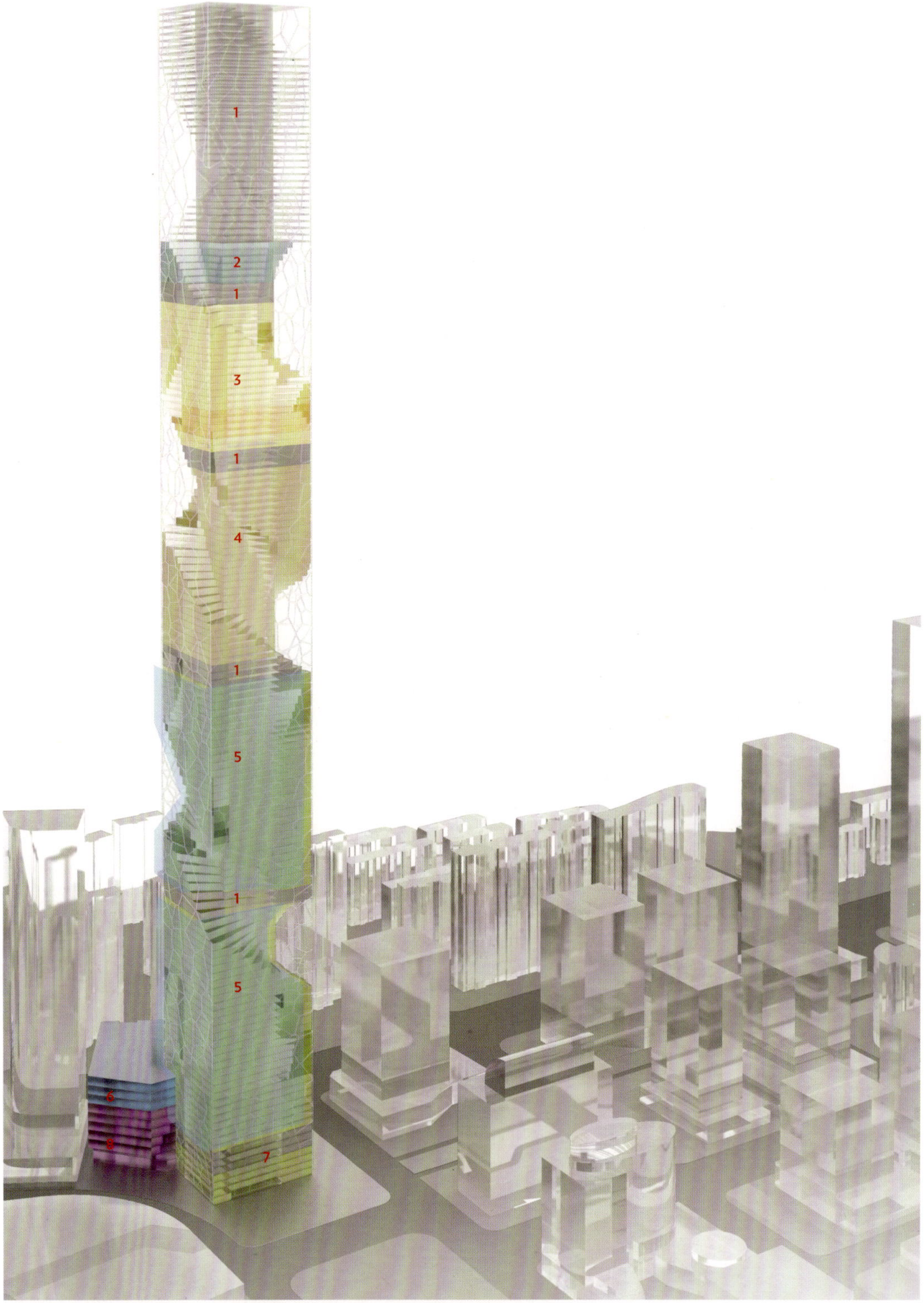

PROGRAM DIAGRAM

1. Observation
2. Club
3. Hotel
4. Apartment
5. Office
6. Conference Center
7. Parking/MEP/Loading
8. Retail

1 Dubai

Dubai, United Arab Emirates

1 Dubai

Dubai, United Arab Emirates

1 Dubai is a trio of supertall towers of staggered heights, each reaching at least 600 meters. The three towers are linked together, creating one of the tallest and largest vertical city networks in the world.

SERVICES
Architecture

CLIENT
Meraas Development

FUNCTION
Mixed-use

FACTS
1000+ m height
1,784,257 sm building area

A city within a city, the giant mixed-use project was designed as the centerpiece of Dubai's Jumeirah Gardens development, a site at the center of Dubai. On its tripedal base, 1 Dubai rises over a canal that forms an oasis in the center. Viewers can gaze up through the great atrium-like space between the three towers. At night, a virtual "fourth tower"—a giant beam of light—lances up through the atrium, creating a shining beacon at the city's center.

On special occasions, the oasis transforms itself into one of the world's most unique event and performance spaces with a floating stage that is surrounded by barges that double as seating banks. There is a state-of-the-art sound and light show featuring giant holograms that are projected in the air and on the building's mosaic-like glass and aluminum skin.

High above, a series of three-story sky bridges, or "plazas in the sky," connects the towers as they taper upward. The skybridges afford breathtaking views of the Gulf and the city and functionally help stabilize the towers structurally and facilitate interfloor circulation between them.

1 Dubai includes two world-class (five- and six-star) hotels, office and retail space and some of the world's highest condominiums—including a number of exclusive, double-height penthouse units in the top levels of the three towers. In corner penthouse units, columns are removed at the corners for unobstructed views. The tallest tower also features one of the world's highest club and observation halls.

Other facilities and amenities include two trading floors with 8.4 meter (18 feet) floor-to-ceiling heights; ballrooms; conference facilities; and a spa with full-size basketball courts, volleyball courts, and an Olympic-sized swimming pool.

1 Dubai also takes full advantage of a variety of cutting-edge sustainability technologies, with special emphasis on photovoltaics to generate solar energy.

SITE CONTEXT PLAN

TALL BUILDING STRATEGY

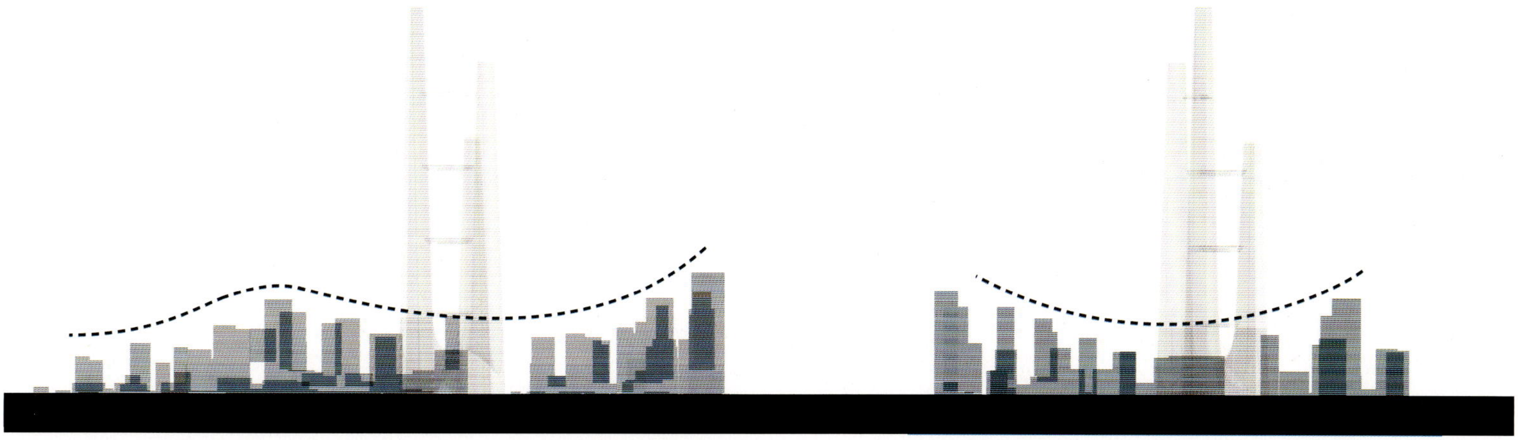

FRAMEWORK PLAN

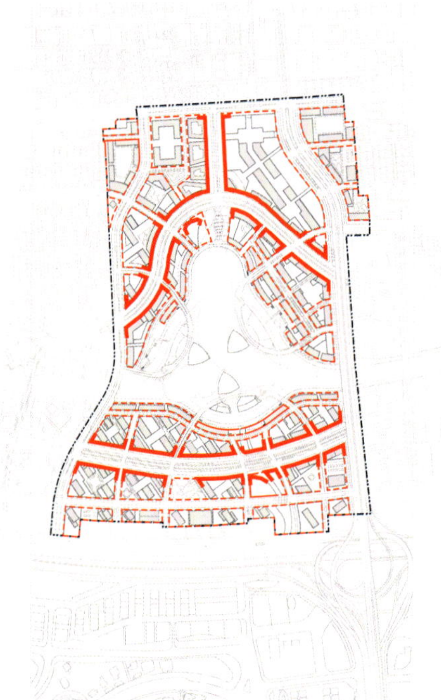

LOT LINE RELATIONSHIP

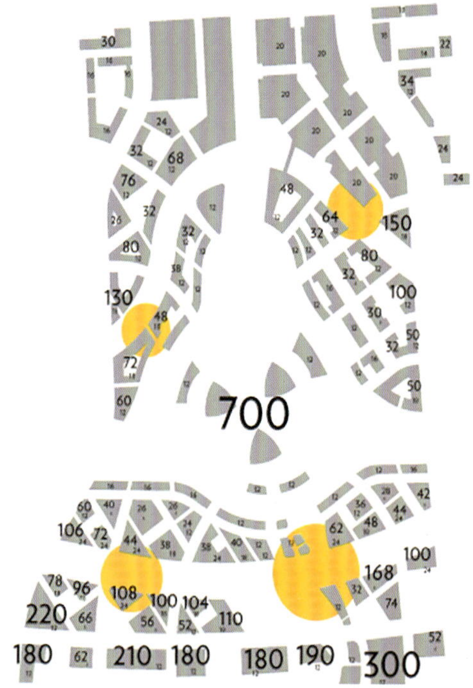

TALL BUILDING STRATEGY

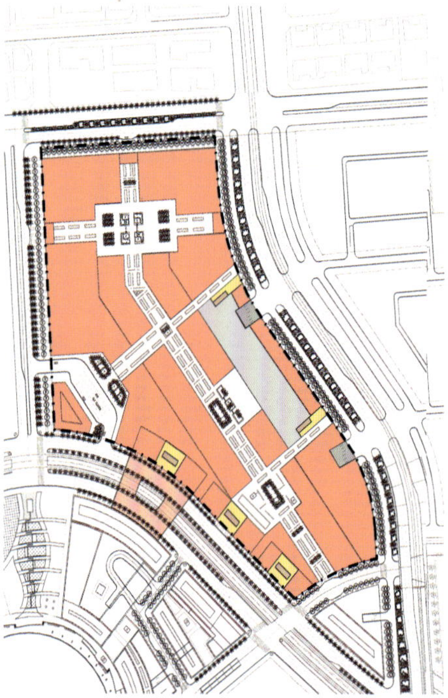

GROUND-USE PLAN

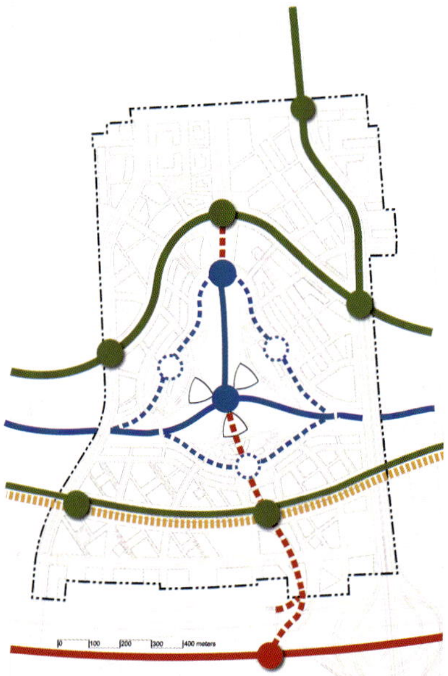

TRANSIT SYSTEMS

OVERALL LANDSCAPE PLAN

"OUTSIDE" LANDSCAPE

"INSIDE" LANDSCAPE

OUTSIDE LANDSCAPES INCLUDE WATERFRONTS AND STREETSCAPES

INSIDE LANDSCAPES CREATE QUIET, SHADED ENVIRONMENTS FOR PEDESTRIANS AND RESIDENTS

Initial structural studies indicate that significant benefit in the behavior of the buildings can be achieved by linking the buildings together through the use of the bridges. The bridges are not deep enough to transfer over-turning moment, however, shear can be transferred through the bridges between the towers, which will allow for the smaller two towers to effectively stiffen the more slender Tower 1, subtly. Additionally, the bridge links may have a benefit to the dynamic behavior of the towers by effectively linking together the inertia of the three towers, which naturally (due to the height and stiffness difference) would respond differently to dynamic loads like wind. This will be confirmed by wind tunnel testing as the project proceeds. Preliminary studies indicate that the linking of the towers would reduce the drift of the tallest tower by 15 percent.

LINKED TOWERS
STRUCTURAL MODEL

WIND DISPLACEMENTS
-15% STIFFER

WIND AXIAL STRESS

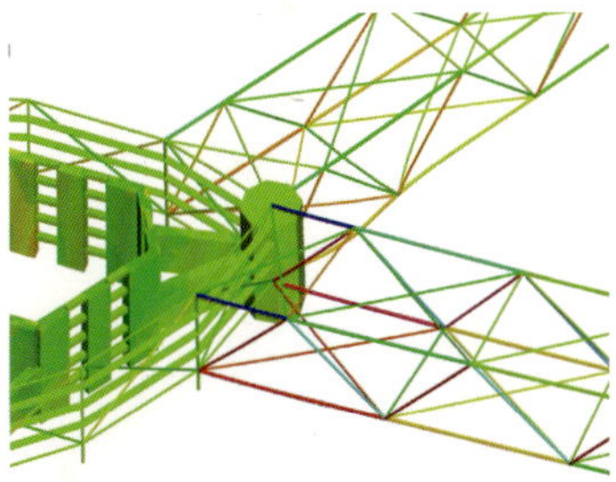

BRIDGE AXIAL STRESS

LINKED TOWERS LATERAL ANALYSIS

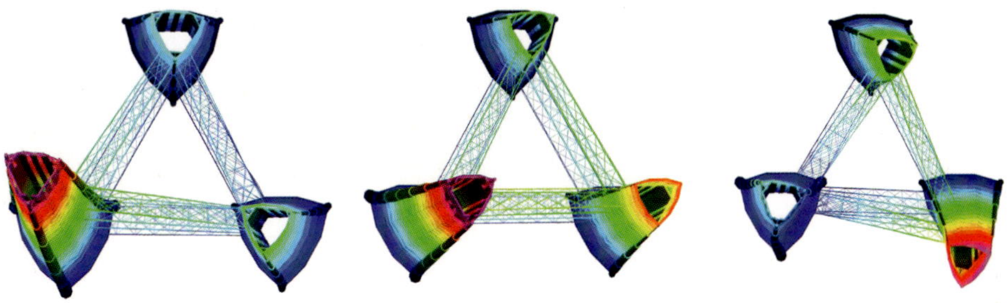

MODE 1
T = 12.5 SECS

MODE 2
T = 11.5 SECS

MODE 3
T = 8.1 SECS

LINKED TOWERS DYNAMIC ANALYSIS

1 Park Ave.

Dubai, United Arab Emirates

1 Park Avenue

Dubai, United Arab Emirates

1 Park Avenue, a 550-meter, 116-story tower with a trio of podium buildings at its base, is a signature feature of Dubai's Jumeirah Gardens development. With its undulating sculptural form, the tower aims to be one of the city's most poetic and evocative structures.

SERVICES
Architecture

CLIENT
Meraas
Development

FUNCTION
Mixed-use

FACTS
550 m height
600,000 sm
building area

It is also an example of cutting-edge sustainable design; 1 Park Avenue's transparent skin will feature a high-performance exterior wall that controls the transfer of heat and light from outside with the help of a high-tech system of light shelves and light-sensor-activated shades. Shading fins jut out above each floor, shading the glass beneath, which allows for a more transparent curtain wall and adds visual texture to the building skin. Integrated photovoltaic cells will harvest solar energy.

The approximately 600,000 sm mixed-use complex houses premium offices, condominiums and service apartments, along with the world's highest luxury hotel. Its three podium buildings, whose flowing form complements the tower's own, provide offices and support for the hotel in a park-like setting.

Besides its distinctive sculptural form, the tower features an exclusive club/observatory space at the top, with a 20-story-high dome and two restaurants. The hotel features a multi-story atrium. At the tower's base, visitors will enter through a soaring, multi-story lobby with double-decker elevators and a series of elevated and suspended glass walkways.

The tower's undulating form means that each floor plate is different from all the others, even though all are trisymmetrical. Some floor plates are almost round, while others resemble a triangle imposed on a circle. Each has ample access to views and daylight.

Other facilities and amenities include a business center in the tower's residential zone; a health club, Olympic-sized swimming pool, ballrooms and meeting rooms in the podium buildings; lush landscaping with fountains and other water features throughout the development site; and four levels of underground parking.

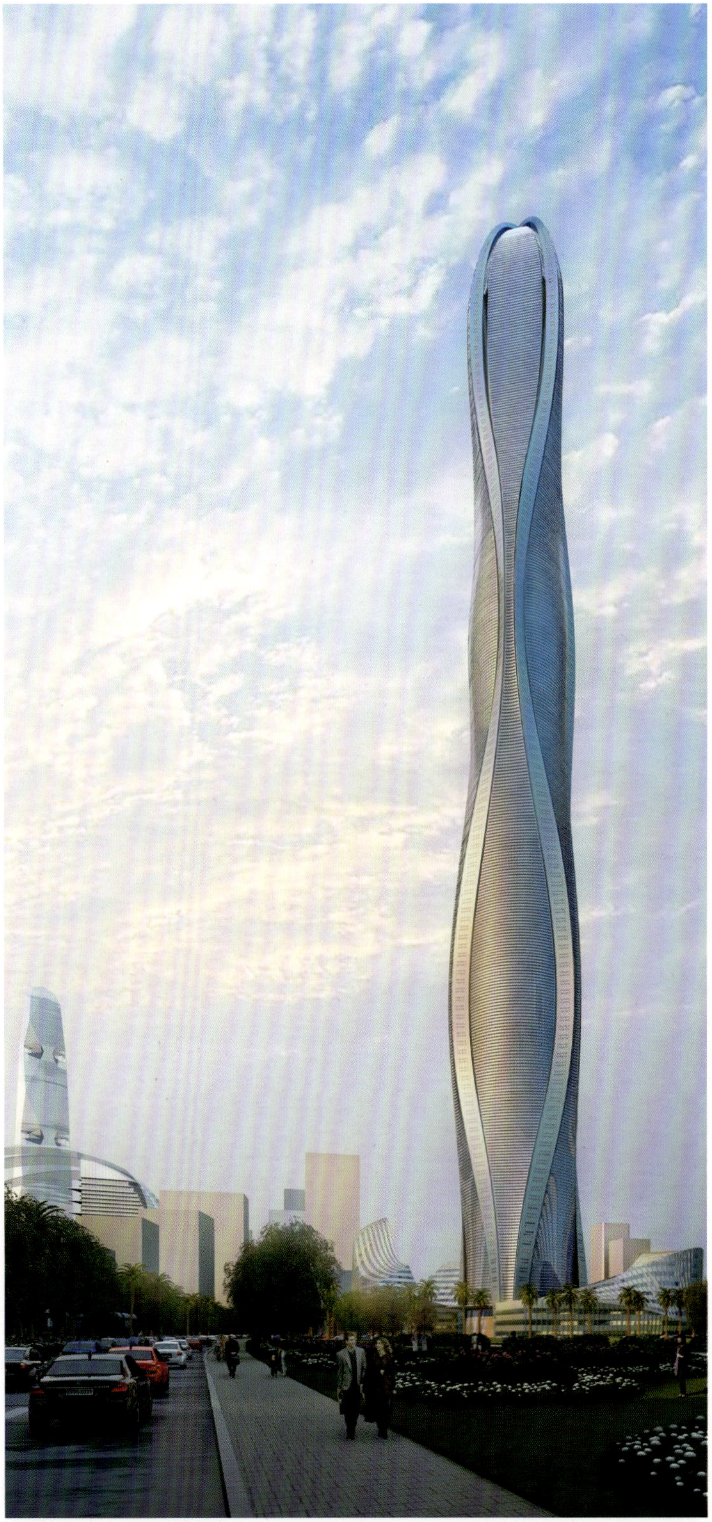

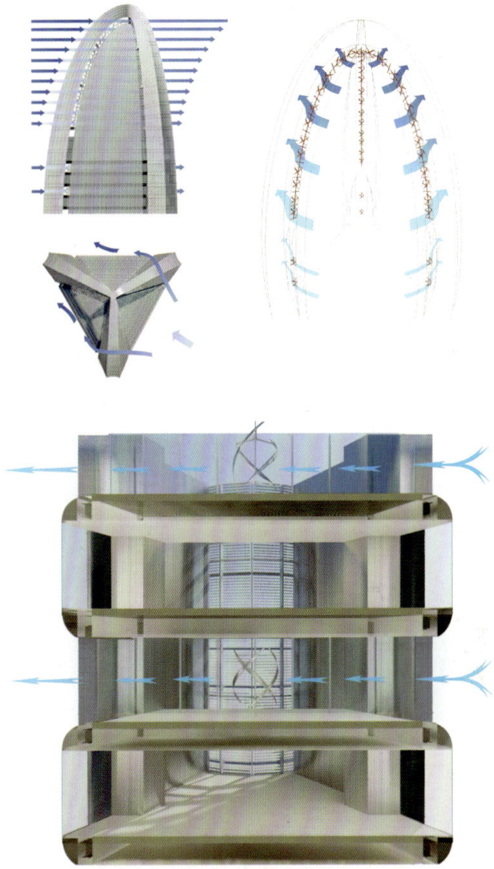

BUILDING INTEGRATED WIND TURBINES

Twelve vertical axis wind turbines are contained within each of the three slots between the mega-columns and the dome at the top of the tower. Maintenance access to the turbines is via ladder cages inside the mega columns. The location of the turbines was studied and optimized using CFD modeling; the shape of the structure allows wind to be channeled into the turbine area, so the turbines are placed near the top of the tower, where they have the highest wind speeds and minimize any vibration issues or disruption to the building occupants. The turbines are a visible representation of the futuristic design and the sustainable aspirations of the tower as 21st-century structure.

SECTION + TYPICAL FLOOR PLANS

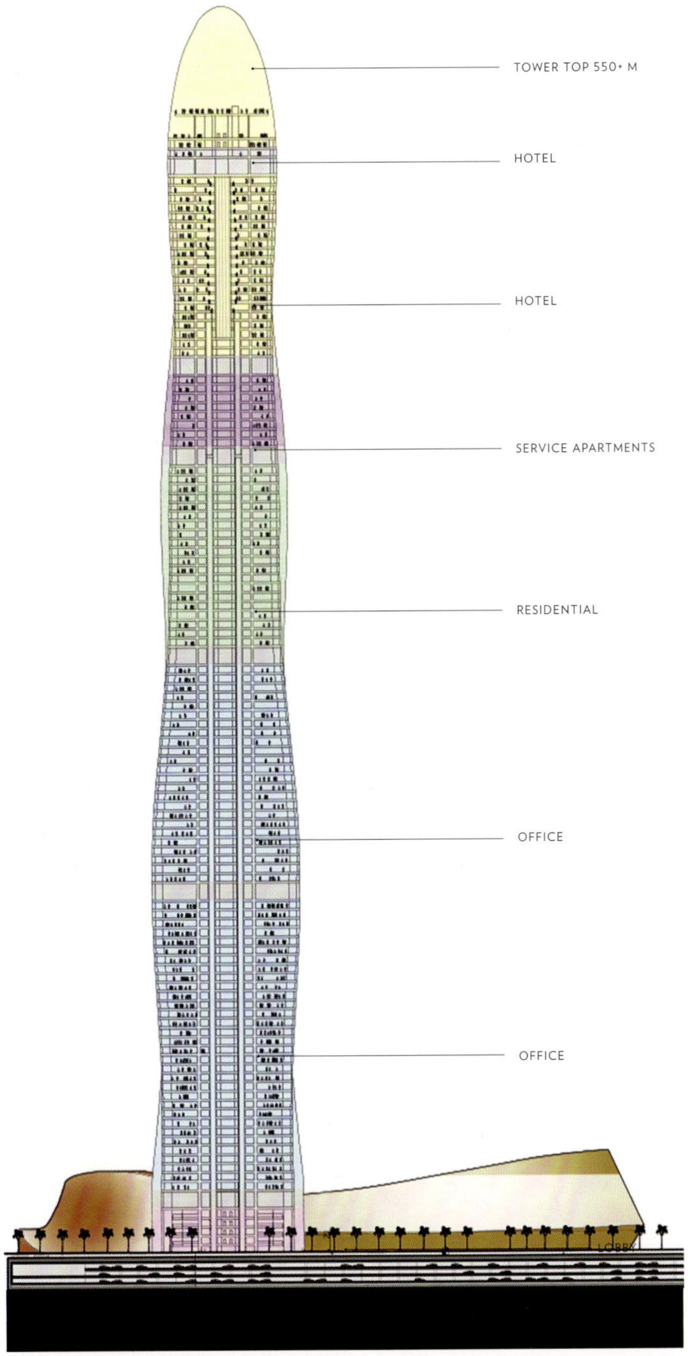

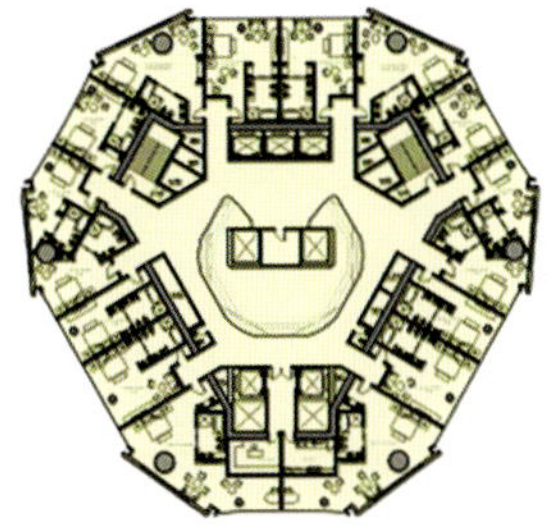

TYPICAL HOTEL

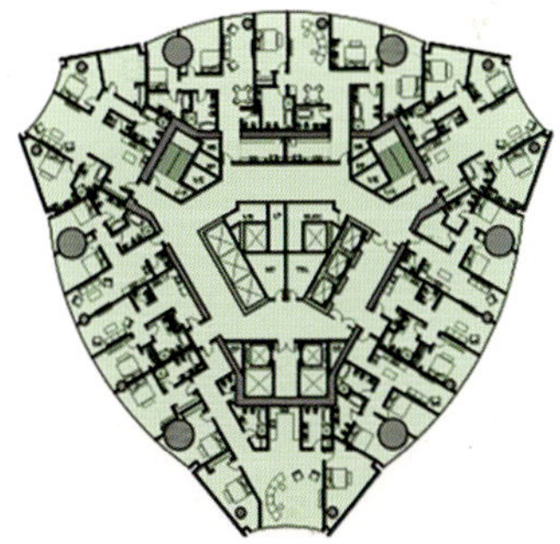

TYPICAL RESIDENTIAL

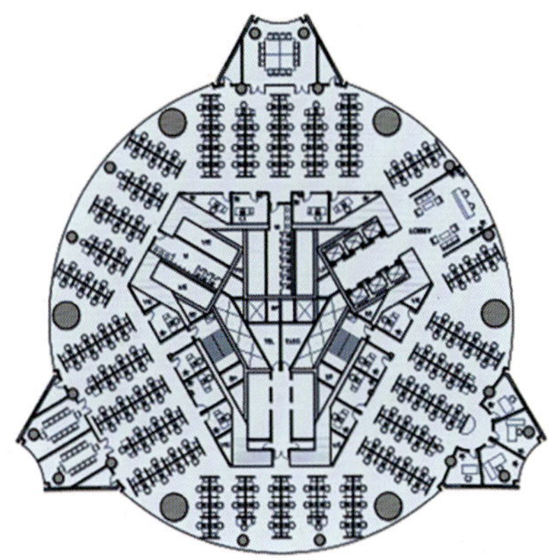

TYPICAL OFFICE

Park Gate

Dubai, United Arab Emirates

Park Gate

Dubai, United Arab Emirates

Park Gate is a 464,515-square-meter mixed-use development—including offices, retail, and a hotel—that creates a visual portal into the adjacent Jumeirah Gardens in Dubai.

SERVICES
Architecture

CLIENT
Meraas Development

FUNCTION
Mixed-use

FACTS
37 stories
464,515 sm area

The project's six gently curving towers, arranged in facing pairs connected at the top by three vaulted canopies, surround a unique urban oasis inspired by the Middle East's ancient and modern souks—covered markets that also serve as places to rest and socialize.

This central plaza, further protected by micro-canopies, boasts expanses of drought-tolerant greenery and reflecting pools. From balconies and sky gardens in the surrounding towers, users will enjoy inspiring overlooks of this outdoor "great hall," which features indigenous, salt-water-tolerant plants (reducing energy needed to desalinate water) and reflecting pools that also act as thermal sinks, absorbing heat during the day and releasing it at night.

High above, the main canopies perform three sustainability functions at once: harvesting solar energy through photovoltaics on top; creating shade, which will reduce heat gain in the towers and can reduce temperatures on the ground by 10 to 15 degrees; and incorporating trellises from which hanging plants will grow in a thriving microclimate irrigated by a graywater misting system. The canopies are semi-permeable (70 percent closed, 30 percent open) to allow dappled light through to ground level.

In the towers, whose sculpted form completes the curvature of the canopies, more sustainable design features and strategies are deployed. The towers are oriented to limit solar exposure and allow circulation of gulf breezes through the development. Landscaped sky gardens on some floors provide access to the outdoors and allow natural light to penetrate the interiors.

The towers on one side of the development are 37 stories tall, while the others are 34 stories tall, creating an asymmetrical effect. The towers are oriented to turn slightly in toward each other, heightening the sense of ensemble. Shading elements on the tower exteriors reduce solar heat gain.

SUSTAINABILITY SECTION

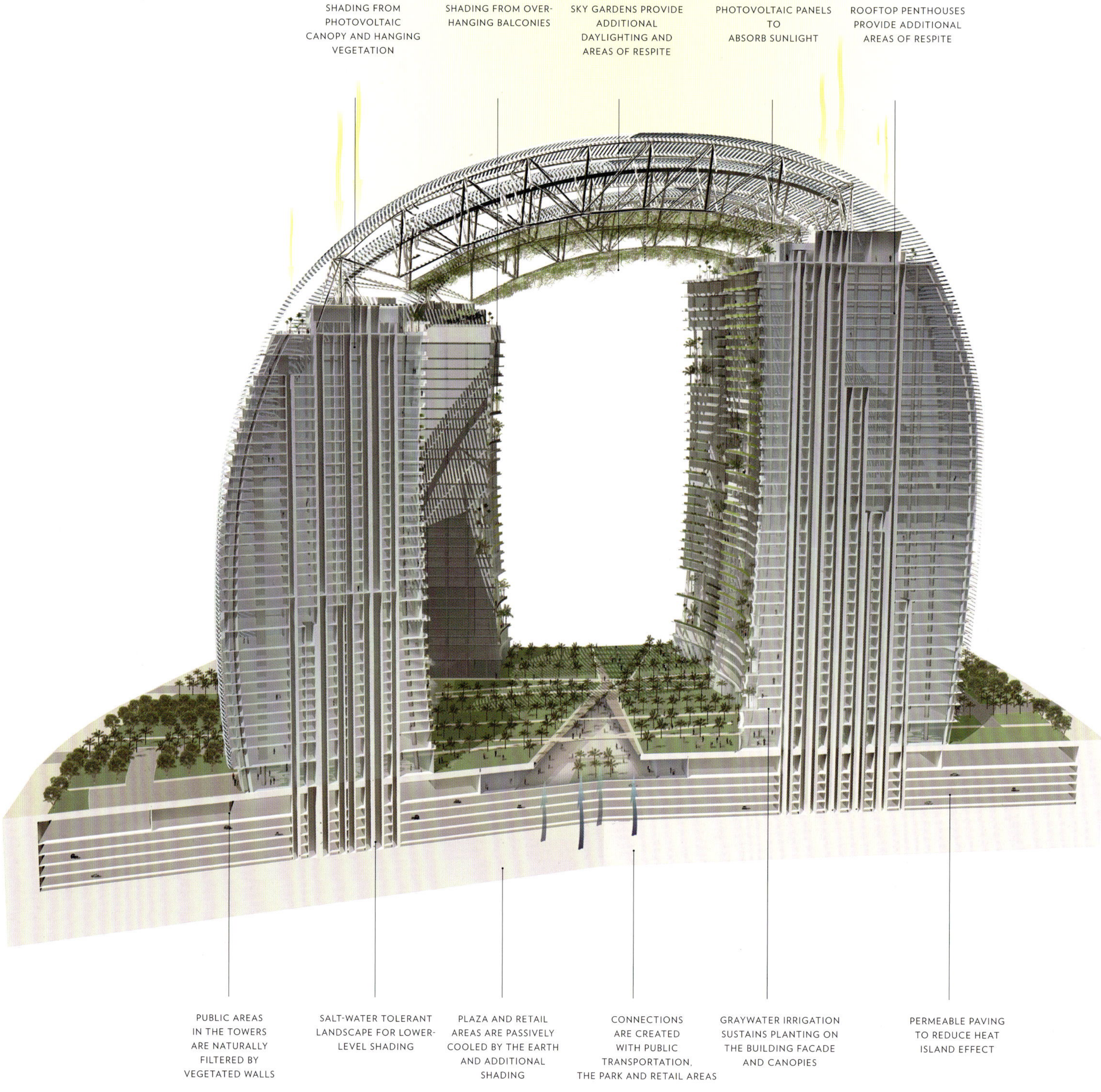

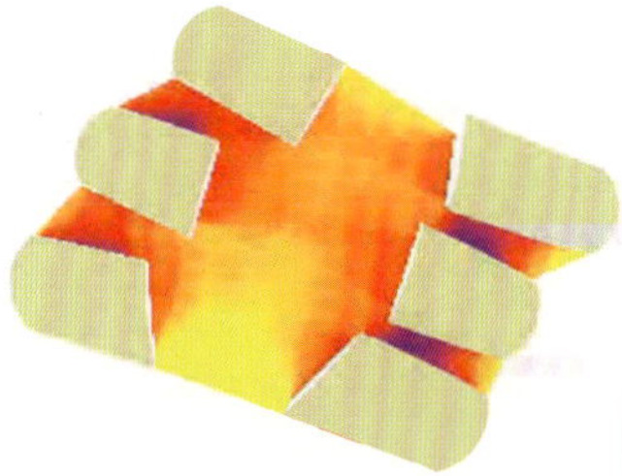

ANNUAL SOLAR EXPOSURE
WITHOUT CANOPY

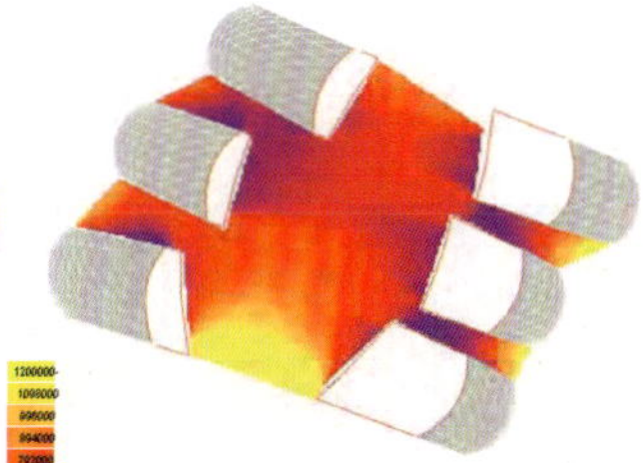

ANNUAL SOLAR EXPOSURE
WITH CANOPY

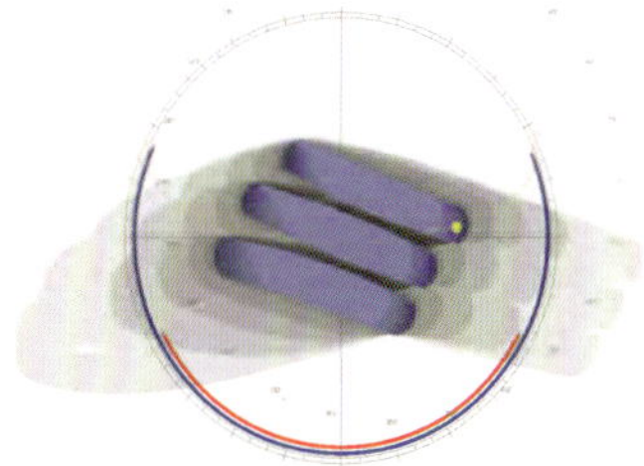

SUMMER SHADOWS

CANOPY SHADING

The climate of Dubai dictates that after air conditioning, shading is the most effective way of tempering the climate. By providing a roof covering the interior area of the site a comfortable environment is created for its inhabitants.

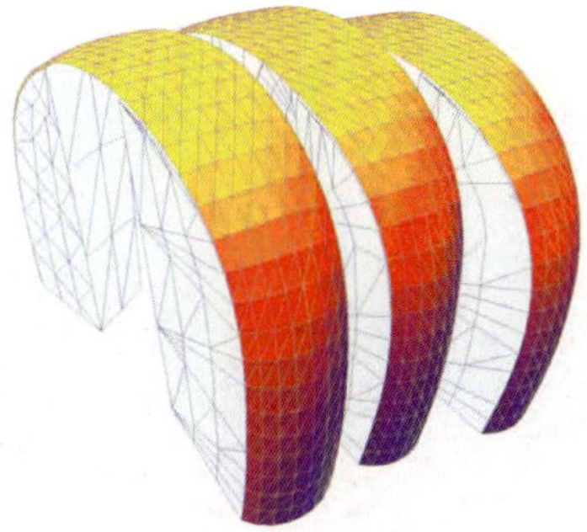

ANNUAL SOLAR EXPOSURE

PHOTOVOLTAICS

It is estimated that the annual energy provided by PV in the canopy could potentially be enough to offset the entire annual lighting demand for the residential towers.

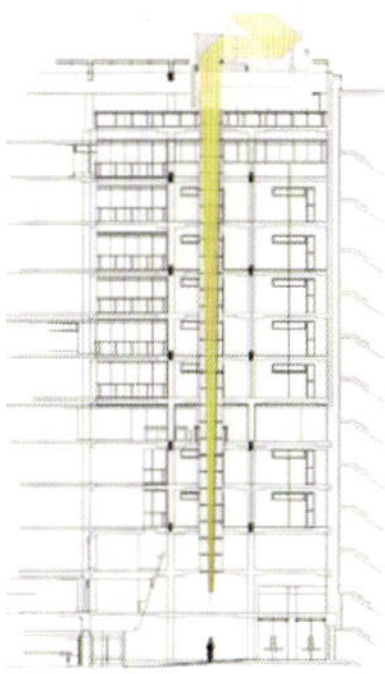

DAYLIGHT

Daylight penetration to the atria could be maximized by integrating a Heliostat system. This technique consists of reflecting direct sunlight, abundant in the UAE, via a combination of mirrors into the atria. This strategy will not only save lighting energy consumption but also improve occupant's comfort.

Meraas Tower

Dubai, United Arab Emirates

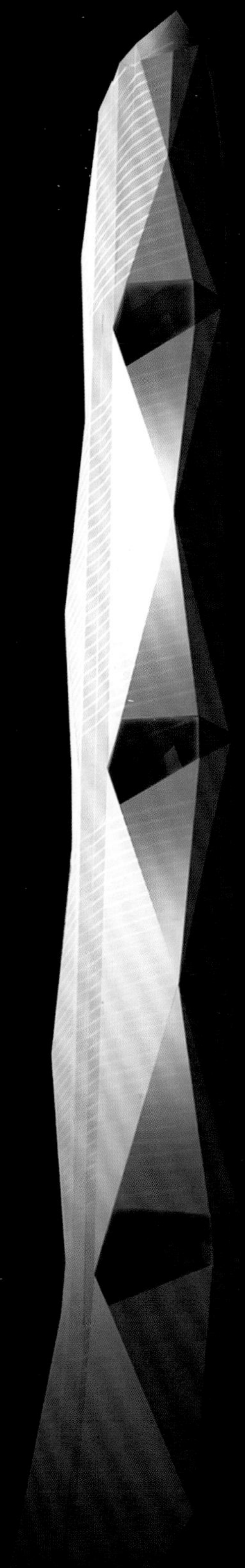

Meraas Tower

Dubai, United Arab Emirates

Meraas Tower combines simple geometric principles with new and emerging technologies to create a modern, soaring "tower of light" for the city of Dubai.

SERVICES
Architecture

CLIENT
Meraas
Development

FUNCTION
Mixed-use

FACTS
500 m height
300,000 sm
building area

Like a prism, the 112-story tower has a series of faceted surfaces that increase light and air traveling through the building. The faceted shapes maximize energy generation, balance natural light and offer 360-degree views. They also create natural atrium spaces as the building ascends, allowing for the creation of naturally lit sky gardens that activate the tower's form.

Exposing the intermediate floors gives the illusion that the structure is composed of four smaller towers stacked on top of one another, creating a "vertical city."

Meraas Tower includes 300,000 square meters of hotel, convention, commercial, and retail spaces. The 15-story hotel features a ballroom, prefunction facilities and soaring lobby atrium topped by an elegant, lushly landscaped sky lobby.

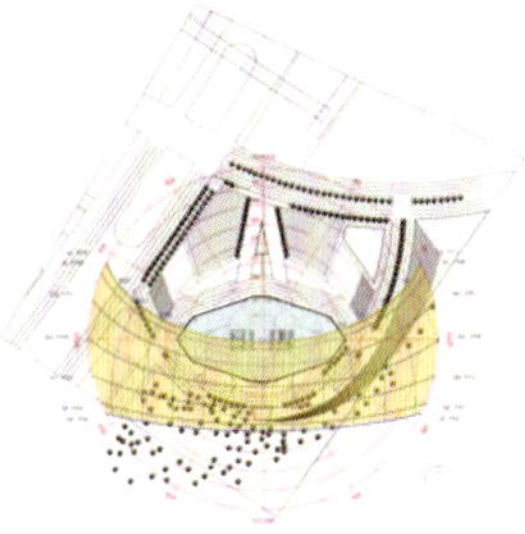

SOLAR PATH

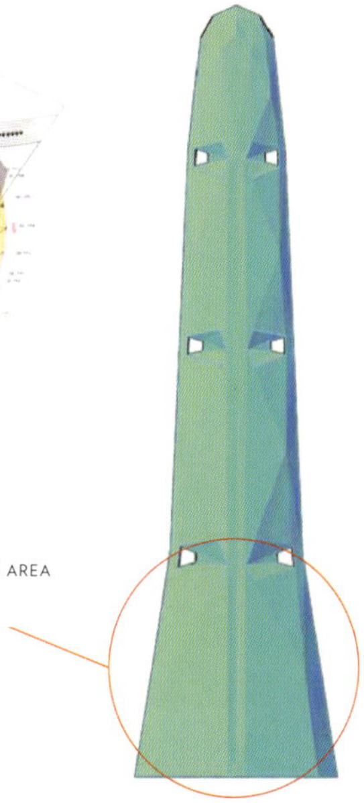

DAYLIGHTING ANALYSIS AREA OF STUDY

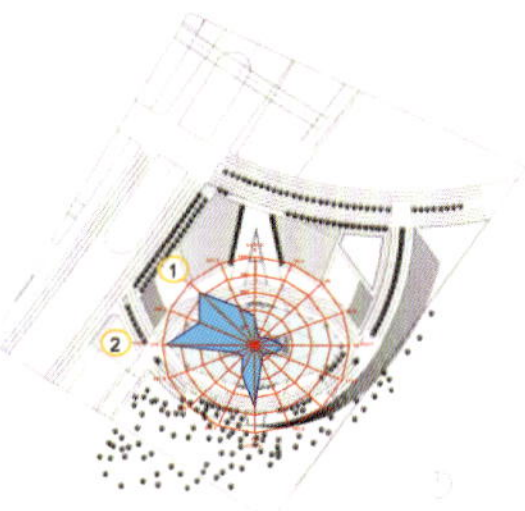

PREVAILING WIND DIRECTION

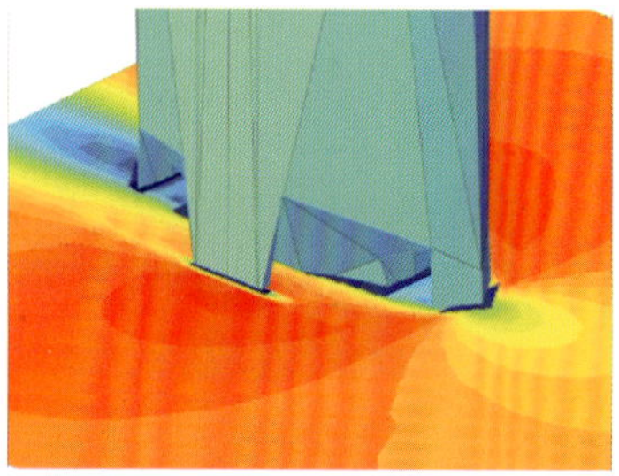

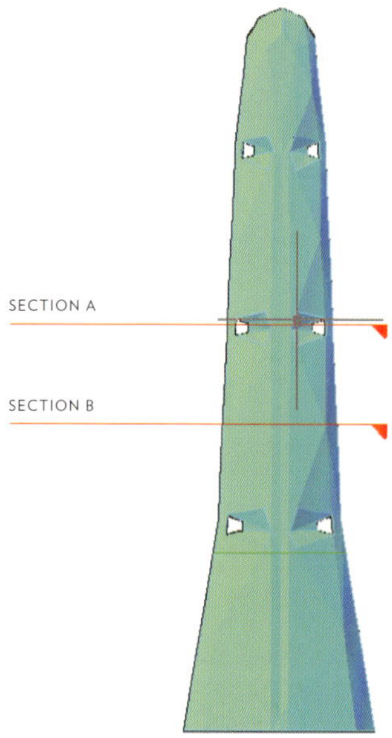

ATRIUM DAYLIGHT

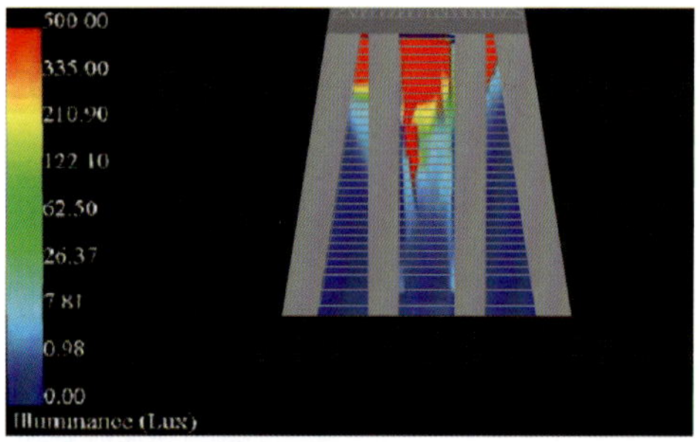

SPRING (MARCH 21, 2009 @ NOON)
AVERAGE ILLUMINANCE WITHIN ATRIA: 94 LUX

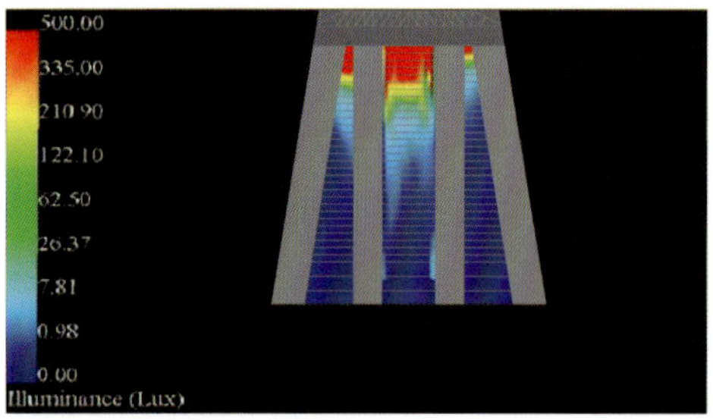

SUMMER (JUNE 21, 2009 @ NOON)
AVERAGE ILLUMINANCE WITHIN ATRIA: 35 LUX

WIND ENERGY

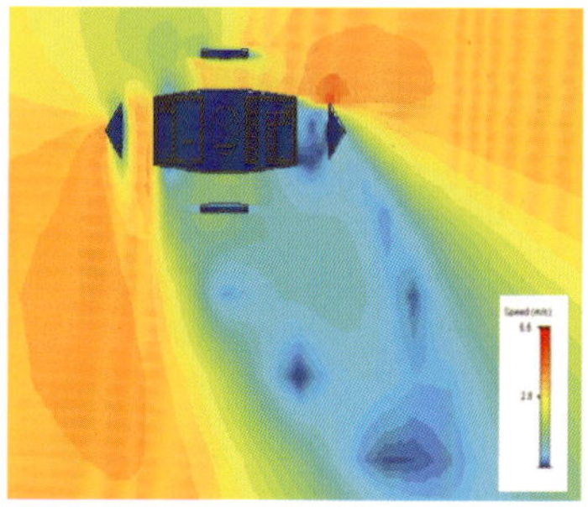

PLAN-A DIRECTION 1

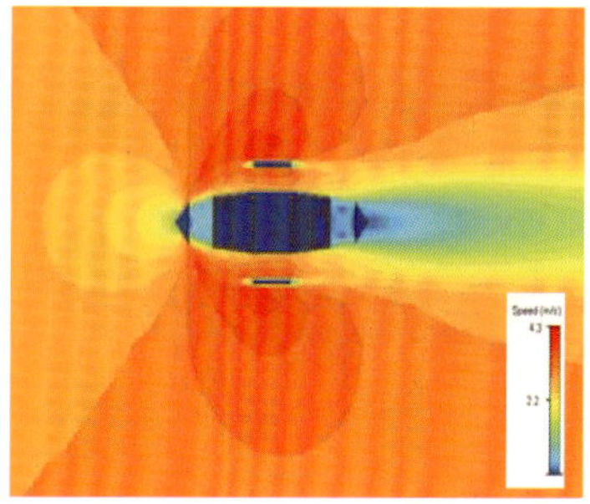

PLAN-A DIRECTION 2

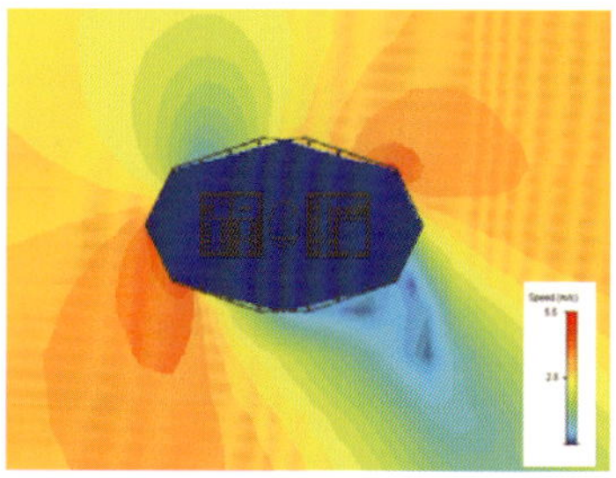

PLAN-B DIRECTION 1

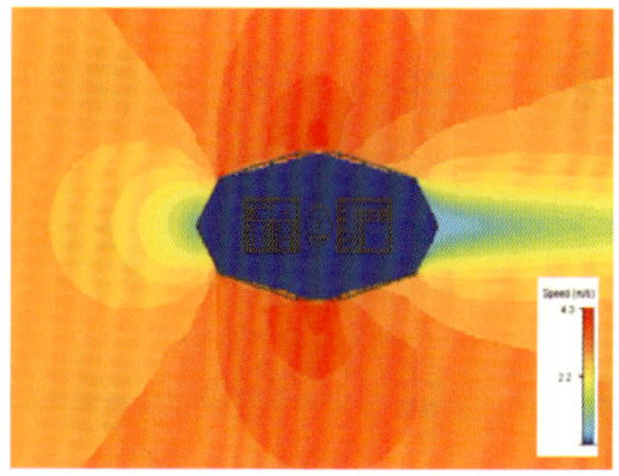

PLAN-B DIRECTION 2

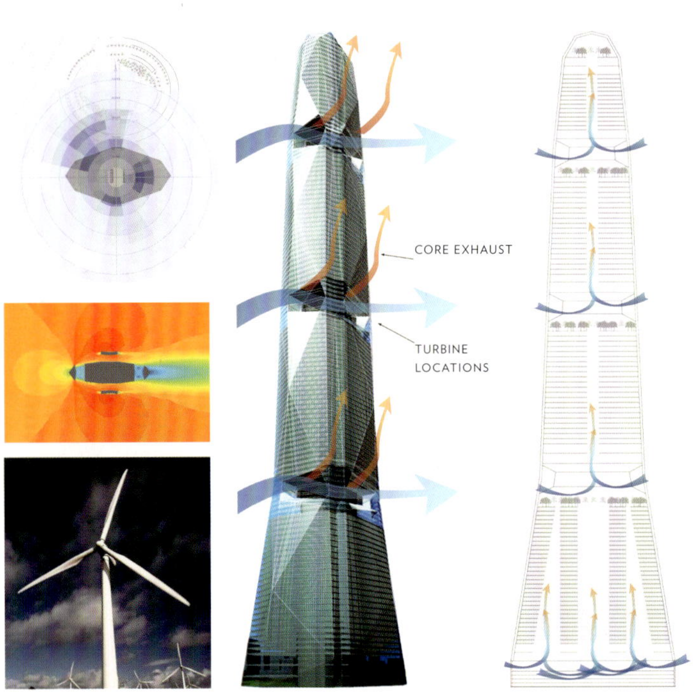

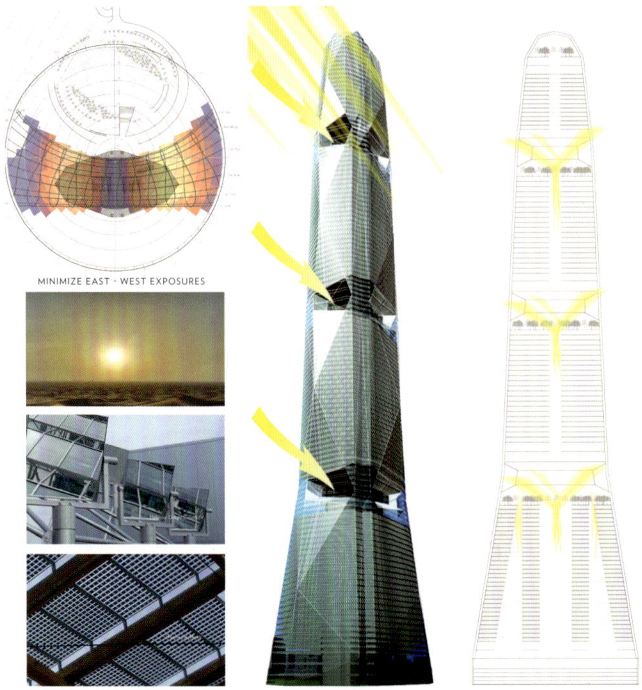

NATURAL DAYLIGHTING FOR ATRIUM SPACE

SKYGARDEN LOCATIONS

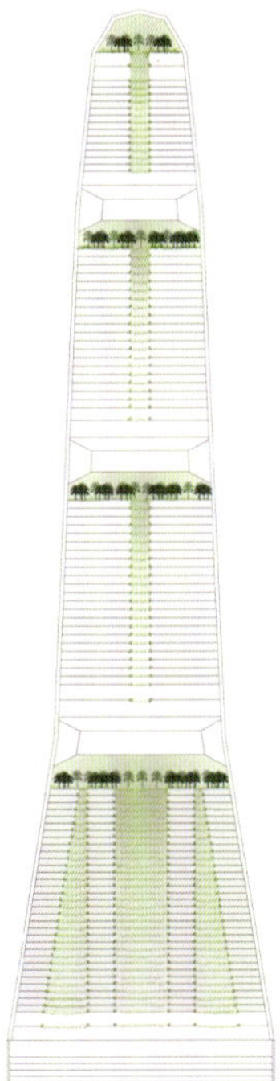

SKYGARDEN AND VEGETATED ATRIUM

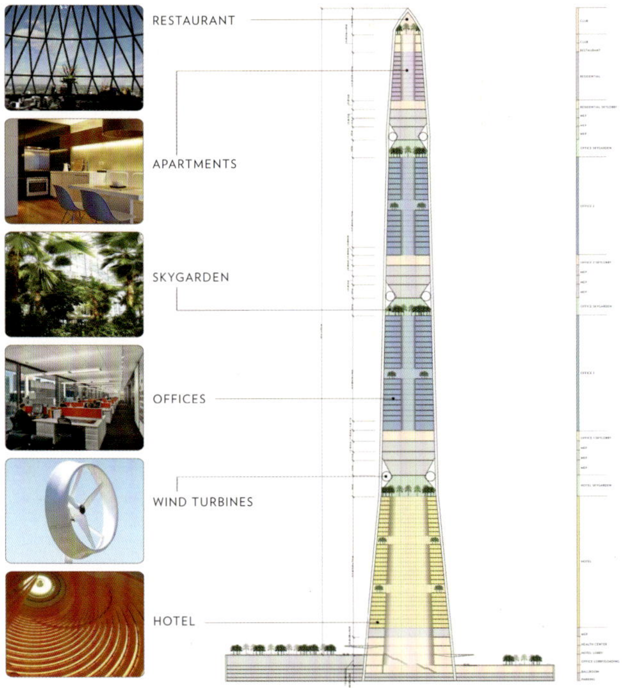

ADRIAN SMITH + GORDON GILL
ARCHITECTURE

BUILDING INTEGRATED WIND TURBINE + SKY GARDEN

Mile-High Tower

Various Locations

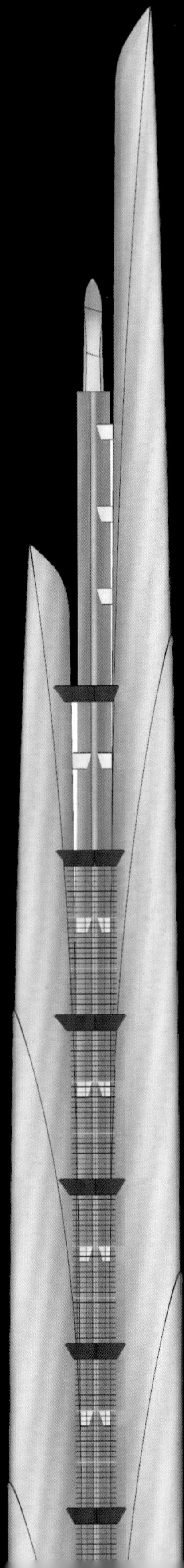

Mile-High Tower Prototype

Various Locations

Over the past 10 years, AS+GG has explored several concepts for a mile-high tower. Each prototype is a design exercise to study the structural and architectural viability of constructing a mixed-use, mile-high tower.

SERVICES
Architecture

CLIENT
Confidential

FUNCTION
Mixed-Use

FACTS
1 mile height

The first concept is designed for Chicago, Illinois and for a specific site at the intersection of the north branch and main stem of the Chicago River on a plot known as Wolf Point. The design was completed with the idea that a megatall tower can increase taxes, create new employment opportunities, and increase economic activity in the area directly around the tower.

Although the design was presented to various potential developers, there was little interest. AS+GG looks forward to the opportunity to find another special site for this special building.

The second and third concepts are designed for a site in Mecca, Saudi Arabia. The client was looking for a building that honors the pilgrimage that Muslims strive to take at least once in their lifetime. The tower is a triumph of modern technology, while paying homage to this holy tradition.

While the proposal has not yet been acted upon, the goal to build a Middle East mile-high tower is still in discussion.

ADRIAN SMITH+GORDON GILL
ARCHITECTURE

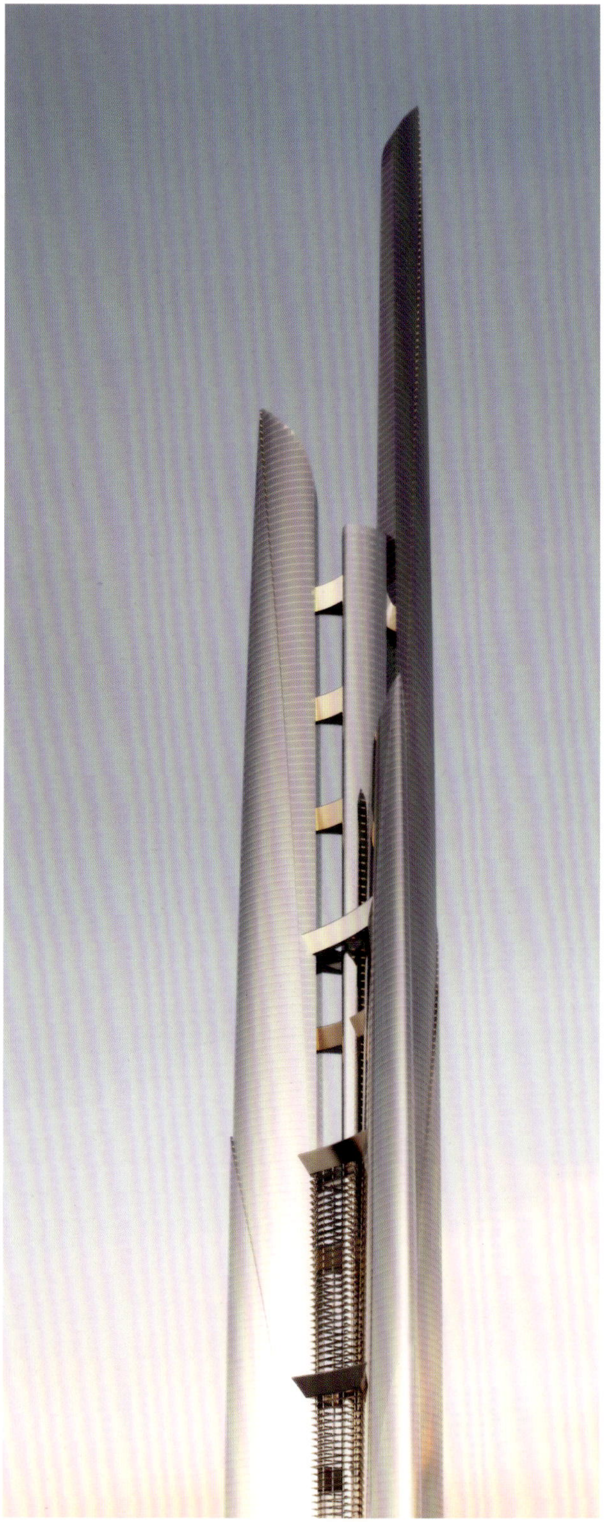

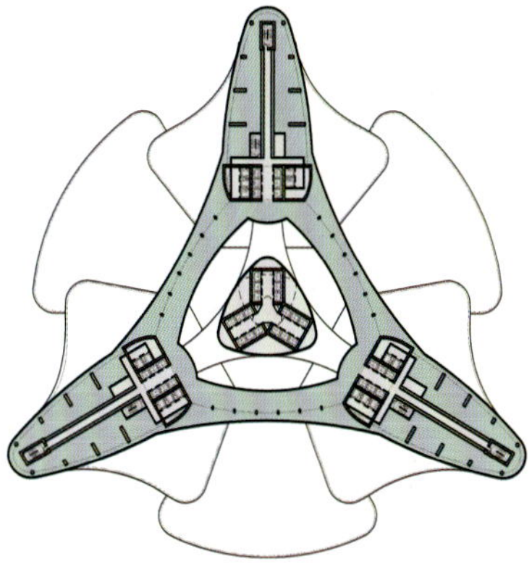

TIER 3 BRIDGE

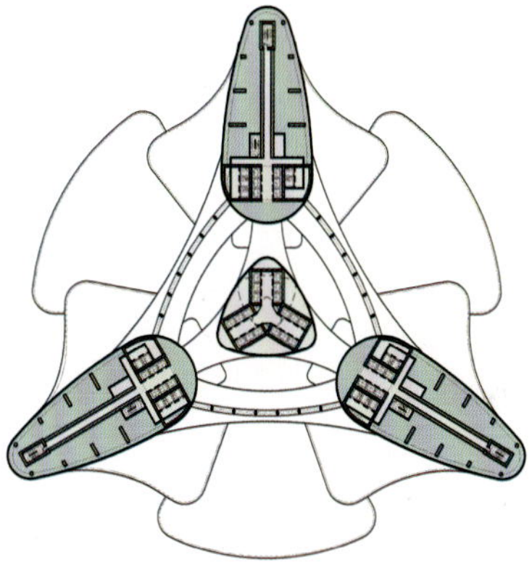

TIER 3

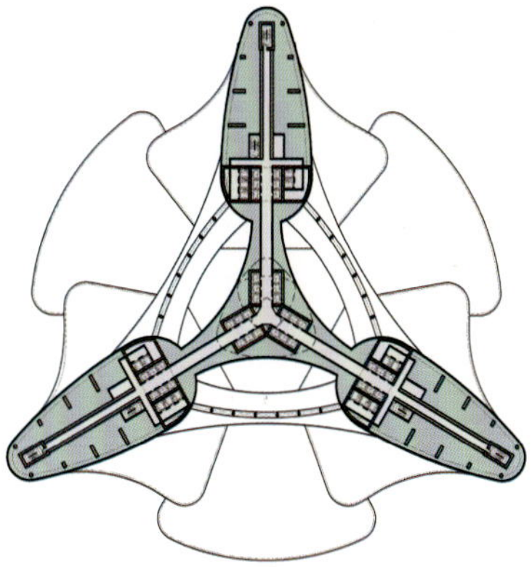

TIER 3 UMBILICAL

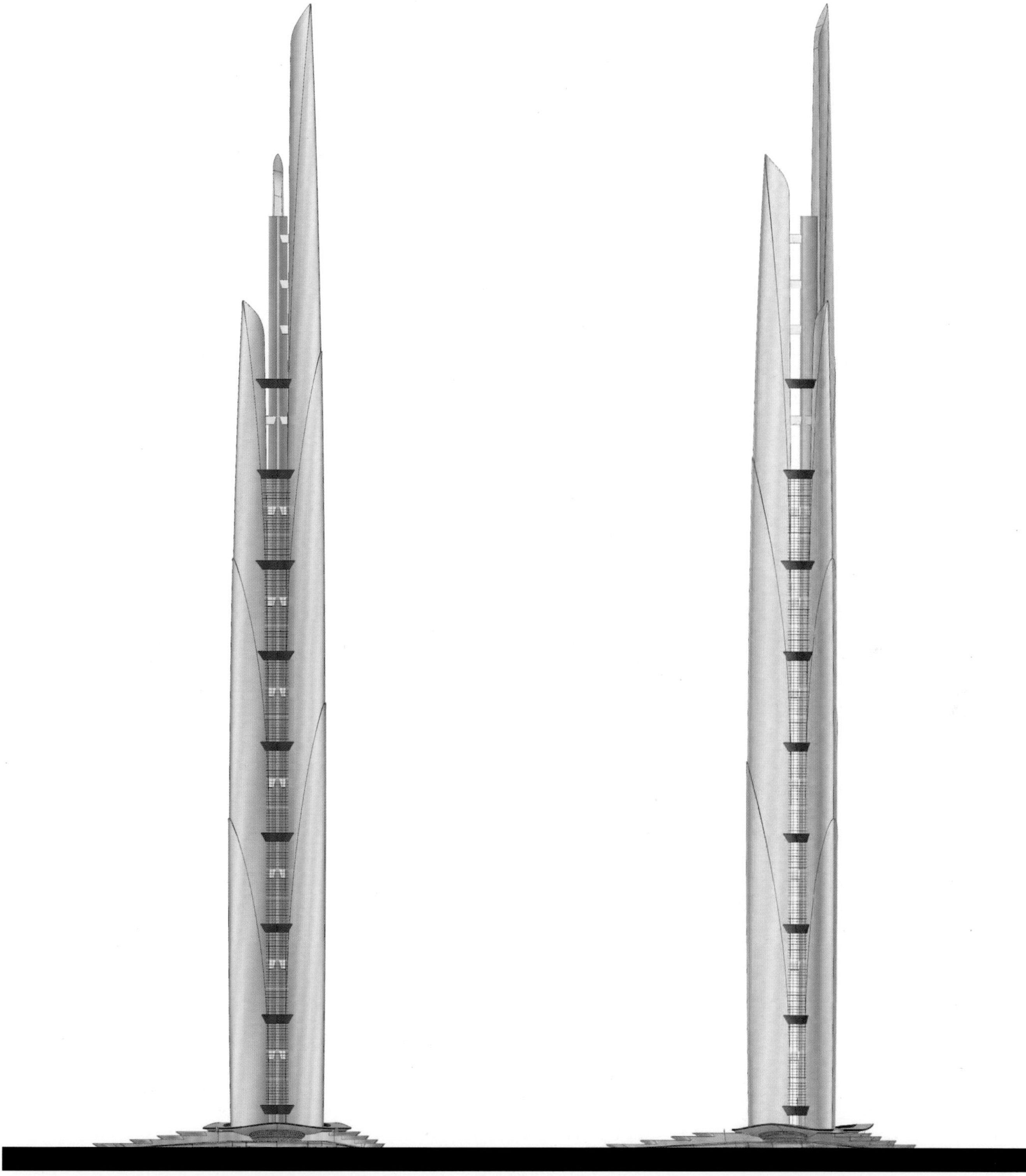

Clean Tech Tower

Chicago, Illinois

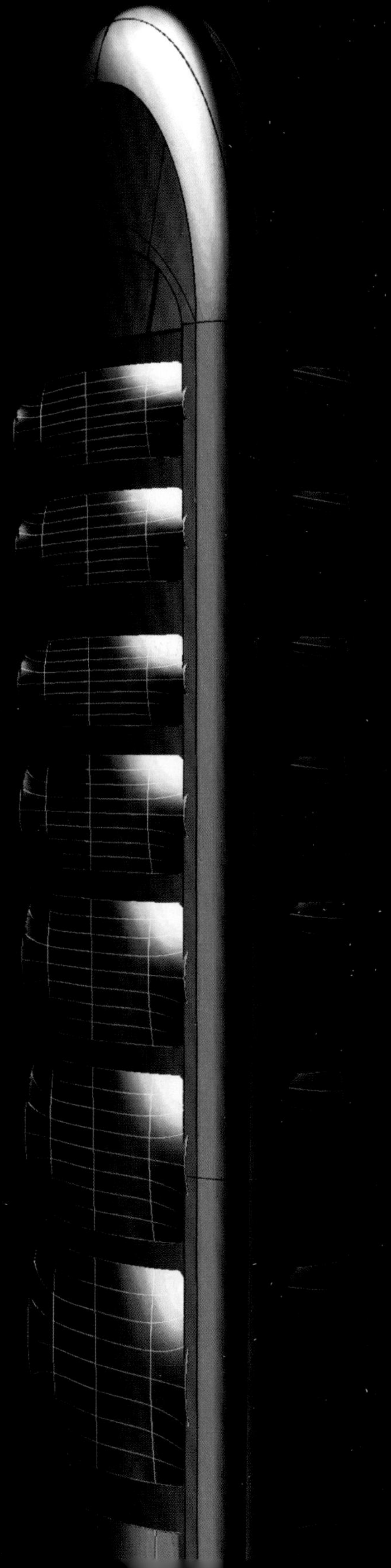

Clean Technology Tower

Chicago, Illinois

Clean Technology Tower is a high-performance, net-zero-energy mixed-use development designed both for a specific site in Chicago and as a prototype to demonstrate sustainable architecture principles that can be applied around the globe.

SERVICES
Architecture

CLIENT
N/A

FUNCTION
Mixed-Use

FACTS
2.5 million sf

Building on the concept of biomimicry, Clean Technology Tower uses advanced sustainability systems and strategies to foster a symbiotic relationship with its environment. Sited and formed to harness natural forces, the tower refines conventional methods of capturing those forces to increase efficiency.

Wind turbines at the building's corners capture wind at its highest velocity as it accelerates around the tower; the turbines become denser as the tower ascends and wind speeds increase. At the tower's apex, where wind speeds are highest, a domed double roof cavity captures air, creating a large wind farm; negative pressures ventilate the interior. The dome is shaded by photovoltaic cells that capture the southern sun.

While the prototype design is specific to Chicago, its guiding principles and applied technologies are universal. Clean Technology Towers could be built around the world, and each would be distinctly formed in response to its particular site.

The Chicago design features about 1.8 million square feet of office space, 300,000 square-feet of hotel space, a spa, and street-level retail. Office space is located on high floors to maximize views and take advantage of natural daylight. Dedicated elevators provide access for both office and hotel tenants to all of the tower's amenities. The tower's domed top offers unrestricted skyward views, creating a grand atrium space.

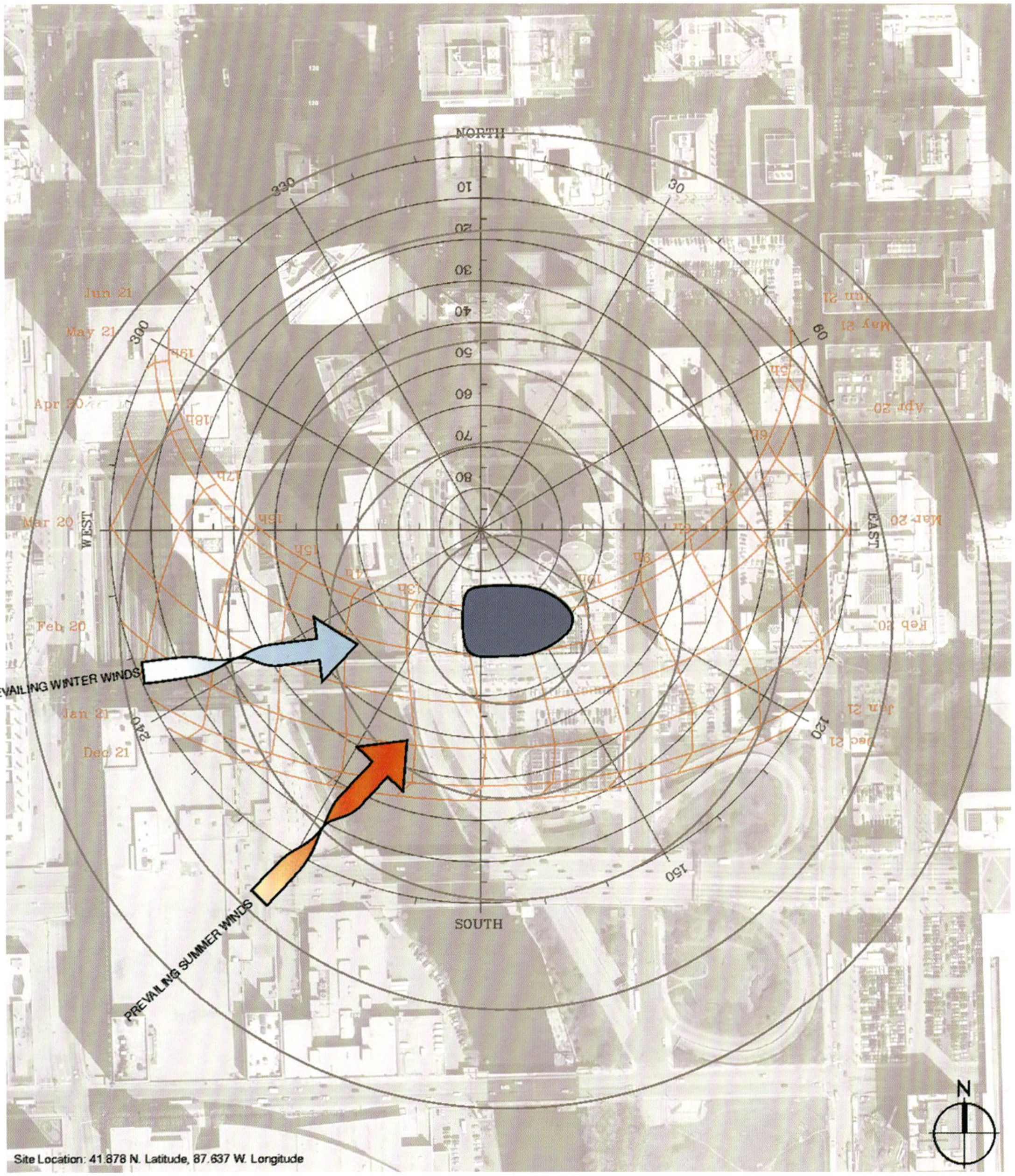
NORTH
SOUTH
EAST
WEST
PREVAILING WINTER WINDS
PREVAILING SUMMER WINDS
Jun 21
May 21
Apr 20
Mar 20
Feb 20
Jan 21
Dec 21
Site Location: 41.878 N. Latitude, 87.637 W. Longitude
N

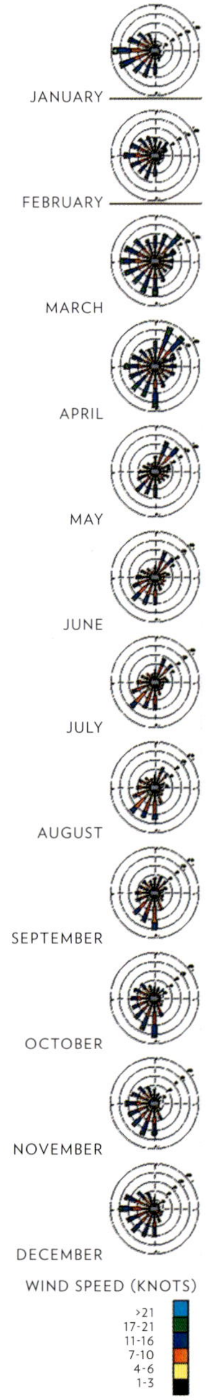
JANUARY
FEBRUARY
MARCH
APRIL
MAY
JUNE
JULY
AUGUST
SEPTEMBER
OCTOBER
NOVEMBER
DECEMBER
WIND SPEED (KNOTS)
>21
17-21
11-16
7-10
4-6
1-3

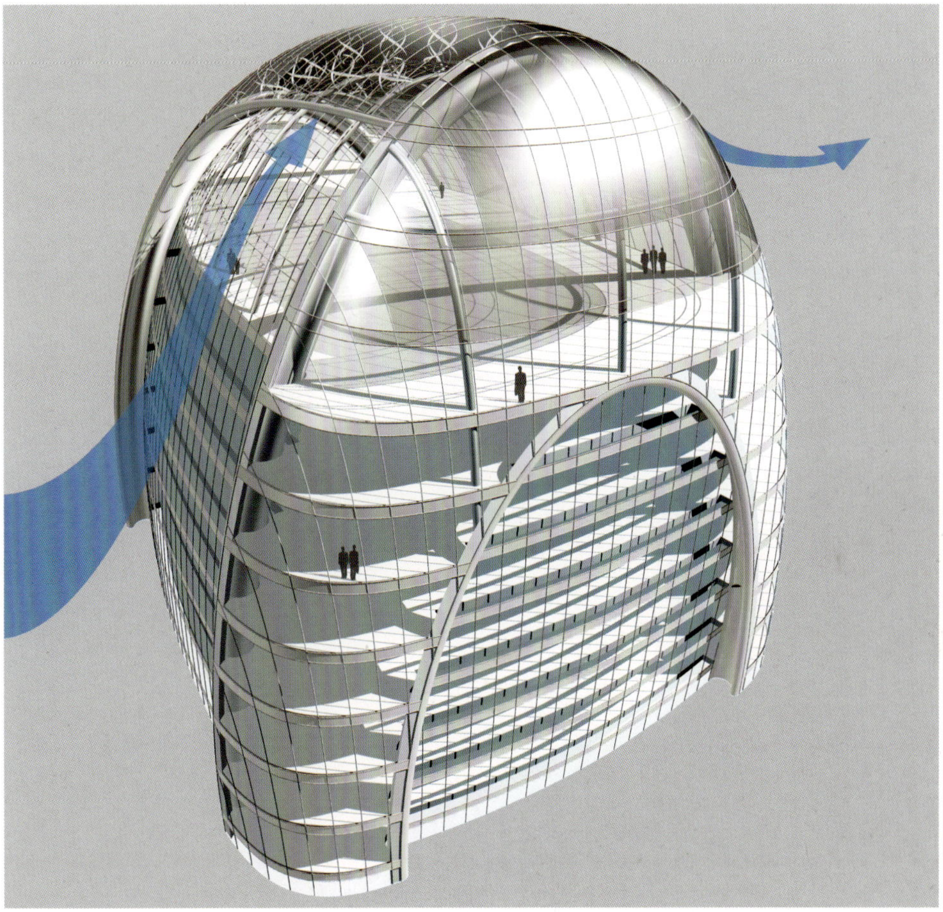

BUILDING INTEGRATED
WIND TURBINES

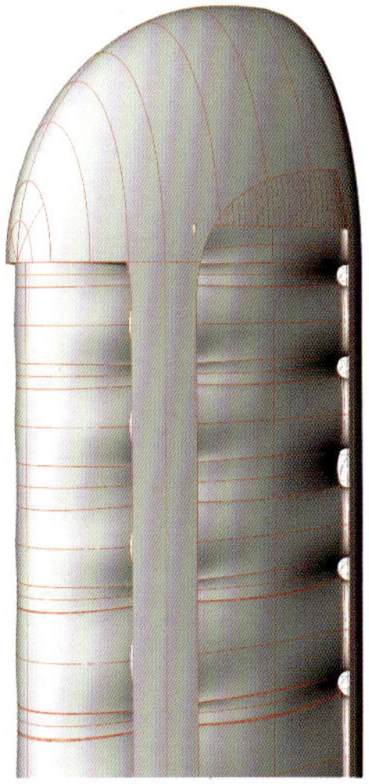

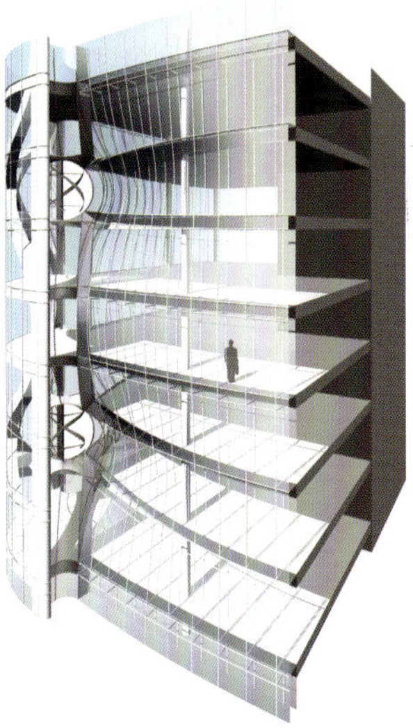

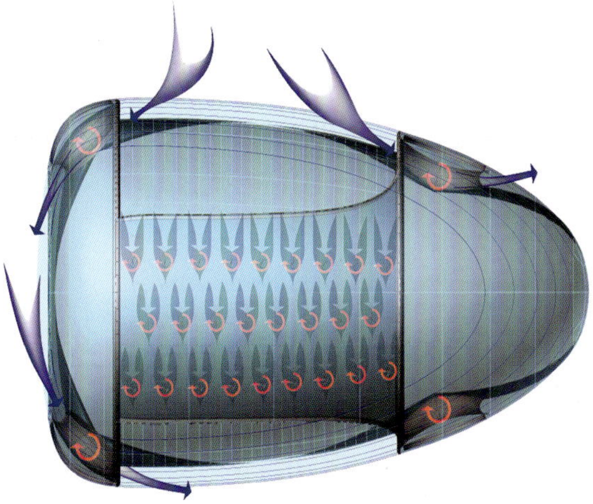

FKI Tower

Seoul, Korea

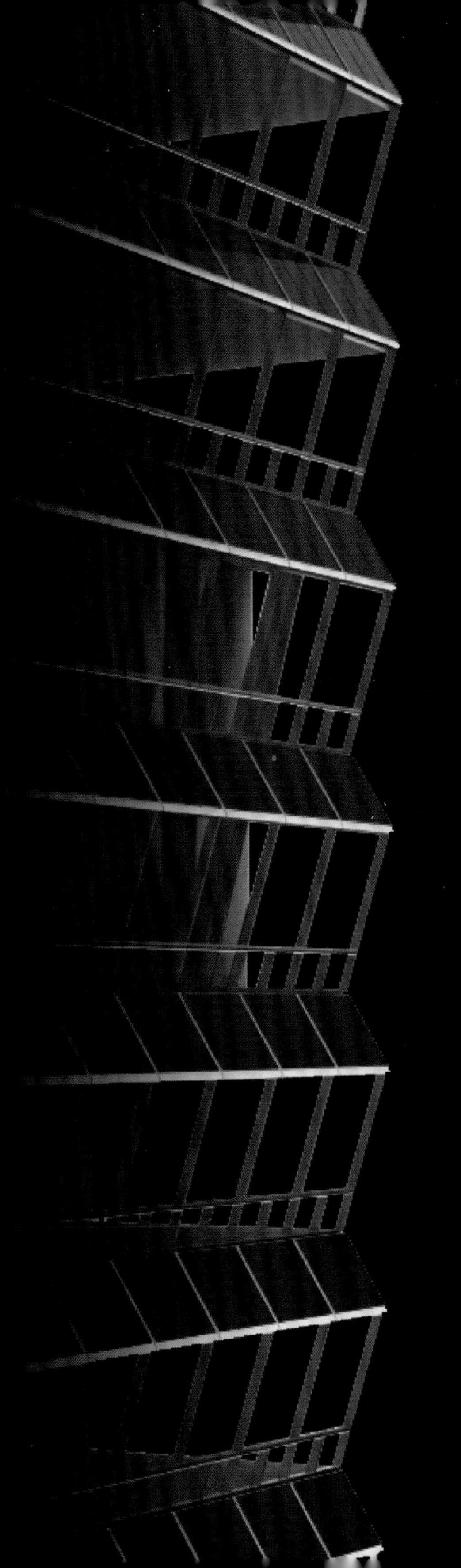

FKI Tower

Seoul, Korea

SERVICES
Architecture
Interior Design

CLIENT
Federation of Korean Industries

FUNCTION
Office

FACTS
244 m height
170,104 sm area

AWARDS
The American Architecture Prize, Architectural Design | Tall Buildings, Winner, 2017

Re-Thinking the Future, Sustainability Award, First Award, Commercial, 2016

AIA Chicago, Divine Detail Award, FKI Tower BIPV, 2016

The Chicago Athenaeum, International Architecture Award, 2016

The Chicago Athenaeum, Green Good Design Award, Green Architecture, FKI Tower, 2015

Civic Trust Awards, International Winner, 2015

Korean Architecture Award, Excellence Award, 2014

Korea Presidential Commission on Architecture Policy, Korea Green Building Award, 2014

Chicago AIA, Distinguished Building Award, Citation of Merit, 2014

CTBUH, Best Tall Building Asia and Australasia, Finalist, 2014

Structural Engineers Association of Illinois, Excellence in Structural Engineering Award, Winner, Best Project $150 million and over, 2014

Architizer A+ Award, Office Building High Rise, Finalist, 2014

Completed in December 2013, FKI Tower is a major addition to the skyline of Seoul. The tower's position guarantees spectacular views, adding to the world-class setting similar to New York's Central Park or Chicago's Magnificent Mile.

The 50-story, 240-meter tower features an innovative exterior wall, designed specifically for the project. The building's unique skin helps reduce internal heating and cooling loads and collects energy through photovoltaic panels that are integrated into the spandrel areas of the southwest and northwest facades.

FKI Tower's exterior wall system combines maximum access to views, energy-efficiency strategies and energy-generation technologies. By angling the spandrel panels 30 degrees toward the sun, the amount of energy collected by the photovoltaic panels is maximized. Below the spandrel panels, the vision panels are angled 15 degrees toward the ground, minimizing the amount of direct sun radiation and glare. The end result is a unique folded exterior texture that is both purposeful and visually distinctive. Benefits include a reduction of glare and heat gains from direct sunlight, while maintaining a high level of indirect light. With the exception of the early morning and the late afternoon periods, the building is able to use the geometry of the exterior wall to self-shade the perimeter spaces that would normally be inundated with direct sunlight. This gives the building occupants the flexibility to open the shades and allow indirect natural light.

The tower's interior includes several indoor garden and atrium spaces that enhance the workplace environment with natural elements of wood, bamboo, and other native plants. The interior of the building takes advantage of the floor-to-ceiling windows of the exterior wall, offering an abundance of natural light to office spaces and corridors as well as extensive views of neighboring Yeoido Park, the Han River, and the surrounding city.

FKI Tower also features an expansive rooftop atrium garden that also has custom photovoltaic panels. The ideal angle of the panel placement on the roof was studied in detail. In a relatively unconfined space photovoltaic panels are angled upward at 30 degrees but within the limited area of FKI's roof, it was determined that a 10-degree angle allowed for more panels to be installed closer together, minimizing the effect of the panels casting shadows on each other and ultimately producing more solar energy for the building. When analyzing the roof skylight photovoltaic panels, it was equally important to account for self-shading so that enough natural light would be let into the sky garden below. The garden is planted with Korean Boxwood, a lush and hearty shrub that is also low-maintenance. The rooftop atrium has several seating and viewing areas that tenants can sit and enjoy views of the surrounding city.

EXTERIOR WALL DETAILS

1. Silver-Anodized-Aluminum Curtain-Wall System
2. Panel-Fixed Joint
3. Customized Photovoltaic Panel/Rain Screen
4. Panel-Fixed Joint
5. Low-E Insulated Glass
6. Panel Movement Joint
7. Operable Window
8. Water-Tight Metal-Insulated Panel
9. Ventilated And Drained Void

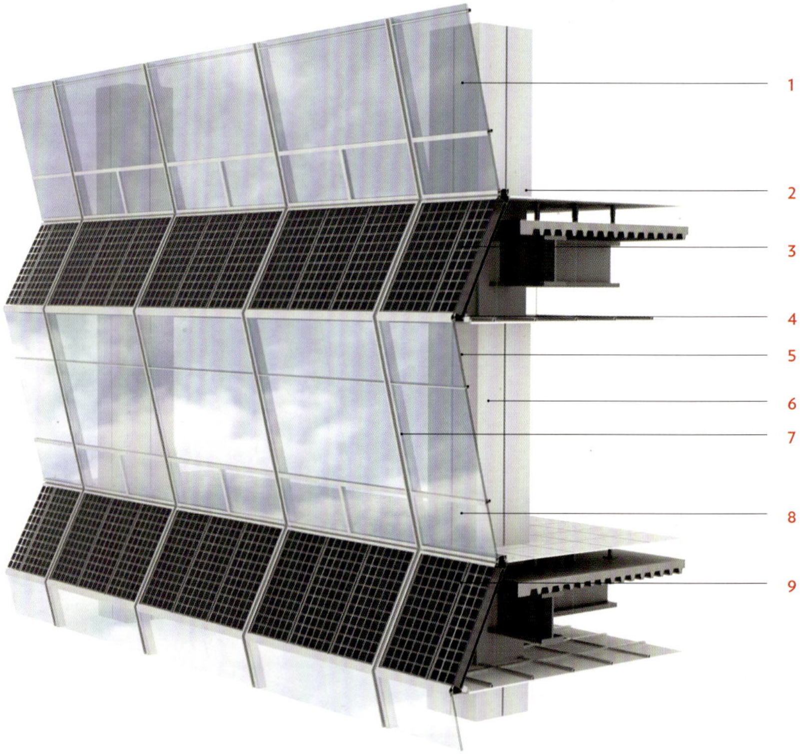

GLARE MITIGATION

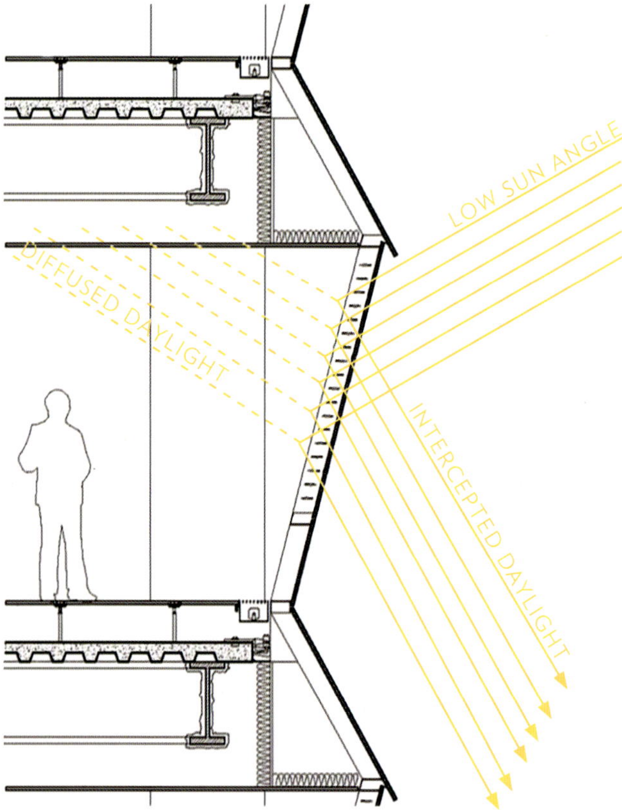

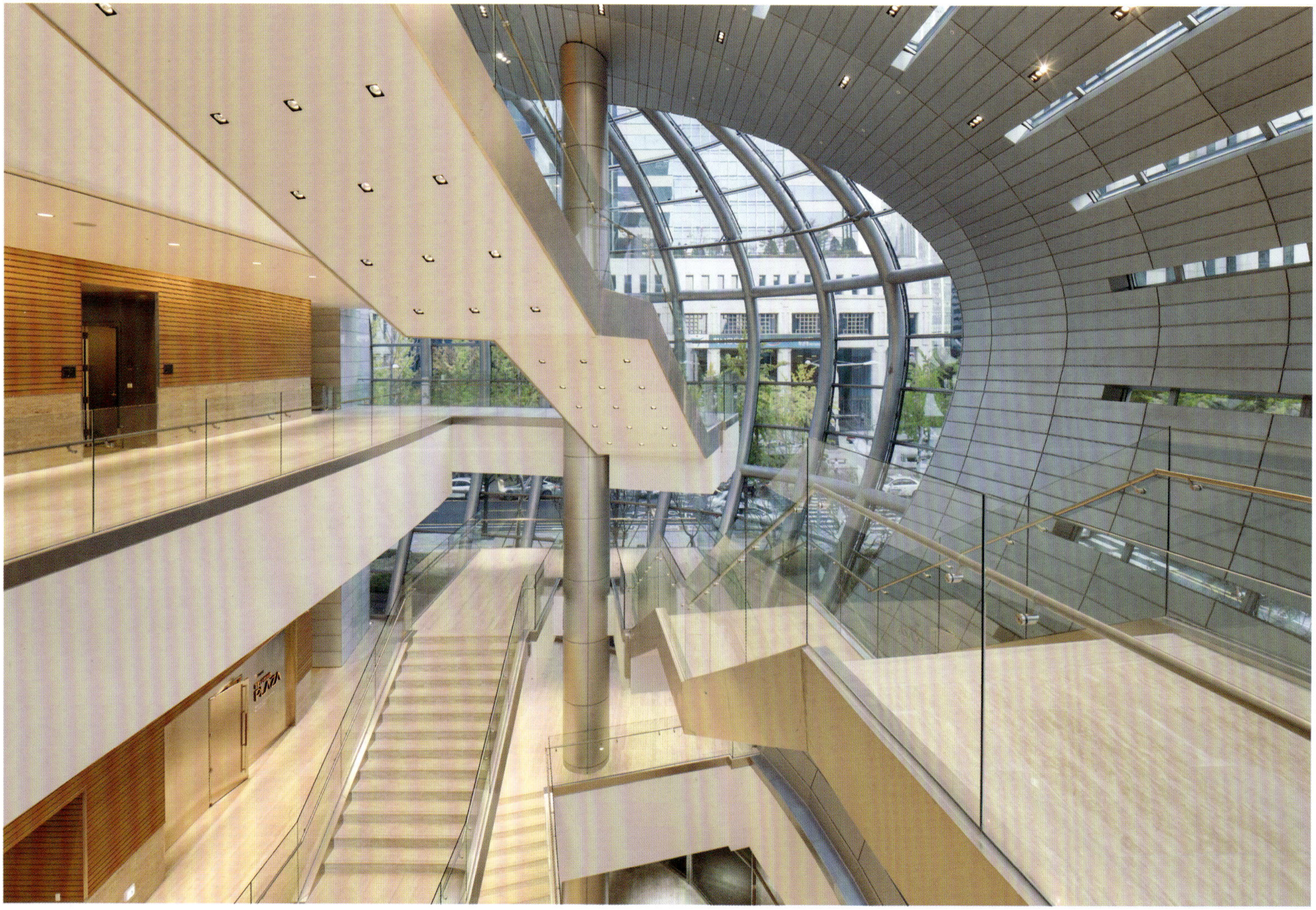

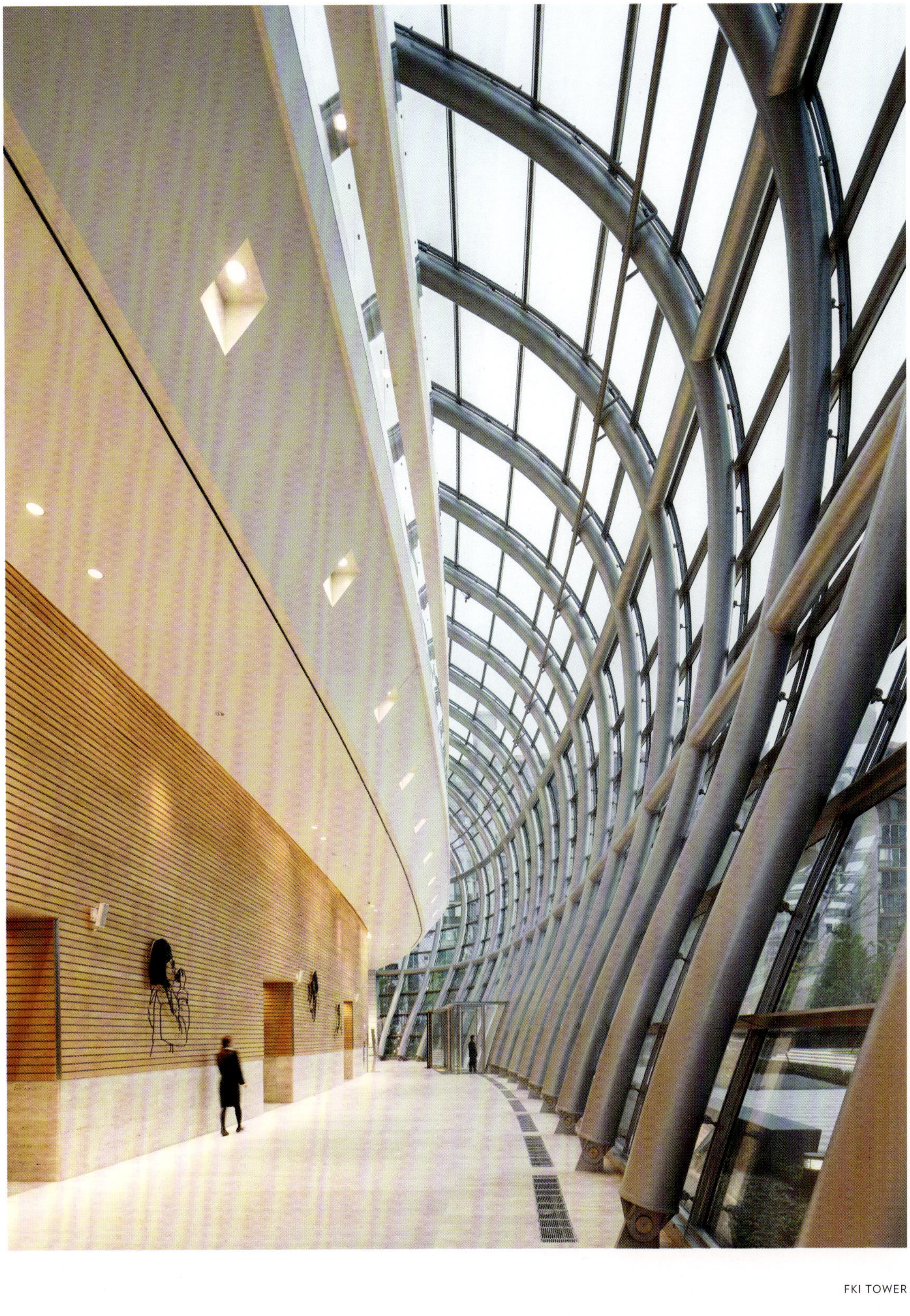

Gang Xia Tower

Shenzhen, China

Gang Xia Tower

Shenzhen, China

Gang Xia is the newest icon of Shenzhen's Futian Central District. The 198-meter, 43-story tower with softly curved corners makes a powerful architectural statement that is at once dynamic and elegant, contemporary and timeless.

SERVICES
Architecture
Interior Design

CLIENT
Shenzhen Xiangjiang Real Estate Co., Ltd.

FUNCTION
Mixed-use

FACTS
198 m height

For occupants and visitors, the experience of the building is defined by its simplified floor plate, spacious 4.5-meter floor-to-floor heights, landscaped gardens, and windows with spectacular westward views of the adjacent Civic Center Park, a focal point of the city's sparkling new business district.

The primary design challenge was to maximize views of the park—which requires an overall north-south orientation for the tower—while mitigating heat gain from the harsh morning and afternoon sun. To meet this challenge, AS+GG's design team developed a unique steel-and-glass envelope for the tower that features a unified grid system of unitized curtain wall panels of standard dimensions, each with recessed high-performance glass about 300 mm deep. The modular fenestration system, with four smaller-proportioned windows stacked vertically on each floor, allows for significantly shallower louvers. The system also reduces the percentage of glazing in the building envelope, increasing its insulation value.

The tower's other sustainability features include daylight harvesting, high-efficiency lighting and HVAC, and a suite of water-saving systems including low-flow or no-flow fixtures, graywater and condensate reclamation, and rainwater capture.

The floor plate of less than 2,000 square meters is compact and efficient, eliminating the need for fire zone separations and other features that can increase building costs. It adheres rigidly to the constraints of idealized lease spans, elevator service quality, overall energy efficiency, and high-quality elemental materials.

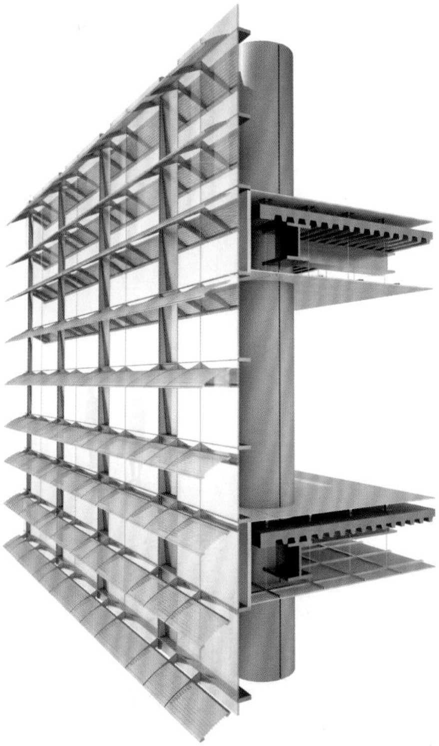

EXTERIOR WALL DETAILS

FENESTRATION SOLAR ANALYSIS

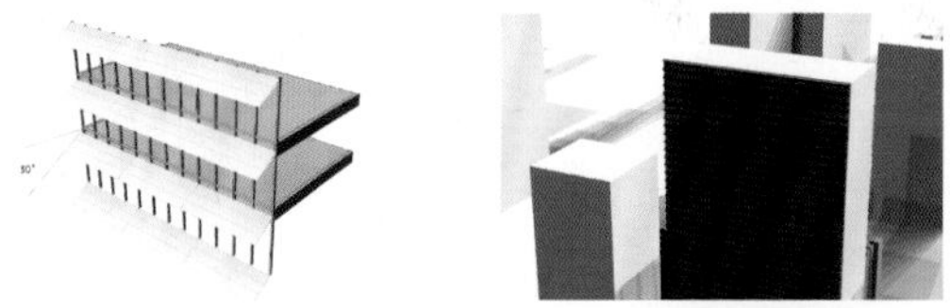

HORIZONTAL LOUVERS ANGLE 30° DOWN

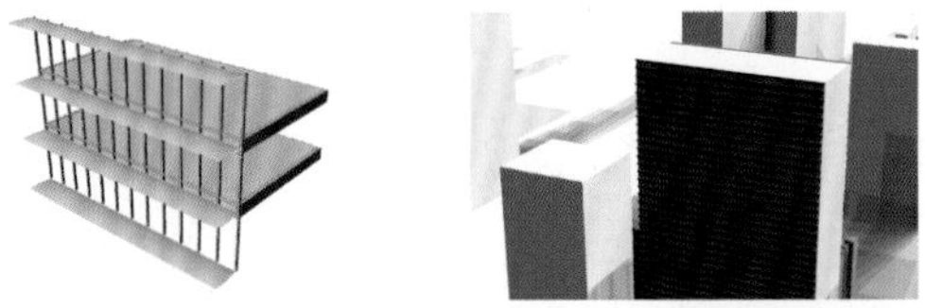

HORIZONTAL LOUVERS ANGLE 0

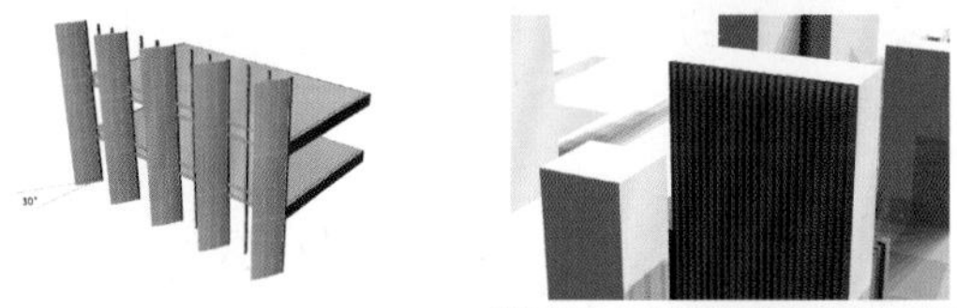

VERTICAL LOUVERS ANGLE 30° NORTH

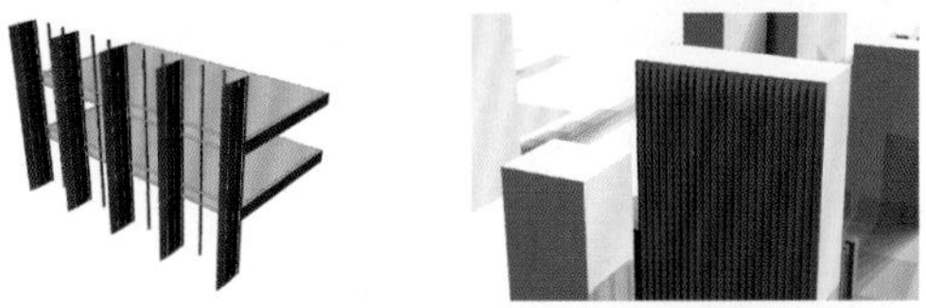

VERTICAL LOUVERS ANGLE 0

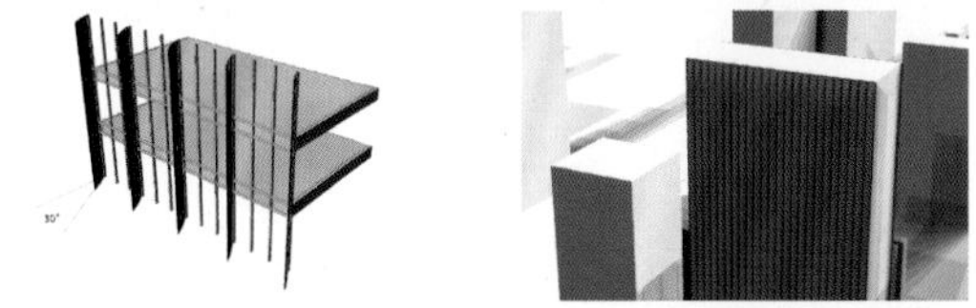

VERTICAL LOUVERS ANGLE 30° SOUTH

Zhongzhou Holdings

Shenzhen, China

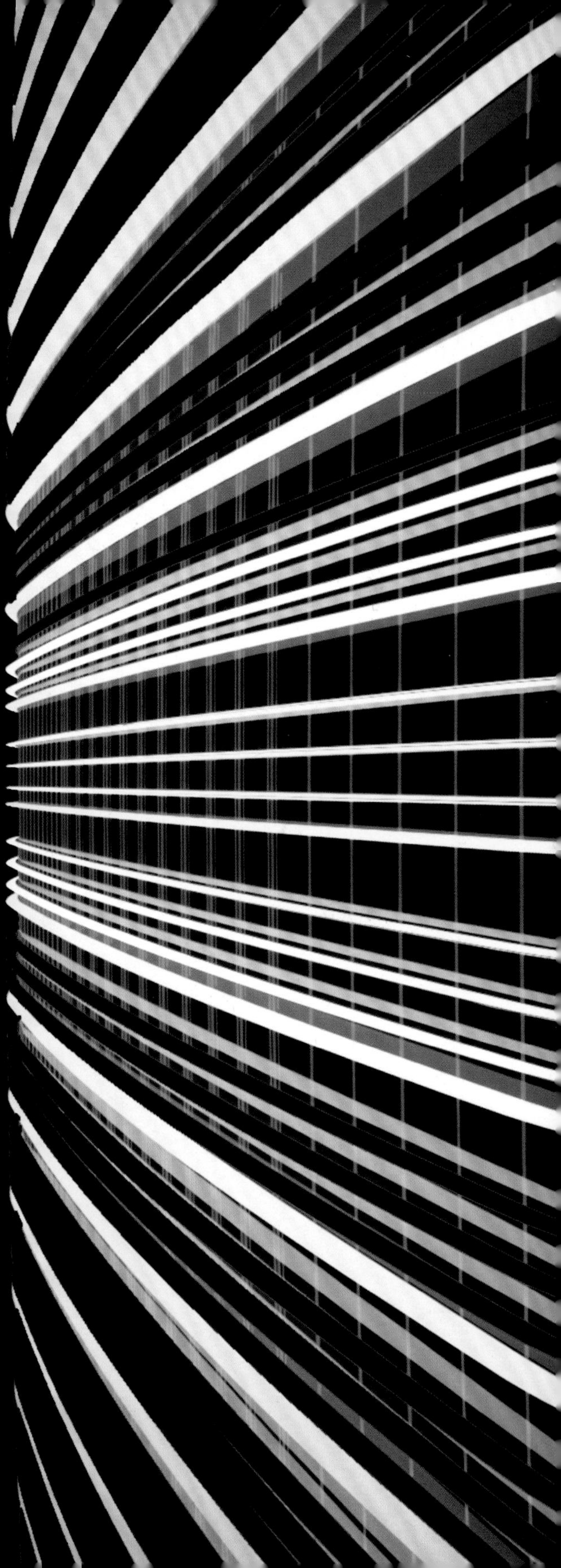

Zhongzhou Holdings Financial Center

Shenzhen, China

Shenzhen's Zhongzhou Holdings Finance Center is a mixed-use complex located in Shenzhen's Nanshan Culture District, consisting of a multi-purpose podium, a 300-meter-tall office and hotel tower, and a related 160-meter-tall residential tower.

SERVICES
Architecture
Facade Design

CLIENT
Shenzhen Xiangjiang
Real Estate Co., Ltd

FUNCTION
Mixed-use

FACTS
300 m height

AWARDS
CTBUH, Best Tall Building in Asia or Australia, Finalist, 2016

The simple form and fluid skin of the towers is sleek and modern and presents a dynamic image for the district, as well as Shenzhen at large. The design demonstrates a highly-refined collection of multi-purpose, performance based solutions and coincidental aesthetic discoveries that were built and can be maintained on a modest budget.

Early in the design process, a series of solar studies were completed to establish the performance of the design as a base-case scenario to improve the towers' energy performance and user comfort levels. The studies included incident (direct) solar heat gain analysis, diffuse (indirect) solar heat gain analysis, daylighting analysis, radiance analysis, wind-pressure mapping, view analysis, and social and program mapping. The resulting shape was a gently curving facade that helps the light be evenly distributed among the interior, increasing daylighting while minimizing solar gain.

Zhongzhou Holdings Financial Center represents the intersection between performance and function. It expresses an understanding of local environmental conditions through the intense refinement of passive technologies to create a timeless architectural expression. The building's facade was strategically designed to work within the site's dense urban environment and it's unique design helped the building achieve a LEED-Gold rating. The building also has numerous atria and break spaces to increase the comfort level of tenants.

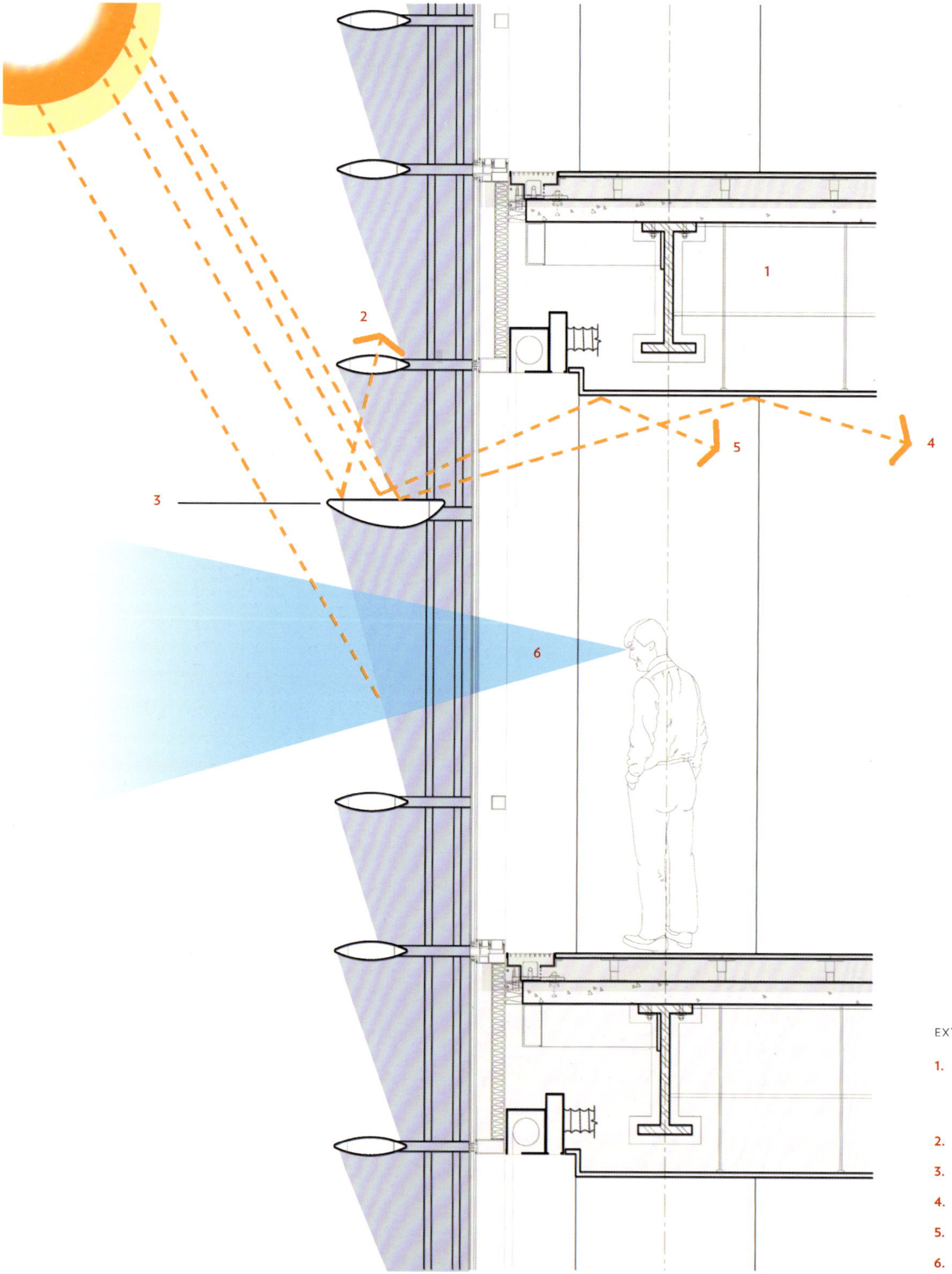

EXTERIOR WALL DIAGRAM

1. Structural Glazed Low-E Insulating Unit with Frit Pattern and Sun Shade / Light Shelf
2. Reduces Glare
3. Daylighting Louver
4. Shade Reduces Solar Heat
5. Interior Natural Light
6. Transparent Views

Vantone Center

Tianjin, China

Vantone Center

Tianjin, China

Vantone Center Tianjin is a new corporate headquarters and one of the most sustainable buildingGols in Tianjin, China. At 185-meters tall, Vantone Center is one of the taller structures in downtown Tianjin's thriving Central Business District.

SERVICES
Architecture

CLIENT
Beijing Vantone Real Estate Co., Ltd.

FUNCTION
Office

FACTS
185 m height

Design to reach LEED-Platinum or Gold certification, Vantone Center consists of 64,000 sm above-grade, Class-A office and high-end retail space, along with an additional 30,000 sm below-grade retail and parking. The building also features a soaring, 27-meter-tall private club for building tenants.

The tower's elegantly twisting, faceted form signifies the rising importance of Tianjin, while the undulating pattern of the cladding of the north and south facades evokes both the rippling surface of the Haihe River, two blocks to the east, and the region's tradition of bamboo weaving. The south facade provides stunning views of the Tianjin business district's planned central park; a sunken garden at the base of the building will provide an underground connection to the park and its planned subterranean retail complex.

A two-story, high-end retail podium on the north side of the building complements the area's bustling shopping district and offers a handsome amenity on its publicly accessible green roof and restaurant terraces.

The tower's sustainability features include a high-performance, high-thermal-mass exterior wall system with alternating metal and inward-angled glass panels that block solar heat gain, and extensive use of self-shading and daylight harvesting. The east and west facades use alternating metal and glass panels that balance solar heat blocking, optimized shading for the low-angled morning and afternoon sun, and the availability of views of the park to the south.

ADRIAN SMITH+GORDON GILL
ARCHITECTURE

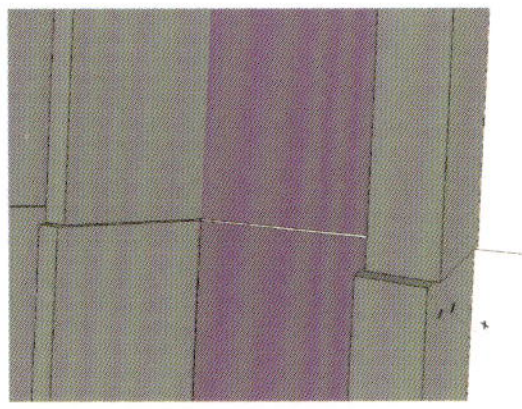

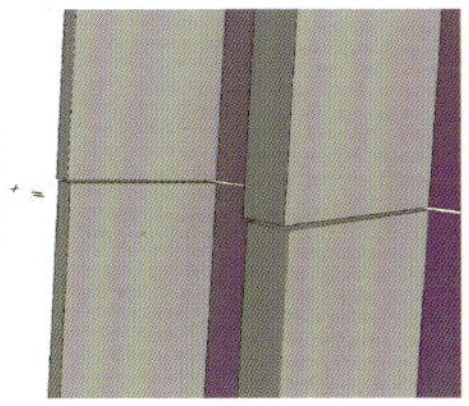

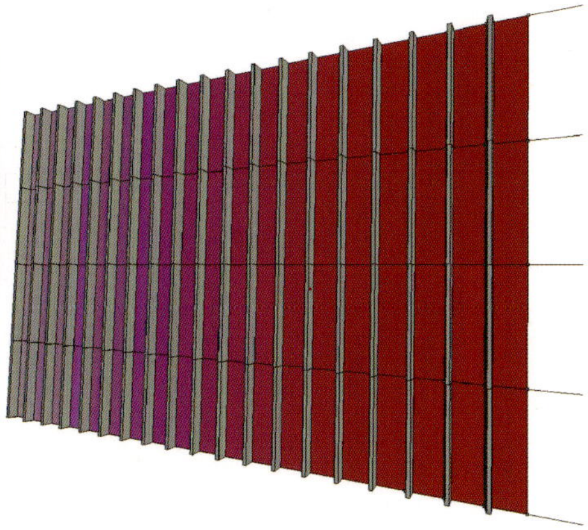

WEST WALL WITH FINS
PERSPECTIVE

EAST WALL WITH FINS
PERSPECTIVE

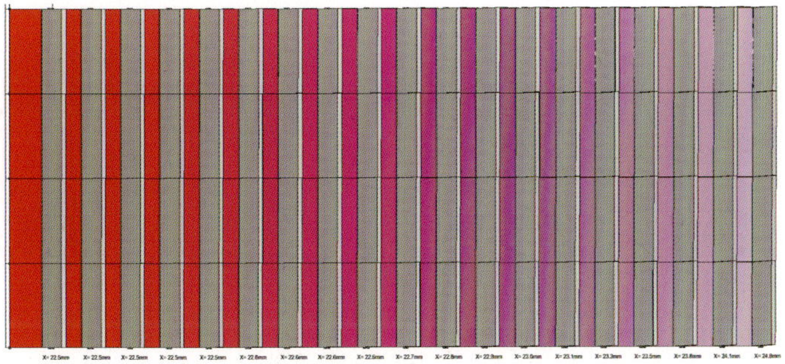

WEST WALL WITH FINS
ELEVATION

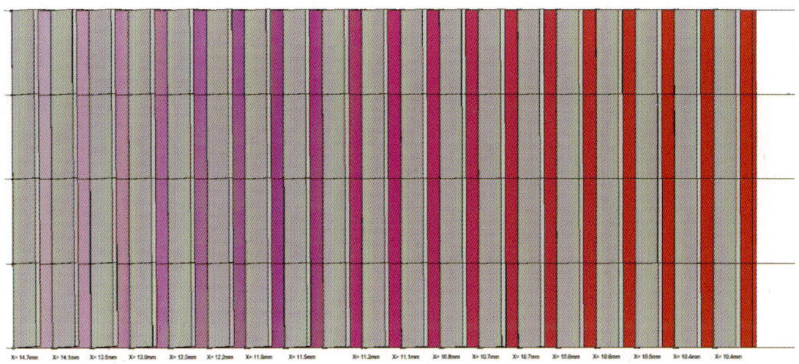

EAST WALL WITH FINS
ELEVATION

WEST WALL WITH FINS
PLANS

EAST WALL WITH FINS
PLANS

160 Front

Toronto, Ontario

160 Front Street

Toronto, Ontario

The new iconic tower, now under construction, will forever alter the Toronto skyline with a shape that is designed specifically for the site at 160 Front Street.

SERVICES
Architecture
Interior Design

CLIENT
Cadillac Fairview

FUNCTION
Mixed-use

FACTS
111,483 sm

The building's form is sculpted in response to extensive environmental analysis, one of which includes that the main axis of the building ideally be oriented parallel to the direction of the site's prevailing winds, minimizing its resistance to the wind's lateral loads. A significant amount of time was spent on analysis. The resulting design is tapered both at the top and the bottom, assisting the structure when resisting wind, minimizing its effect on the pedestrian realm, and creating a spacious respite to the compressed neighboring sidewalks.

160 Front Street is contextually integrated to the street grid of Toronto's urban fabric and enhances the pedestrian experience by creating broader sidewalks with landscaped areas both on Simcoe Street and Front Street. The adjacent six-story masonry heritage building is renovated and integrated into the architecture and program of the tower, providing an historical perspective to the tenants of the building.

The building incorporates a state-of-the-art exterior wall with other passive sustainable strategies, helping the building achieve both LEED® Platinum and WELL Building Standard® certification. To ensure continued sustainability monitoring, once completed, 160 Front Street will be subject to the rigorous standards of Green at Work® by Cadillac Fairview, the client's award-winning sustainability program.

The interior features an expansive 33-foot tall lobby with floor-to-ceiling glazing and stone finishes. Throughout the building, 9-feet-6-inch x 2.9-meter ceiling heights, with floor-to-ceiling glass, have spectacular views of Toronto's skyline and offer an amazing quality of light for flexible and efficient workspaces. Daylight harvesting controls help the building yield significant savings in lighting energy consumption and maximize the energy-saving potential of the building's high-performance curtain wall system.

160 Front Street is also incorporating unparalleled amenities including a green roof at the podium level and several outdoor 'inlets' with tenant access from their workspaces. The building is tailored for business. It is designed to specifically appeal to quality conscious tenants seeking to relocate to a world-class building, in a world-class city, with a bold and distinctive Architecture that serves to enhance the tenant's corporate identity.

The tower is designed by AS+GG in collaboration with B+H Architects as the Architect of Record and has 111,000 sm of leasable Class-A office space; 4 levels of below-grade parking for 340 cars; and bike storage for 450 bikes. Construction began in 2019 and is scheduled for completion in 2023.

ADRIAN SMITH + GORDON GILL
ARCHITECTURE

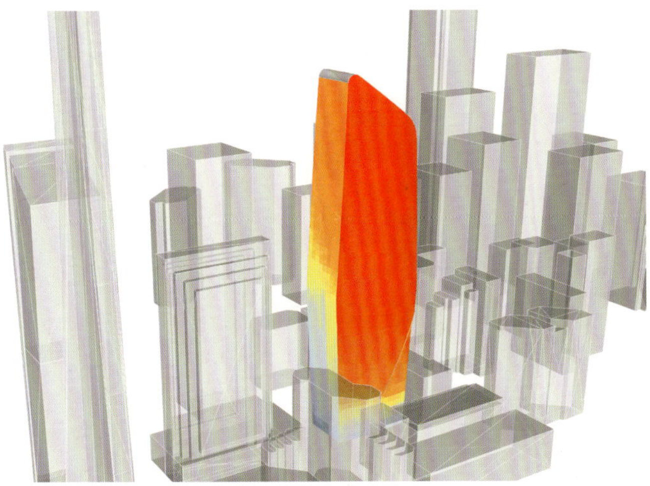

SOUTHWEST VIEW

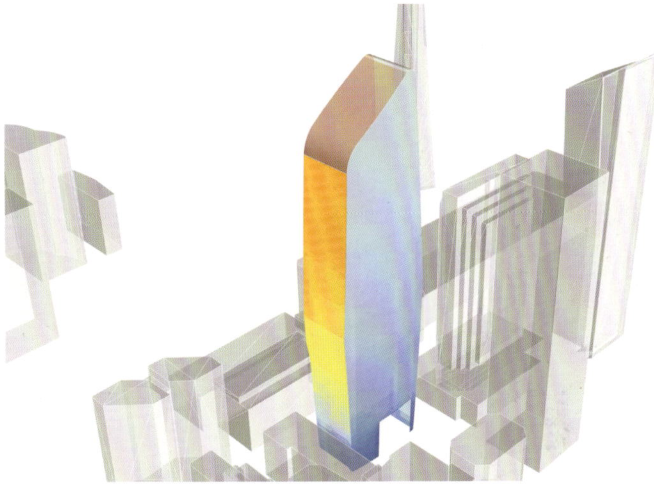

NORTHEAST VIEW

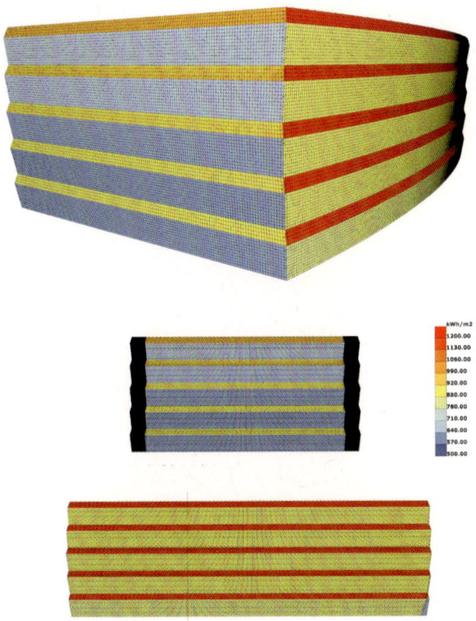

ANNUAL RADIATION ANALYSIS
SAWTOOTH 10 DEGREES DEEP

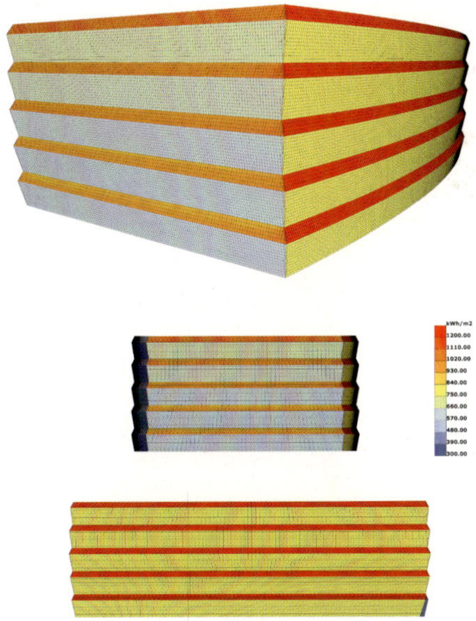

ANNUAL RADIATION ANALYSIS
SAWTOOTH 550MM DEEP

Ahlamana

Riyadh, Saudi Arabia

Ahlamana

Riyadh, Saudi Arabia

Located on the periphery of the King Abdullah Financial District (KAFD) and next to a major expressway, Ahlamana will be one of the primary gateways into the overall development.

SERVICES
Architecture
Interior Design

CLIENT
Saudi Binladin Group

FUNCTION
Mixed-use

FACTS
78 m height office
105 m height residential

Ahlamana, which is the Arabic word for "our dream," a reference to an Arabic figure that informed the design, consists of a 78-meter-tall office tower and a 105-meter-tall residential tower, with the towers connected by two retail podium structures. Ahlamana's podium will also feature KAFD's only outdoor restaurant.

Ahlamana's chief sustainability strategy is its deployment of a louvered travertine screen wall that protects the office tower's western facade from the harshest solar radiation. The residential tower also presents a mostly solid stone wall toward the west, minimizing solar heat gain and reducing energy consumption for air-conditioning. On the other sides of the structure, the facade consists of mostly high-performance vision glass alternating in a subtle pattern with mostly opaque-frit glass panels, allowing for stunning views of KAFD toward the north and south while reducing solar heat gain.

Ahlamana's other sustainable elements include district cooling, solar hot water, energy-efficient lighting and equipment, a graywater collection system and highly efficient HVAC and MEP systems.

Hilal Tower

Riyadh, Saudi Arabia

Hilal Tower

Riyadh, Saudi Arabia

The design of Hilal Tower, a 32-story, 138-meter-tall mixed-use tower that accommodates office, residential, and retail functions, is informed by its prominent site within the King Abdullah Financial District (KAFD) master plan.

SERVICES
Architecture
Interior Design

CLIENT
Saudi Binladin Group

FUNCTION
Mixed-use

FACTS
138 m height

Building occupants will enjoy spectacular views of the development's central plaza and shopping district as well as a museum and a grand mosque Hilal Tower—whose name features the Arabic word for "crescent," a reference to the building's C-shaped window frames—is also oriented on its site in relation to the path of the sun, with increased shading elements on the southern facade to protect against solar heat gain. The northern facade, which enjoys the best views, features a higher percentage of vision glass.

Hilal Tower's other sustainability features include a locally manufactured stone-and-glass exterior wall system that uses shading elements and high thermal mass, solar hot water cells, which provide hot water for the residences, and water conservation systems that collect and re-use graywater for landscape irrigation. The building's overall energy performance will be about 44 percent above ASHRAE standards.

The tower's tapered stepping pattern relates to its program, with the largest floorplates at the lower levels devoted to retail and offices, and the smallest floorplates on the higher levels used for residences. Hilal Tower is topped by a full-floor luxury penthouse unit with rooftop garden.

CONSTRUCTION, 2017

830 Brickell

Miami, Florida

830 Brickell

Miami, Florida

830 Brickell will be the first new office tower to launch in Miami in nearly a decade. The 57-story, 724-foot-tall tower introduces a premium commercial to the city's booming financial district and seeks to reinvent the workplace lifestyle for the highest-caliber of global workforce.

SERVICES
Architecture
Interior Design

CLIENT
OKO Group

FUNCTION
Office

FACTS
57 stories
724 ft height

AS+GG's aim was to elevate the architectural expression of the building to the level of museum-quality art. Set in Miami's Brickell neighborhood, 830 Brickell is at the center of the city's most exciting cultural, culinary, and retail experiences.

The tower has spectacular panoramic ocean and city views, floor-to-ceiling windows, and column-free spans. The progressive environmentally efficient design will reach LEED Silver certification and features has state-of-the-art digital infrastructure with Wired certification.

The building will have unprecedented lifestyle offerings for a commercial tower, which will promote out-of-the-box collaboration, work-life balance, and wellness.

Amenities include a rooftop restaurant and two-story bar on the 56th and 57th floors, and a 30th floor sky lobby with a health and wellness center and first-class conference facility, parking with electric vehicle charging stations, cafés, and retail.

Tenants have direct, walkable access to Brickell City Center, Mary Brickell Village, and Downtown Miami offering a suite of upscale hotels and restaurants. Known as the city's financial district, Brickell is a rapidly transforming neighborhood for residents, tourists, and businesspeople. Vertical construction on 830 Brickell is now underway.

High Tech Park

Shenzhen, China

High Tech Park

Shenzhen, China

AS+GG's design for High Tech Park in the Nanshan District of Shenzhen, China, consists of three research and factory towers 100 meters to 120 meters in height; three separate chairman villas; and a linked podium building two stories tall that contains retail space, restaurant space, and a roof garden.

SERVICES
Architecture

CLIENT
Centralcon

FUNCTION
Mixed-Use

FACTS
119 stories

In addition to several buildings, there is a public central open space of about 5,000 sm. The architectural design is limited to the exterior wall for the towers, retail podium, chairman villas, and to the design of the landscape for the entire plot.

The site is designed to emphasize the importance of the public central space and its relationship to the surrounding buildings, clearly directing views and circulation paths to the tower and retail entry points. The main feature of the public central space is a sunken garden that is shaped by the influence of the towers, villas, and podium geometries. This responsive architectural move allows the space to relate physically to the surrounding buildings and promotes clarity of circulation and spatial relationships. The sunken garden space is aligned with the main circulation axis through the site, which runs north-south, acknowledging the main entry points and bringing pedestrians through the site into a variety of landscaped areas. Daily users and visitors will enjoy a rich variety of urban furniture, lighting, natural stone materials and selected vegetation around the whole site.

The design of the exterior wall attempts to optimize the natural environmental conditions with the goal of achieving balance and harmony with the development's users and climate. The fact that the tower's massing and orientation were already determined by the local architect presented a challenge when considering optimal orientation for energy performance. That said, the exterior wall design focuses on delivering a simple, yet compelling exterior wall system that is easy and economical to implement/maintain. Modular panels of standard 1500 mm widths are the underlying system on which variations are applied. A special module is used at the tower corners to define the edges, and it is expressive of the highly refined design. Within each module there are sub-mullions, both vertical and horizontal, that will vary their location across the facade.

While most of the tower facades display a simple and softly undulating exterior wall, the main tower entries present an opportunity to explore the exterior wall's potential to become more active and articulated, and to respond to the ground level and pedestrian scales. The variable sub-modules within the 1500 mm module starts to merge and become more uniform as the tower wall reaches the ground and the entry area. The module then becomes 750 mm, and this finer module is then implemented throughout the site and landscape design as a unifying element.

Renaissance District

South Bend, Indiana

Renaissance District

South Bend, Indiana

AS+GG is leading the new campus design of the former Studebaker corridor, located on the southwest edge of downtown South Bend in an area known as the Renaissance District, for Union Station Technology Center, the largest data center in northern Indiana and the second largest carrier hotel in the state.

SERVICES
Architecture

CLIENT
Union Station
Technology Center

FUNCTION
Research + Development

FACTS
1.3 million sf

AWARDS
The Chicago
Athenaeum, Green
Good Design, Green
Architecture, 2018

With construction waste being the highest contributor to consumer solid waste in the United States, the reuse of existing building stock is essential to environmental protection. The Renaissance District reuses and revitalizes the existing Studebaker buildings to take advantage of its Cartesian logic and structural strength to extend its life for another 100 years.

The Studebaker corridor redevelopment provides a platform for a new wave of data and technology companies to thrive in South Bend. The redeveloped area will be part of a mixed-use campus consisting of more than one million square feet of Class A office, education, technology, research grade manufacturing, data center, and live-work spaces.

The Studebaker Corporation was the nation's fourth largest automobile manufacturer, employing as many as 23,000 people in South Bend prior to its closure in 1963. The adaptive reuse of South Bend's only remaining Studebaker manufacturing facility and its surrounding area honors the legacy of the company that built South Bend and embodies the continuity of innovation that began in the mid-1800s. That innovation will now live on by transforming a once abandoned facility into a large scale, sustainably designed tech hub that promises to spur a second economic boom for South Bend and the surrounding region.

The data center, which opened its doors in 2019, is a well-lit space with 45-foot ceilings. This height and overall volume encourages collaborative discovery and innovation from a full range of company types including tech startups, creative workshop spaces, and design firms. The full program is still evolving and more than 3,000 people are expected to become tenants of the building.

Current tenants include CupPrint, an Irish company that uses technology to print customized paper cups in a way that is quick and cost effective; enFocus, a nonprofit group that partners with local businesses to create fellowship opportunities for recent graduates; F Cubed, a biotech firm that develops diagnostic devices and test kits for environmental, food safety, medical and other applications; South Bend Code School, which provides training and Web-development skills to prepare people for tech jobs; and Trek10, a technology firm that develops and manages cloud-based computing for businesses.

Renovating and converting the former Studebaker auto plant and its four associated buildings into a modern tech park capitalizes on the fiber-optic data infrastructure at Union Station. South Bend has an abundance of installed "dark fiber," or unused fiber optic cables. A major corridor of high-speed fiber optic cable travels from New York to Chicago, with a major corridor, passing right under the old Studebaker factory, which will help entice corporate entities from across the nation. Tax increment financing from the city and funding from the state's Regional Cities program have helped fuel the project.

PHASE 1 COMPLETED, 2019

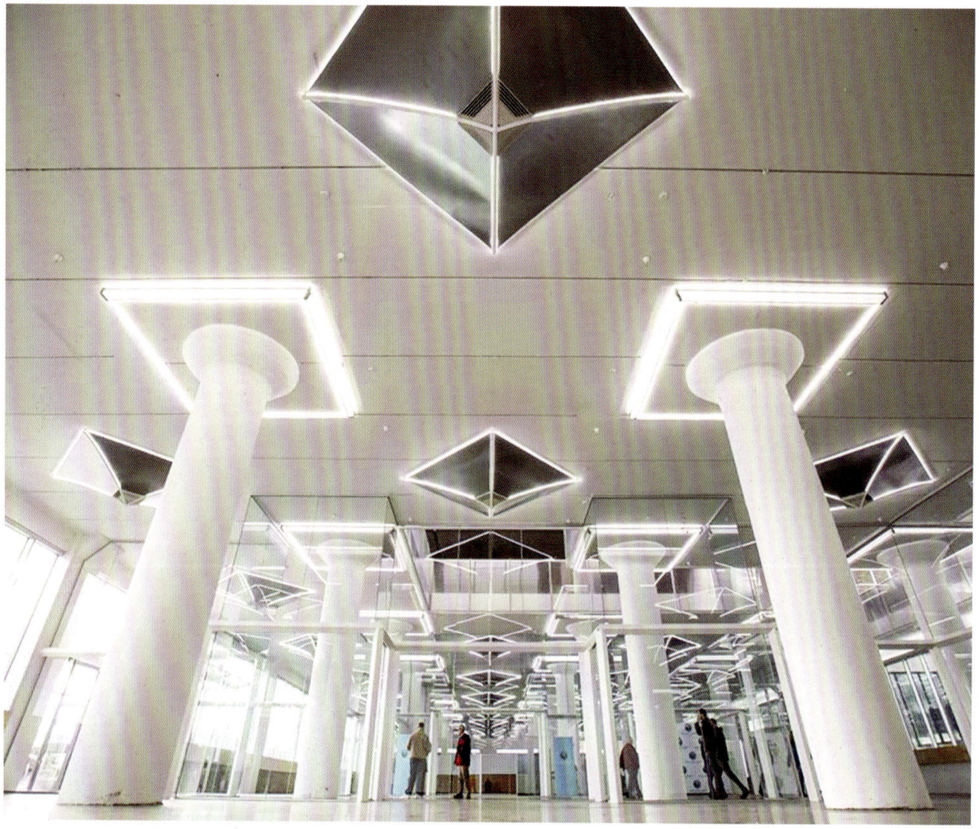

Masdar HQ

Abu Dhabi, United Arab Emirates

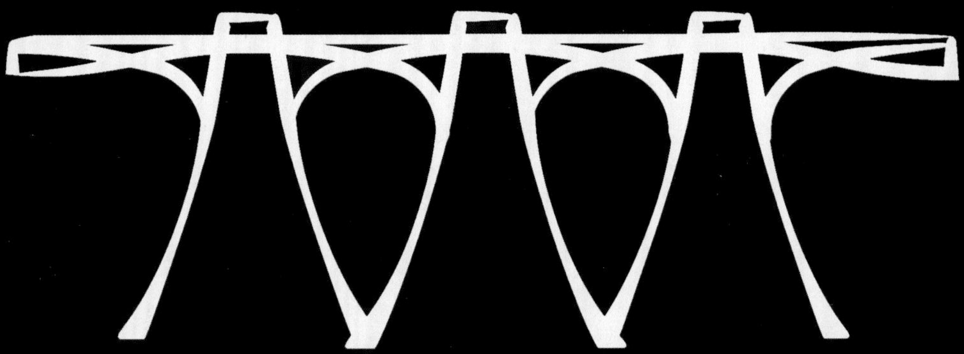

Masdar Headquarters

Abu Dhabi, United Arab Emirates

Masdar Headquarters is designed as the world's first mixed-use, positive-energy building, using sustainable design strategies and systems to produce more energy than it consumes.

SERVICES
Architecture
Interior Design
Master Planning

CLIENT
Masdar

FUNCTION
Commercial

FACTS
7 stories height
134,662 sm

AWARDS
International Property Awards, Arabian Property Award for Architecture, Mideast Region, 2010

Cityscape Architectural Awards, Environmental Award, 2008

Middle East Architect Awards, Green Project of the Year, 2008

Construction Week Awards, Sustainable Design Award, 2008

The seven-story, 134,662-square-meter structure, which includes landscaped areas, accommodates commercial, retail, and cultural uses. The building's form, sculpted in response to extensive environmental analysis, adapts the ancient science and aesthetics of Arabic wind towers, screens, and other vernacular architecture, which emphasize natural ventilation, sun shading, high thermal mass, courtyards, and vegetation.

Masdar HQ's signature architectural feature is a collection of eleven wind cones which provide natural ventilation and cooling (drawing warm air up to roof level, where wind moves it away) and form oasis-like interior courtyards and/or flexible spaces, each with its own theme, at ground level. The cones also provide soft daylighting for the building's interiors.

Other key sustainability design features, systems, and strategies include a vast roof canopy, which provides natural shading and incorporates one of the world's largest photovoltaic and solar-panel arrays, which simultaneously harvest solar energy while solar thermal collectors provide solar cooling. The roof's undulating understructure facilitates the roof pier's structural performance.

High-thermal-mass exterior glass cladding provides solar heat blocking while remaining transparent for views. Thermal technology in the project also includes earth ducts that reduce the temperature of outside air and provide underground pedestrian passages that connect public garden space with the proposed mass-transit system. And a lush sky garden on roof level creates a microclimate that includes water features and restful community spaces landscaped with indigenous vegetation.

Masdar HQ was designed as the world's greenest mixed-use building, yielding zero carbon emissions and zero waste—both liquid and solid—and a sustainable measure beyond LEED platinum. It was designed to consume 70 percent less water than typical mixed-use buildings of the same size, and be the lowest energy consumer per square meter for a modern Class A office building in a hot/humid climate.

It was also designed to be the first building in history to generate power for its own assembly via one of the world's largest arrays of photovoltaics on its roof canopy, providing shade for workers during construction of the structure's lower levels.

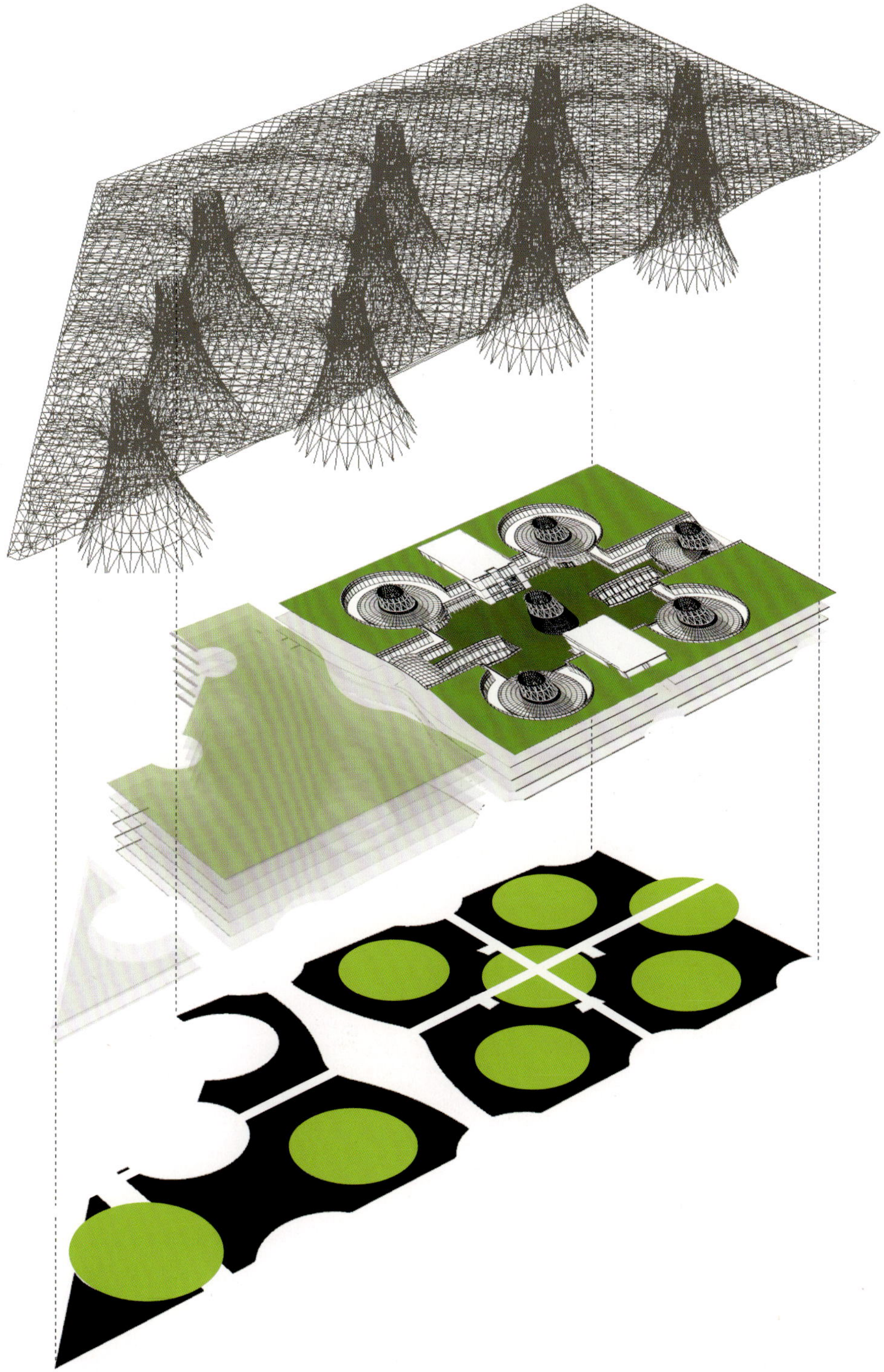

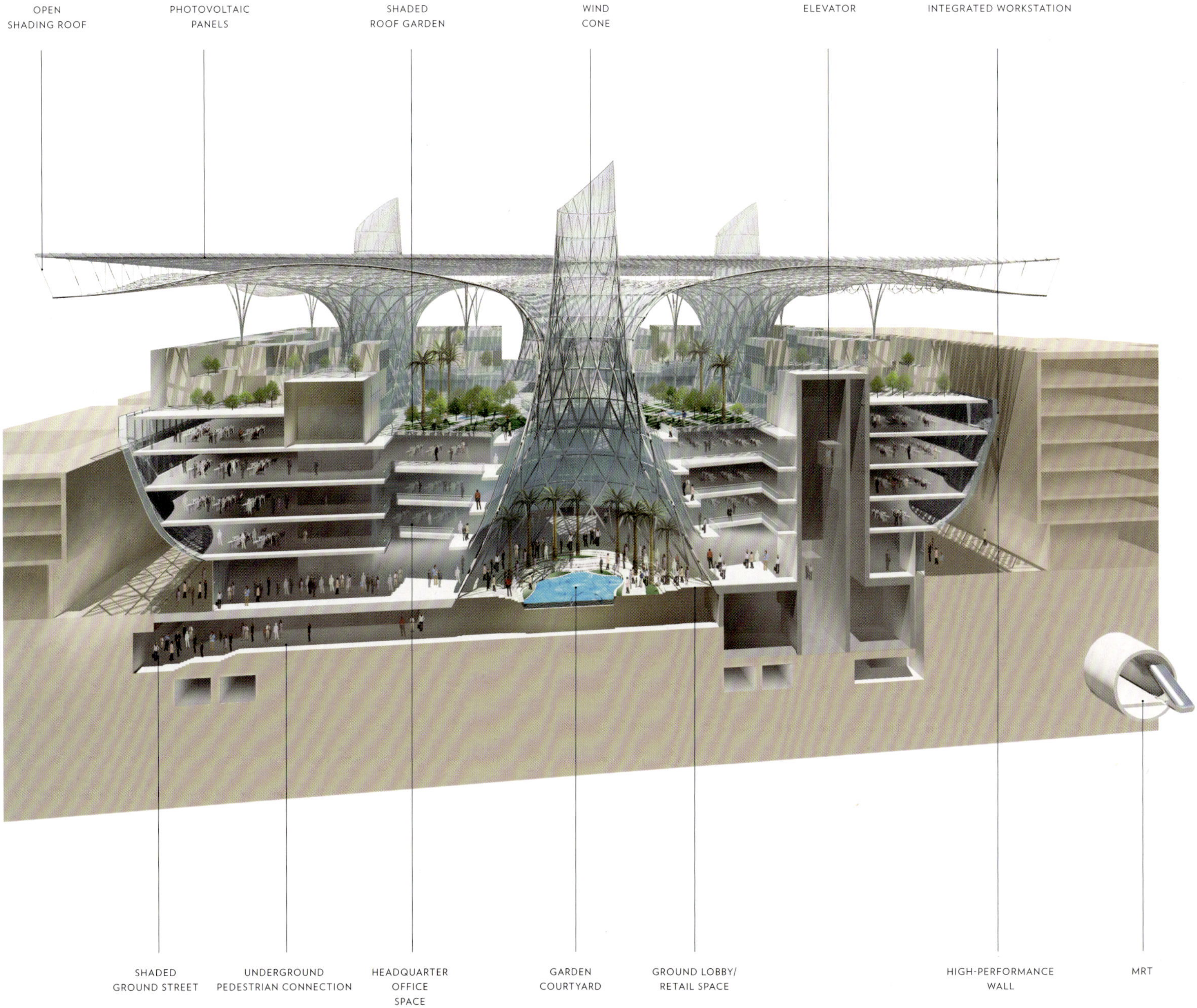
OPEN
SHADING ROOF
PHOTOVOLTAIC
PANELS
SHADED
ROOF GARDEN
WIND
CONE
ELEVATOR
INTEGRATED WORKSTATION
SHADED
GROUND STREET
UNDERGROUND
PEDESTRIAN CONNECTION
HEADQUARTER
OFFICE
SPACE
GARDEN
COURTYARD
GROUND LOBBY/
RETAIL SPACE
HIGH-PERFORMANCE
WALL
MRT

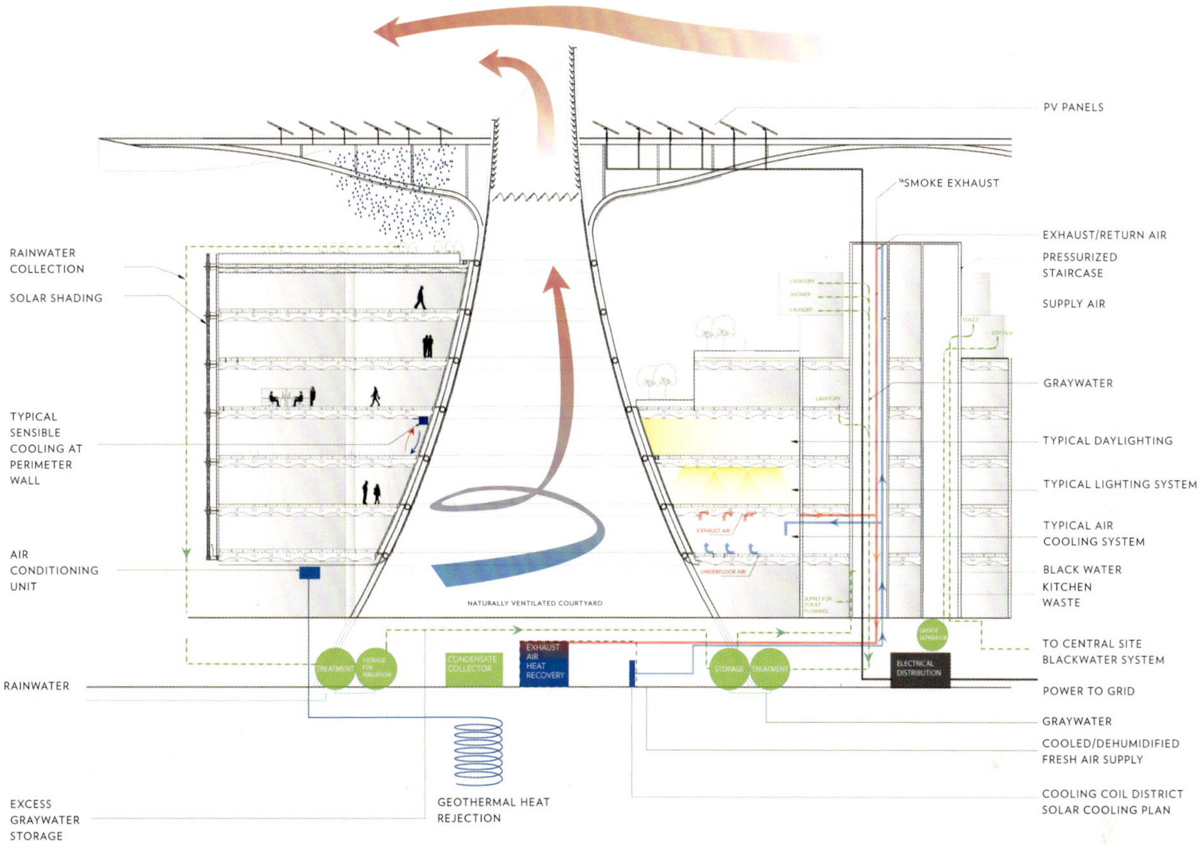
PV PANELS
SMOKE EXHAUST
RAINWATER COLLECTION
EXHAUST/RETURN AIR
PRESSURIZED STAIRCASE
SOLAR SHADING
SUPPLY AIR
GRAYWATER
TYPICAL SENSIBLE COOLING AT PERIMETER WALL
TYPICAL DAYLIGHTING
TYPICAL LIGHTING SYSTEM
TYPICAL AIR COOLING SYSTEM
AIR CONDITIONING UNIT
BLACK WATER KITCHEN WASTE
NATURALLY VENTILATED COURTYARD
TO CENTRAL SITE BLACKWATER SYSTEM
TREATMENT
STORAGE
CONDENSATE COLLECTOR
EXHAUST AIR HEAT RECOVERY
STORAGE
TREATMENT
ELECTRICAL DISTRIBUTION
RAINWATER
POWER TO GRID
GRAYWATER
COOLED/DEHUMIDIFIED FRESH AIR SUPPLY
EXCESS GRAYWATER STORAGE
GEOTHERMAL HEAT REJECTION
COOLING COIL DISTRICT SOLAR COOLING PLAN

RETAIL
OFFICE
OFFICE CIRCULATION
OFFICE CORE
RESIDENTIAL
RESIDENTIAL CORE
RESIDENTIAL CIRCULATION
PUBLIC CIRCULATION
MEP

Xiamen Oceanfront Center

Xiamen, China

Xiamen Oceanfront Center

Xiamen, China

Inspired by President Xi Jinping's directives focusing on innovation, entrepreneurship, and ecological stewardship, the design of this waterfront stadium complex is a gateway that welcomes people from around the world to connect, create, compete, and prosper.

SERVICES
Architecture

CLIENT
Xiamen City Planning Commission

FUNCTION
Cultural

FACTS
600 hectares

The design builds on the legacy of Xiamen, the anchor city of the South China Sea. The region is recognized for its natural beauty, cultural arts, and tourism industry, and is positioned to become a global destination for international sport and exhibition events.

The master plan includes 600 ha of land and 7,000,000 sm of buildings that are organized to maximize the value of the oceanfront location, elevating the visitor and athlete experience. A major sports park, convention center, and entertainment district anchor the site. A new transit hub provides commuter access during event, and non-event days throughout the year.

Multi-level pedestrian walkways and bridges interconnect the entire district, creating a walkable site that is also serviced by on-demand shuttles with drop-off locations distributed throughout. An oceanfront park with recreational areas are available to residents and visitors with views to Xiamen Island. The park is activated by the Fisherman's Village and ferry terminal to the north, yacht marina in the center and sports park to the south.

Bordering the park is a world-class Athlete Village that is further connected to the sports facilities by streets, parks, and trails. A pedestrian-oriented, Ramblas-type street is lined with creative offices, shops, and galleries to enhance the entrepreneurial district. Adjacent is a mixed-density residential community with larger-scale office, medical, and cultural uses that are located along the major roadways and transit routes.

SITE PLAN

STREET ALIGNMENT: REALIGN STREET TO CREATE OCEANFRONT PARKLAND

OCEANFRONT PARK: CREATE PUBLIC RECREATION AREAS WITH VIEWS TO XIAMEN ISLAND

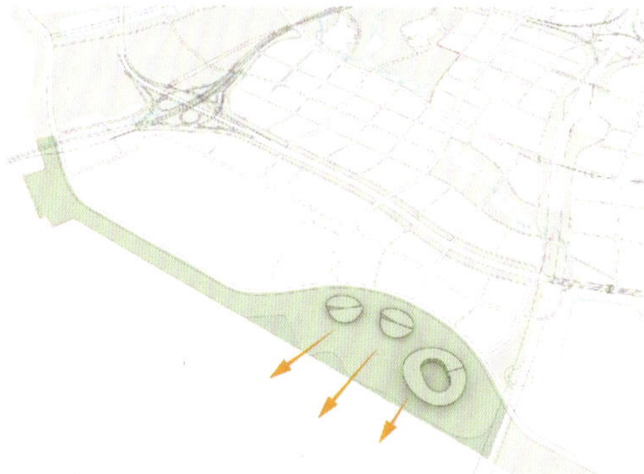

SPORTS VENUE LOCATIONS: LOCATE SPORTS VENUES ON WATERFRONT TO CREATE LANDMARK IDENTITY

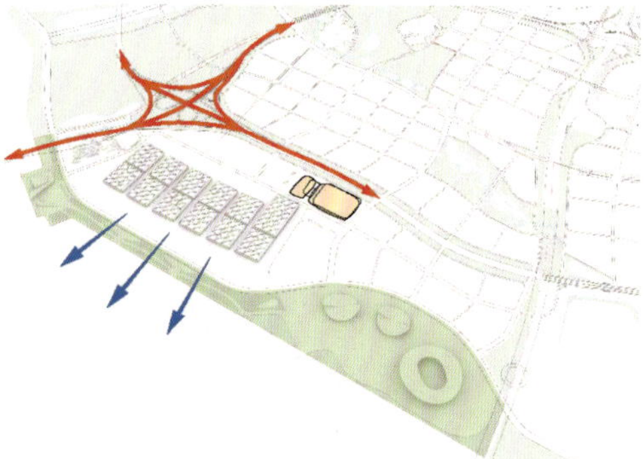

CONVENTION CENTER LOCATION: LOCATE CONVENTION CENTER ADJACENT TO HIGHWAY, IN CLOSE PROXIMITY TO THE WATERFRONT

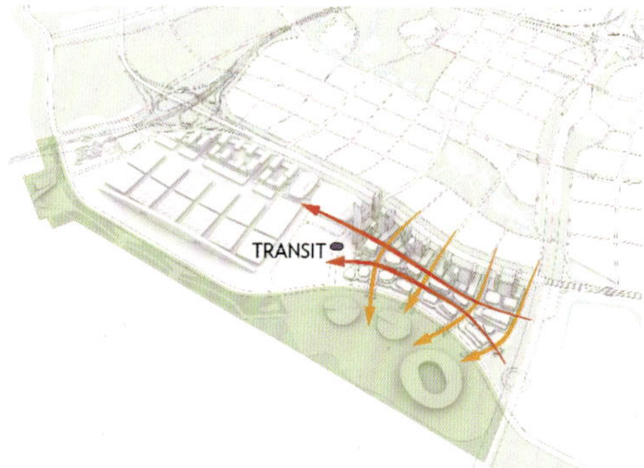

ENTERTAINMENT/TRANSIT HUB: ACTIVATE AREA WITH MIXED-USE ENTERTAINMENT DISTRICT LINKED TO TRANSIT

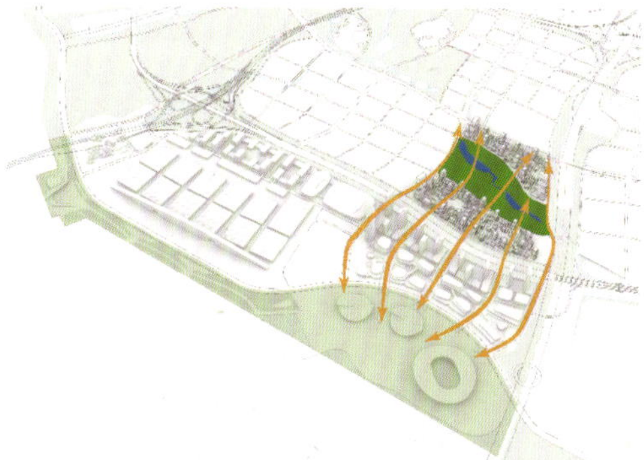

ATHLETE VILLAGE: PROVIDE HOUSING FOR ATHLETES IN CLOSE PROXIMITY TO FACILITY

ENTREPRENEURIAL DISTRICT: CULTIVATE CULTURE AND COMMERCE IN MIXED-USE, LIVE/WORK ENVIRONMENT

GREEN NETWORK: LINK ALL DISTRICTS WITH GREENWAYS, PARKS, AND TRAILS

Incheon Airport

Seoul, Korea

Incheon International Airport Competition

Incheon, Korea

AS+GG's competition design for Incheon Airport's Terminal II is a celebration of Korea's cultural heritage and success. The form of the terminal, a curved aerodynamic shape, is reminiscent of traditional Korean building roof lines, reinforcing the cultural heritage.

SERVICES
Architecture
Interior Design

CLIENT
Incheon International Airport Corporation

FUNCTION
Infrastructure

FACTS
700,000 sm area

The expansion of Incheon International Airport offers a new opportunity to draw visitors, create excitement, and set a new precedent as an airport of the future. As air travel expands around the world, the role of airports is changing—Incheon isn't just a place for travelers to embark on their journeys, it's part of the journey.

An airport of the future is a transportation hub—an extension of the city which it serves, as well as a city in itself—where thousands of employees serve millions of passengers every year. The integration of the airport as part of the airport city, and as part of Seoul, is key. Incheon International Airport is a symbol of Korea and is an opportunity for people from around the world to experience Korea, even if they are only visiting for a short time. The visit should be a unique, memorable experience; after all, the terminal is effectively, for many people, the gateway to Korea. The new design for Terminal II incorporates lessons from Terminal I in terms of its successes, along with intelligent planning for future expansion and new excitement in its design.

The visual experience continues with skylights that begin at the main departure hall and can still be seen by passengers in the arrival hall as well as in the vertical circulation room. Their shape will lead passengers in a directional flow along the main circulation route through the terminal to the boarding gates. Throughout the day the skylights will project artistic patterns and colors of light onto the walkway below, providing a unique, shared-artistic experience for the visitor; one which they will take with them long after their visit to Incheon.

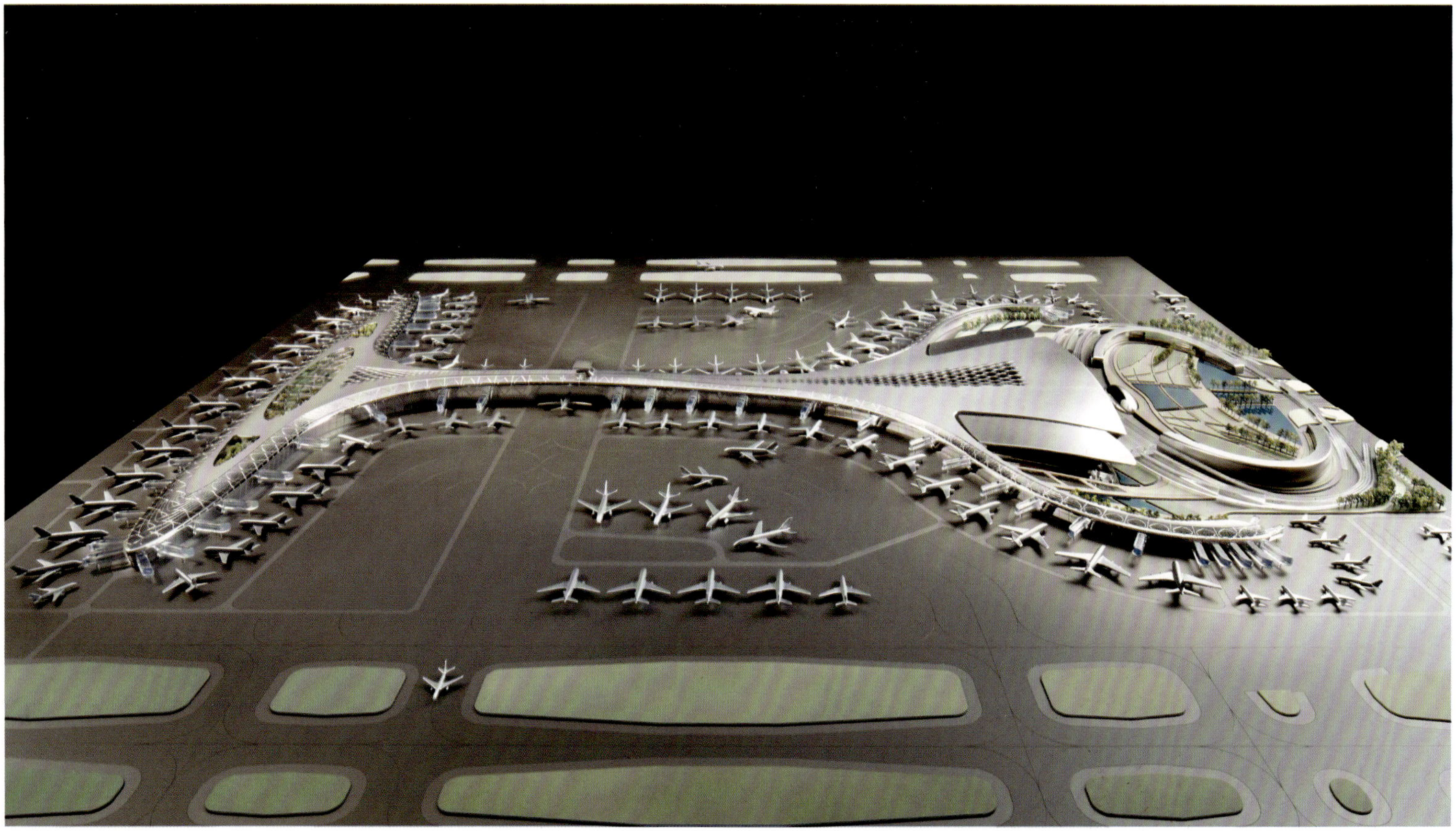

DEPARTURES LEVEL 5 + 6

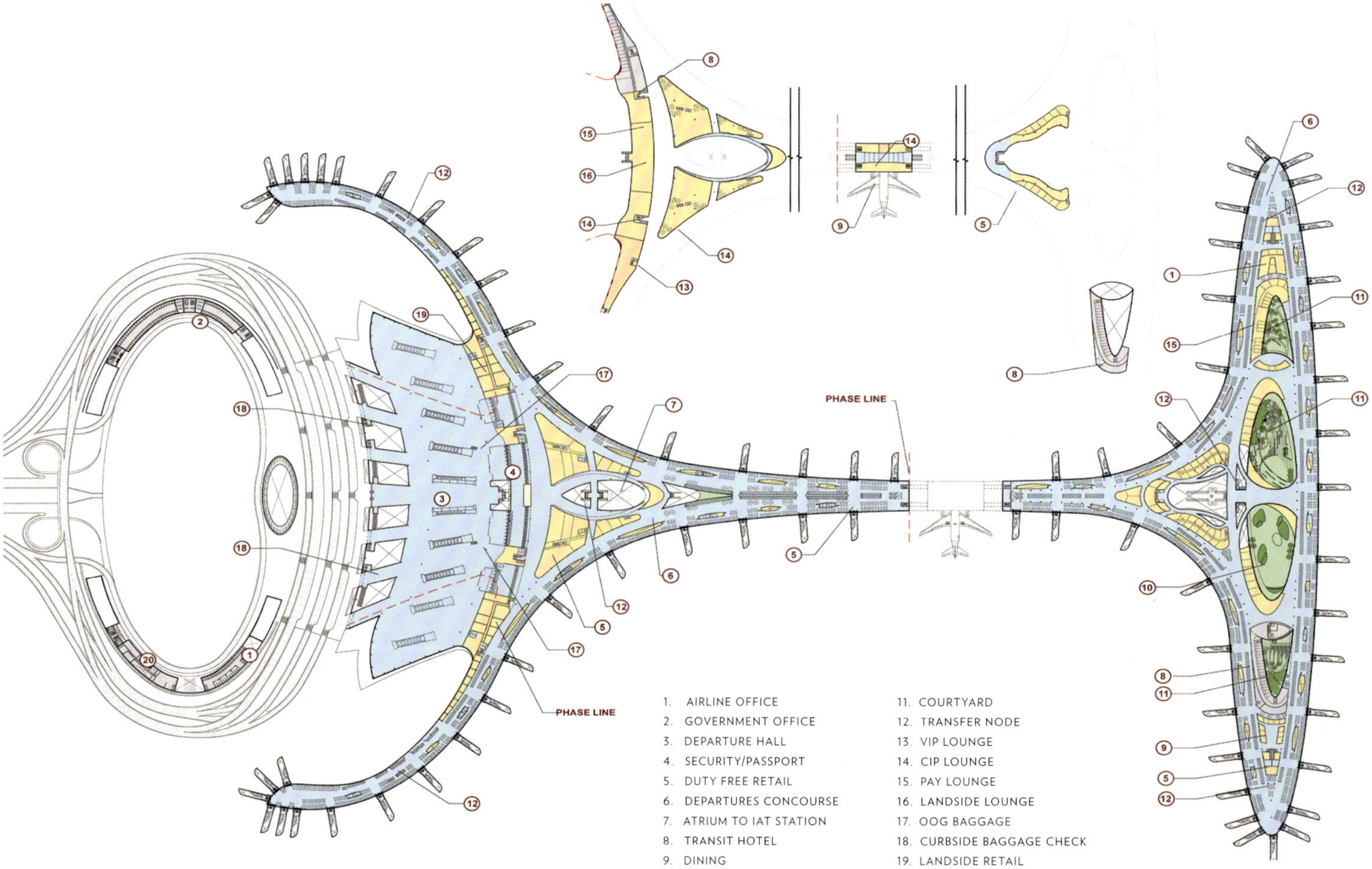

1. AIRLINE OFFICE
2. GOVERNMENT OFFICE
3. DEPARTURE HALL
4. SECURITY/PASSPORT
5. DUTY FREE RETAIL
6. DEPARTURES CONCOURSE
7. ATRIUM TO IAT STATION
8. TRANSIT HOTEL
9. DINING
10. DRIVING RANGE
11. COURTYARD
12. TRANSFER NODE
13. VIP LOUNGE
14. CIP LOUNGE
15. PAY LOUNGE
16. LANDSIDE LOUNGE
17. OOG BAGGAGE
18. CURBSIDE BAGGAGE CHECK
19. LANDSIDE RETAIL
20. EMPLOYEE WELFARE FACILITY

SPINE CONCOURSE

VIEW INSIDE BRIDGE

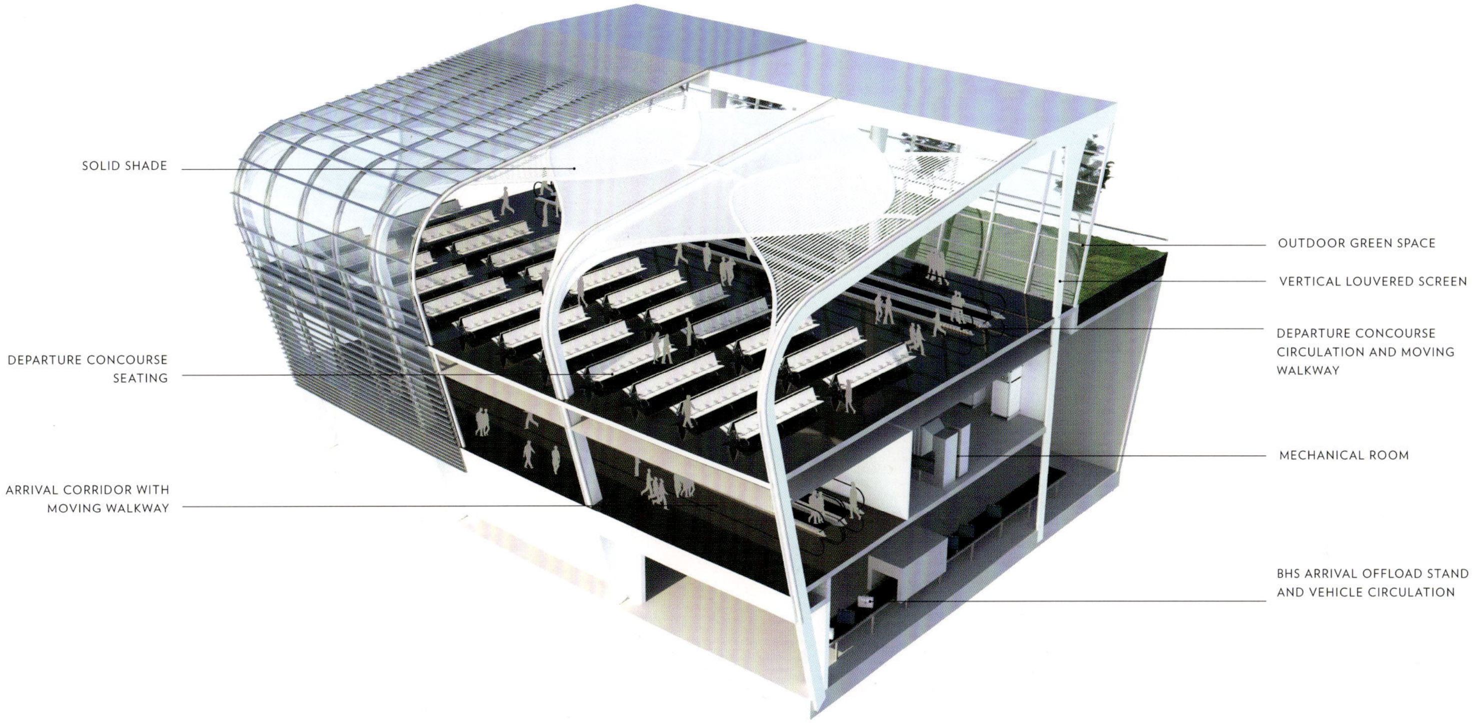
SOLID SHADE
DEPARTURE CONCOURSE SEATING
ARRIVAL CORRIDOR WITH MOVING WALKWAY
OUTDOOR GREEN SPACE
VERTICAL LOUVERED SCREEN
DEPARTURE CONCOURSE CIRCULATION AND MOVING WALKWAY
MECHANICAL ROOM
BHS ARRIVAL OFFLOAD STAND AND VEHICLE CIRCULATION

TRAIN STATION

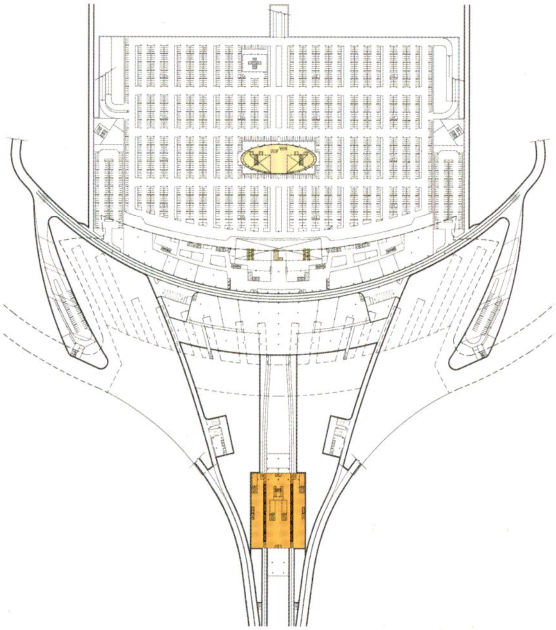

SOUTH RETAIL VIEW

Kellogg School of Management

Evanston, Illinois

Kellogg School of Management

Evanston, Illinois

AS+GG's competition design for the new Kellogg School of Management at Northwestern University aims to reinforce and advance the school's position as a global leader with a true international center that inspires and cultivates the business leaders of tomorrow.

SERVICES
Architecture
Interior Design

CLIENT
Northwestern University

FUNCTION
Educational

FACTS
350,000 sf

AWARDS
The Chicago Athenaeum, Green Good Design Award, Green Architecture, 2015

Kellogg is known worldwide as a leader within business and academic communities, and a pioneer of collaborative learning. AS+GG's design for Kellogg's new global hub reflects its leadership within these fields in every way: from stunning architecture to innovative integrations of technology to spaces that allow for new kinds of interaction.

The design takes full advantage of the building site, embracing an organic form and addressing each aspect of its surroundings including the campus, the lakefront and lagoon, the adjacent buildings, and an adjoining site available for future expansion. The result is an iconic, permeable space that encourages discourse, allows flexible teaching configurations, and a new public square for the entire community.

The challenge of the project from a programmatic and site standpoint is maintaining compression and collaborative space while increasing the exterior perimeter to foster views and admit natural light. From an efficiency standpoint, the new design is effective both in plan and in section. It is modular, it is flexible, and it is accessible.

Entrance to the building is accessible from multiple avenues to create a true collaborative gathering space. Five major points of access become "five points of transparency," at the lakefront, the lagoon, the adjacent buildings, the historic campus, and the future campus. By responding to these five points, the new building represents flexibility and identity without jeopardizing cost or functionality.

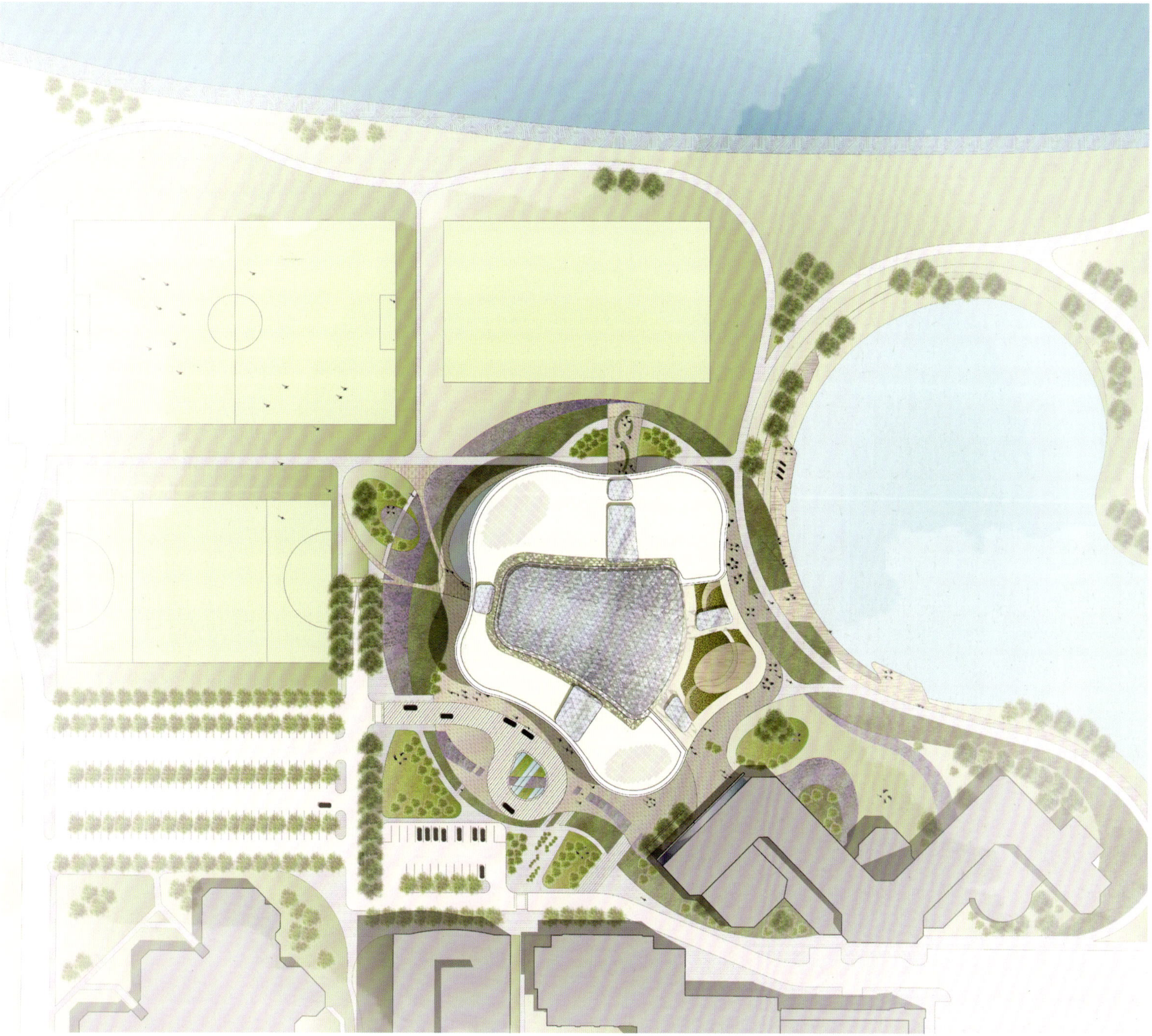

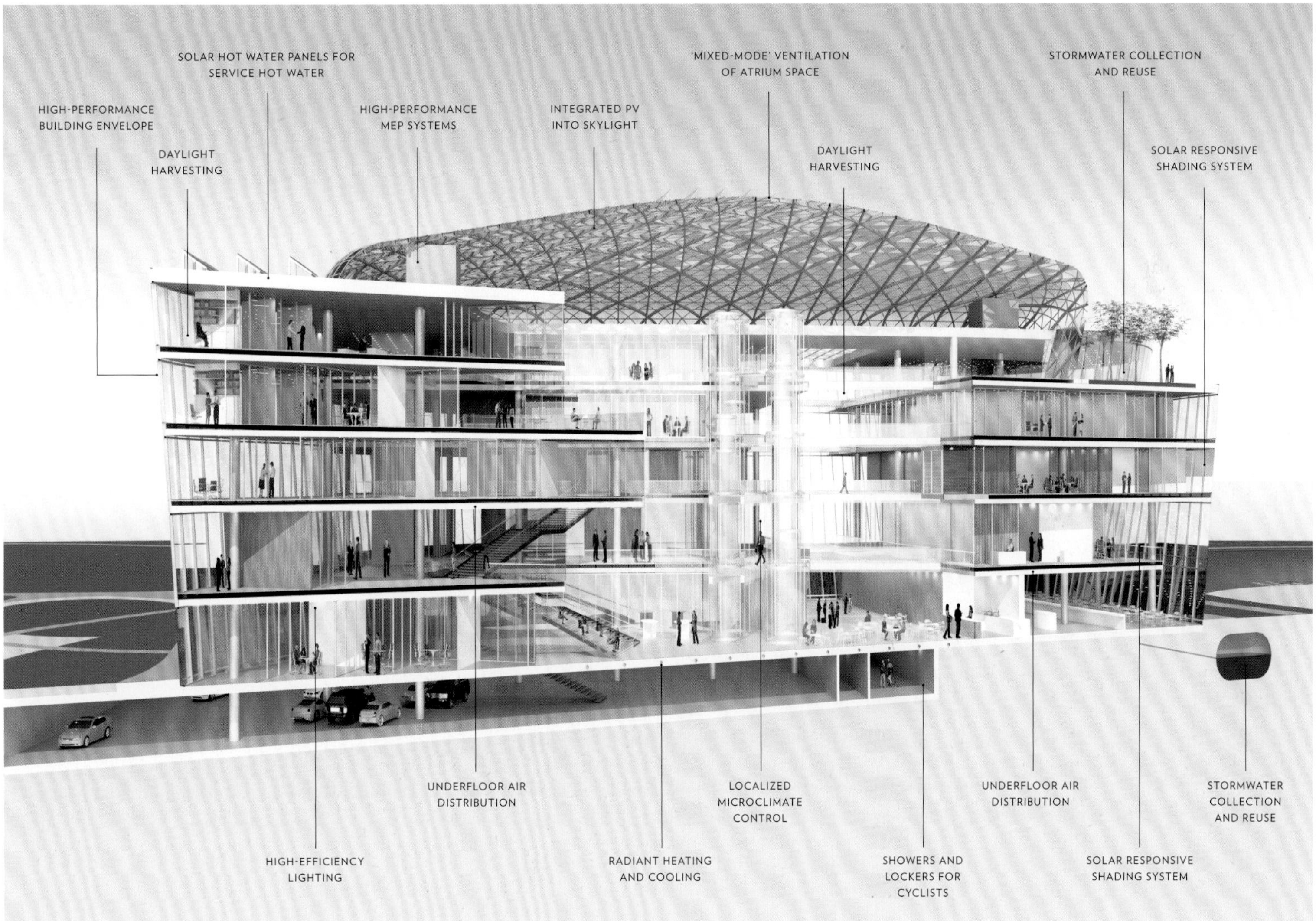

SOLAR HOT WATER PANELS FOR SERVICE HOT WATER
HIGH-PERFORMANCE BUILDING ENVELOPE
DAYLIGHT HARVESTING
HIGH-PERFORMANCE MEP SYSTEMS
INTEGRATED PV INTO SKYLIGHT
'MIXED-MODE' VENTILATION OF ATRIUM SPACE
DAYLIGHT HARVESTING
STORMWATER COLLECTION AND REUSE
SOLAR RESPONSIVE SHADING SYSTEM
UNDERFLOOR AIR DISTRIBUTION
LOCALIZED MICROCLIMATE CONTROL
UNDERFLOOR AIR DISTRIBUTION
STORMWATER COLLECTION AND REUSE
HIGH-EFFICIENCY LIGHTING
RADIANT HEATING AND COOLING
SHOWERS AND LOCKERS FOR CYCLISTS
SOLAR RESPONSIVE SHADING SYSTEM

ADRIAN SMITH + GORDON GILL
ARCHITECTURE

THE GLOBAL AGORA

The grand atrium space at the building's center serves as a marketplace for the exchange of ideas and collaboration between members of the international school community. In addition to providing strong visual connections to the lake front, the lagoon, the campus, and adjacent buildings, the atrium is also a common space that is democratic and non-hierarchical—a place for cross-pollination across the community.

GETTING OUT OF THE BOX

The collaborative spirit across disciplines and international borders results in a fluid and open approach to dialogue. The form and nature of the building supports this ideology, representing a new standard in business education: breaking away from the architectural box and the boundaries that confine thought. The open views, visual connections, and the central public square support this ideology, allowing for intellectual face-to-face discourse, meaningful discussions, and learning experiences.

Kuwait University

Shadadiyah, Kuwait

Kuwait University Master Plan

Shadadiyah, Kuwait

This dramatic, top-rated competition entry for Kuwait University's central administrative facilities complex—a subdistrict of the main campus—includes an administration building, a conference center, a convocation hall, a cultural center, a library, a visitor center, and a grand mosque.

SERVICES
Architecture
Master Planning

CLIENT
Kuwait University

FUNCTION
Education

FACTS
152,713 sm
building area

AS+GG's scheme is an integrated complex of buildings that promotes accessibility, creates a strong dialogue between the buildings and the landscape, allows for unparalleled views of the campus, and takes full advantage of the benefits of light and shade.

On the eastern side of the campus, the adjacent central administration building and cultural center share a sloped roof plane, unifying the two buildings into a single volume. On the western side, the adjacent conference center and library mirror this form, creating a dialogue between the main campus buildings.

The campus recalls traditional regional design in a number of contemporary ways. We explore the duality of light and shade, a central design theme in the desert landscape, by creating courtyards and shaded spaces, indoors and outdoors. Islamic-inspired geometric patterns are incorporated in courtyard trellises and building facades, resulting in dappled light patterns and shadows.

The scheme's energy performance represents a modern vision of proven vernacular responses to an intense climate. The building guards itself and the lower public realm from intense high-angled sun through responsive angled facades, reducing solar gains by over 20 percent with an expansive roof system, which by being permeable, allows for controlled daylight penetration and ventilation. To further take advantage of the climate, solar energy is harnessed through a 19,000 sm building-integrated photovoltaic system, which will generate approximately 4,560 MWh of electricity.

The building also makes use of regional planning principles with an inward-focused design incorporating landscaped courtyards. Through shading and integral landscaping, temperatures are moderated throughout the day, allowing cooler air to sink into the courtyard at night, which is then stored by the monolithic thermal mass walls, allowing a further reduction in temperature throughout the following day.

These passive strategies are coupled with intelligent dynamic control of an energy-management system, including occupancy and carbon dioxide sensors; energy recovery via total enthalpy wheels and desiccant dehumidification systems; daylight dimming ballasts; and variable-speed, electrically-commutated smart motors on fan coil units that will prevent excessive fan energy while improving thermal comfort and acoustics.

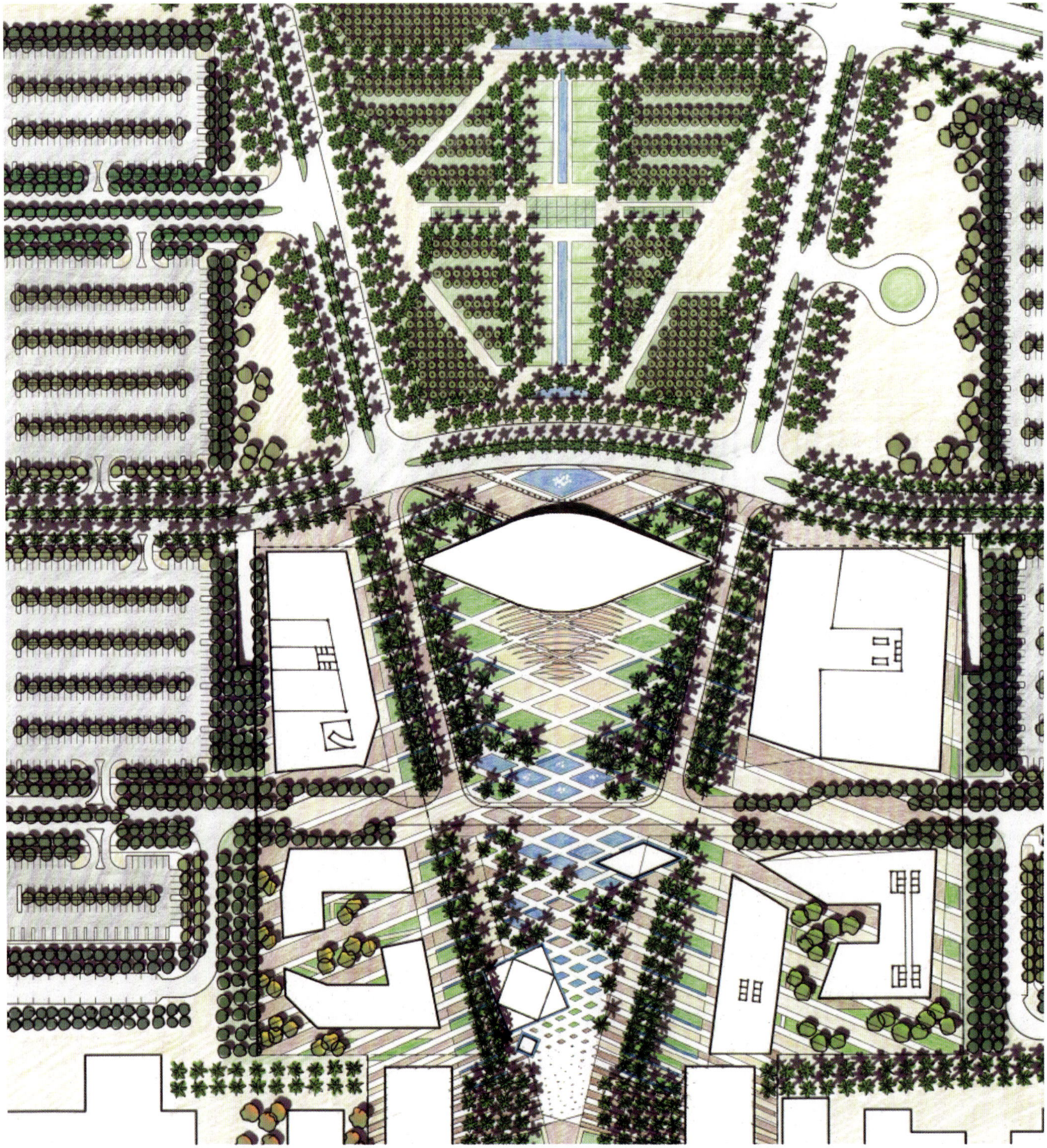

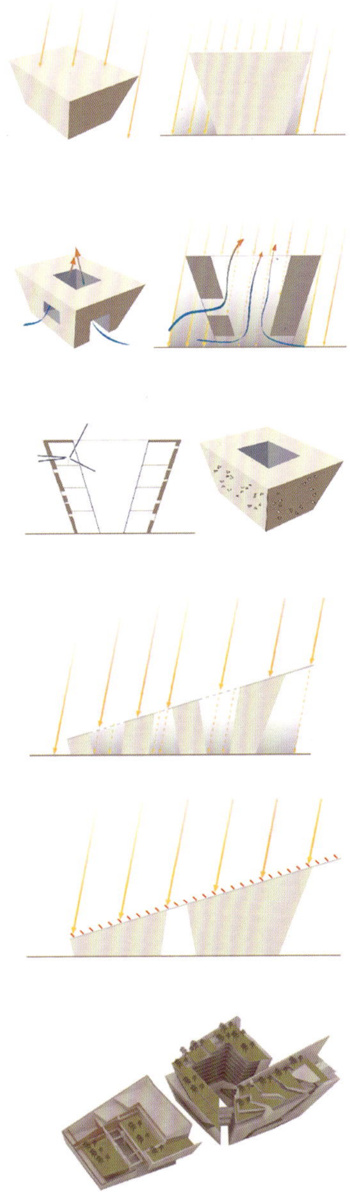

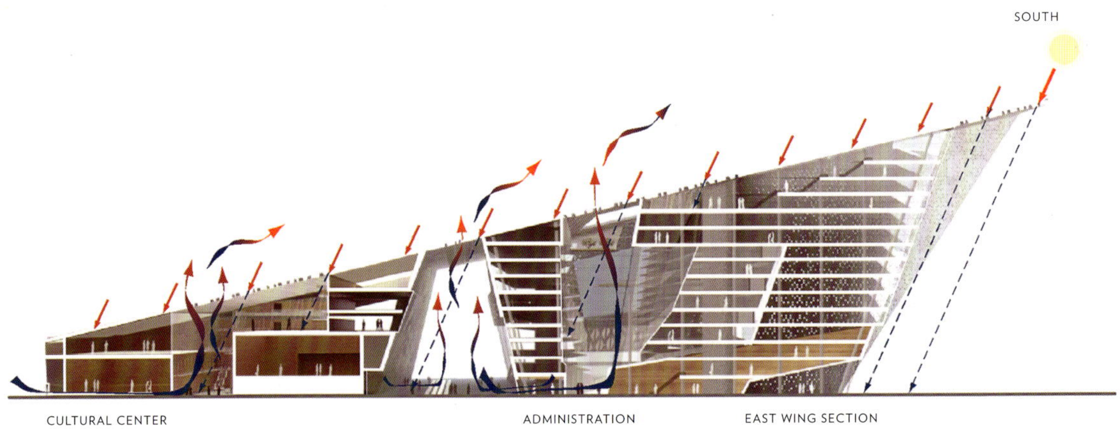
SOUTH
CULTURAL CENTER
ADMINISTRATION
EAST WING SECTION

SOUTH
LIBRARY
CONFERENCE CENTER
WEST WING SECTION

HIGH PERFORMANCE BUILDING ELEMENTS

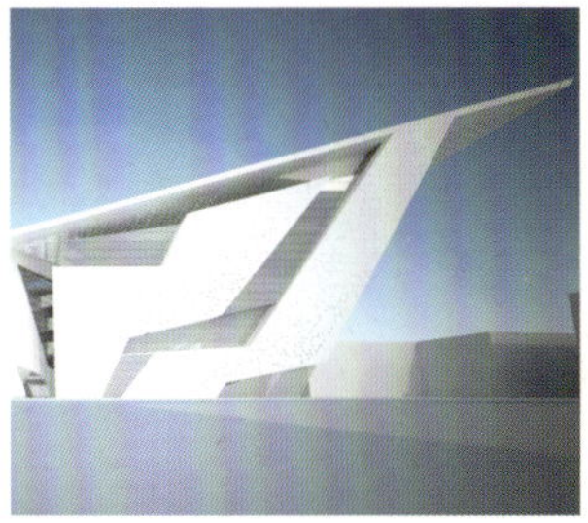

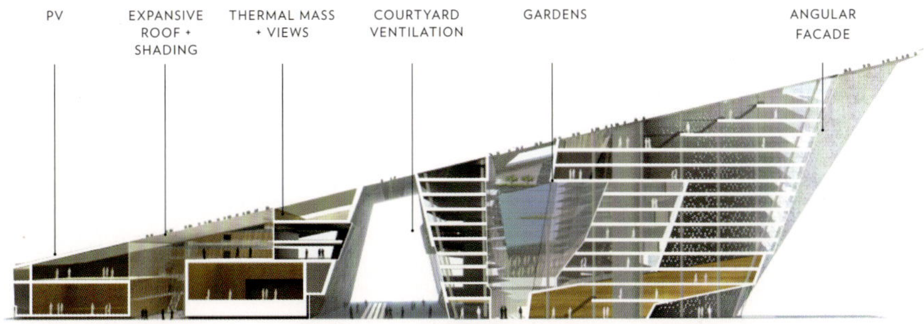

PROTECTIVE BUILDING ELEMENTS

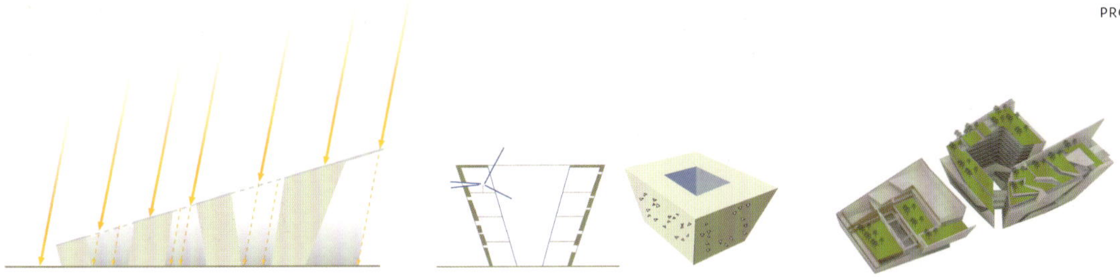

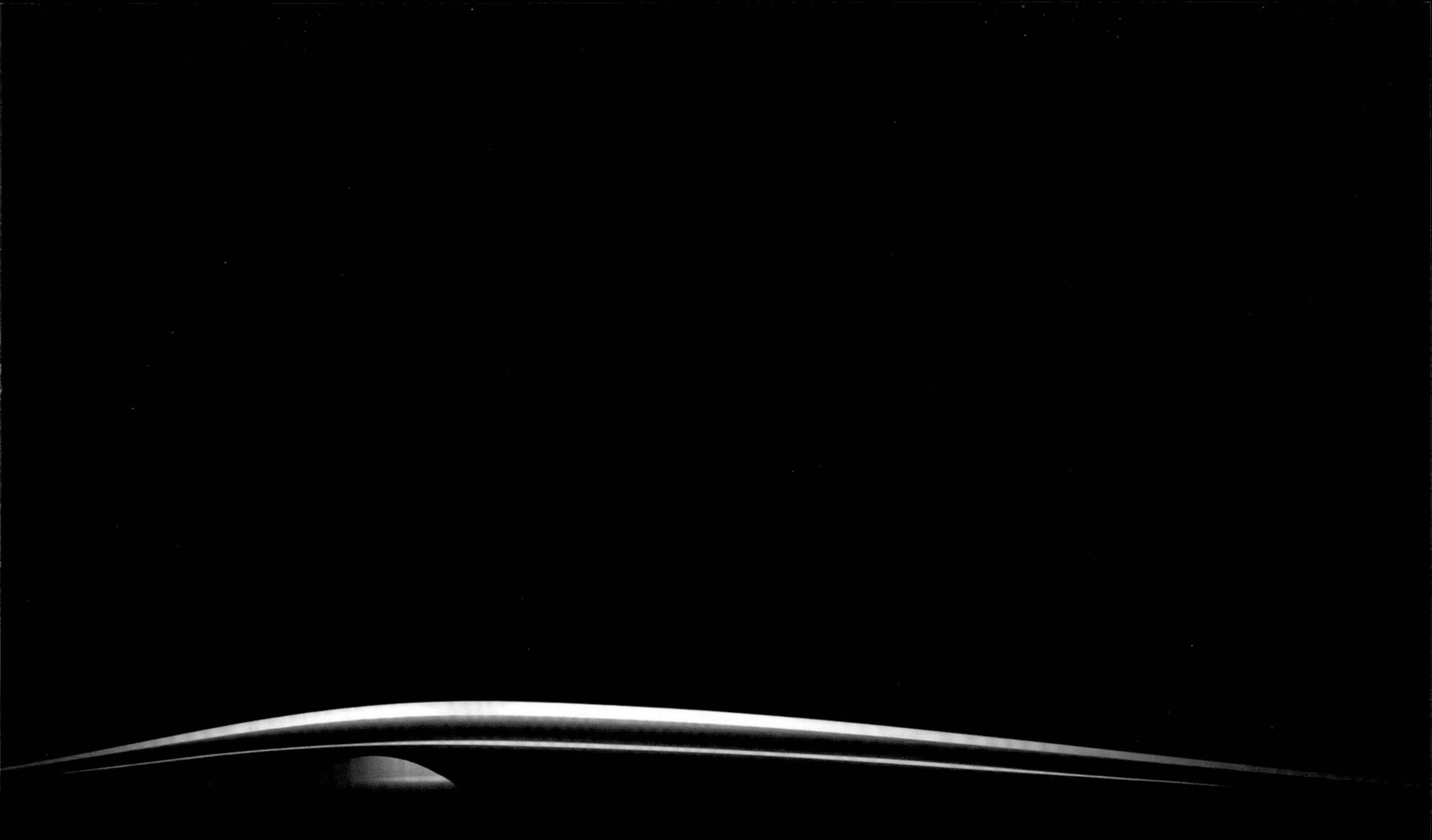

KAPSARC

Riyadh, Saudi Arabia

KAPSARC

Riyadh, Saudi Arabia

AS+GG's competition entry for a research facility is designed to engage the intense climatic conditions of its desert setting and incorporate vernacular design strategies into cutting-edge architecture and engineering systems.

SERVICES
Architecture

CLIENT
Saudi Arabian Oil Company

FUNCTION
Research

FACTS
180,722 sm building area

AWARDS
The Chicago Athenaeum, American Architecture Award, 2012

AIA Chicago, Unbuilt Design, Honor Award, 2011

The design's evocative dune-like shape maintains a predominantly north-south aspect ratio, allowing for enhanced control of daylight and views. The exterior form catches and drives wind into a labyrinth that is integrated into the building's foundation system, which allows for the pre-tempering of air and rejection of airborne particulate. This pre-cooled air is then fed to the air-handling plants serving the independent buildings of the superstructure or to the external street that joins with water features and landscaping to allow passive cooling.

The building's skin, which uses the high-performance, lightweight polymer ethylene tetrafluoroethylene (ETFE), is designed to have high-corrosion resistance and strength over a wide temperature range. The cladding is also designed to intelligently respond to solar radiation and wind. The lower floors engage the inward-sloping skin, allowing for direct views with minimal thermal penalty. The upper floors disengage from the skin, allowing for a climatic buffer and the integration of a photovoltaic energy field to enhance buoyancy-driven wind-flow through the street.

Power for the building is completely supported by solar energy; hydrocarbon-based power at night is offset by the building-integrated photovoltaic system during the day on an annual basis. Sater scarcity is addressed in the region through stringent requirements for washroom fixtures, controlled evaporation of water features, and reduced heat rejection demands from cooling towers.

A variety of outdoor shaded and protected areas and courtyards are designed for social interaction and informal activities. The central Al Mamsha circulation space encourages sustainable transit and creates a walkable thoroughfare. The benefits of this circulation include establishing relationships that encourage spontaneous communications and collaboration, especially between disciplines.

The plant materials selection features indigenous species chosen for low water requirements. Interior atria and spaces within the spine of the building are planted and include water features to promote comfort and human restoration. The irrigation design minimizes the use of potable water by collecting and storing stormwater and condensation from the mechanical coils and pipes within the air cooling system, treating waste water for irrigation, and collecting and recycling irrigation water. Reclaimed condensate is used in the fountains and water channels to further cool the interior spaces.

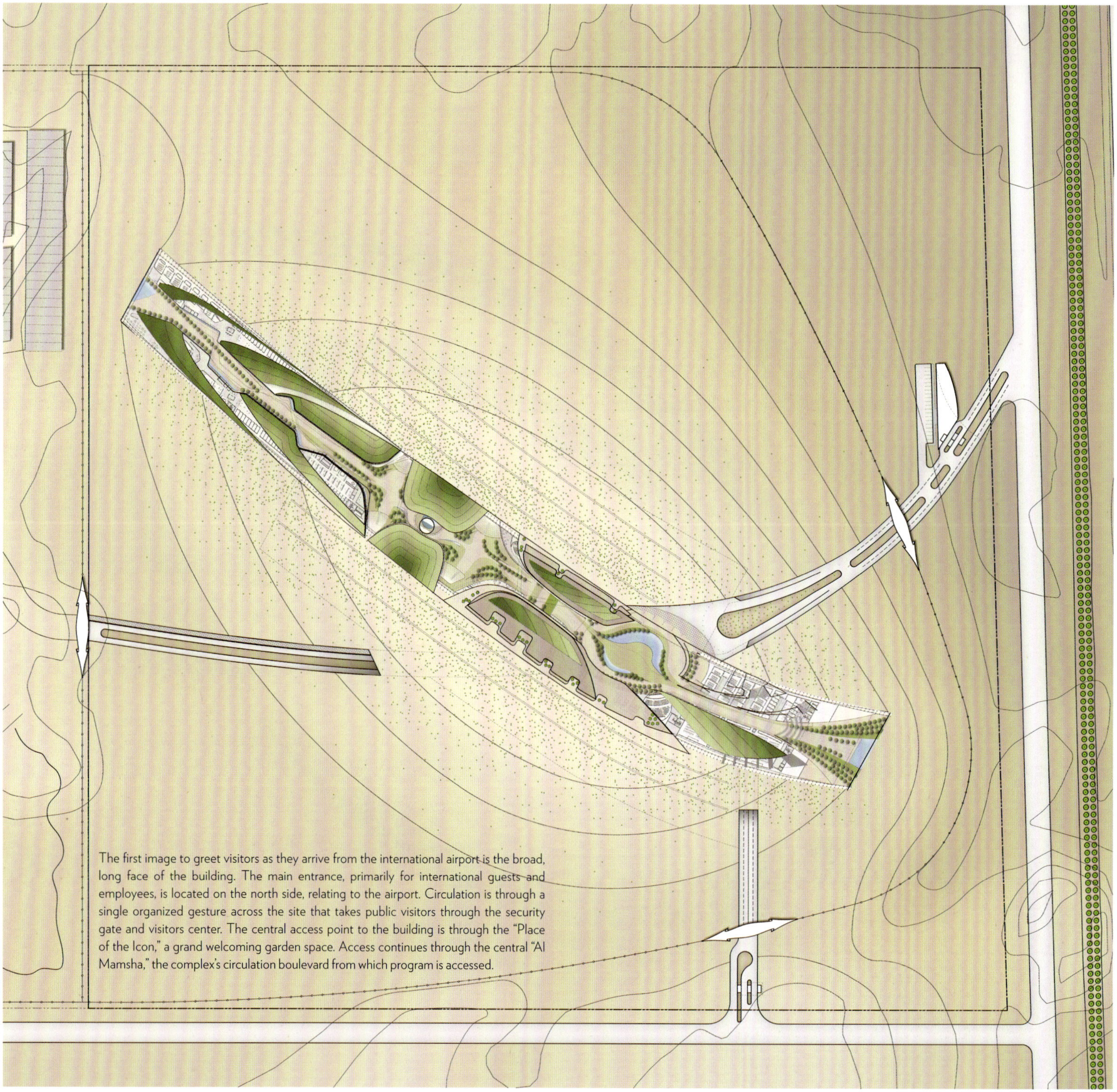

The first image to greet visitors as they arrive from the international airport is the broad, long face of the building. The main entrance, primarily for international guests and employees, is located on the north side, relating to the airport. Circulation is through a single organized gesture across the site that takes public visitors through the security gate and visitors center. The central access point to the building is through the "Place of the Icon," a grand welcoming garden space. Access continues through the central "Al Mamsha," the complex's circulation boulevard from which program is accessed.

PLACE OF ICON

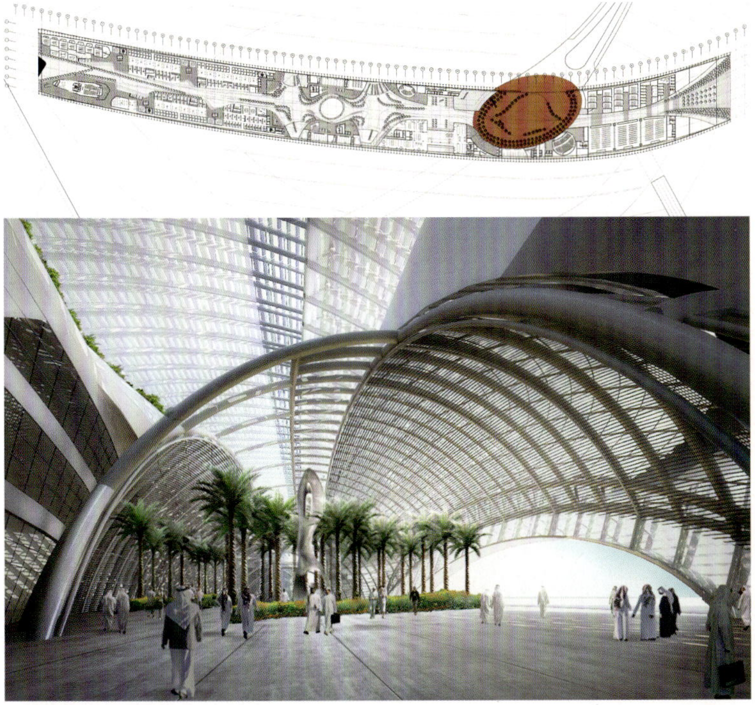

PLACE OF WORSHIP

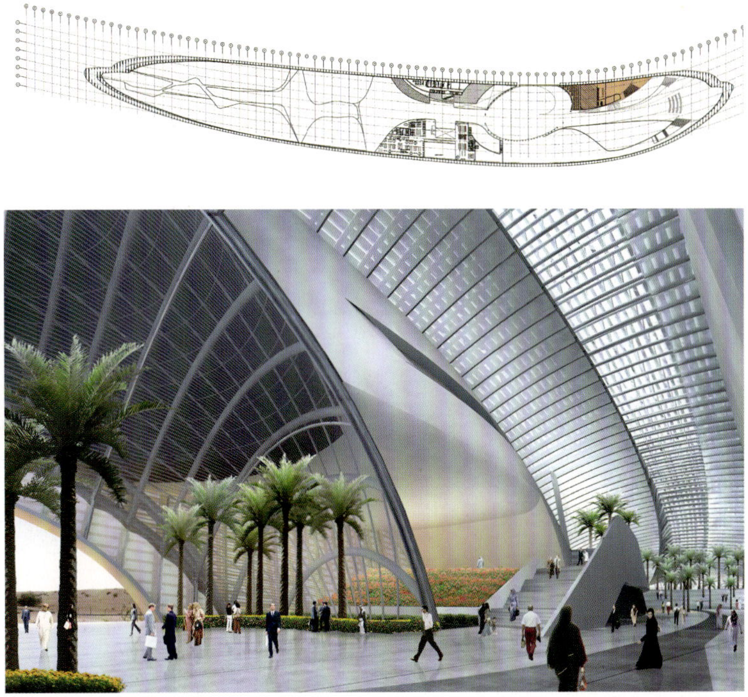

LIBRARY

EXHIBITION HALL

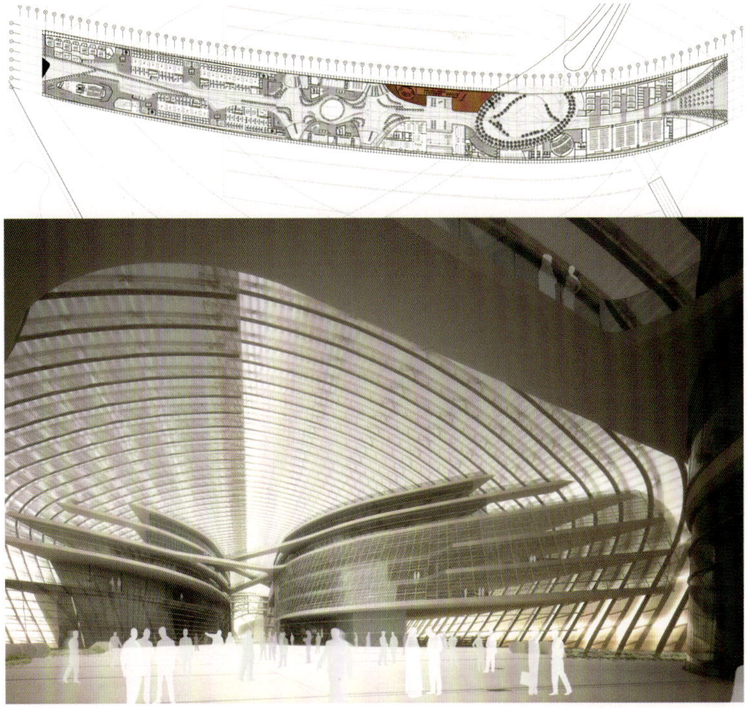

SUSTAINABILITY SECTION

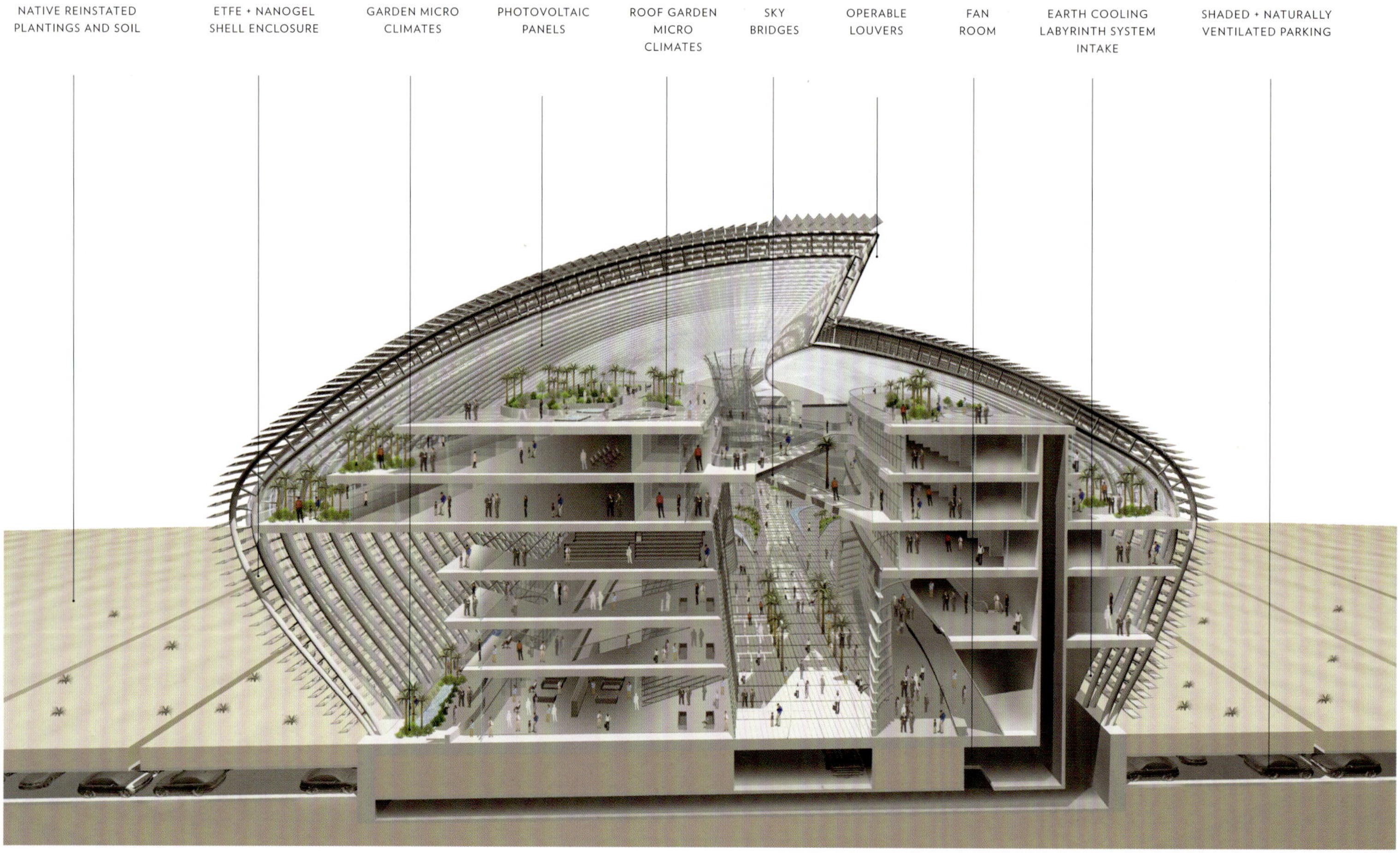

USE OF AIRFLOW

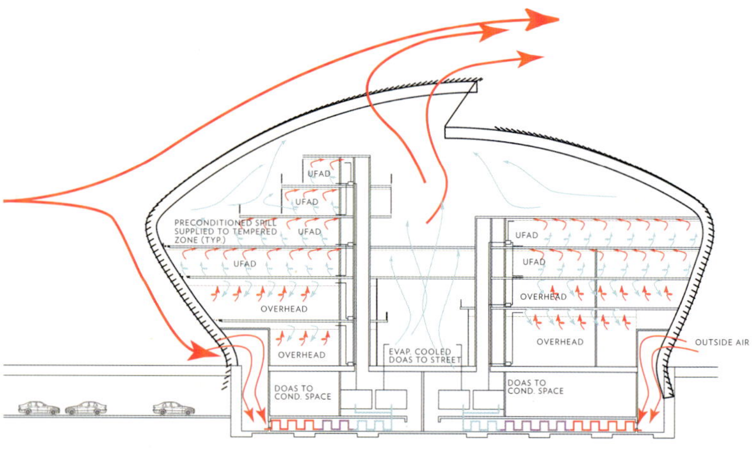

USE OF DAYLIGHTING

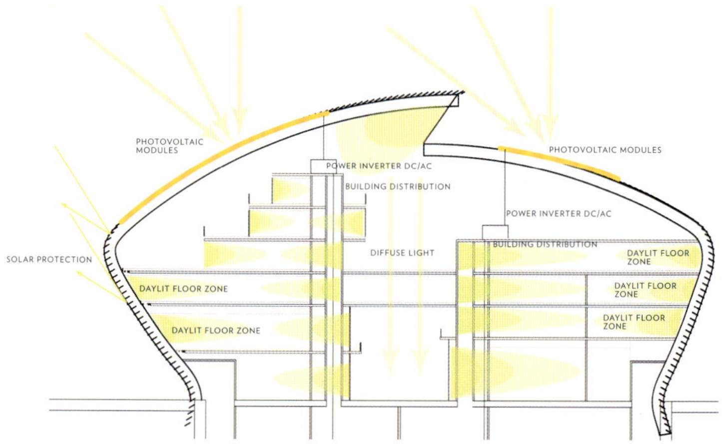

WIND PATTERN STUDY

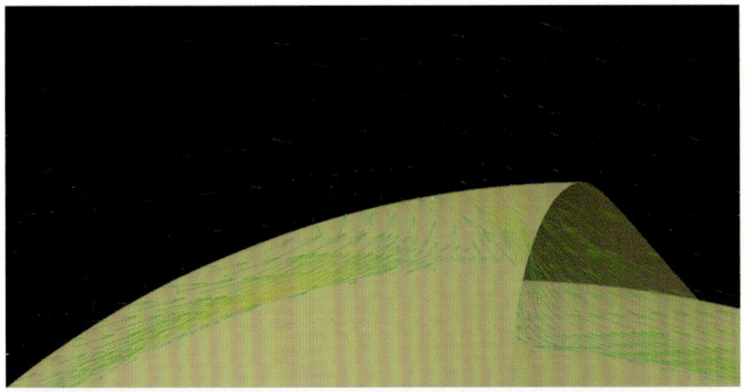

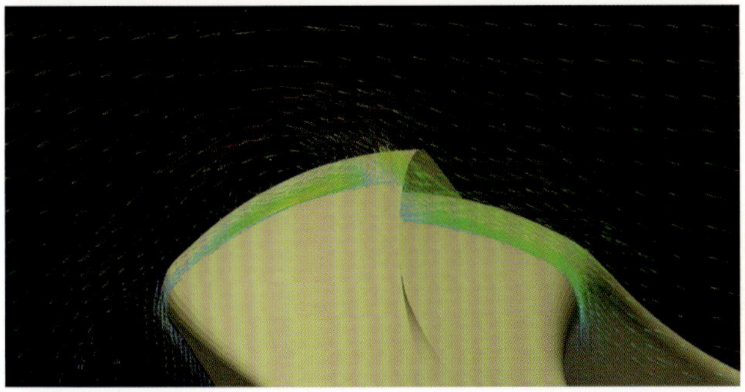

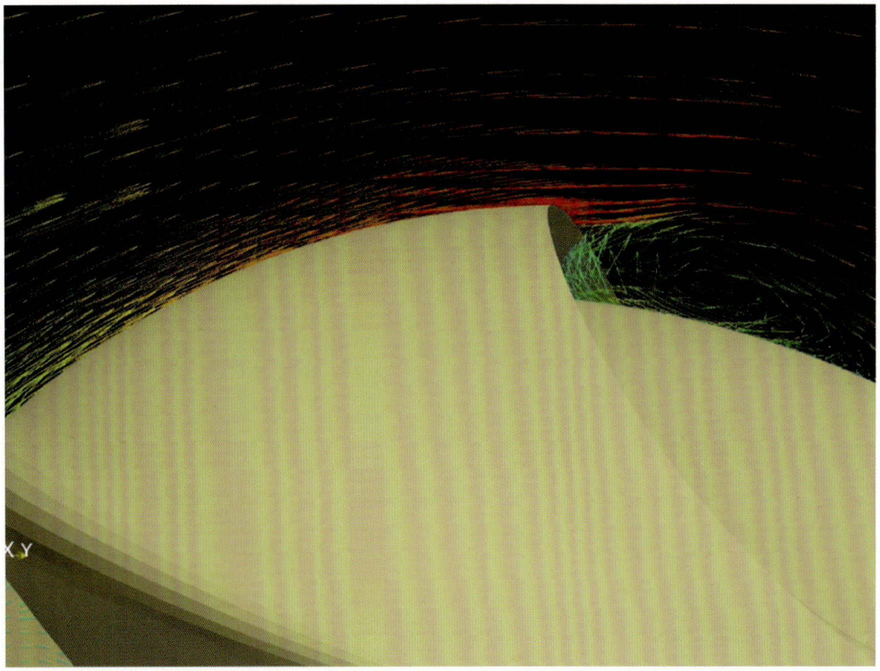

SOUTH BY SOUTH WEST WINDS

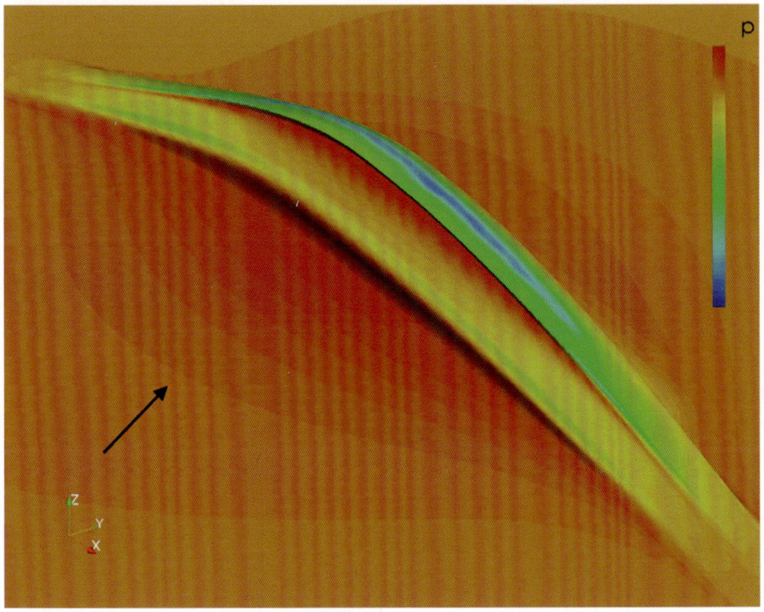

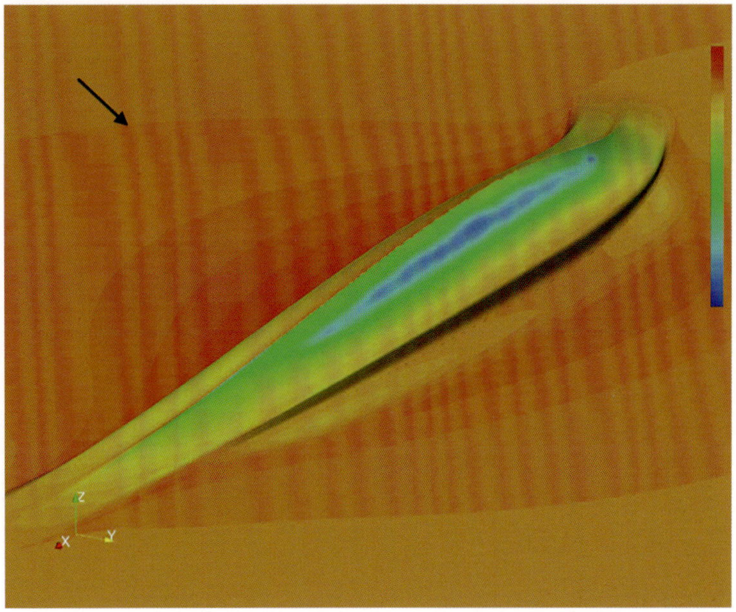

ARROW INDICATES WIND DIRECTION

RED CONTOURS INDICATE POSITIVE PRESSURE

BLUE CONTOURS INDICATE NEGATIVE PRESSURE

WEST ELEVATION: TOTAL RADIATION

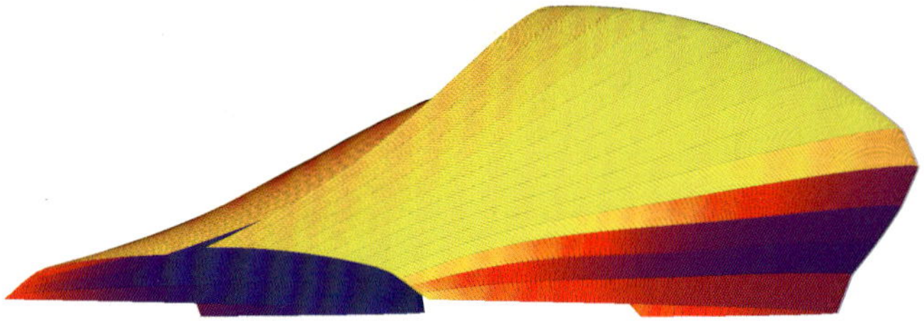

EAST ELEVATION: TOTAL RADIATION

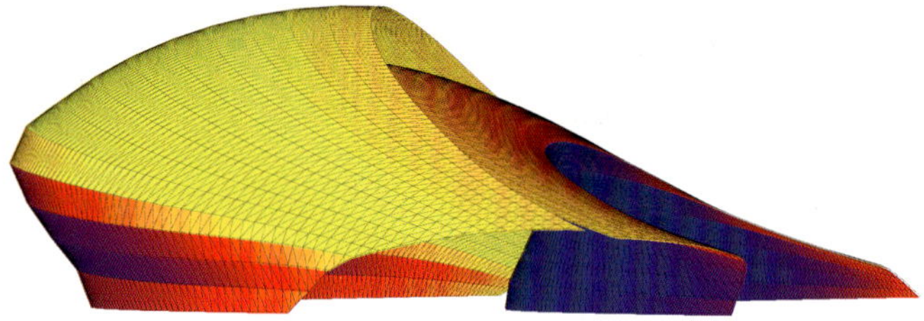

SOUTH ELEVATION: TOTAL RADIATION

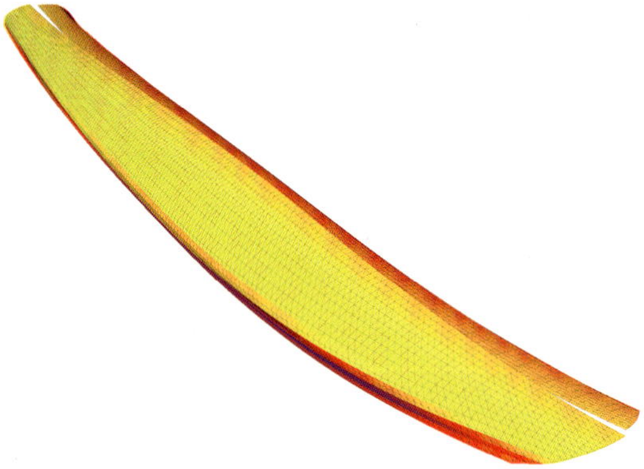

BUILDING PV PLACEMENT

GEO-EXCHANGE LABYRINTH COOLING SYSTEM

PREVAILING WINDS FROM THE NORTH

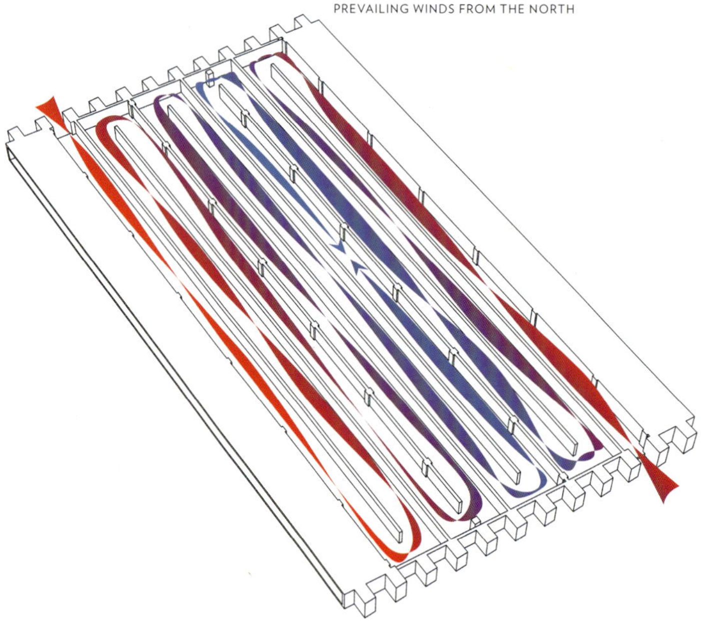

PREVAILING WINDS FROM THE SOUTH

The Yard at Chicago Shakespeare Theater

Chicago, Illinois

The Yard at Chicago Shakespeare Theater

Chicago, Illinois

The Yard at Chicago Shakespeare Theater is a next-generation performance venue that reflects Chicago Shakespeare's multi-faceted artistic vision.

SERVICES
Architecture

CLIENT
Chicago Shakespeare Theater

FUNCTION
Cultural

FACTS
33,000 sf

AWARDS
AIA Innovation Awards, Stellar Architecture, Honorable Mention, 2017

The American Architecture Prize, Honorable Mention in Architectural Design, Cultural Architecture, 2017

The project features a new flexible theater and glazed two-story lobby and reception space, with magnificent views of Lake Michigan, that connects to the existing theater at Navy Pier. Consisting of 33,000 sf of space, the project introduces a global trend in theater architecture that focuses on resourceful, sustainable, and adaptive design. The new theater is artfully tucked beneath the existing signature white tent and above the existing parking garage. The new theater shares existing stage house and backstage support spaces.

To mitigate glare and heat, the lobby facade uses electrochromic glass. Designed with daylight sensors on the roof, the facade gradually tints when sunlight passes across its southern face. This unique solution is highly sustainable and will reduce heat gain and cooling needs. The geometry of the faceted curve creates dynamic reflections, inviting passersby to interact with the facade, heightening the theatrical experience. The "theatrical" nature of the facade is akin to the raising of the curtain, as it will be primarily tinted throughout the day becoming clearer in the evenings as the sun sets and the performances begin.

Another innovation is the theater's flexible egress system that allows seating towers to be configured into nine different arrangements, adjusting the range of seating capacity from 250 to over 850 seats. The mobility of the seating towers is achieved through the incorporation of air casters at the base of each structure.

SHAKESPEARE

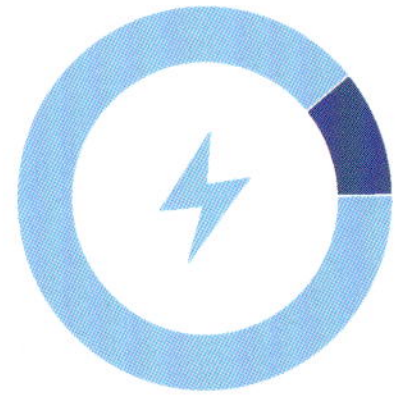

11%
Total
Energy
Reduction

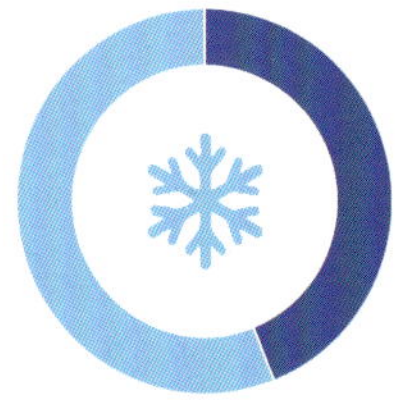

44%
Cooling
Demand
Reduction

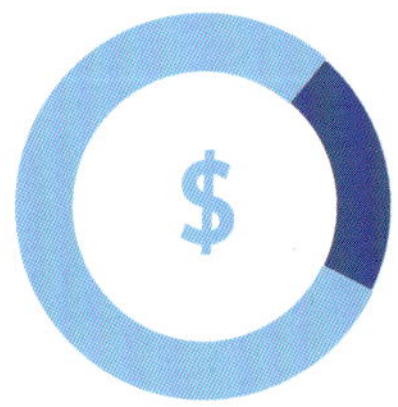

21%
Operating Cost
Reduction

Glass was selected for the main facade of the lobby to create an architectural relationship between the existing and new buildings as well as to capture and frame views in both directions. To combat against the intense southern exposure on this curtain wall, electrochromic glass was an excellent material option, capable of reducing the life cycle operational costs for the project. Traditional low-e glass would require a larger HVAC system first cost as well as increase energy usage, lighting and cooling costs, and peak-demand charges. However, with electrochromic glass the thermal heat gain is reduced significantly, thereby reducing the cooling loads, particularly in the summer months.

SUMMER MORNING

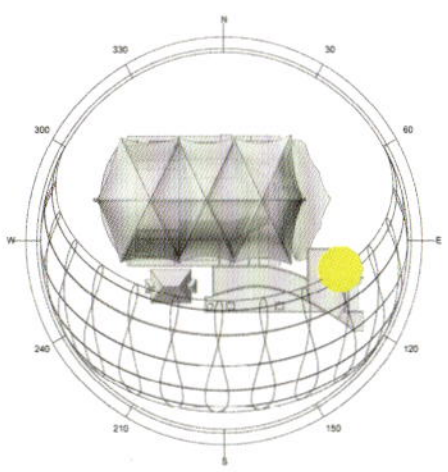

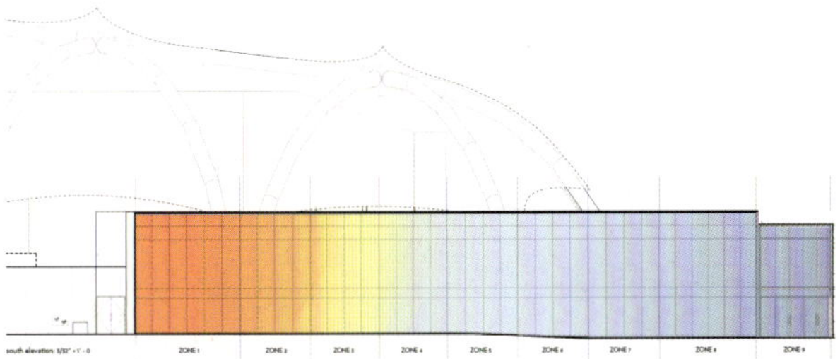

Conventional glass
Summer morning solar gain: 16 kW

16 kW

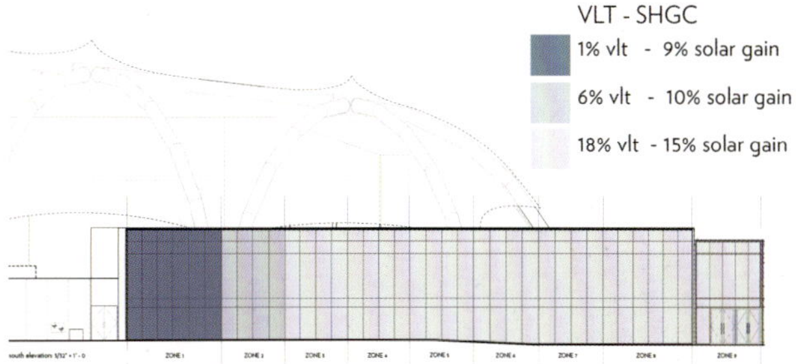

SageGlass
Summer morning solar gain: 3 kW
(81% reduction)

3 kW

SUMMER NOON

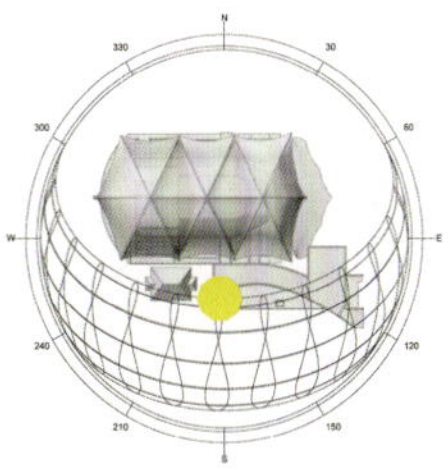

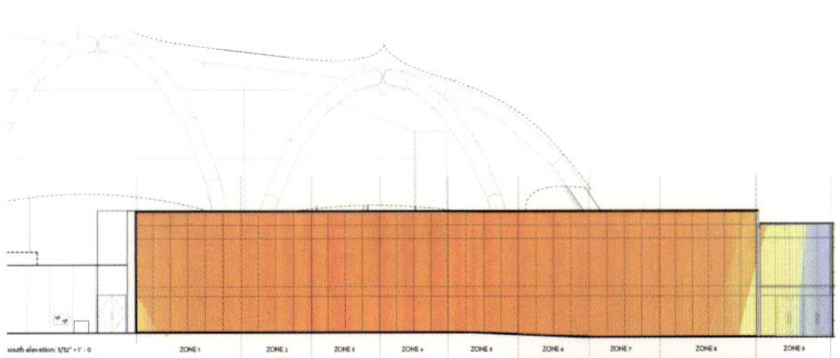

Conventional glass
Summer noon solar gain: 29 kW

29 kW

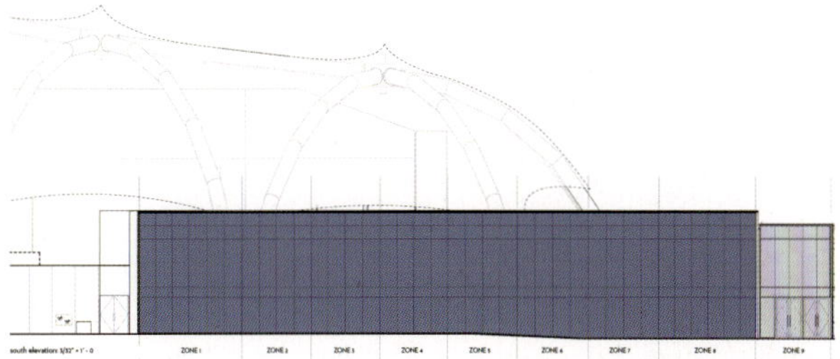

SageGlass
Summer noon solar gain: 5 kW
(83% reduction)

5 kW

SUMMER AFTERNOON

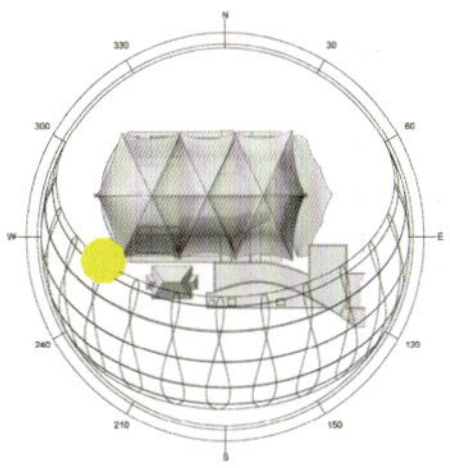

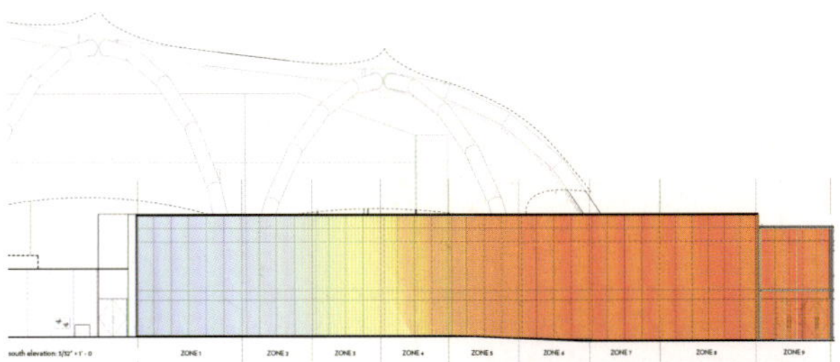

Conventional glass
Summer afternoon solar gain: 33 kW

33 kW

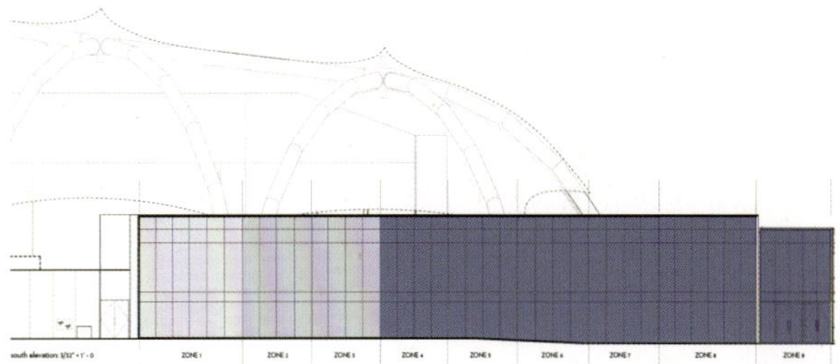

SageGlass
Summer afternoon solar gain: 6 kW
(81% reduction)

6 kW

LOBBY

MEZZANINE

FLEXIBLE THEATER
SMALL END ON
80 OCCUPANTS

FLEXIBLE THEATER
THRUST
623 OCCUPANTS

Chicago
Architecture
Center

Chicago, Illinois

Chicago Architecture Center

Chicago, Illinois

Opened in August 2018, the new Chicago Architecture Center is the city's newest must-see cultural destination and home to everything architecture in Chicago.

SERVICES
Architecture

CLIENT
Chicago Architecture Center

FUNCTION
Cultural

FACTS
1860 sm

AWARDS
National AIA, Interior Architecture Award, 2022

AIA Chicago, Interior Architecture Award, Citation of Merit 2020

The 20,000-square-foot center at 111 East Wacker Drive is a one of a kind Chicago experience. Visitors can find world-famous river and walking tours, educational programs and new interactive exhibits that reveal the stories behind the city's architectural wonders. Visitors will see first hand how Chicago's design legacy has changed skylines around the world.

Visitors to the CAC will be greeted at the box office and orientation center on the ground level before choosing to taking an expert, docent-led tour or viewing the innovative exhibition spaces developed and executed by museum planning and design firm, Gallagher & Associates at your own pace. The premier exhibit is located in the Skyscraper Gallery on the second floor, in a dramatic space with 40-foot-tall windows overlooking the Chicago River and the Michigan Avenue Bridge. The exhibit features supersized-scale models of famous skyscrapers from Chicago and around the world including AS+GG's 40-foot-tall model of Jeddah Tower, which will be the world's tallest building when completed in 2020.

The Chicago: City of Architecture Gallery, located on the first floor, will tell the story of how Chicago became the epicenter of modern architecture and design. The popular Chicago Model exhibit has expanded from the previous CAC space from 1,300 to 3,000 buildings and now features a film and light show that illuminates the model to illustrate Chicago's early growth, rebirth after the Great Chicago Fire, first-ever skyscrapers, and today's modernist masterpieces of steel and glass.

20
50
CHICAGO
ARCHITECTURE
CENTER

CHICAGO:
CITY OF ARCHITECTURE

THE 606
2015
NORTHERLY ISLAND
2015

Steppenwolf

Chicago, Illinois

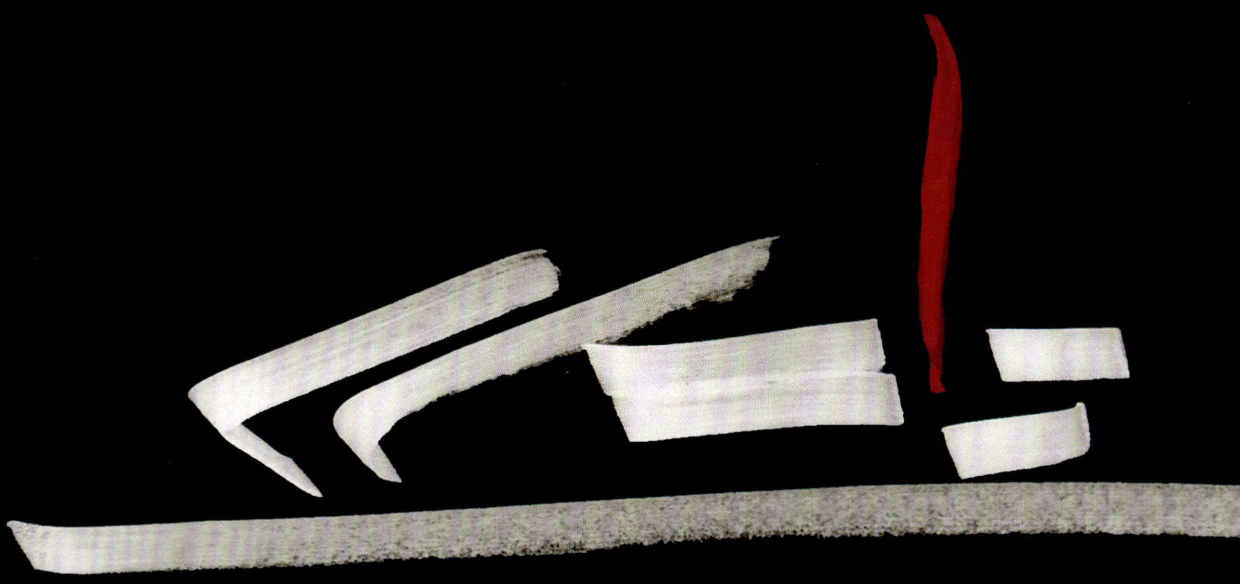

Steppenwolf Theatre Expansion

Chicago, Illinois

The 50,000 sf Steppenwolf Theatre Expansion includes a new in-the-round theater and education center and is now named the Liz and Eric Lefkofsky Arts and Education Center.

SERVICES
Architecture
Interior Design
Urban Planning

CLIENT
Steppenwolf Theatre Company

FUNCTION
Cultural

FACTS
5,574 sm

The transformed Steppenwolf campus will change the way Chicagoans and visitors experience the company's cutting-edge theater when in-person performances return in late 2021.

Steppenwolf's Liz and Eric Lefkofsky Arts and Education Center is the largest new permanent cultural asset to open in the City of Chicago in 2021. The $54 million building project is part of Steppenwolf's multi-phase $73 million campus expansion, and includes Steppenwolf's first-ever dedicated education space, The Loft, encompassing the entire fourth floor of the new building.

The expansion will introduce new relationships with its patrons, neighborhood, and Chicago as a whole. Architecturally, the design is carefully stitched into its neighborhood context, recognizing the significance of its presence along Halsted Street, while respecting its neighbors.

At the heart of the center is an intimate and state-of-the-art 400-seat theater in the round, one of its kind in Chicago. The concept, based on Collision, that interaction between the actor and the audience serves to establish dynamic and intimate spatial relationships throughout the project.

The theater is only six rows deep, always placing the actor in an intimate relationship with the audience. No audience member will be more than 20 feet from the stage, blurring the lines of actor/audience relationships.

Other improvements include a dedicated education floor for the future of Chicago's youth. Steppenwolf has always had a strong commitment to the social construct and neighborhoods across Chicago. Through its Young Adult Council and Teen Programs, the project took an Education-centric approach to its design by placing the Teens and the future youth of Chicago at the Center of design and in the most prominent spaces.

The program also includes a dynamic lobby space, Steppenwolf's costume shop and other updated production amenities, as well as a wine bar and a sidewalk lounge, increasing the social gathering spaces where artists and audiences converge.

Key elements of the in-the-round theatre include a modular staging system that allows for designers and directors to control the architecture, adjust the capacity, and explore different stage footprints for a variety of audience relationships. Accessibility was at the forefront of the design, including 20 fully integrated wheelchair accessible locations (versus the six that are required by law), as well as an induction hearing loop and improved sight lines for performances featuring ASL Interpretation and Open Captioning.

STEPPENWOLF

LIZ AND ERIC LEFKOFSKY
ARTS AND EDUCATION CENTER

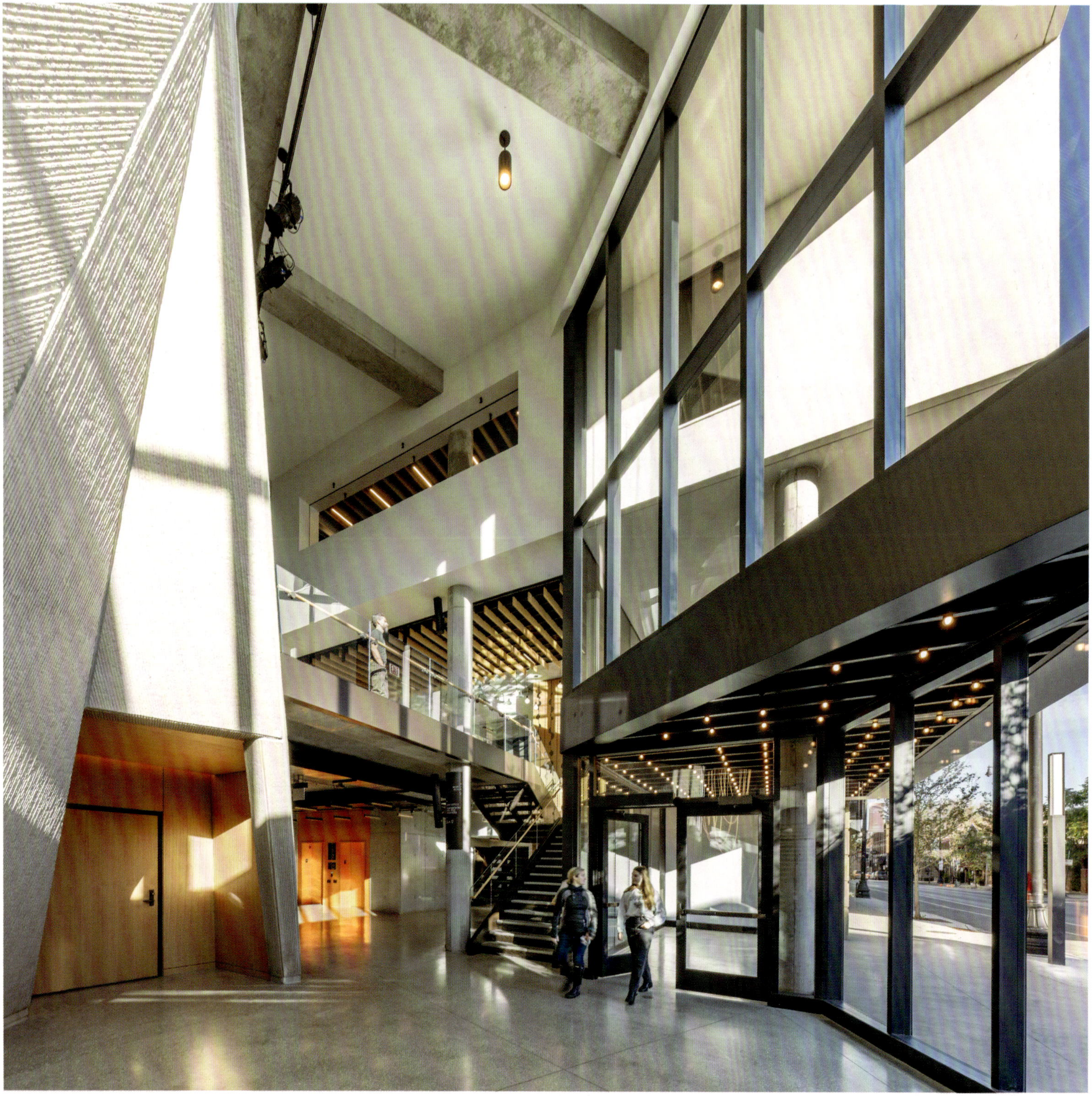

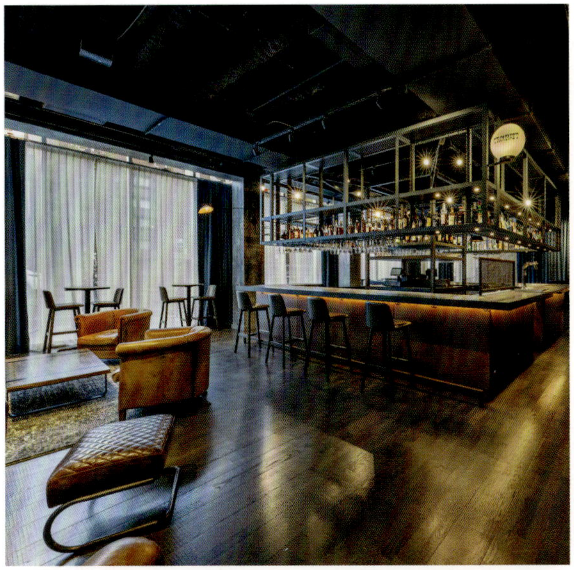

Willow Creek

Glenview, Illinois

Willow Creek North Shore

Glenview, Illinois

The new Willow Creek Community Church is inspired by the form of a seed, a biblical reference that also symbolizes the connection the building's design has to nature.

SERVICES
Architecture
Interior Design

CLIENT
Willow Creek
Community Church

FUNCTION
Cultural

FACTS
6,689 sm

AWARDS
The Chicago
Athenaeum, American
Architecture Awards,
2017

The building shape is symmetrical about the north/south axis, and is designed to strategically use natural light while bringing the experience of the outdoors to the building occupants.

The auditorium space is located at the center of the building and acts as an anchor as the lobby, offices, classrooms, and café spaces surround the it, connected by a large circulation area. The design features two main circulation paths which help to form a courtyard between the classroom and office wings and the auditorium.

A multipurpose room at the end of the classroom wing is symmetrical to the auditorium, forming a smaller version of the main auditorium, reinforcing the strong relationship between the youth fellowship activities and the main auditorium where the Sunday services take place. The Harvest Café space, located in front of the auditorium, is used for large, more casual meetings and as a gathering space on Sundays for those who wish to watch the service on video screens. It may also be used for weddings or funerals, and has direct access to the front terrace.

The outdoor space is designed and programed so that members of the church are encouraged to experience nature during their visit. The large front terrace has views onto the retention pond. A canopy wraps the front of the building in order to shade the facade and provide protected seating area.

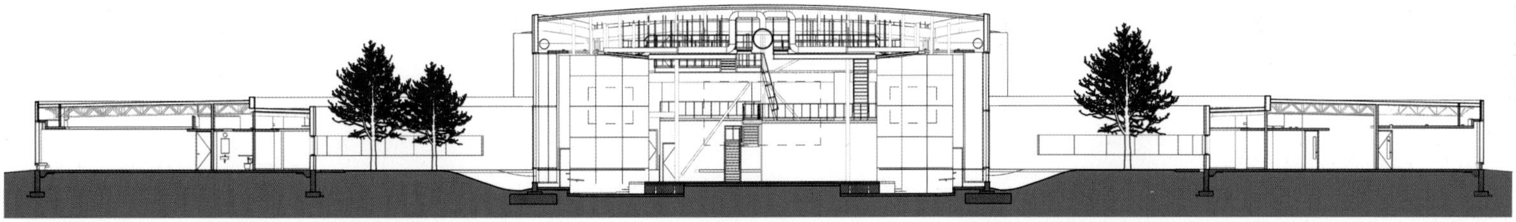

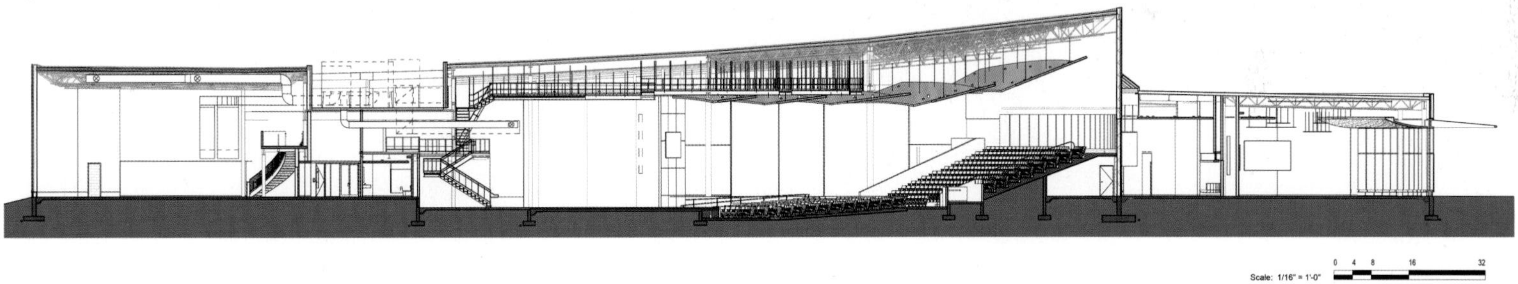
Scale: 1/16" = 1'-0"
0 4 8 16 32

FLOOR PLAN

1. Youth Group Worship
2. Circulation
3. Auditorium
4. Prefunction
5. Cafe
6. Storage
7. MEP
8. Classrooms
9. Office
10. Adult Education
11. Courtyard

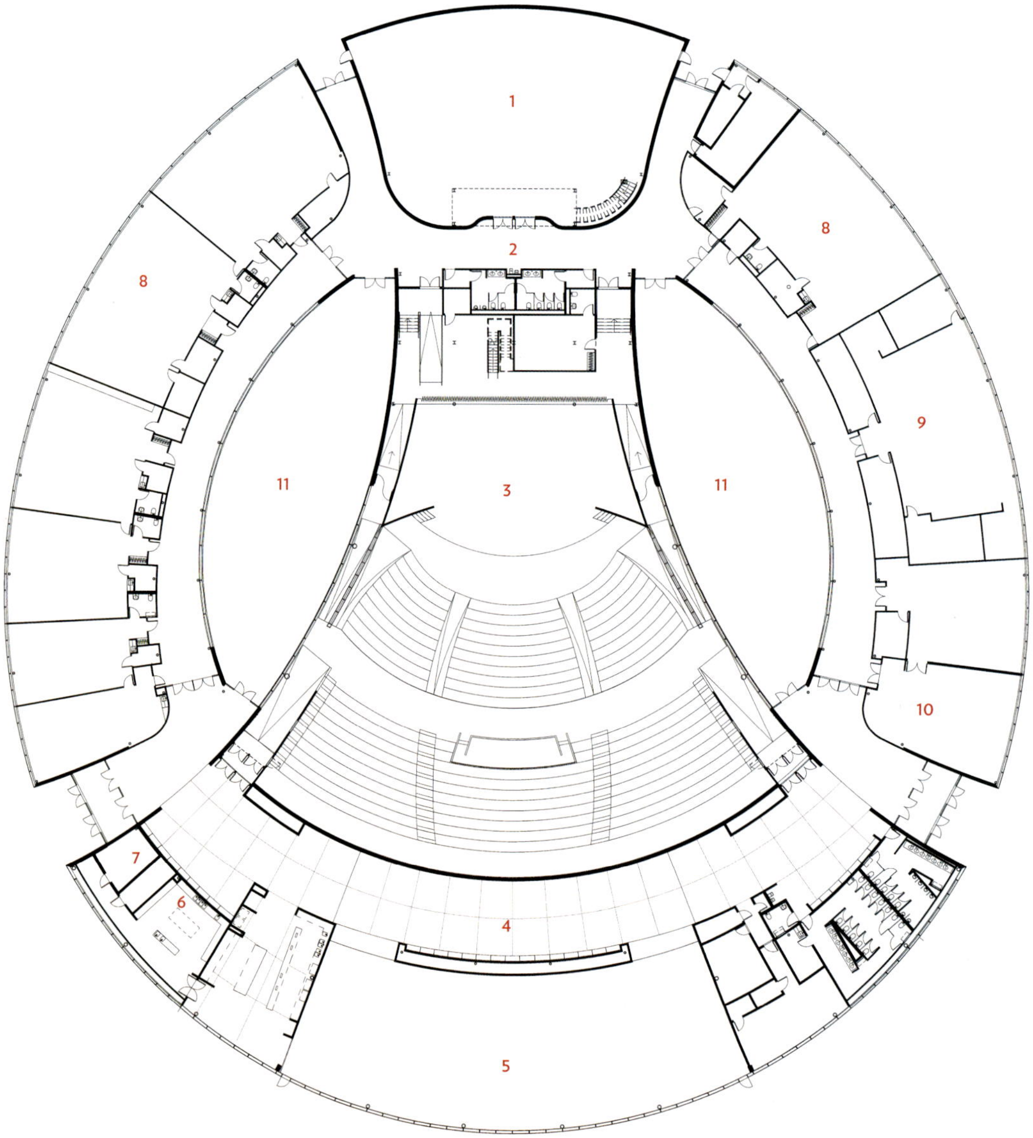

Welcome Center
COME
&
SEE
EASTER
AT
WILLOW CREEK

CAFE

CORRIDORS

Matrix Gateway Complex

Dubai, United Arab Emirates

Matrix Gateway Complex

Dubai, United Arab Emirates

Designed as both an urban gateway and an independent self-sustaining city, this 42-story prototype is designed to be one of the greenest, most aesthetically striking and technologically innovative mixed-use buildings in the world.

SERVICES
Architecture

CLIENT
Meraas Development

FUNCTION
Mixed-use

FACTS
382,127 sm building area

AWARDS
AIA Chicago, Design Excellence, Unbuilt Category, 2010

P/A Award, Architect Magazine, 2010

The Chicago Athenaeum, American Architecture Award, 2009

The Chicago Athenaeum, International Architecture Award, 2009

A 180-meter cube designed on an 18-meter supergrid, the prototype contains many of the components of a great urban center: a hotel with fitness and conference centers, retail and office spaces, cultural and religious facilities, and waterfalls and lush green terraces. Each component takes the form of a moveable module connected to one of five central cores that are visible from the outside through a semi-transparent exterior skin enveloped with a blend of screens and photovoltaic cells.

The prototype was designed to rest on a cove, harbor, or lake and functions as a bridge through a 54 sm aperture in the building. Drivers journey across the bridge from one land mass to another by passing through the building and emerging in either direction to spectacular views of the city skyline.

The building's its high-tech skin blocks solar heat gain and generates power from sunlight and a condensate collection system converts humidity from the air into drinking water. The surrounding water naturally cools the environment around the structure, while waterfalls and breezes flowing through the screens also make the interior feel cooler.

The prototype's structural concept is elegant and simple. Floor systems are composite steel framing hung from the cores—four are concrete and one is steel—and are supported by a hat truss roof system. The truss also engages the concrete cores to act in unison when subjected to lateral wind loads. Hanging steel column supports are provided for most floors on an 18 sm grid. Floor framing spans between column grid-lines allow large 18 sm free spans.

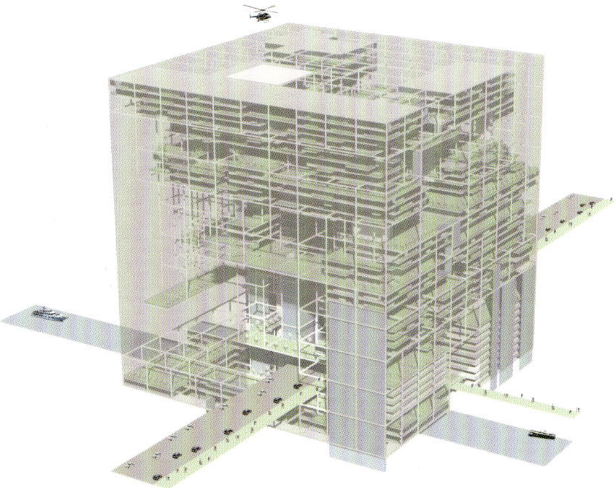

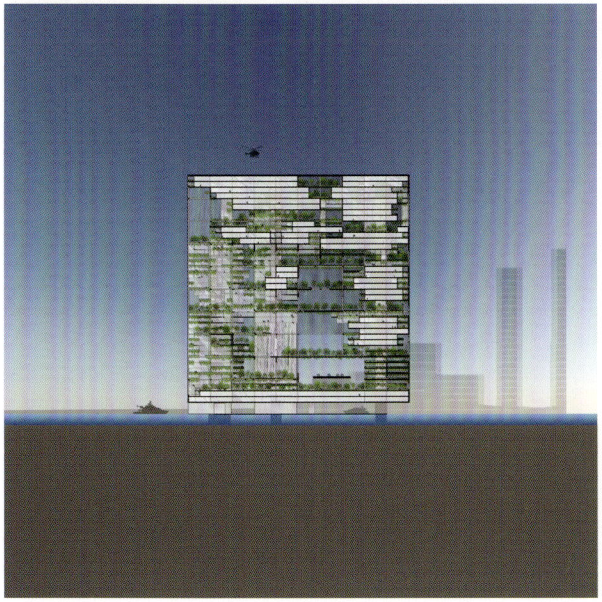

PROGRAM

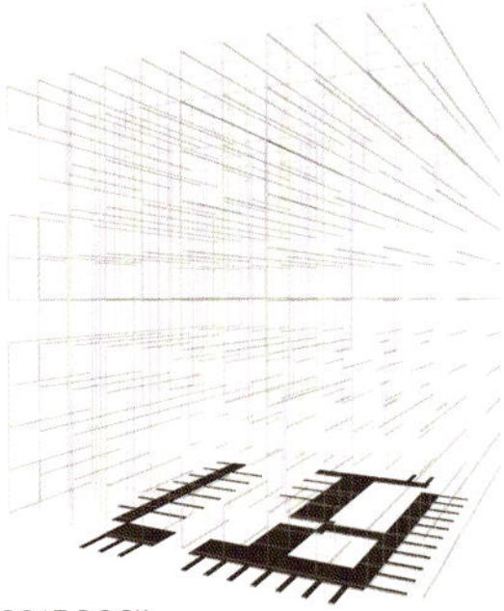

BOAT DOCK

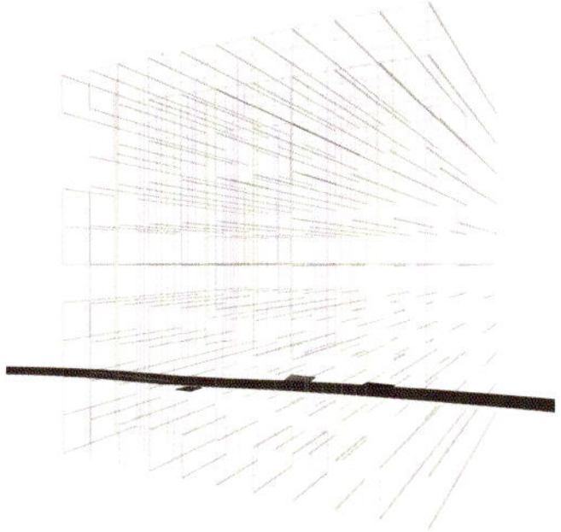

BRIDGE

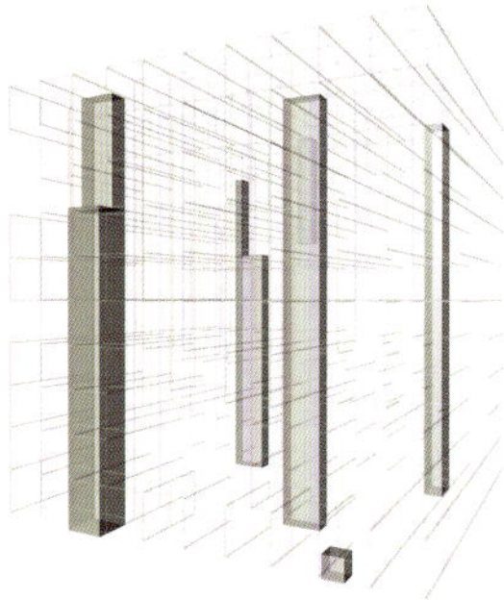

CORES

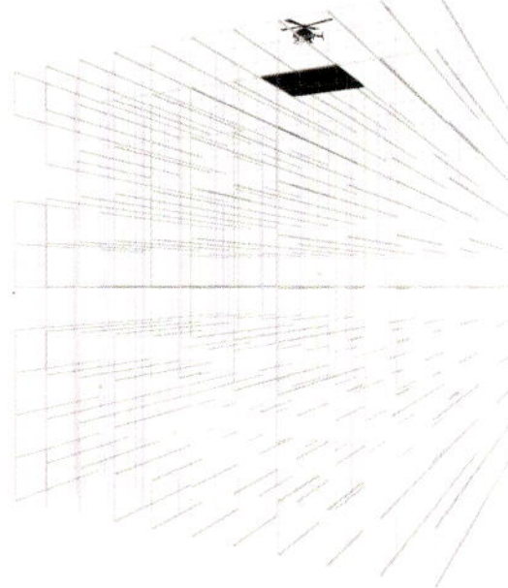

HELIPAD

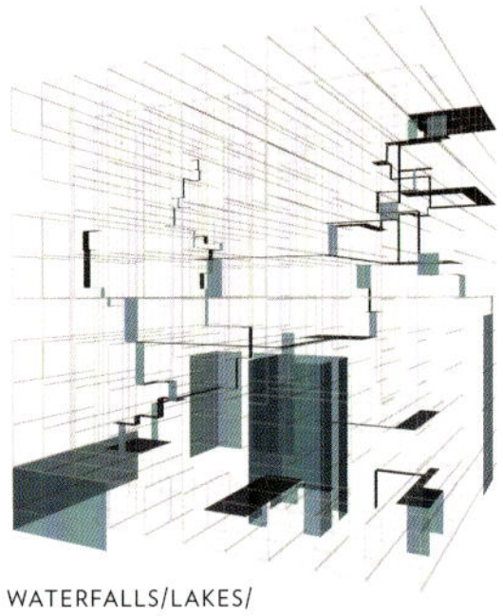

WATERFALLS/LAKES/STREAMS

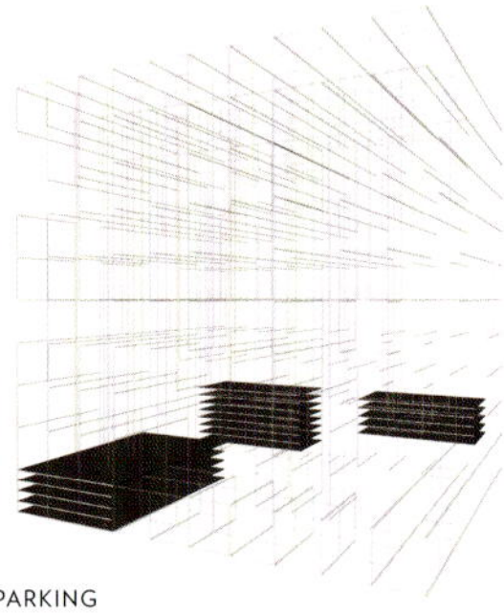

PARKING

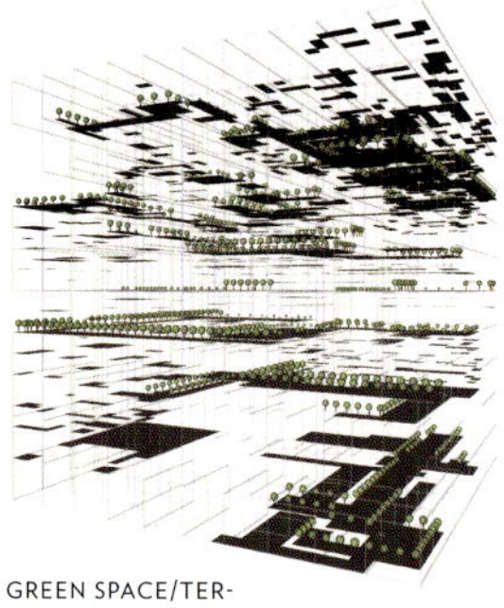

GREEN SPACE/TERRACES

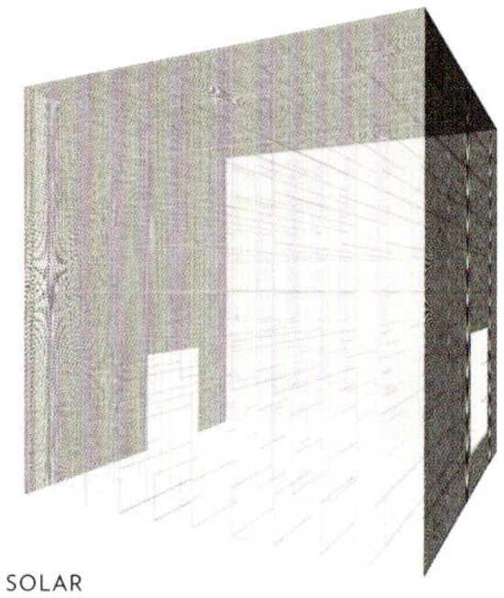

SOLAR SCREEN

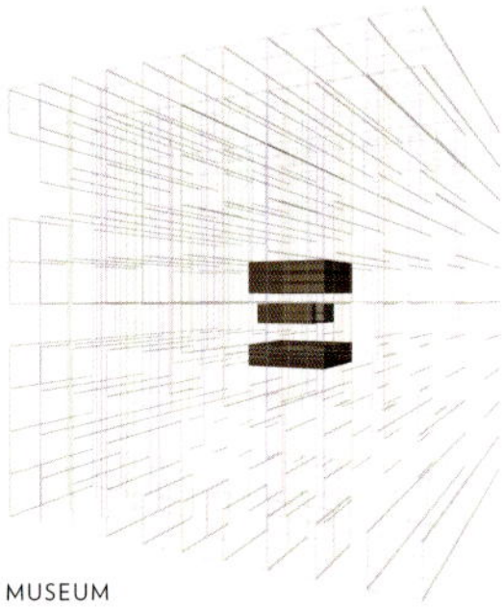

MUSEUM

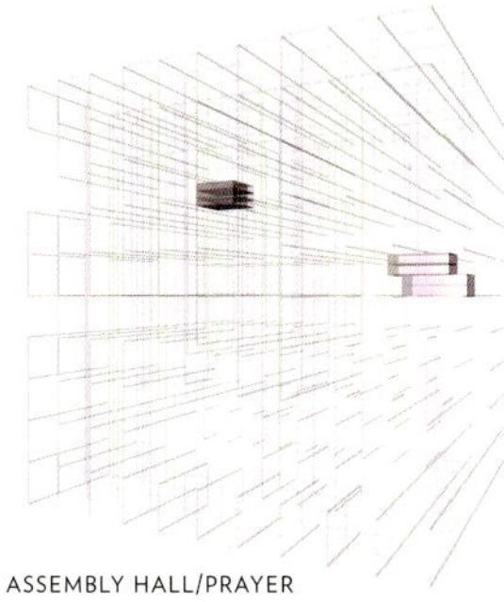

ASSEMBLY HALL/PRAYER HALL

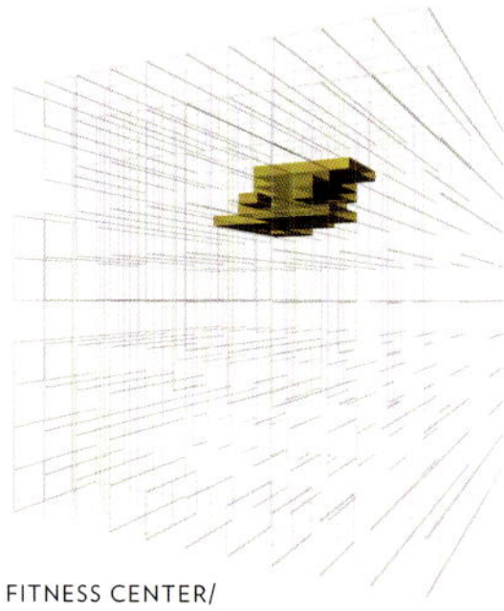

FITNESS CENTER/AMENITIES

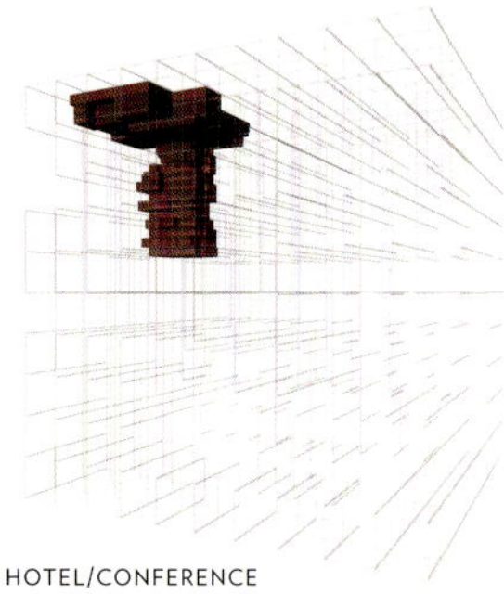

HOTEL/CONFERENCE CENTER

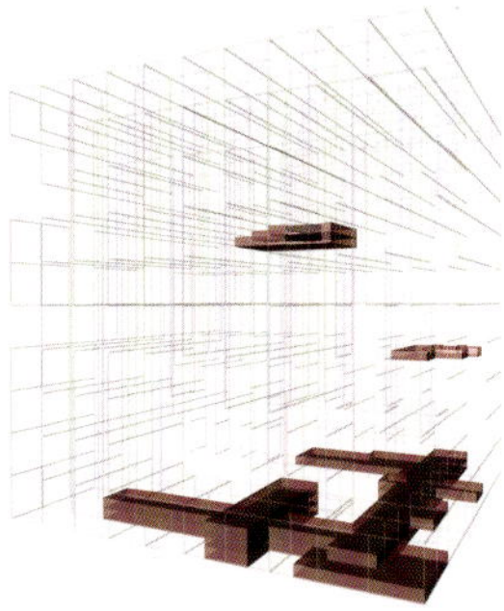

RETAIL/RESTAURANT

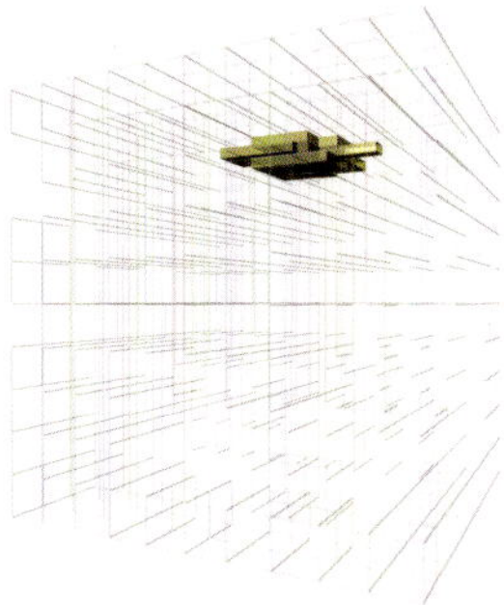

EDUCATIONAL

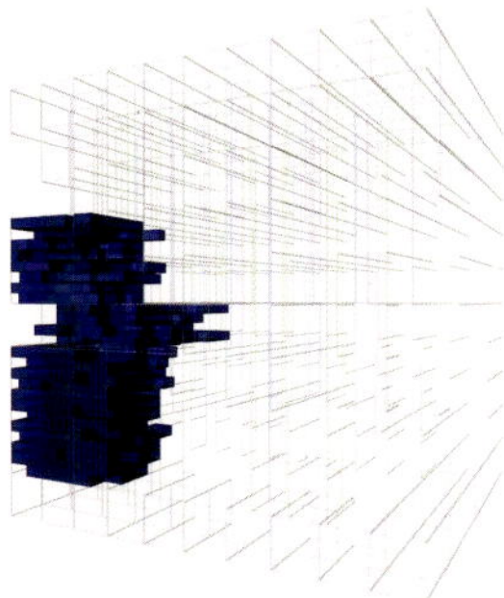

OFFICE

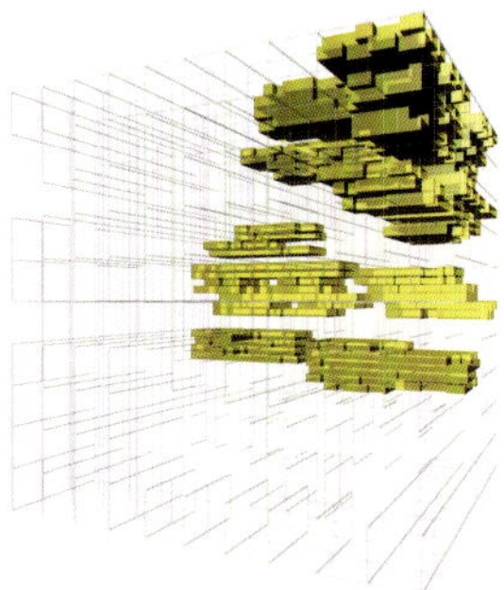

RESIDENTIAL

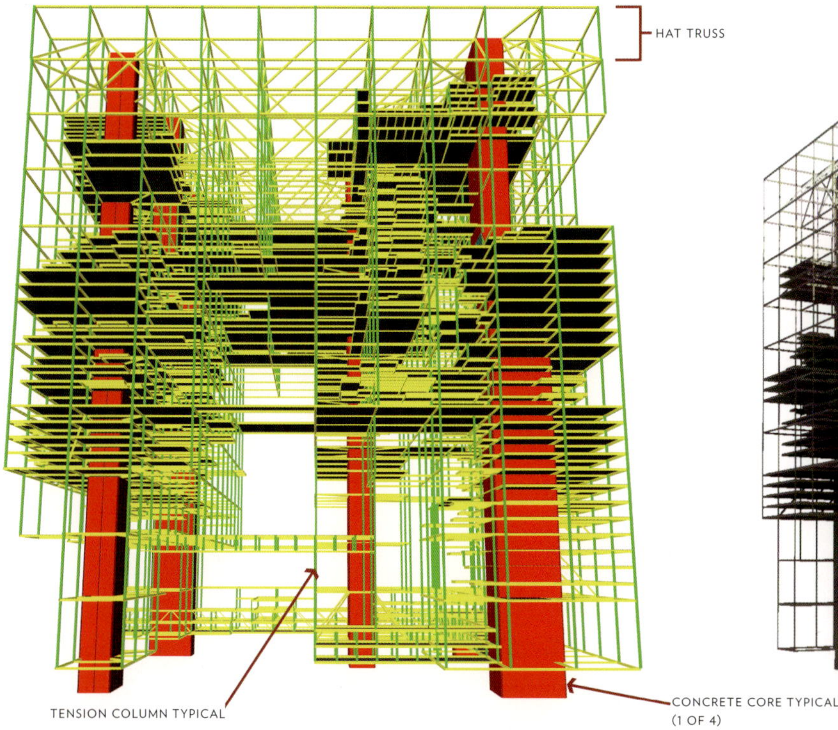

3D STRUCTURAL ANALYSIS MODEL

3D REVIT MODEL

TRUSS AND CORE DEFLECTED SHAPE

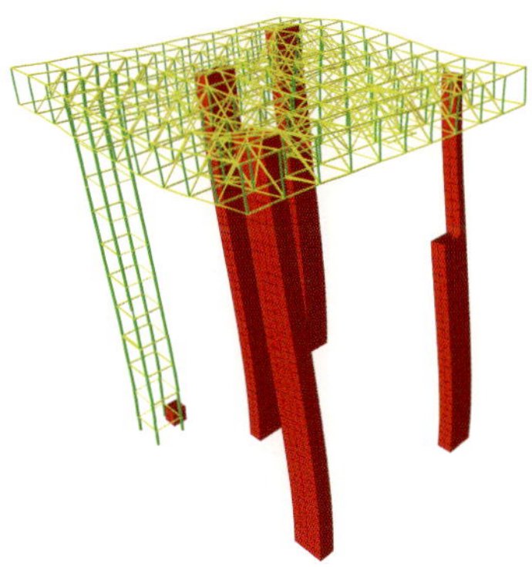

WIND IN X-DIRECTION

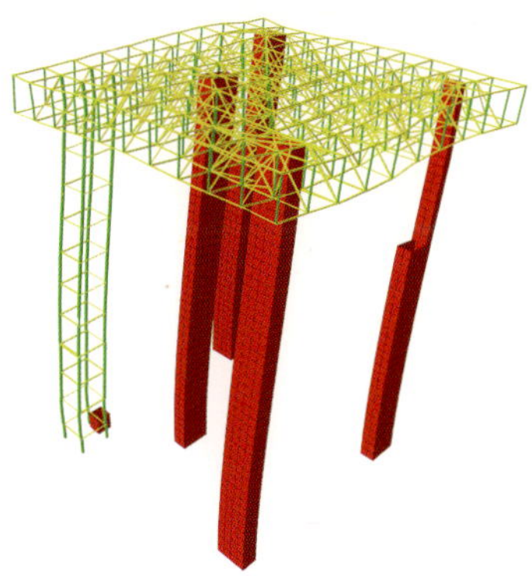

WIND IN Y DIRECTION

Wings Museum

Dubai, United Arab Emirates

Wings Museum

Dubai, United Arab Emirates

A simple but arresting image from nature—a bird skimming over the surface of a body of water—is the inspiration for this prototype of a museum on a lake or ocean harbor.

SERVICES
Architecture

CLIENT
Meraas Development

FUNCTION
Cultural

FACTS
375,000 sm building area

With its wings unfurled as if in midflight, this powerfully poetic structure is an evocation of the natural world at its most graceful, dynamic, streamlined, and ecologically interdependent. When combined with concepts from automobile and product design, the design for the Wings Museum is a sculptural, asymmetrical form that is echoed in its interior by two great atria that feel equally organic.

The building is highly sustainable. Covered with photovoltaic cells, the entire roof structure protects the underside of the building from the harshest sunlight. That, in turn, allows for a more transparent curtain wall, which features a graduated frit pattern based on the building's structural geometry.

The elegance of the building's form is made possible by its complex structure, which involves a system of belt trusses and large columns necessary to support cantilevers of up to 100 meters. A grid of exterior steel members is mirrored inside the building, creating a tube-within-a-tube. The interior diagrid allows the floor plan to be supported with simple spans and achieves a column-free interior space.

The tension face of the structure is reinforced by a belt truss, which occurs at each floor to resist forces that would pull the surface flat, and it provides a support edge for the long-span trusses supporting the interior atrium floors.

CFD ANALYSIS

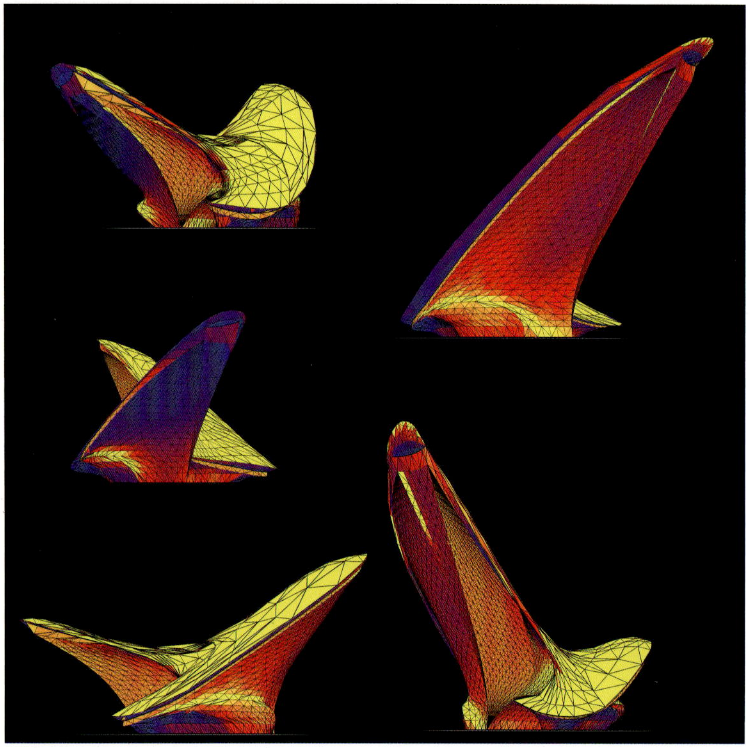

Crystal Center

Dubai, United Arab Emirates

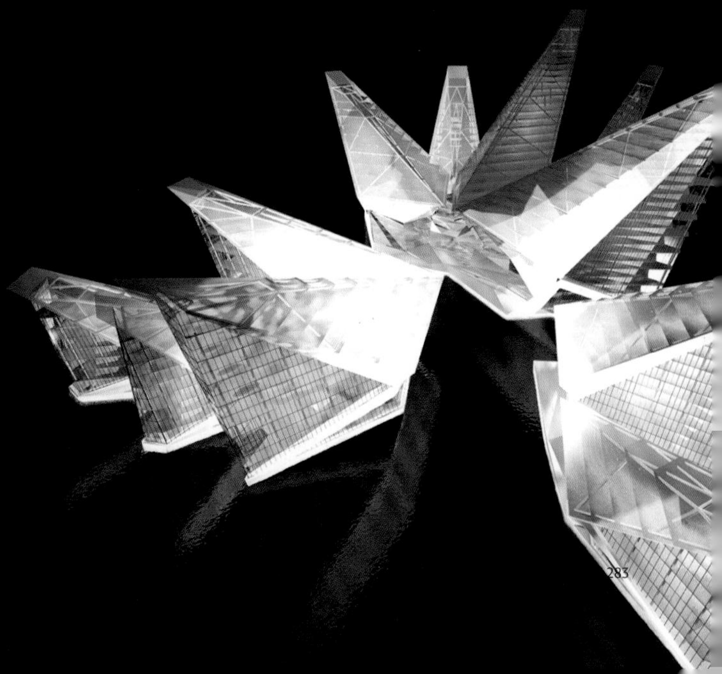

Crystal Center

Dubai, United Arab Emirates

Eleven crystalline structures of varying size, with cantilevers of up to 230 feet over the water, are joined at a base largely concealed beneath the surface, creating the illusion of the structures as independent.

SERVICES
Architecture

CLIENT
Meraas Development

FUNCTION
Cultural

FACTS
180,000 sm

This prototype is design to be located in a tidal basin so that some hards—or crystals—are accessible across the base at low tide. At high tide, the base, which also contains a parking podium accessed from the mainland by a tunnel, is submerged. At the rear of the circle of structures, a series of plazas—one large, two smaller—is enclosed, creating a grand civic space complete with water features.

Inside the structures, the cantilevers create stunning interior spaces for occupants to enjoy extraordinary views while experiencing a sense of being suspended above the water. The cantilevered roofs also allow the building to shade itself in a hot climate, which allows for greater transparency in the glass curtain walls beneath.

This low-maintenance passive sustainability strategy is assisted by mesh shading screens on the building envelope that reduces solar heat gain and protects a series of rear-facing terraces and balconies.

The structure of this complex building is surprisingly rational, using standard members for a building of its size. Many of the floor slabs are hung from a series of exterior steel trusses at the rear of the crystals. The trusses, which provide lateral stability and define the structure's tapering profile, are balanced and propped by uniquely inclined concrete cores.

Willis Tower Greening

Chicago, Illinois

Willis Tower Modernization

Chicago, Illinois

AS+GG's retrofit and greening plan for Chicago's tallest tower uses a variety of active and passive sustainable technologies to modernize the 1973 landmark and to increase its energy efficiency.

SERVICES
Architecture

CLIENT
US Equities Realty, Inc.

FUNCTION
Commercial

FACTS
140,000 sm building area

The plan reduces the base building electricity use by 80 percent—including energy savings and co-generation—equivalent to 68 million kilowatt hours or 150,000 barrels of oil per year. The modernization demonstrates how to save a significant amount of energy and improve the occupant experience of an existing building during a large-scale 21st-century modernization.

Key components of the greening/modernization project include:

- Efficiency improvements to the building's exterior envelope and 16,000 single-pane windows. Sustainability plans for the building call for a window replacement and glazing program. Strategies to achieve a thermal break of the curtain wall are also being investigated. These upgrades can achieve a savings of up to 50 percent of heating energy.
- Mechanical systems upgrades in the form of new gas boilers that utilize fuel cell technologies, which generate electricity, heating and cooling at as much as 90 percent efficiency. Mechanical upgrades also include new high-efficiency chillers and upgrades to the distribution system.
- The tower's 104 high-speed elevators and 15 escalators modernized with the latest technology to achieve 40 percent reduction in their energy consumption.
- Water savings realized with conservation initiatives through upgrades to restroom fixtures, condensation recovery systems, and water efficient landscaping, which reduces water usage by 40 percent and saves 24 million gallons of water each year.
- Lighting upgrades through advanced lighting control systems and daylight harvesting and an advanced lighting control system that automatically dims lights in tenant spaces based on the amount of sunlight entering through the windows. Combined, these upgrades save up to 40 percent of lighting energy consumption.
- Renewable energy like wind and solar, and technologies like green roofs to be tested. Wind turbine can take advantage of the tower's height and unique set-back roof areas. Solar hot-water panels can heat water for the building. Green roofs, which would be among the tallest in the world, can sustain high-altitude conditions and can be tested to reduce storm water runoff, improve insulation, help mitigate the urban heat island effect, and provide pleasant vistas for tenants overlooking the areas.

Willis Tower Hotel

Chicago, Illinois

A 50-story, five-star hotel on the south side of the Willis Tower plaza was designed to operate using part of the energy savings from the modernization and draws net-zero energy from the power grid.

A new skydeck entry is located within the hotel building's podium and is integrated with retail along Jackson Street. Visitors enter in the same location, but can take escalators to the Skydeck attraction on LL2 to decrease wait times. The escalators are underneath an attractive glass dome that connects Willis Tower to the new hotel. Direct access to the outdoor plaza and restaurants is also provided for skydeck visitors.

The new hotel features a host of green/sustainable features, including:

- Sky Gardens
- Solar Deck
- Double-walled Exterior
- Green Roofs + Planting Terraces
- Building-Integrated Wind Turbines
- Efficient Systems
- Sustainability standard designed for a LEED Gold rating

The 500-unit hotel's amenities include an elegant lobby, dining room, pool and spa; modern conference facilities with direct connection to sky terraces and green roof gardens on multiple levels; an 8,000-square-foot grand ballroom; top-of-the-line finishes made with renewable and/or recycled materials; new retail storefronts along Jackson and Franklin; and a grand outdoor plaza featuring landscaped terraces that connect the hotel to Willis Tower.

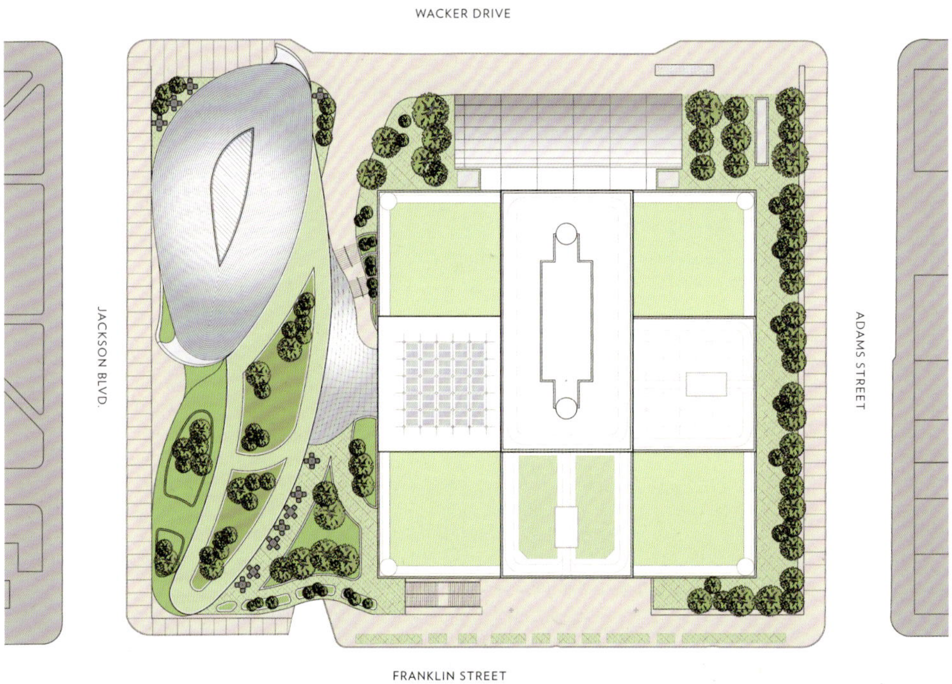
WACKER DRIVE
JACKSON BLVD.
ADAMS STREET
FRANKLIN STREET

A MODERNIZED ICON

HOW

MODERNIZATION + GREEN STRATEGIES

EXTERIOR WALL

The insulation value of the exterior wall system, which consists of more than 16,000 windows and metal panels, will be upgraded. These upgrades are estimated to save up to 60% of heating energy.

MECHANICAL SYSTEMS

The mechanical systems will be upgraded to save energy through higher efficiency equipment, stack effect reduction and the introduction of fuel cell boiler plants.

DAYLIGHTING

By expanding daylight harvesting, Willis Tower will save electrical energy and improve the work environment. Proposed methods include advanced lighting controls, higher ceilings, light shelves, and more efficient light fixtures.

GREEN ROOFS

Green roofs at Willis Tower will be the highest in the united states, reducing storm water runoff, improving insulation, and helping to mitigate the urban heat island effect.

WATER SAVINGS

Willis Tower will upgrade its plumbing systems using the latest technology to reduce its water usage by up to 24 million gallons annually.

OPERATIONS + MAINTENANCE

Willis Tower has introduced several new operational policies, including green cleaning, a bike-sharing program, bike storage, and a new recycling policy. The tower is also pursuing LEED Certification for existing buildings.

SOLAR HOT WATER

Solar hot water panels at the 90th-story roof level will help provide water for the building's restrooms. They will also be the highest solar panels in the United States.

WIND TURBINES

Taking advantage of the tower's height and location, wind testing will be performed at the highest roofs, to help advance the use of building integrated wind power in existing structures.

VERTICAL TRANSPORTATION

Willis Tower's elevator equipment will be modernized to provide greater energy efficiency and continued reliability.

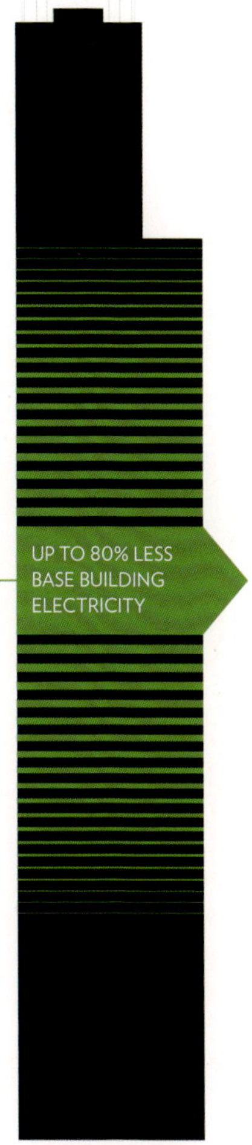

=

WHY

CONSERVES MORE THAN 68,000,000 KILOWATT HOURS PER YEAR, OR:

5,000,000 FEWER MILES OF HIGHWAY DRIVING

+

50,000 FEWER BARRELS OF CRUDE OIL

+

A HOTEL USING NET ZERO ENERGY FROM THE GRID

+

ELECTRICITY FOR 2,500 AVERAGE CHICAGO HOMES

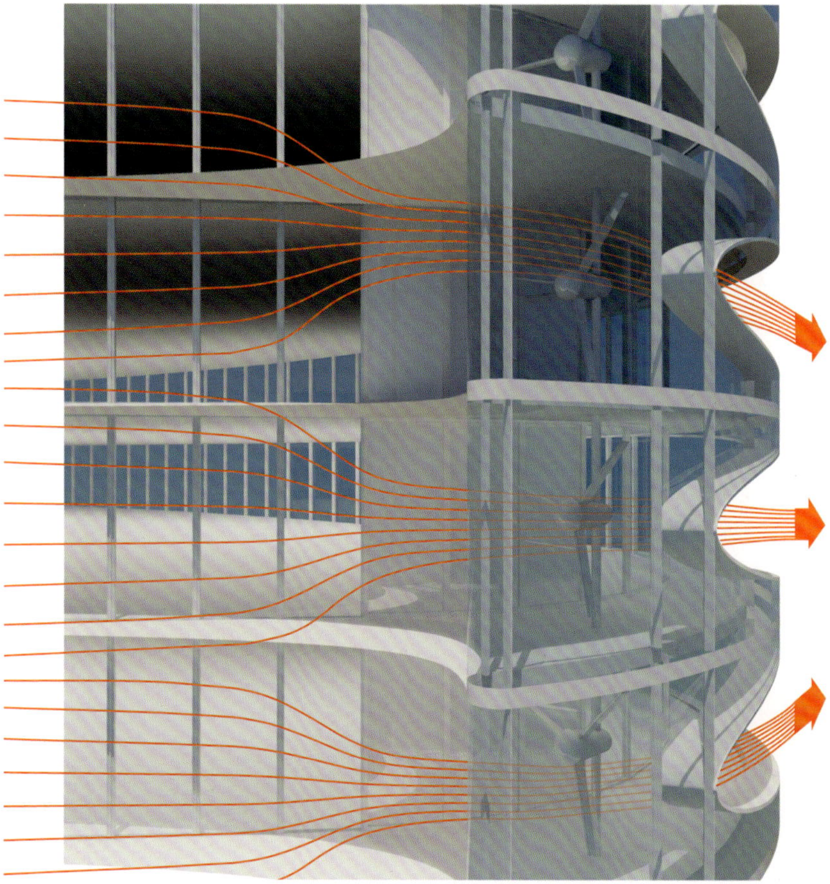

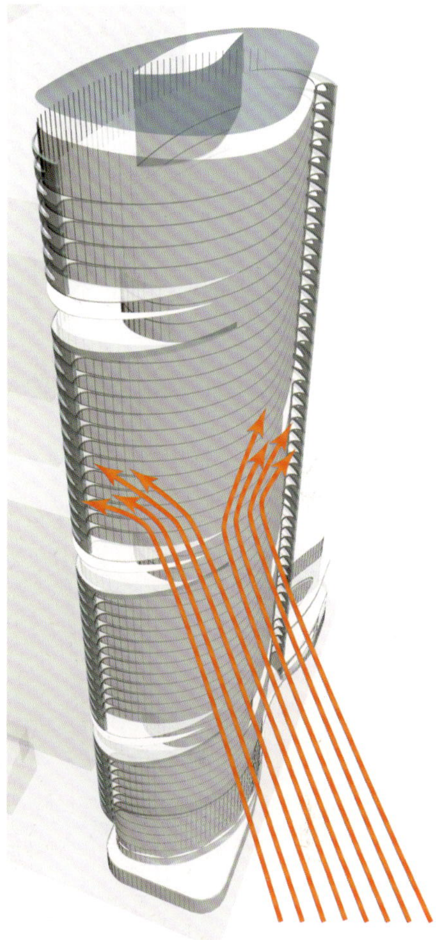

CLEAN POWER GENERATION

Wind turbines are integrated into the building's architecture to maximize its power output. The hotel building is shaped like a wing to capture prevailing wind from the southwest as it flows over the smooth front facade. Wind is channeled into the turbine openings, accelerating its speed and increasing the output of the wind turbines

The building also functions as a shield to block unpleasant wind from the plaza below. A Computational Fluid Dynamic (CFD) model, shown to the far right, illustrates how the building controls the wind.

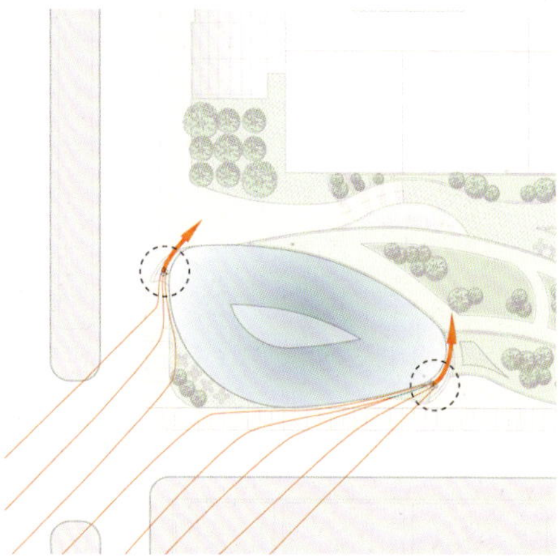

PLAN

WIND SPEED: 30 MP
SECTION: 305 FEET ABOVE GROUND

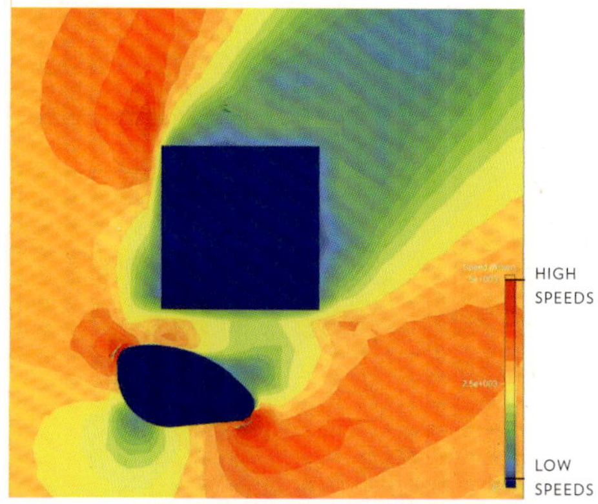

CFD MODEL

Waldorf Astoria

Beijing, China

Waldorf Astoria

Beijing, China

The new Waldorf Astoria in Beijing is a contemporary interpretation of the Forbidden City, China's most important historical treasure. The luxury hotel is located in the heart of downtown Beijing, next to Wang Fu Jing, the famous high-end walking shopping district, two blocks west of the Forbidden City.

SERVICES
Architecture

CLIENT
COFCO Limited

FUNCTION
Hospitality

FACTS
36,397 sm building area

AWARDS
AIA Chicago, Divine Detail Award, Bronze Facade, 2017

Civic Trust Awards, International Winner, 2015

AIA Chicago, Distinguished Building Award, Citation of Merit, 2015

The Chicago Athenaeum, American Architecture Award, Waldorf Astoria Beijing, 2015

HD Awards, Winner, Hotel Luxury | Upscale, Waldorf Astoria Beijing, 2015

Stylistically the influence is seen in the hotel's symmetry, prominent eaves, and generous use of bronze. The attention to detail is crucial to the design. Vertical frames and roof eaves are shaped, detailed, and strongly connected at the corners to reiterate the profile of traditional Chinese roof soffit silhouettes.

The intention is to subtly evoke Chinese architecture through the use of materials with a strong sense of richness. The exterior is featured with bronze—a royal material that expresses the luxury, dignity, and legend of the Waldorf brand, and reflects the character of the site location. The superframe, connecting the roof and anchoring building corners, recalls the symmetry and steady character of Chinese traditional architecture.

Bronze is used in large areas of the walls, as well as on window mullions, small clad sunshades, and perforated screens on the exterior wall. Other high-end, traditional materials are used to the same effect such as the local gray granite used as an additional exterior wall material, recalling the historic charcoal bricks of Beijing's traditional residential streets.

Luxury is evident in the orientation of the facade. The bay windows are floor-to-ceiling, allowing guests to enjoy superior city views from each guest room. The windows also create a unique viewing room area with screens for guests to enjoy a special living experience in Beijing. The orientation of the facade is equally important to the comfort of the building users and the environmental sensibility of the project. The shading frame system created for each room provides the character of the hotel but it also protects the building and minimizes the solar heat gain from all directions.

The design team worked closely with the client, COFCO, to re-shape the building massing while advancing the program and re-establishing the building structure and its interior layout grid. The end result is a beautifully done building that is contextual to the city, environmentally efficient, and true to the Waldorf Astoria brand.

WALDORF ASTORIA

WALDORF
ASTORIA

EXTERIOR WALL DETAILS

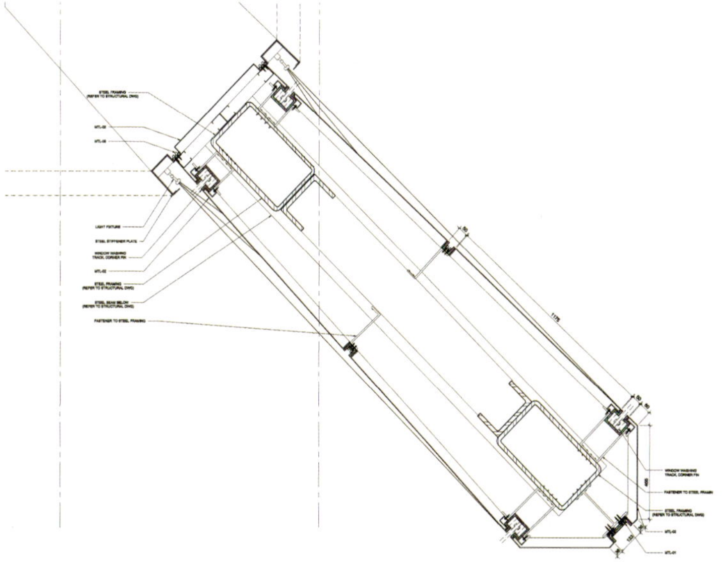

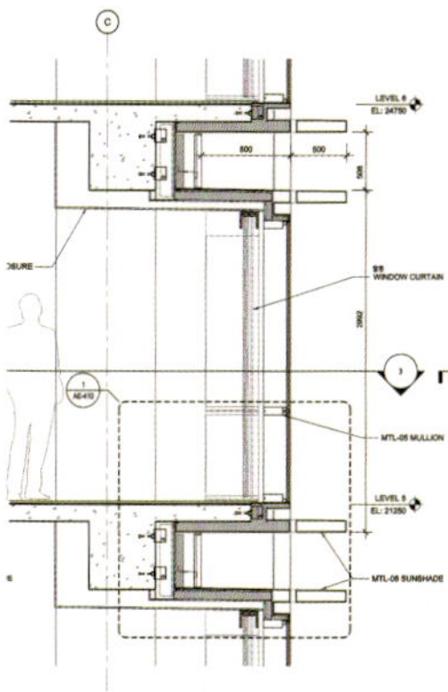

ENLARGED SECTION 4

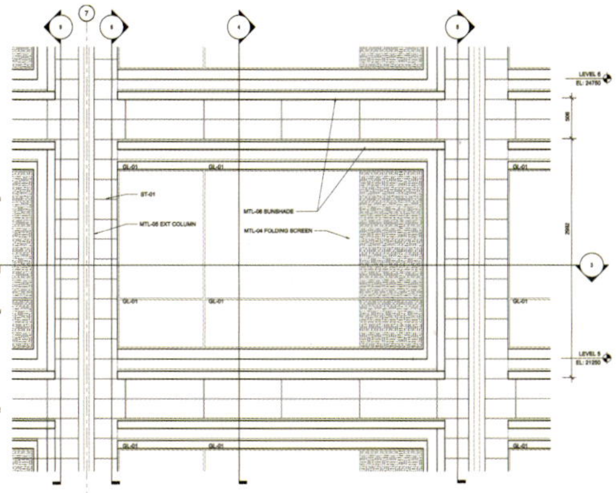

ENLARGED ELEVATION 1

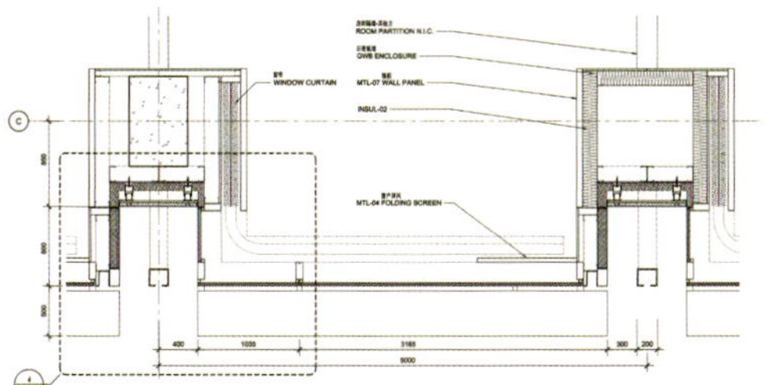

ENLARGED PLAN 3

金鱼胡同
JINYU Hutong

Hotel Atlantic

Dubai, United Arab Emirates

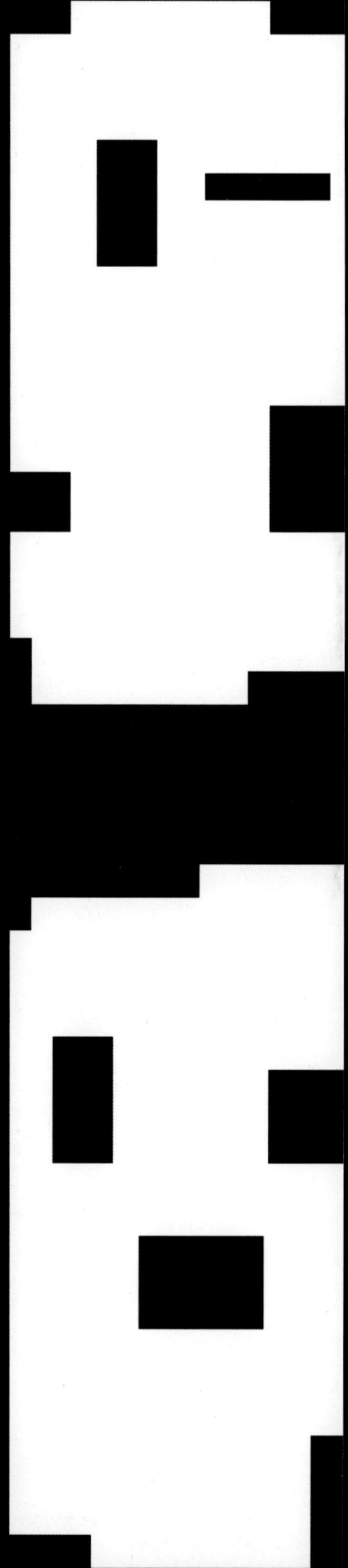

Hotel Atlantic

Dubai, United Arab Emirates

Hotel Atlantic is designed for a site in Dubai as a contemporary interpretation of a world-class resort. The complex provides a unique vision for a technologically advanced destination that dazzles visitors while offering the best in comfort, style, and luxury.

SERVICES
Architecture
Master Planning

CLIENT
Kerzner International
Management

FUNCTION
Hotel

FACTS
152 m height

AWARDS
WAN Awards, Future Projects Commercial Award, Winner, 2017

The Chicago Athenaeum, International Architecture Award, Hotel Atlantic, 2015

The hotel's design is based on a linear composition of two buildings sited parallel to the beach, with a 35-story residential tower to the east and a 35-story hotel tower to the west, each offering unique views from all rooms.

The main feature of the tower design is a canopy veil that frames the buildings, extending off the towers by 10 meters on each side. The canopy unites the composition of the two towers and provides shading to the public spaces below. The veil also acts as a lighting awning for the buildings, creating another dimension that adds to the depth of space to the complex. The north and south canopy facades have light options to punctuate the glass at regular intervals, highlighting the canopy's structural elements. The color of the buildings can also be changed with the light system.

The canopy is designed to be constructed using an assembly of steel columns and beams that are rigidly connected to create a frame structure that is "tuned" to an optimal stiffness and is sympathetic to the behavior of the tower to avoid incompatibilities under wind and seismic events, as well as longterm shortening of the tower. The basic stability of the frame out-of-plane is provided by a network of steel stubs or props that attach back to the reinforced-concrete tower. These attachment points are anticipated at the tower slab edges that align with the exterior canopy frame and at column lines on the roof level that align with the canopy grid overhead.

Another priority of the canopy design is to reduce solar heat gain while maintaining natural lighting levels and wind movement that contribute to creating a comfortable indoor and outdoor environment. The interior spaces are inherently sustainable through simple, cost-effective design moves and system controls that include abundant use of responsibly sourced natural materials and occupancy linked environmental controls such as interior shades and lighting.

The landscape design playfully integrates the square geometry of the building into subtle patterns of different sized squares and rectangles, which form the landscape of pools, seating, sun-bathing, and green areas. Small level changes are utilized to enhance the spaces around the pools. Cabanas are located to maximize views without blocking views to and from the swimming pools.

Sanya Resort

Hainan Island, China

Sanya Haitang Bay Resort

Hainan Island, China

Inspired by the famous rock formation, Fiver-Finger Mountain, at the heart of Hainan, the new resort towers form an iconic family of varied and intriguing structures, transforming Sanya Haitang Bay Resort into a hospitality retreat unlike any other in the world.

SERVICES
Architecture
Master Planning

CLIENT
Ju Yuan Properties
Development Ltd

FUNCTION
Hotel

FACTS
117,000 sm site

The tower's design is unified as a single gesture, creating a dynamic and memorable shape against the sky. Each tower his optimized to accommodate its individual program and project parameters, creating an effortless and luxurious experience for visitors and guests

The luxurious resort features two separate hotels and a condo hotel tower. The southern part of the site has a seven-star hotel, complete with full amenities and a complex of ultra-luxury villas, while a five-star hotel tower, also with resort amenities, is located at the northern most part of the site.

The overall master plan is organized around a slender body of water, strategically positioned to provide sea views from a maximum number of buildings and units, as well as invite meandering walking paths to the beach, and delightful site areas for each respective building. The towers feature textured facades to offer guests unique and distinct experiences within each unit, and each building features indoor/outdoor blended spaces for guests.

The Hotel A portion of the site is arranged within an irregular and undulating cellular framework. This allows for an organic order without a hard-lined grid. Villas are arranged at the south of the site and are free from the towers shadows. Resort amenities are linked along a winding network of walking paths adjacent to the seawater lagoon.

The area designated for Hotel B is arranged on overlapping line grids, creating a denser experience toward the beachfront. An angular patchwork results from this overlap, creating a rich texture for building organization, woven gardens, paths, and pools. The buildings are predominantly oriented southeast for optimum views and solar access. The architecture and patterns on the Hotel B site provide variety and contrast to the more curvilinear gesture of the Hotel A property.

At 163 meters tall, the striking form of the Hotel A Tower is the dominant image on the skyline welcoming visitors approaching from the airport and downtown Sanya. The tower features a rich and highly detailed layout, designed to provide an unmatched experience and level of service to guests.

Visitors are greeted with a breathtaking view of the sea through an opening at the entrance to the grand hotel lobby. The tower incorporates deep crevices and facets in its facade, as well as cantilevered end units. These unique elements provide a variety of spaces at the outboard ends of the hotel's extra wide units, designed to allow each guest uninterrupted and unmatched views of Haitang Bay.

The seaside facade of each unit is comprised of wall-to-wall and floor-to-ceiling glass. Protection from the sun and any strong winds is provided by 1.5-meter-deep extensions comprised of stone and glass.

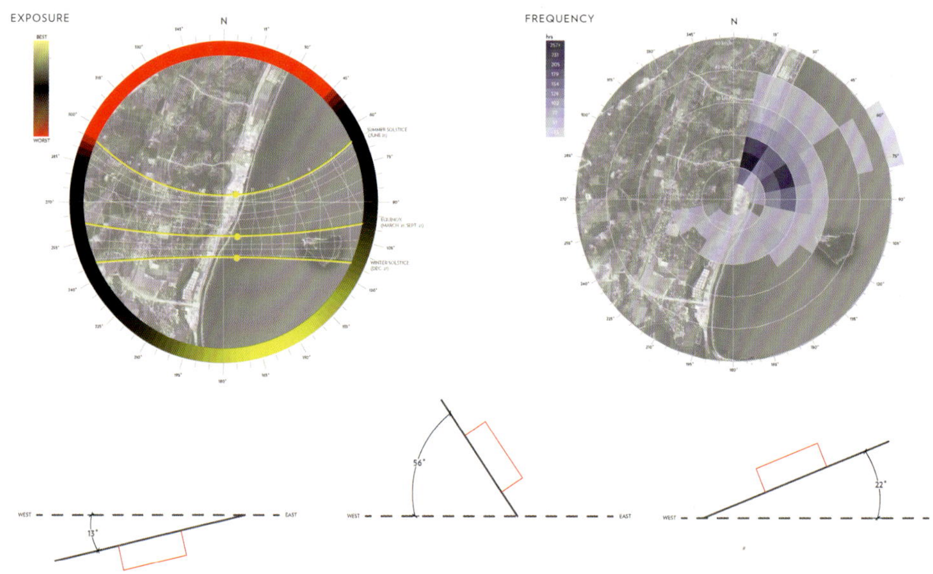

CLIMATE ANALYSIS

SITE PLAN

MASTER PLAN

1. Security Checkpoint
2. Restaurant + Bar
3. Tower A
4. Tower B
5. Tower C
6. Lobby
7. Restaurant
8. Conference
9. Pool
10. Beachfront Pavilion
11. Tennis Court
12. Fitness Center
13. Wedding Chapel
14. Banquet Hall
15. Executive Lounge
16. Spa
17. Villa Lobby + Conference
18. Villa Recreation
19. Villa Fitness
20. Villa Restaurant
21. Villa Bar

Lakeside Residential Towers

Chicago, Illinois

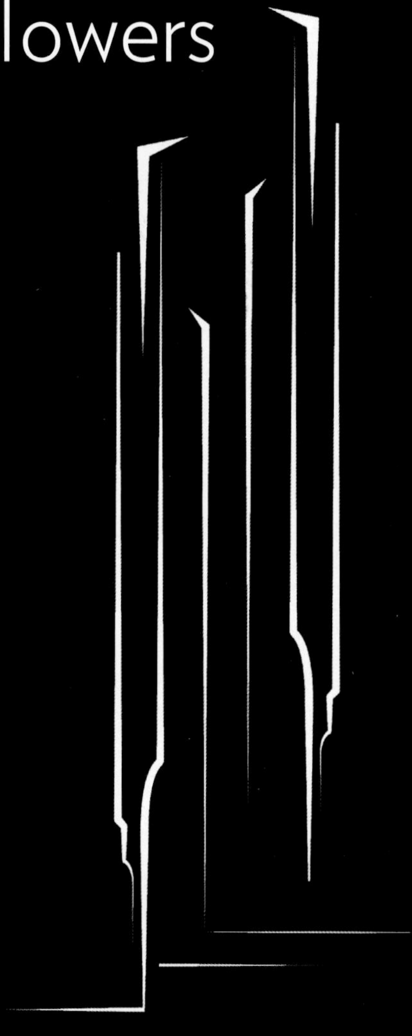

Lakeside Residential Towers

Chicago, Illinois

The conceptual design for Lakeside Residential Towers is a luxury two-tower residential complex that responds to the site's constraints as opportunities rather than obstacles.

SERVICES
Architecture

CLIENT
Related Midwest

FUNCTION
Residential

AWARDS
Architizer A+ Awards, Residential-Unbuilt - Multi-Unit Housing, Finalist, 2018

The Chicago Athenaeum, American Architecture Awards, (As Confidential Residential Development,) 2017

Units are carved out of slopping areas of glass, giving each unit a unique character that has exceptional views toward the lake, river, or surrounding city, while minimizing views into adjacent buildings.

The shaping of the tower massing at the lower and higher levels also enhances wind performance, providing significant structural savings. Carving back the tower's lower levels increases the amount of sunlight, expands views and significantly reduces the wind impact on the outdoor amenity areas.

Amenities are designed to be resort like with a world-class fitness facility, a series of lounges, sports rooms, private dining rooms, a screening room, a technology room, exterior BBQ grilles and Cabanas, private sun decks, pools, and gardens. The amenities are situated in close proximity to views of the river and the city beyond.

Sustainable design strategies include rainfall harvesting and condensate recovery with graywater collection, treatment, and storage. The reclaimed water is used in landscape irrigation and in common areas for toilet flushing. On site water is also be used to facilitate the rejection of heat from the central chilled water plant.

PODIUM ORGANIZATION

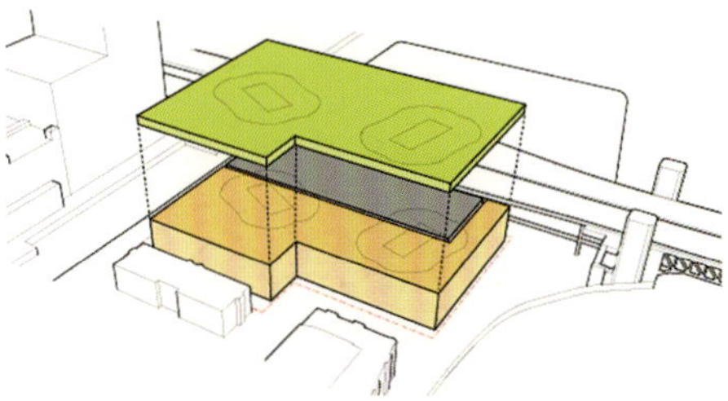

SERVICE + AMENITY USES SCREEN THE MAIN THRUWAY

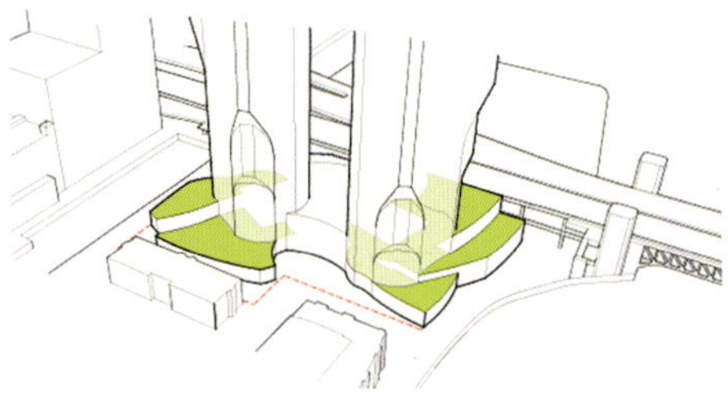

CONNECT INDOOR + OUTDOOR AMENITY FEATURES

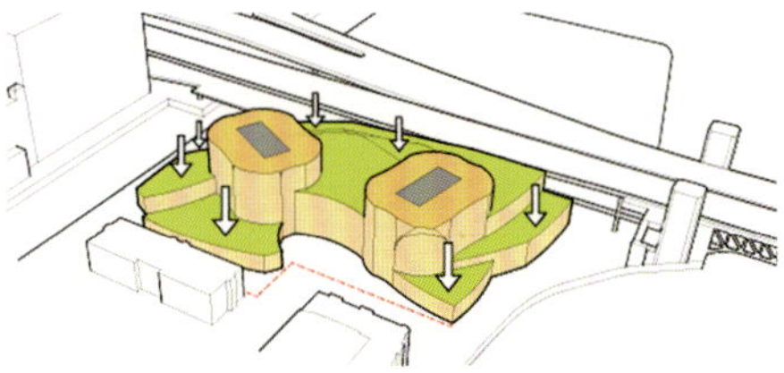

TERRACE AMENITY TO DEMARCATE APARTMENT + CONDO AREAS AND DIRECT VIEWS TO RIVER

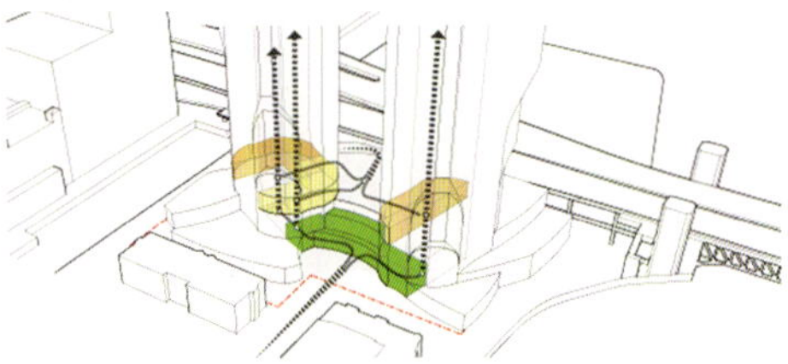

CONNECT UPPER + LOWER ARRIVAL THROUGH WINTER GARDEN

The importance of creating an exceptional arrival experience for residents is a major design factor for all residential tall towers. The design approach delivers a landmark stature arrival with lobbies that are elevated across the street to deliver glorious views of the water. The design appeals to a wide demographic that includes urban professionals, empty nesters, and families, providing progressive urban living at a variety of scales that is balanced with connections to nature and a focus on well-being.

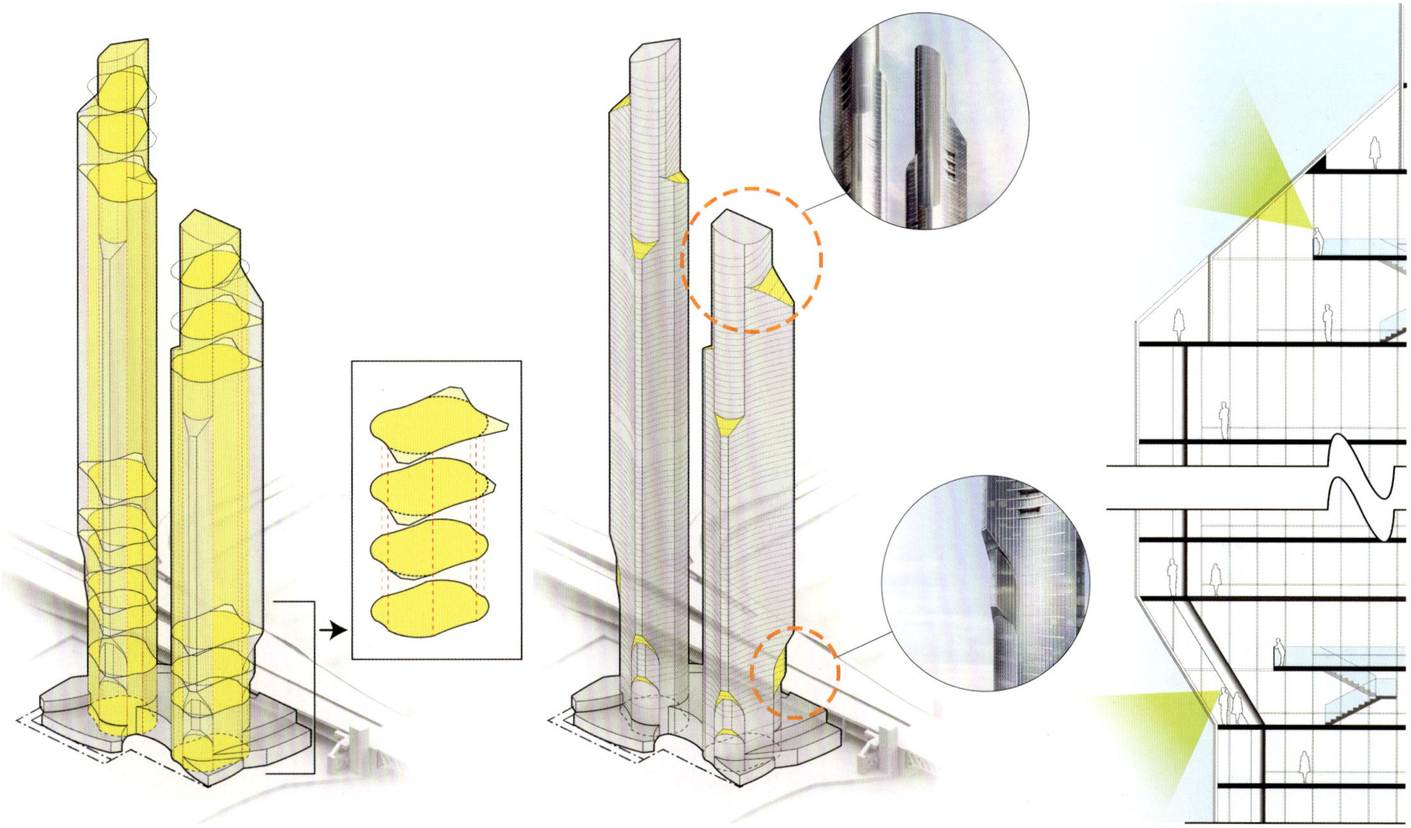

The building form creates unique high-value spaces with visual connections to the ground and sky distributed vertically throughout the towers.

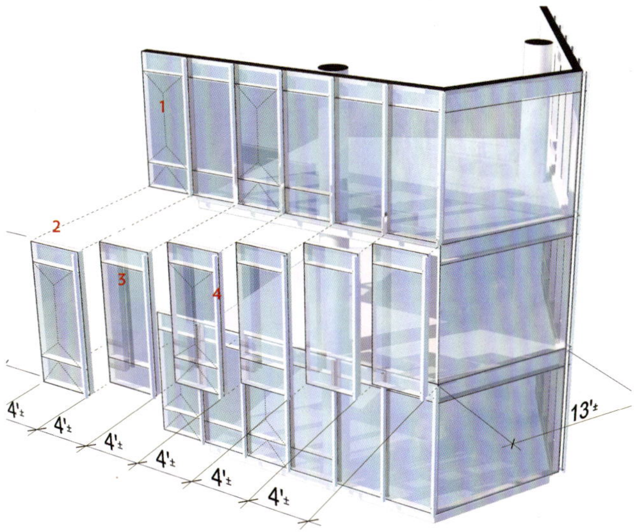

UNITIZED CURTAIN WALL SYSTEM

1. Integrated operable window upper and/or lower glazing panel
2. Fully unitized aluminum curtain wall frame
3. Painted metal panel shadow box
4. Extruded aluminum fin clad with 2mm 316 stainless polished finish

Una Residences

Miami, Flordia

Una Residences

Miami, Florida

Una Residences is a new 47-story condominium tower, designed for OKO Group, in Miami's South Brickell neighborhood. Once completed, Una will have spectacular views of Florida's coastline including Biscayne Bay, Fisher Island, and the Biscayne Islands.

SERVICES
Architecture
Interior Design

CLIENT
OKO Group

FUNCTION
Residential

FACTS
47 stories

AWARDS
The Chicago Athenaeum, American Architecture Award, 2021

The tower is an iconic new vision that seeks to reinvent South Brickell, the 1970s birthplace of modern high-rise living in Miami. Brickell Avenue, named for early Miami founders William and Mary Brickell, is known by insiders as Miami's "Park Avenue" with its scenic canopy of ancient oaks, shaded sidewalks, ease of access to the city's financial district, award-winning restaurants, luxury retailers, and cultural and sporting venues. AS+GG's design for Una sets the modern standard of living in Brickell. Residences reflect the elegant, yet playful, lifestyle of Miami.

The formal aspects of the building are sculptural in nature. It's fluid, organic form speaks to the water, and to Miami's climate, with large flowing terraces that wrap around the building. A sweeping cantilever at the south end of the tower overlooks the amenity spaces on the podium. By placing the amenities on the podium levels, the grounds around the tower are liberated, opening the space for public access to the waterfront. The public access points allow the design a more inviting opening sequence so that the landscaping of the building flows into the landscaping of the park.

AS+GG is also leading the interior design for the tower, ensuring a seamless exterior and interior aesthetic. Inspired by the Riva yacht, a highly crafted wooden sport boat made in Italy, the interior design uses natural materials like leather, wood, and stone, featured in warm colors that contrast with the cool tones of chrome and stainless steel. The palette generates a timeless, classic mood.

Una has 138 elegantly crafted residences that range from two to five bedrooms and are between 1,100 to 4,786 square feet. Each unit features ocean views, a private elevator entry, 10'8" ceiling heights, a chef's kitchens with Gaggenau appliances, master suites with double closets and bathrooms, utility rooms with full-sized washers and dryers, and 10-foot deep expansive terraces that feature effortless "lift-and-glide" floor-to-ceiling doors with glass balcony railings for a seamless indoor-outdoor lifestyle.

Among the many signature elements that enhance the experience are a private marina for bayside excursions, three pools, a state-of-the-art fitness center with yoga and personal training areas. Other luxuries include a dedicated beauty suite for private services, a private resident's dining/party room, a cinema, a kids' splash-pad area and playroom, an owners' lounge and an outdoor lounge, and a 24-hour concierge.

Construction began in early 2020, with an estimated completion date of 2023.

Burj Vista

Dubai, United Arab Emirates

Burj Vista

Dubai, United Arab Emirates

Burj Vista is a sophisticated two-tower residential presence on Dubai's Boulevard, providing tenants with unobstructed, front-row views of Burj Khalifa, the current world's tallest building.

SERVICES
Architecture

CLIENT
Emaar Properties

FUNCTION
Residential

FACTS
236 m height
110,700 sm
building area

AWARDS
AIA Chicago,
Divine Detail Award,
Citation of Merit, Burj
Vista Self-Shading
Balconies, 2021

At 22 and 69 stories, the towers are part of an urban amphitheater plaza that includes high-end retail. The need to maximize views of the Burj Khaifa in each unit while minimizing overall energy consumption and maximizing the comfort of residents were the key design challenges.

Each unit, regardless of size, features a combination of exterior terrace and observation room in a staggered configuration that maximizes views while keeping view obstructions to a minimum. This strategy also helps reduce heat gain in the warm Dubai climate with the terraces and the sloped glass exterior walls maximizing shading, reducing heat gain, and reducing the collection of wind-born sand.

Other sustainable strategies include high-performance coatings on exterior glass; utilizing a significant amount of GFRC cladding systems to minimize the amount of glass; orienting the towers to minimize solar exposure; and connecting landscaped event areas with shaded paths. These architectural decisions make Burj Vista's design specific to its program, location, and massing configuration, giving it a distinctive identity with high-performance characteristics.

Other features of the project include high-end finishes in all interiors; a semi-protected lounge area with decorative water features open to a landscaped garden; an indoor pool; and ready access to Burj Khalifa, Dubai Mall, Burj Lake Promenade, World Trade Center, and Sheikh Zayed Road.

EMAAR

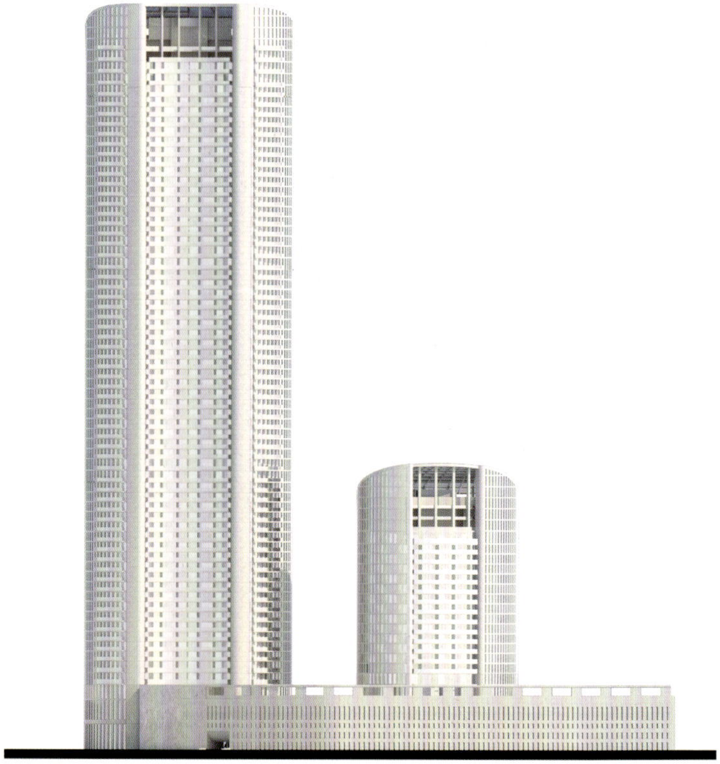

WEST ELEVATION

EAST ELEVATION

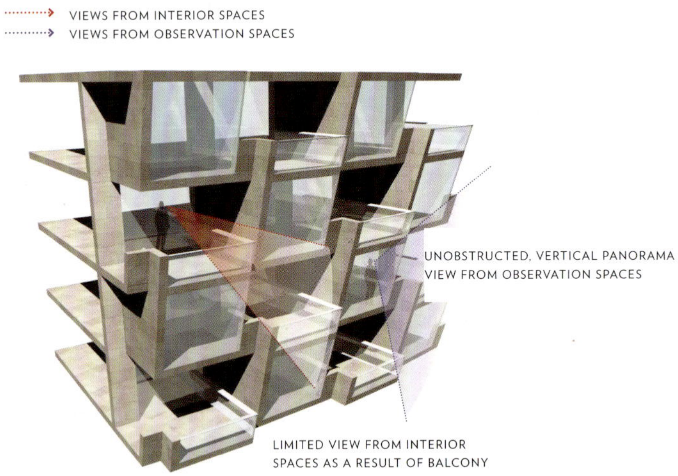
VIEWS FROM INTERIOR SPACES
VIEWS FROM OBSERVATION SPACES
UNOBSTRUCTED, VERTICAL PANORAMA
VIEW FROM OBSERVATION SPACES
LIMITED VIEW FROM INTERIOR
SPACES AS A RESULT OF BALCONY

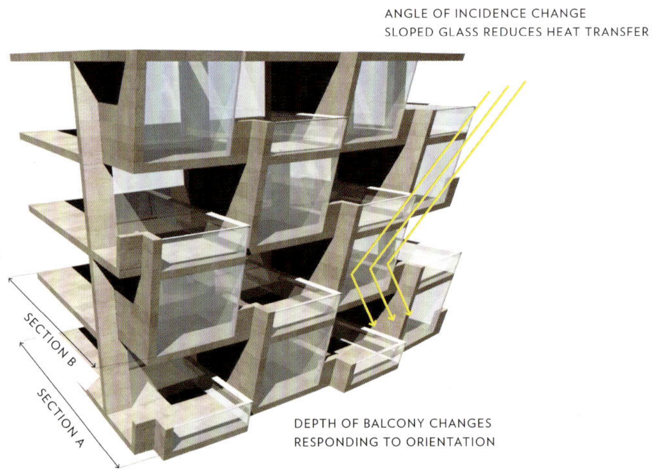
ANGLE OF INCIDENCE CHANGE
SLOPED GLASS REDUCES HEAT TRANSFER
SECTION B
SECTION A
DEPTH OF BALCONY CHANGES
RESPONDING TO ORIENTATION

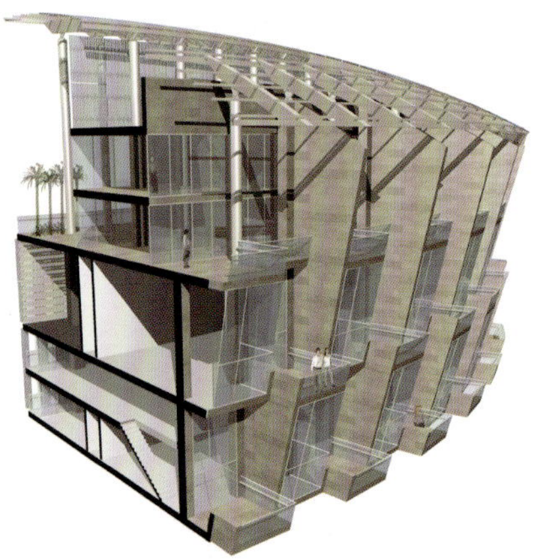

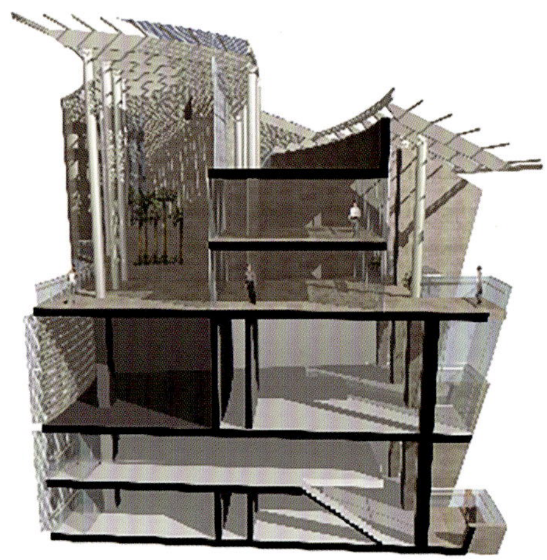

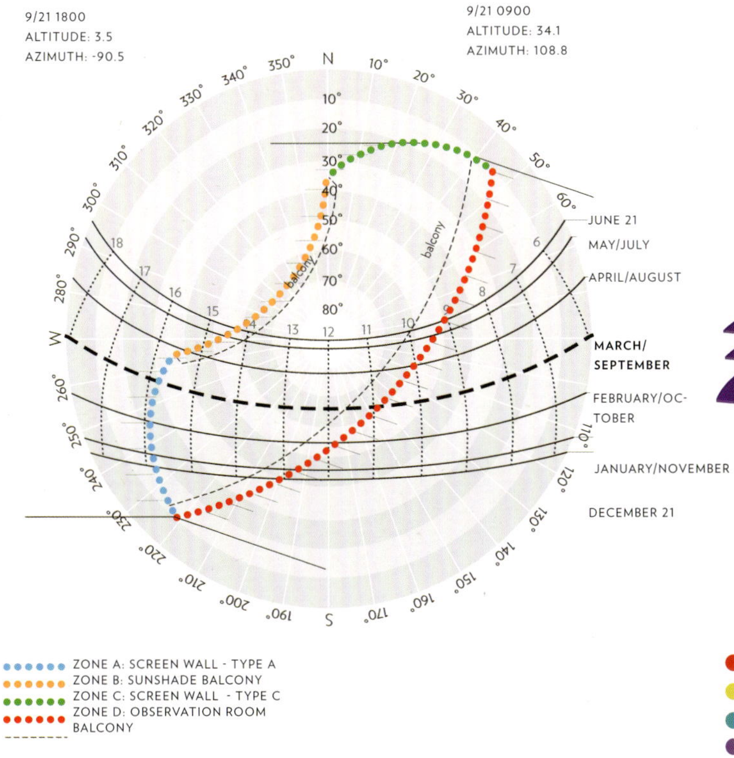
9/21 1800
ALTITUDE: 3.5
AZIMUTH: -90.5
9/21 0900
ALTITUDE: 34.1
AZIMUTH: 108.8
N
W
S
balcony
balcony
JUNE 21
MAY/JULY
APRIL/AUGUST
MARCH/
SEPTEMBER
FEBRUARY/OC-
TOBER
JANUARY/NOVEMBER
DECEMBER 21
ZONE A: SCREEN WALL - TYPE A
ZONE B: SUNSHADE BALCONY
ZONE C: SCREEN WALL - TYPE C
ZONE D: OBSERVATION ROOM
BALCONY

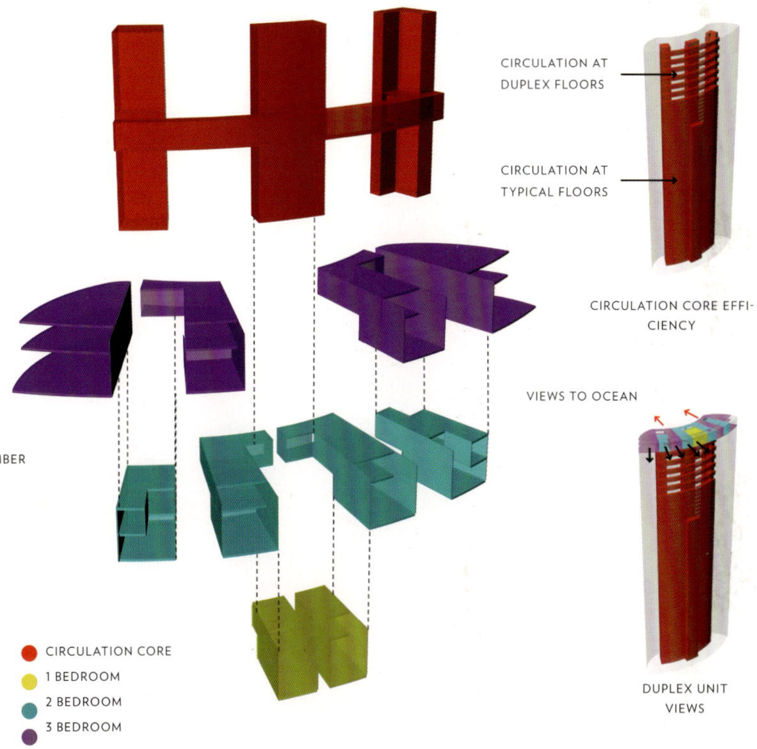
CIRCULATION AT
DUPLEX FLOORS
CIRCULATION AT
TYPICAL FLOORS
CIRCULATION CORE EFFI-
CIENCY
VIEWS TO OCEAN
DUPLEX UNIT
VIEWS
CIRCULATION CORE
1 BEDROOM
2 BEDROOM
3 BEDROOM

The Mansion

Dubai, United Arab Emirates

The Mansion

Dubai, United Arab Emirates

The Mansion is a 60-story, 340-unit luxury residential tower in Dubai that has spectacular, unobstructed views of the Burj Khalifa, the world's tallest building, and its related lake fountain.

SERVICES
Architecture

CLIENT
Emaar Properties

FUNCTION
Residential

FACTS
227 m height
82,807 sm
building area

Embracing a sense of duality, the Mansion is both a gateway between commercial and residential zones in the Burj Khalifa development and an aesthetically striking work of architecture designed to respond to its environmental context with a delicate balance of solidity and transparency.

Located on the inlet of the lake, the Mansion features a unique scalloped northwest facade with a subtle, alternating pattern in the placement of its double-glazed floor-to-ceiling windows and adjacent balconies. This both maximizes views and creates a dynamic woven texture, like a fabric made of glass. Corner units have 270-degree views with northeast and southwest balconies; the top six levels contain units with rooftop terraces.

The 227-meter-tall tower's continuously curving northeast facade, which faces the Burj Khalifa and the lake, provides sun shading to respond to various solar exposures. The southwest facade, which faces the Boulevard, has the greatest exposure to the sun and is protected with openings in the stone and a pre-cast concrete exterior wall that is located and sized to maximize solar shading. The building is designed to earn a minimum rating of LEED Silver.

Indoor amenities include a fully equipped health club, a multipurpose room, and a business center. A bridge near the tower's base connects to a retail and restaurant complex that opens onto a terraced dining area that opens onto the lake park promenade.

Verre
Crate & Barrel

Vancouver Residences

Vancouver, British Columbia

Vancouver Residences

Vancouver, British Columbia

Vancouver Residences is designed as a highly efficient, dense residential development in the heart of the city. The project supports a series of sustainable objectives in line with Vancouver's Ecodensity Charter, which aims to greatly improve the city's "eco-footprint," and encourages residents to live more sustainably.

SERVICES
Architecture

CLIENT
Emaar Properties Canada

FUNCTION
Residential

FACTS
8,400 sm building area

AWARDS
The Chicago Athenaeum, International Architecture Award, 2010

The low-rise residential development features units with high-end, sustainable finishes. Each unit has an outdoor terrace with views to the community gardens and green landscape surrounding the building. A central garden space provides an outdoor lobby entrance and includes water features and lushly landscaped spaces. Other community amenities include a pool, a fitness center, a multi-purpose activity room, and working rooftop gardens for residents.

The natural Vancouver environment is incorporated throughout the project with green walls and permeable paving surrounding the complex. Deciduous trees maximize natural shading and other horizontal shading elements are incorporated into the south facades. The wall system incorporates vertical shading and minimizes direct heat gain on the east and west elevations.

To achieve a reduced eco-footprint a series of goals are defined for the project:

- Reduce energy use by taking full advantage of natural light.
- Reduce travel impact through density, access to public transport, and onsite car-sharing.
- Reduce food choice impact by offering working gardens for onsite food production, composting, and recycling.
- Reduce domestic water use through the integration of water reducing fixtures, systems for rainwater collection, and onsite water treatment.
- Reduce energy consumption through the integration of geothermal systems, thermal massing, solar hot water, passive shading, radiant heat and cooling systems, and energy-efficient appliances and lighting
- Investigate the use of biomass fuel

MEASURING SUSTAINABILITY: ECO-FOOTPRINT = 1.9 GLOBAL HA

TYPICAL ECO-FOOTPRINT:

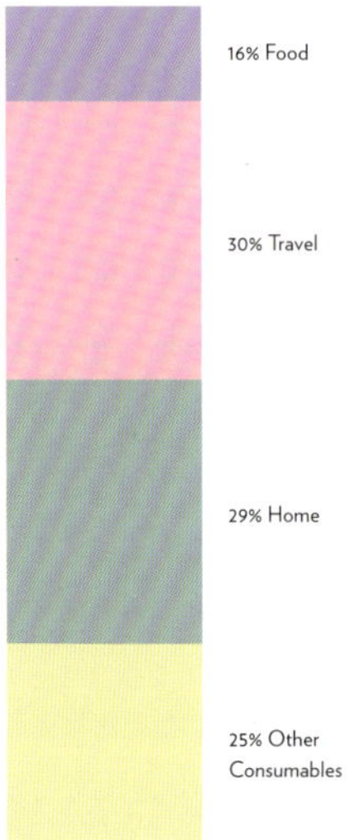

ELEMENTS THAT MAKE UP AN ECO-FOOTPRINT:

Transportation and Travel

- Encourage use of public transportation
- Provide on-site car share
- Reduction of air travel
- Reduction in private automobile use

Water

- Water reducing fixtures
- Rainwater collection
- No potable use for irrigation
- On-site water treatment
- Reduce personal domestic water consumption

House and Garden

- On-site food production
- On-site composting
- Drought-tolerant landscaping

Community Action

- Education program
- Community volunteer program

Energy Consumption

- Sustainable technologies
- Energy efficient appliances and lighting
- Adjust temperature/humidity comfort zone
- Purchase green power
- Live in a smaller, denser footprint

Shopping

- On-site food production
- Use your own re-usable shopping bags
- Reduce consumer purchasing
- Reduce number of household pets

Waste

- Recycling
- Composting

Food

- On-site food production
- Purchase less processed foods
- Purchase foods with less packaging
- Eat locally grown foods
- Eat less meat and dairy

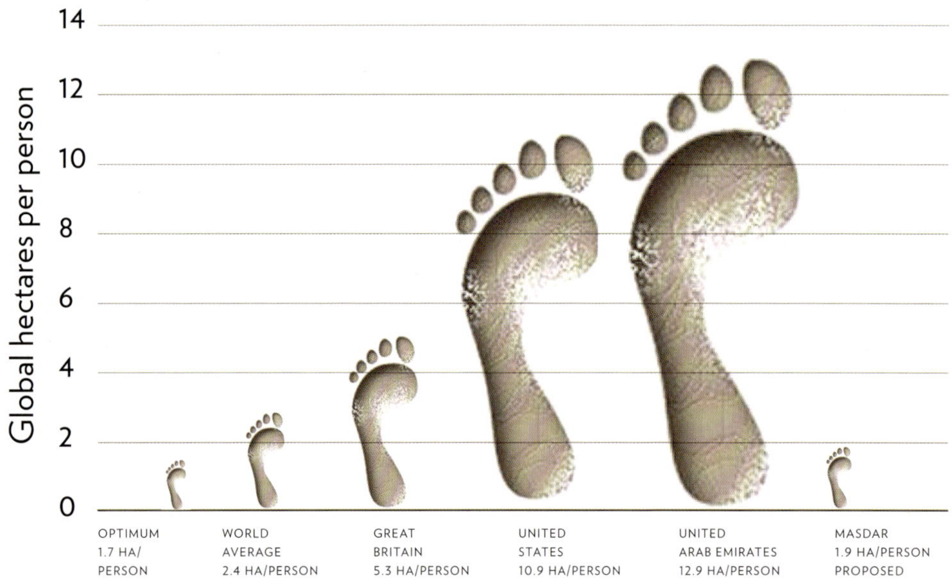

The ecological footprint concept is based on the idea that for every item of material or energy consumption, a certain amount of land in one or more ecosystem categories is required to provide the consumption related resource flows and waste sinks. Based on the goals and strategies proposed for the project, thoughtful design can reduce the inhabitants eco-footprint.

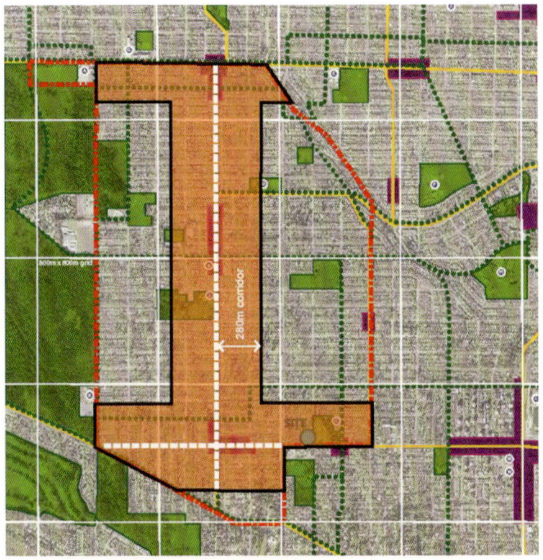

16 UPA DENSITY: SCENARIO 1

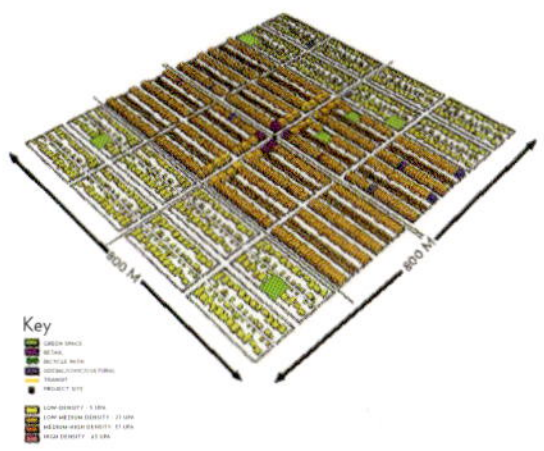

THIS DENSITY ALONG THE TRANSPORTATION CORRIDOR WILL SUPPORT:

- MINIMAL BUS SERVICE
- SMALL CORNER STORE
- SOME SOCIAL/CIVIC AMENITIES

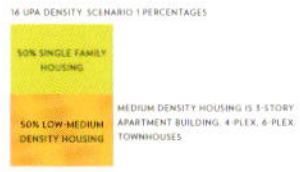

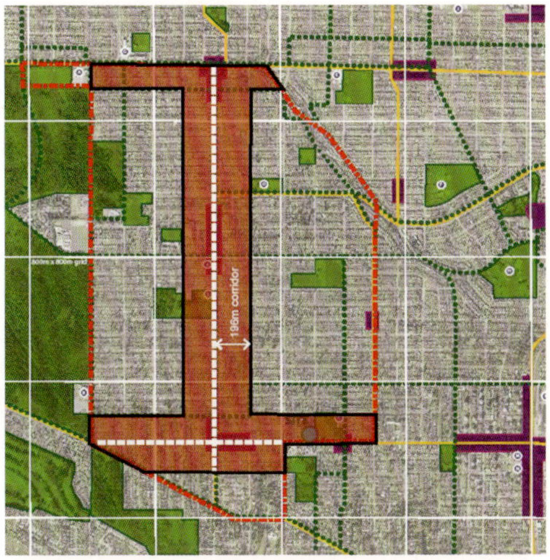

16 UPA DENSITY: SCENARIO 2

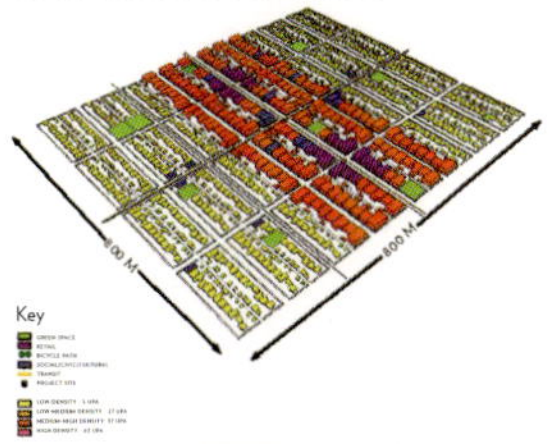

THIS DENSITY ALONG THE TRANSPORTATION CORRIDOR WILL SUPPORT:

- STREET LEVEL RETAIL
- CORNER STORES
- BUSINESS DISTRICT
- SURFACE OR TUCK UNDER PARKING
- TRANSIT STATION AND HIGH FREQUENCY TRANSIT SERVICE
- SUPERMARKET

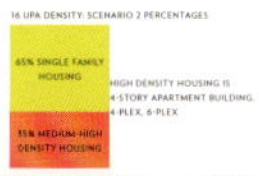

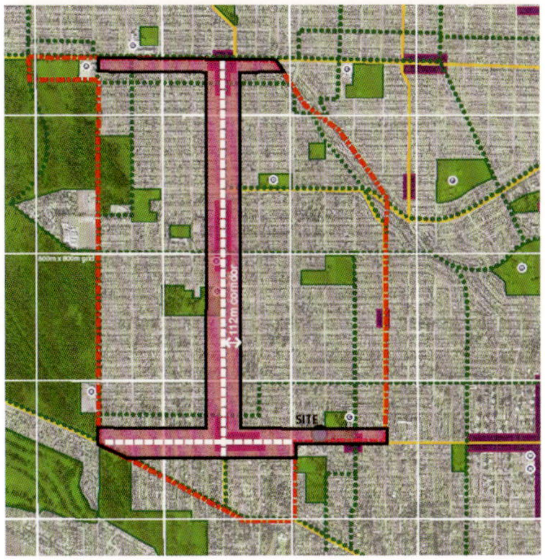

16 UPA DENSITY: SCENARIO 3

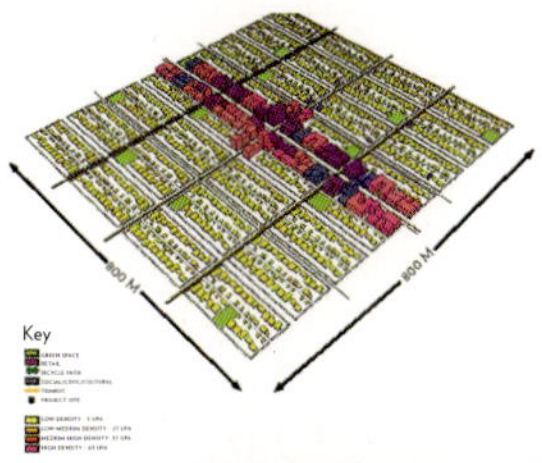

THIS DENSITY ALONG THE TRANSPORTATION CORRIDOR WILL SUPPORT:

- NEW RETAIL + BUSINESS DISTRICT
- SUPERMARKET
- CORNER STORES
- TRANSIT STATION
- HIGH FREQUENCY TRANSIT SERVICE
- NEW TAX REVENUES
- NEW JOBS
- PARKS, SCHOOLS, LIBRARIES
- HEALTHCARE FACILITIES
- RECREATIONAL AND CULTURAL FACILITIES
- INFRASTRUCTURE IMPROVEMENTS
- HABITAT RESTORATION

Guang Qu Lu No. 15 Project

Beijing, China

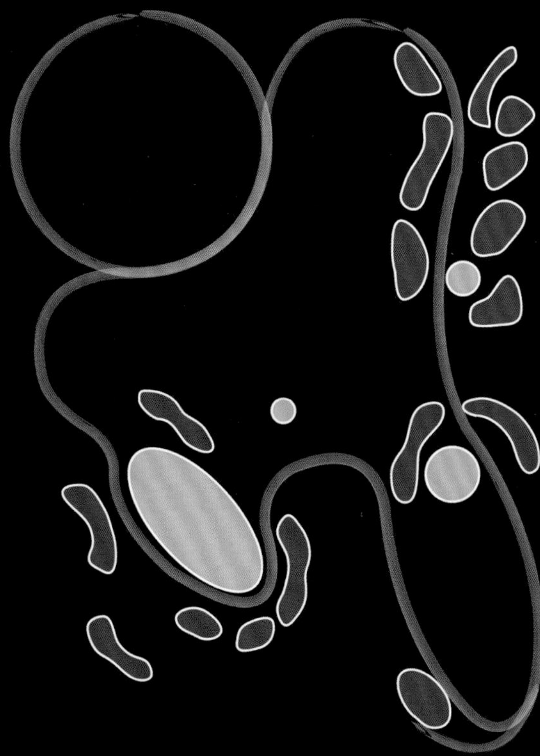

Guang Qu Lu No. 15 Project

Beijing, China

With its curvilinear forms, its collection of buildings of staggered heights at up to 100 meters, and its innovative mixed-use program that includes high-end and low-income housing as well as retail, schools, and a sports park/wellness center, the design for this residential development stands out in its urban context.

SERVICES
Architecture
Interior Design
Master Planning

CLIENT
Franshion Properties

FUNCTION
Mixed-use

FACTS
280,000 sm
building area
160,000 sm area

The development is designed to draw attention throughout Beijing with its contemporary, highly gestural architecture, and organically integrated landscape scheme. The design also provides a full range of lifestyle opportunities for residents to live, play, work, shop and send their children to school, all within the same complex.

The overall plan for the site is built around sinuous gestures that relate to the curving lines of the architecture, linking the various plots together and creating a coherent identity for the development. The theme of integration with the landscape is continued in the buildings' use of green roofs and terraces, and in the plan's acknowledgment of the park to the northeast of the site, as well as a smaller green park to the southeast.

The innovation of the design is most striking on the northwest corner of the development, which features high-end residential units that range from 180-600 square meters. Adjacent is a school complex with a kindergarten and elementary school. On the southwest corner of the development is a sports pavilion that as the development's first-built structure and initially functions as the sales office. The pavilion features an amphitheater, a swimming pool, tennis courts, and basketball courts, as well as as a wellness center/spa, a yoga studio, and a place for meditation.

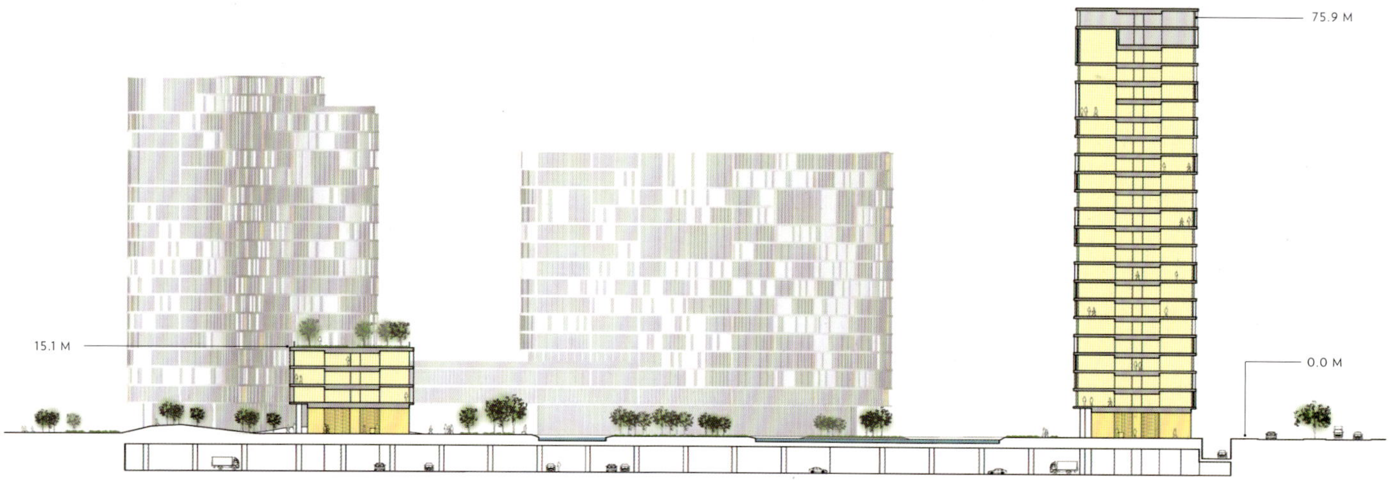
75.9 M
15.1 M
0.0 M

SITE PLAN

Yixing

Yixing, China

Yixing Dongju Development

Yixing, China

The Yixing Dongju Far East Development is a landmark destination for the district. Designed to the highest sustainable standards, this large-scale mixed-use project is also closely integrated with the natural environment.

SERVICES
Architecture
Urban Design

CLIENT
Far East Holding Group

FUNCTION
Mixed-use

FACTS
312,737 sm building area

Yixing Dongju Far East is a modern, floating garden development. The two towers and retail podium are surrounded by a series of interconnected waterways to provide additional site access and a soft, flowing landscape, while referencing the canals that flow throughout the city, the arched shape of a bridge, and the lake directly to the east. The development's curving geometries extend both skyward and outward toward the city, recalling the organic form of a lily flower, whose petals rest on a larger body of water.

Anchoring the development are two towers: a mixed-use office and hotel tower and a neighboring residential tower. The towers connect to the podium roof, which is covered in photovoltaic arrays that create a compelling texture on the roof plane. Similarly, the exterior wall of the office tower features a series of shading devices made out state-of-the-art flexible fabric, which controls natural light while recalling the shapes of lily petals. The tower also contains a conference center and meeting facilities, a ballroom, and a health center. At the apex, an observation space and a club/restaurant offer lake views.

The adjacent residential tower features a series of alternating balconies for each unit to enjoy an outdoor space and balcony view, creating another richly textured exterior facade. The shape, arrangement, and interplay of the balconies evoke the shape of lily petals, an influence that can be found throughout the development. The residential tower connects also to the retail podium.

The intersections of the three sections of retail podium allow for the creation of a central park space, which is active both at the ground plane and at each ascending floor. At night, the park can transform into an entertainment destination, making use of the levels of retail podium and further stepped ground planes at grade to create a dramatic theater space surrounding a myriad of performances in the garden.

Sustainable technologies are integrated throughout the development and contribute strongly to the organic geometric aesthetic. A strong integration with the natural landscape is complemented by other passive technologies including natural daylight, shading, and ventilation. From an active technological standpoint, integrated photovoltaic arrays, solar hot water systems, and high performance equipment and fixtures further contribute to the building's overall sustainability.

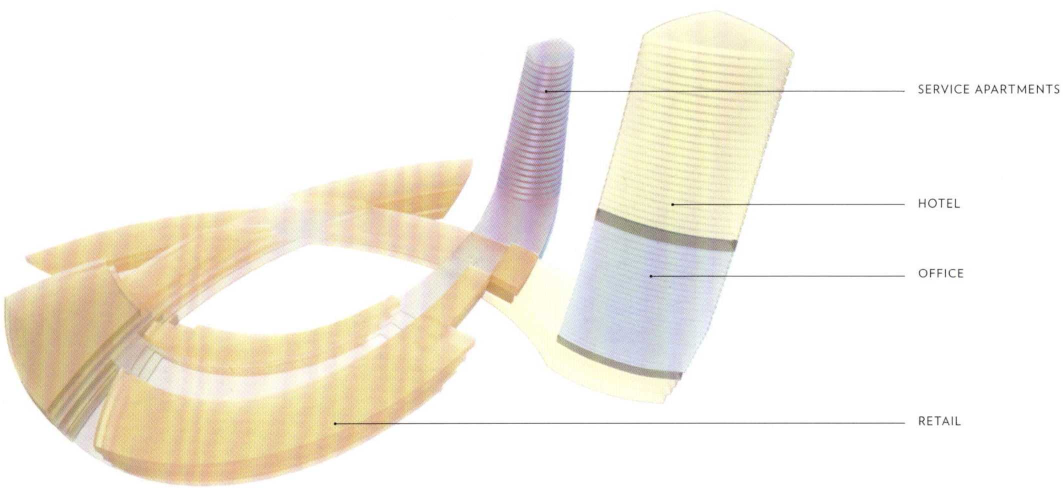

SERVICE APARTMENTS
HOTEL
OFFICE
RETAIL

BUILDING SOLAR STUDY

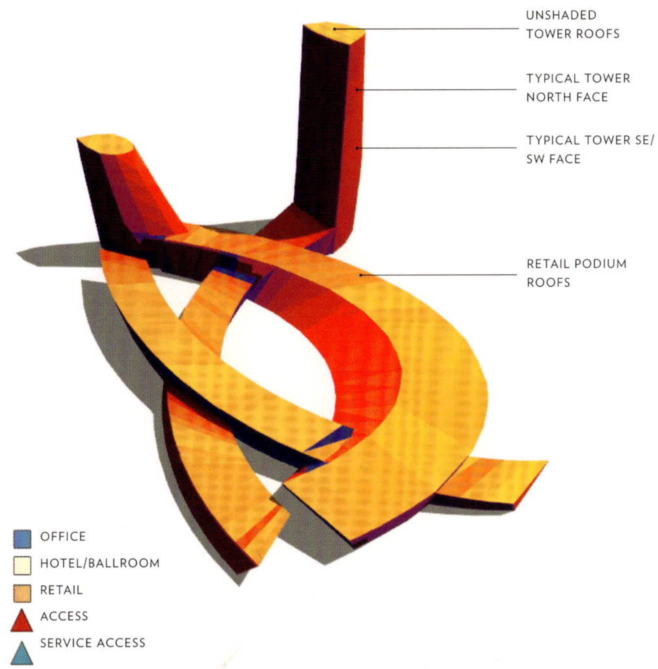

PRELIMINARY WIND STUDY

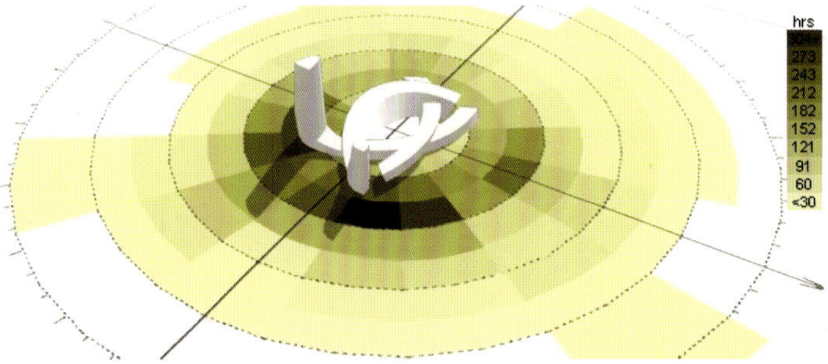

PREDOMINANT WIND DIRECTION
30° NORTH OF EAST @12 MPH

AVERAGE DAILY INCIDENT SOLAR RADIATION

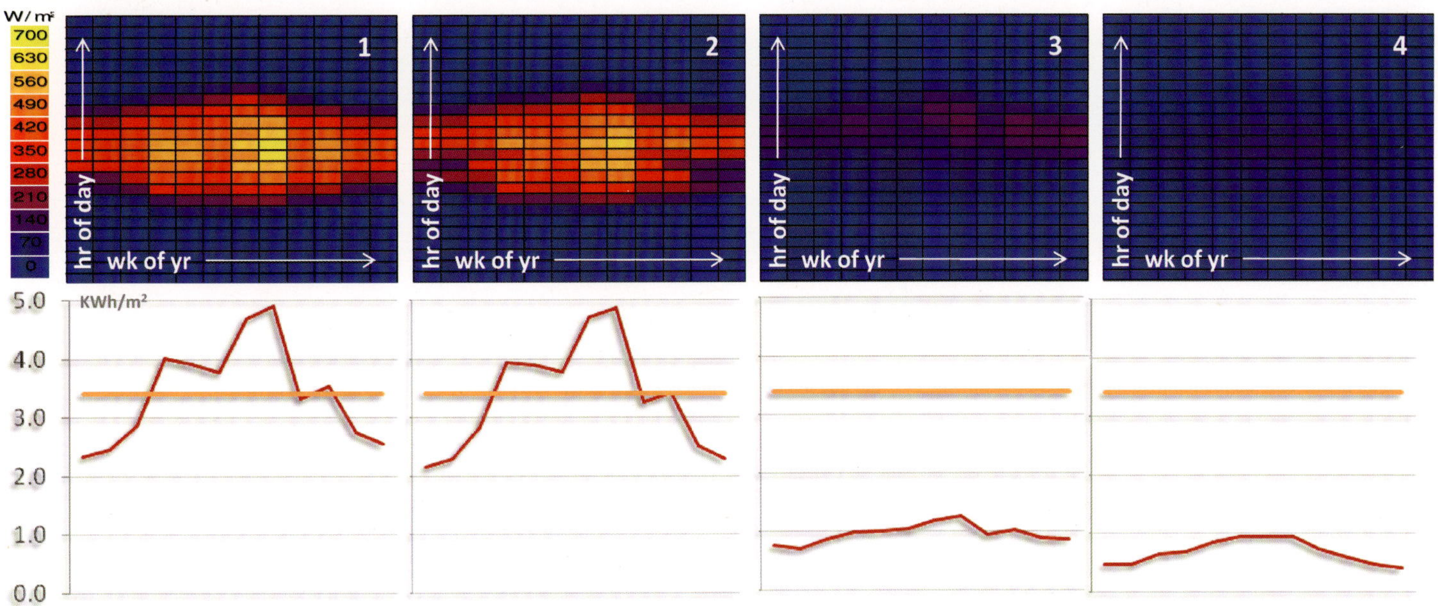

SURFACE ANNUAL AVERAGE
DAILY RADIATION
3.41 KWH/SM/DAY

SURFACE ANNUAL AVERAGE
DAILY RADIATION
3.32 KWH/SM/DAY

SURFACE ANNUAL AVERAGE
DAILY RADIATION
.96 KWH/SM/DAY

SURFACE ANNUAL AVERAGE
DAILY RADIATION
.67 KWH/SM/DAY

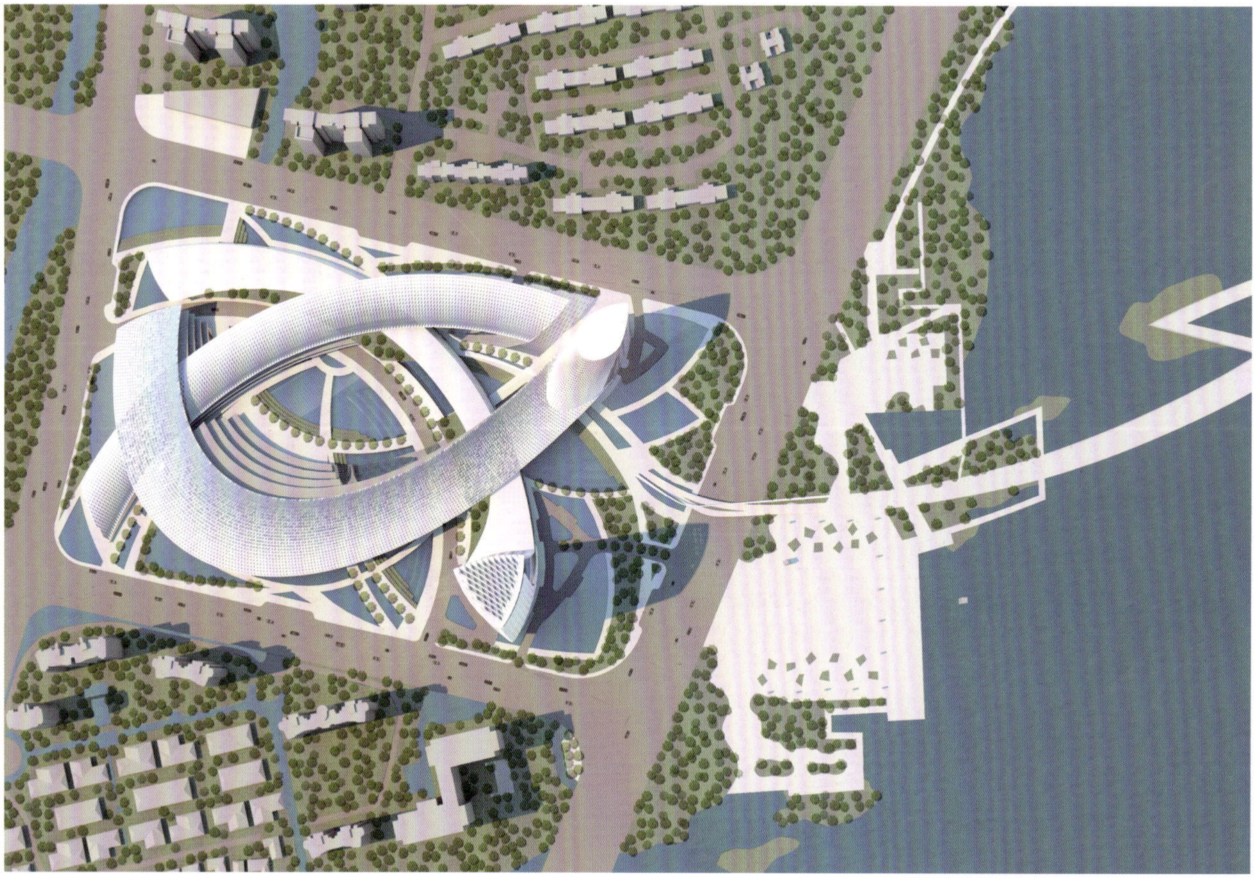

Imperial Tower

Mumbai, India

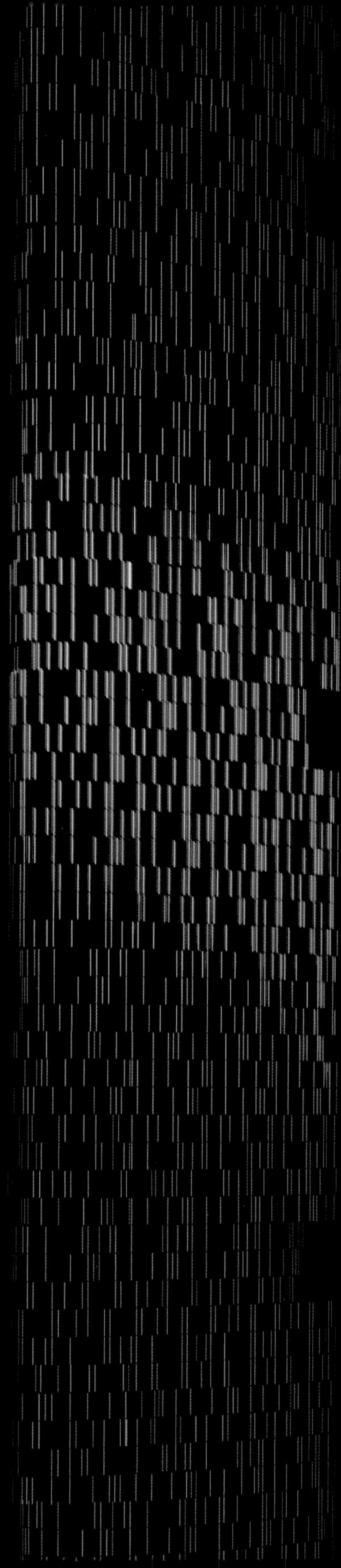

Imperial Tower

Mumbai, India

At 116 stories and 400 meters tall, Imperial Tower is designed to be the tallest building in Mumbai and a prototype for a city. Mumbai is densely developed but is a mostly low-rise metropolis whose urban future revolves around tall residential towers.

SERVICES
Interior Design

CLIENT
SD Corporation
Pvt. Ltd.

FUNCTION
Mixed-use

FACTS
400 m height
116 stories

The softly curvilinear form of this tall, elegantly slender tower is aerodynamically shaped to confuse the wind, minimizing the negative effects of wind action on the tower. Wind vortex shedding is also mitigated by the north- and south-facing sky gardens, which break up wind currents around the tower. The sky gardens also provide unprecedented access to light, views and connection with the natural world that are unprecedented in Mumbai.

Imperial Tower offers the most spacious and luxurious residences in Mumbai. The 76,272 square-meter tower includes 132 residential units that are between 195-1,115 sm, along with serviced apartments of between 72-252 sm. Each of the upper-story condominiums have wide views of the Arabian Sea.

Architecturally, the exterior wall provides a strong visual contrast with the heavy masonry cladding of most of the surrounding buildings. The exterior wall is highly sustainable, blocking heat gain and diffusing direct sunlight in the hot and humid climate of Mumbai.

Sustainability is also evident in the tower's treatment of water, one of the area's most precious resources. Water from mechanical systems is collected and treated as graywater; rainfall is also collected for re-use by the units. High-efficiency mechanical systems, a green-wall podium and the use of native plants in the landscaping and sky gardens also adds to the project's sustainable performance.

ADRIAN SMITH + GORDON GILL
ARCHITECTURE

Elphinstone Mills + Jupiter Mills

Mumbai, India

Elphinstone Mills + Jupiter Mills

Mumbai, India

Elphinstone Mills, a 60-story mixed-use complex, and Jupiter Mills, a 75-story luxury residential tower, are designed for locations in the heart of Mumbai, India.

SERVICES
Architecture

CLIENT
Indiabulls Real Estate Ltd.

FUNCTION
Mixed-use

FACTS
60 stories
75 stories

The Elphinstone Mills complex includes Class A office space and a pedestrian-friendly retail podium. The building is designed to a LEED Platinum standard and creates a new icon in the skyline.

Each floor of the office tower features outdoor terraces and multi-story garden atria, fully integrating the interior workspace with natural elements of the exterior environment. These garden spaces provide tenants with a shaded area for relaxation and socialization. While these outdoor spaces provide abundant natural daylight, the building is oriented to minimize solar gain decreasing the heating effect of direct sunlight and increasing comfort levels for building tenants.

Each atrium space is connected to a central atrium within the building's core. Air flows from the exterior environment into this central chimney space, accelerating as it travels down the atrium toward a series of wind turbines, which generate power for the building.

Residential tower Jupiter Mills maximizes views with 50 stories of residential condominiums from floors 25-75. The building is designed to a LEED Platinum standard.

Dior

ADRIAN SMITH + GORDON GILL
ARCHITECTURE

GROUND LEVEL

LEVEL 1

LEVEL 2

LEVEL 3

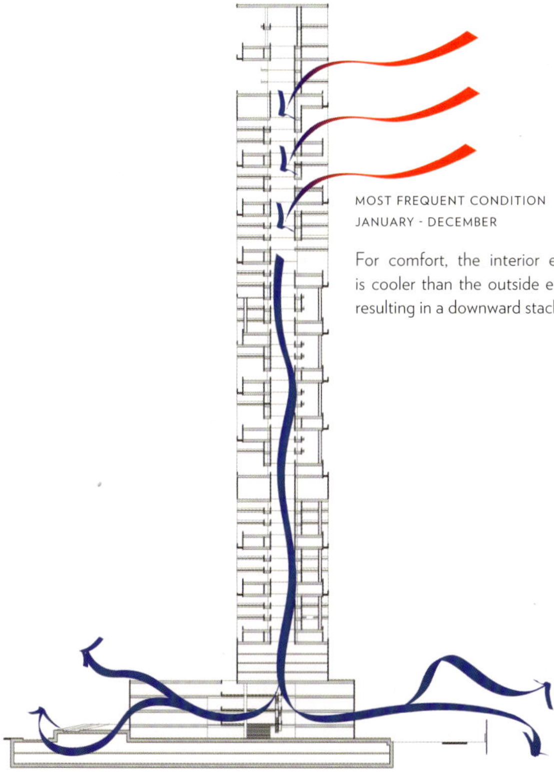

MOST FREQUENT CONDITION
JANUARY - DECEMBER

For comfort, the interior environment is cooler than the outside environment, resulting in a downward stack effect.

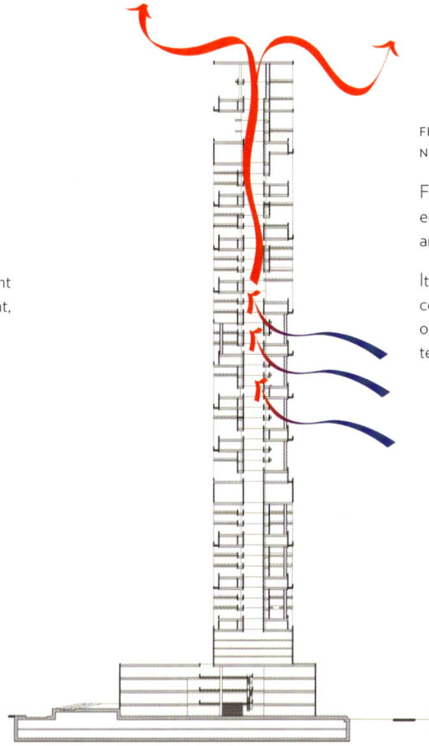

FRINGE CONDITION
NOVEMBER - MARCH

For comfort, the interior environment is warmer than the outside environment, resulting in an upward stack effect.

It is possible that a flip-flop from the downward condition to the upward condition can occur on cooler days or between day and night when temperatures drop to or below 20 C.

NATURAL VENTILATION

Air flow from the terraces and balconies facilitate natural ventilation through the building via the atrium.

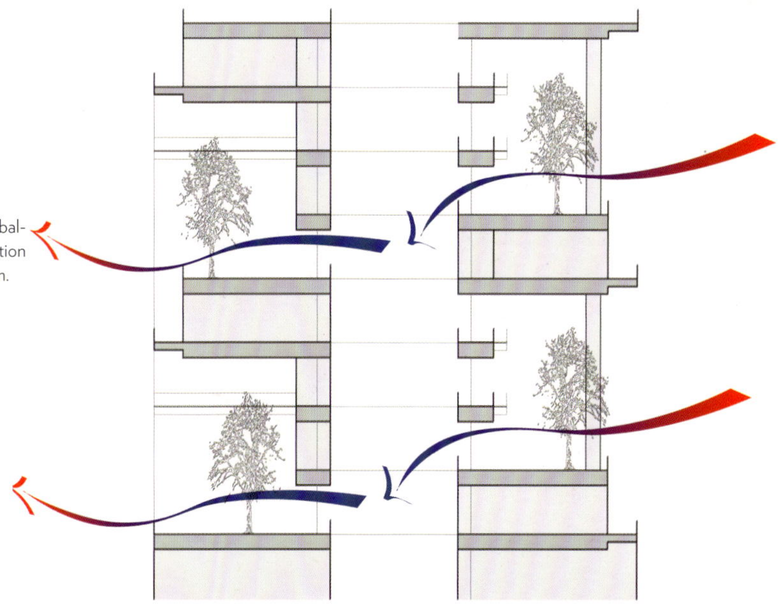

Burj Khalifa Gatehouses

Dubai, United Arab Emirates

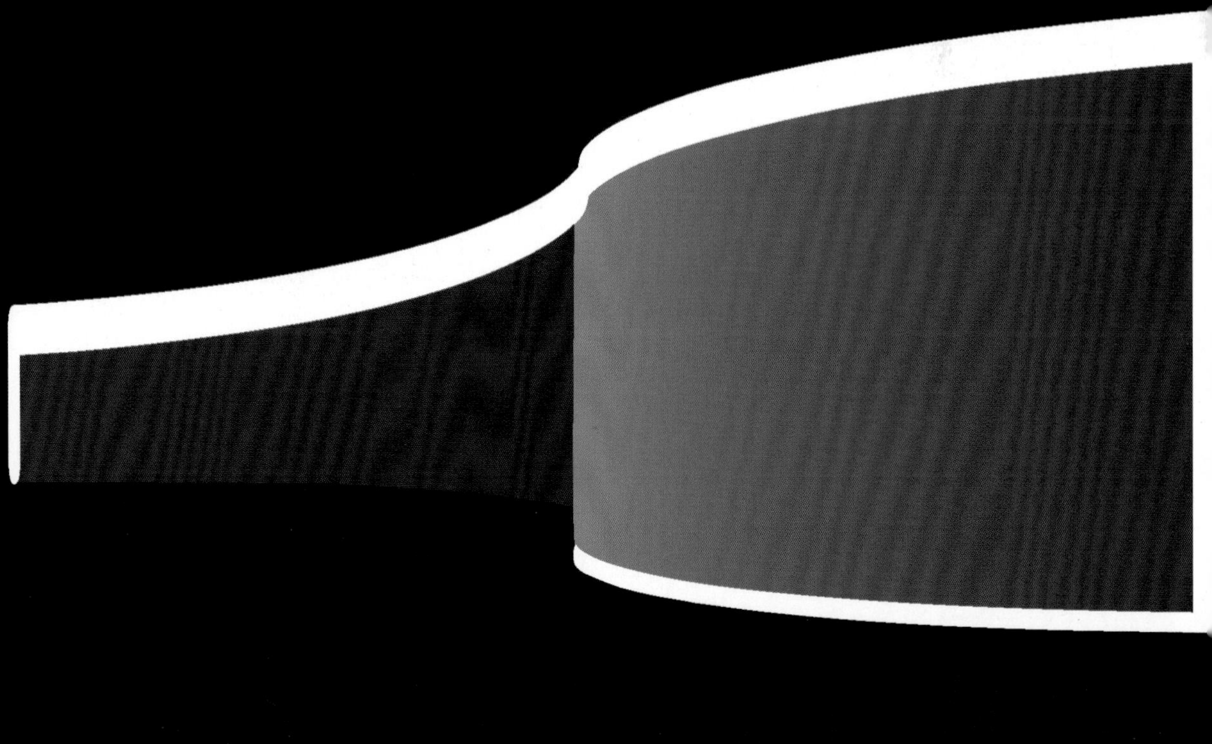

Burj Khalifa Gatehouses

Dubai, United Arab Emirates

A collection of six small, elegant structures act as the gatehouses for the Burj Khalifa to provide key security checkpoints, while maintaining a strong visual connections to the tower.

SERVICES
Architecture

CLIENT
Emaar Properties

FUNCTION
Infrastructure

FACTS
Six gatehouses

AWARDS
The Chicago Athenaeum, International Architecture Award, 2012

Stylistically the gatehouses' curving lines relate to the undulating form of the tower massing and site design. The stainless-steel cladding is similar to that used in the tower's mullions and spandrels, while the panelization echoes the modular framing of the curtain wall.

Each gatehouse has its own function and identity, including the main hotel entrance, the main residential entrance, the office entrance, the office annex entrance, a taxi stand, and the service truck entrance.

The gatehouses feature teak louvers and ceilings for added functionality and contrast with the stainless-steel exterior walls and columns, as well as offices with observation rooms for the security checkpoint staff.

Some of the gatehouses have electronic automobile scanners, the housing for which is also designed by AS+GG. The office windows are glazed with tinted glass that provide additional insulation and glare mitigation while shielding the staff from view.

Solar Canopy

Chicago, Illinois

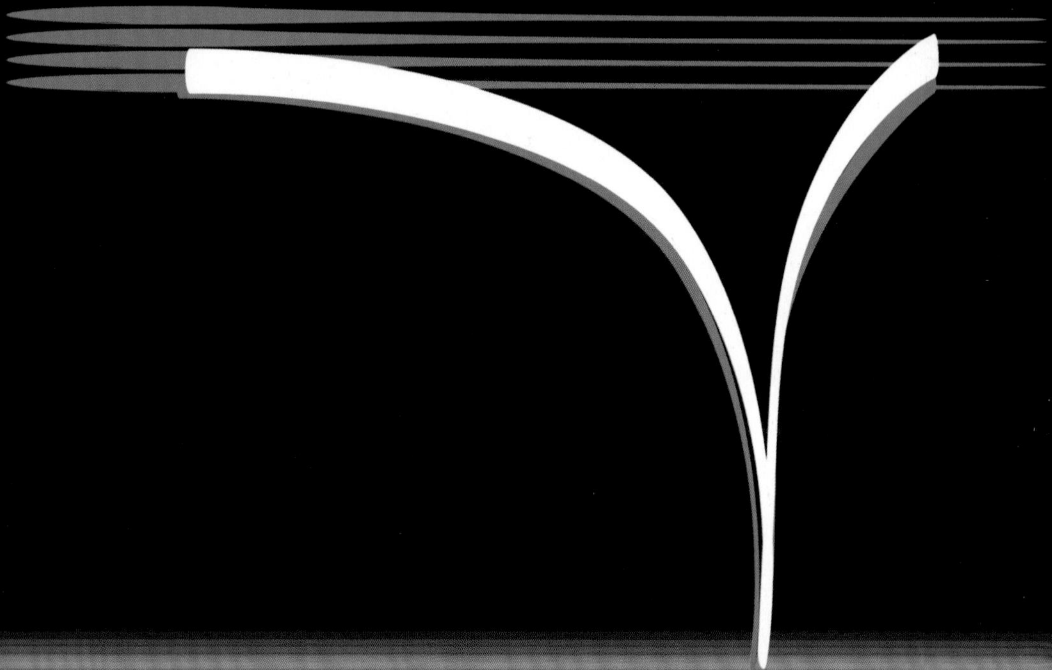

Solar Canopy/EV Dock

Chicago, Illinois

The Solar Canopy/EV Dock harvests solar energy to power electric or electric-hybrid cars, bikes, and scooters. The dock features photovoltaic panels and an integrated conduit through which energy is transferred, either to a power grid or to neighboring buildings.

SERVICES
Architecture

CLIENT
Carbon Day

FUNCTION
Infrastructure

AWARDS
The Chicago Athenaeum, Green Good Design Award, Green Architecture, 2014

American Institute of Steel Construction, IDEAS2 Awards, Excellence in Steel-Frame Building, 2014

The Chicago Athenaeum, International Architecture Award, 2012

The canopy is designed to work as a single structure or multiple structures linked back-to-back. When linked back-to-back, the canopies create a shaded corridor for users in the spaces in between. The canopy also shades vehicles as they are being changed over the course of a workday, offsetting the carbon emissions associated with commuting to work.

The Solar Canopy/EV Dock incorporates a range of photovoltaic technologies at varying orientations to accommodate installations anywhere in the world. Using the industry-standard mono-crystalline PV module, 4,000-6,000 kWh of carbon-free electricity is generated from a structure covering two vehicles. This generates enough energy to provide up to 30,000 carbon-free miles per year, or about the amount required for a 20-mile, or 30-minute, work commute each way, for both cars over a year.

In large-scale applications, employee parking lots can be converted into giant plug-in charging stations, with surplus energy donated or sold to the power grid. The canopy also has the potential to collect rainwater, which is then irrigated to adjacent landscapes or agriculture.

The Solar Canopy/EV Dock, which also incorporates a Columb Technologies charge-point system, was built at Douglas Park and relocated to Northerly Island in 2010, where it is used daily by the City of Chicago to fuel the city's fleet of electric/hybrid vehicles.

SOLAR CANOPY/EV DOCK

FM1034

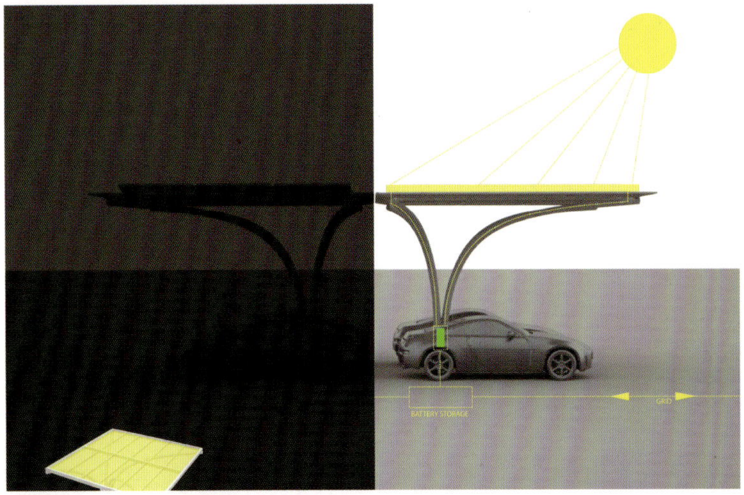

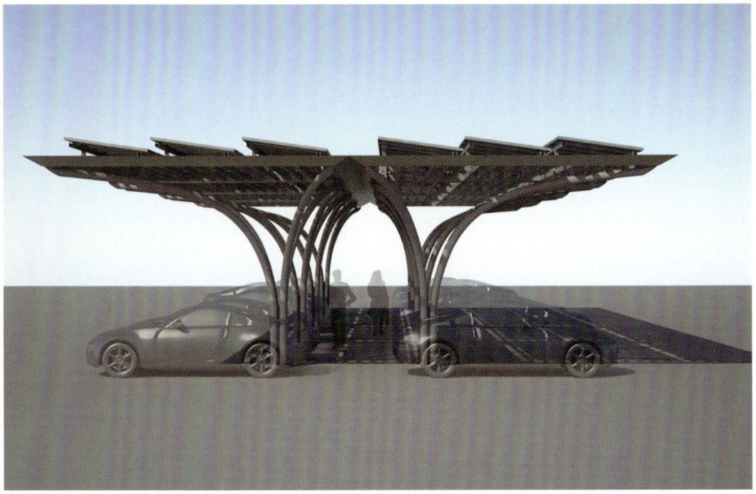

Dubai Bridge

Dubai, United Arab Emirates

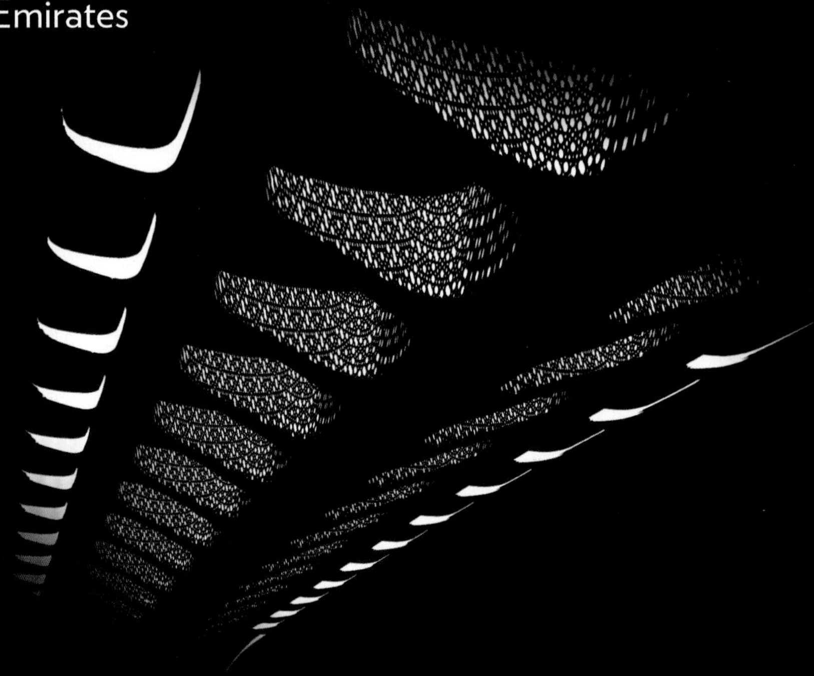

Dubai Bridge

Dubai, United Arab Emirates

Dubai Bridge, designed as a signature feature for Dubai's Jumeirah Gardens development, fuses structural expression, innovative use of materials, and cultural referencing to create one of the most high-performing yet poetically evocative structures of its kind.

SERVICES
Architecture

CLIENT
Meraas Development

FUNCTION
Infrastructure

FACTS
41 m width
210 m length

AWARDS
AIA Chicago, Unbuilt Design, Citation of Merit, 2011

Softly molded in reinforced concrete into a form that suggests the skeleton of a whale from the nearby Arabian Gulf, the 41-meter-wide, 210-meter-long bridge rises to an apex of 14.5 meters above a canal and its twin pedestrian promenades.

The structure is V-shaped in section, with five meters of structural depth in the central spine of the bridge supporting six vehicular lanes and tapering out to cantilevered pedestrian walkways on either side. The vehicular lanes and pedways are separated by an interstitial zone of 10-meter-structural bays that resemble the vertebrae of the whale's spine.

Overall, the bridge has a thin, light edge profile while still providing the substantial structure necessary to support the span. Intermediate support structures on either side of the canal help stabilize the bridge. Unlike other signature bridges that make their grandest architectural gestures when viewed from a distance or from above, Dubai Bridge makes a strong architectural statement to pedestrians, cars, and boats passing beneath it.

Looking up at the structural bays, viewers watch the play of light and shadow on the pristine white inner walls of the larger bays. The ever-changing shadows created by the sun shining through the geometric pattern of the steel-mesh grating, inspired by Middle Eastern Mashrabiya latticework, are made even more dynamic by passing cars. The result is an intimate, captivating relationship between the bridge and the viewers from below.

Sky Ring

Beijing, China

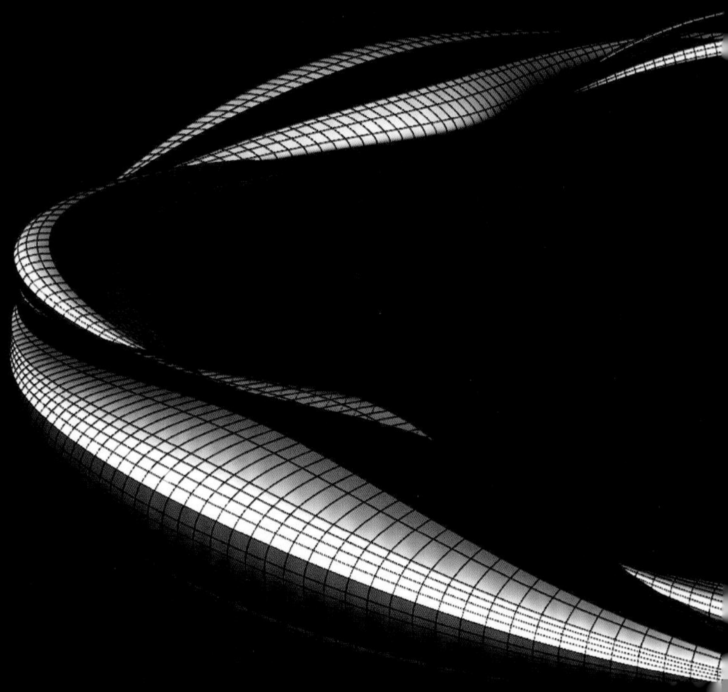

Golden Cross Sky Ring

Beijing, China

The Golden Cross Sky Ring is an flowing urban gateway through one of Beijing's busiest intersections. The design is further proposed as a prototypical pedestrian link at the four major intersections in downtown Beijing.

SERVICES
Architecture

CLIENT
Jingtou Yintai Co., Ltd.

FUNCTION
Infrastructure

FACTS
18,000 sm

AWARDS
The Chicago Athenaeum, International Architecture Award, 2011

Beijing continues expanding its urban structure through a system of wide-ring roads. Although there have been attempts to improve the quality of the streetscape, traffic is still an issue because of the continued increase in the amount of cars. Urban nodes at intersections are not pedestrian friendly and the development of below-grade subway lines further complicate the pedestrian circulation pattern with unclear exits around street intersections.

The Golden Cross, designed for the intersection of East Third Ring Road and ChangAn Ave (also the city's east-west central axis) is famously known as the gateway to the Beijing CBD area. Much of the busy intersection is occupied with luxury mixed-use developments that include offices, hotels, and residences. It is considered an important destination for business, shopping, and viewing the streetscape of famous ChangAn Ave.

Three levels of elevated roads pass through the intersection as a way of organizing the local and express traffic from all directions. It currently takes ten minutes for a pedestrian to pass across the wide streets, navigating through heavy vehicular traffic. The proposed Sky Ring acts as a pedestrian link that allows circulation over the Golden Cross intersection, as well as connects buildings above the street level. The Sky Ring also opens to street level and connects to the subway through four vertical cores that coordinate with existing subway exits.

The form is inspired by the Chinese culture's respect of integrated universal forces and the admiration of a sunlight halo. The Sky Ring is visioned as an urban space with relaxing gardens, a variety of retail stores, and observation decks that create a vibrant new icon for the CBD district and Beijing. The facade has an operable skylight system that opens in the summer to allow natural ventilation and closes in the winter to provide protection.

As a prototype the ring can be scaled to fit different urban scopes. All systems and assemblies can easily be duplicated at any size.

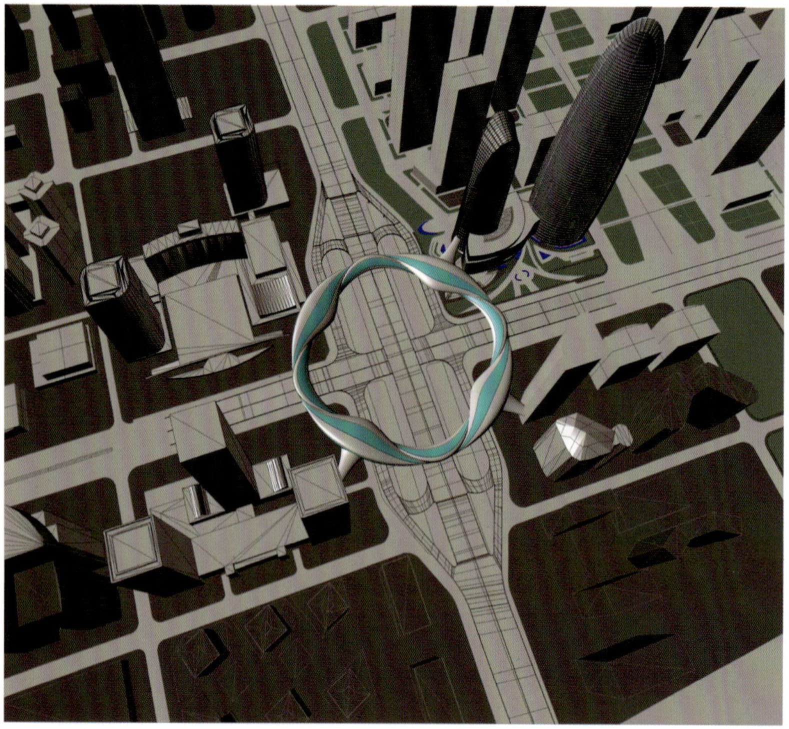

STRUCTURAL CONCEPT

The proposed structural system is a composite structural steel braced system and the roof consist of a light structural steel system. The Sky Ring includes retail space around circulation cores, which also braces the structure of the bridge. Each core consists of concentrically braced walls that provide gravity support and stabilize the bridge. Between the cores over Third Ring Road, additional reinforced columns provide gravity support and laterally stabilize the bridge.

Bridge spans between columns and cores will be achieved by utilization of a series of arched trusses: one truss centered on the support points and two on the sides of the bridge. Initially a series of surface analysis was performed to optimize the shape and to confirm the optimal location of structure to support the bridge. The walking surface and skin surfaces will be diagonalized to ensure a stiff torsion box to resist the twisting induced due to the curved plan of the bridge.

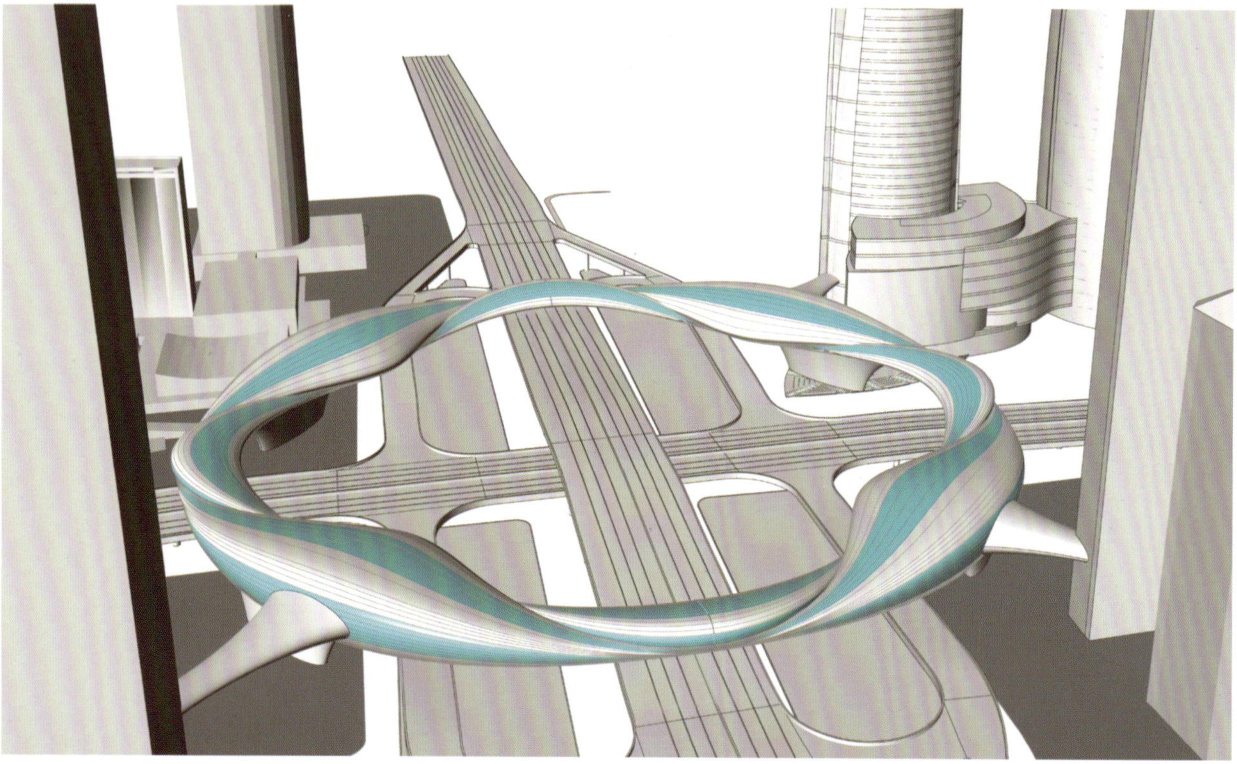

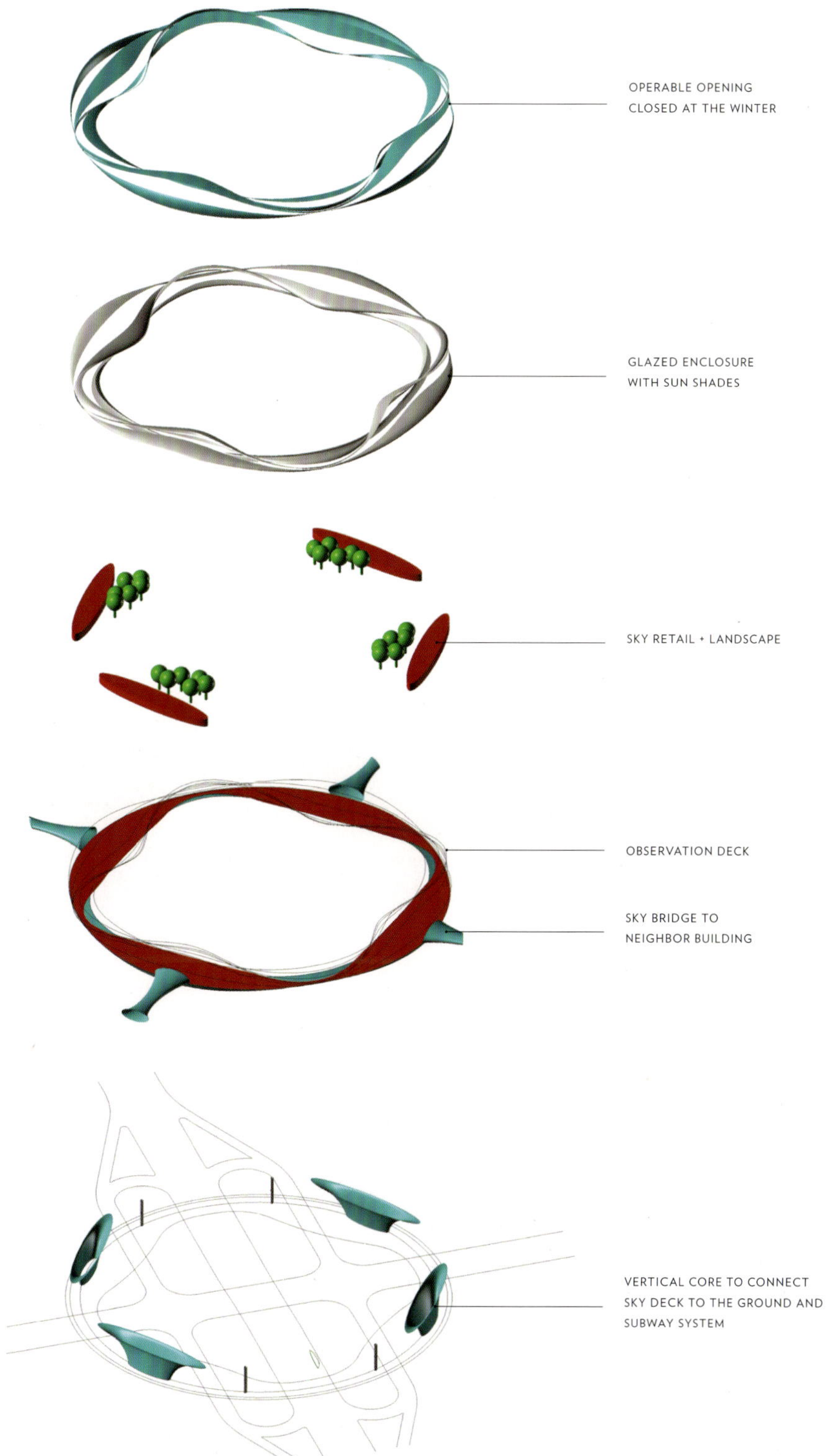
OPERABLE OPENING
CLOSED AT THE WINTER
GLAZED ENCLOSURE
WITH SUN SHADES
SKY RETAIL + LANDSCAPE
OBSERVATION DECK
SKY BRIDGE TO
NEIGHBOR BUILDING
VERTICAL CORE TO CONNECT
SKY DECK TO THE GROUND AND
SUBWAY SYSTEM

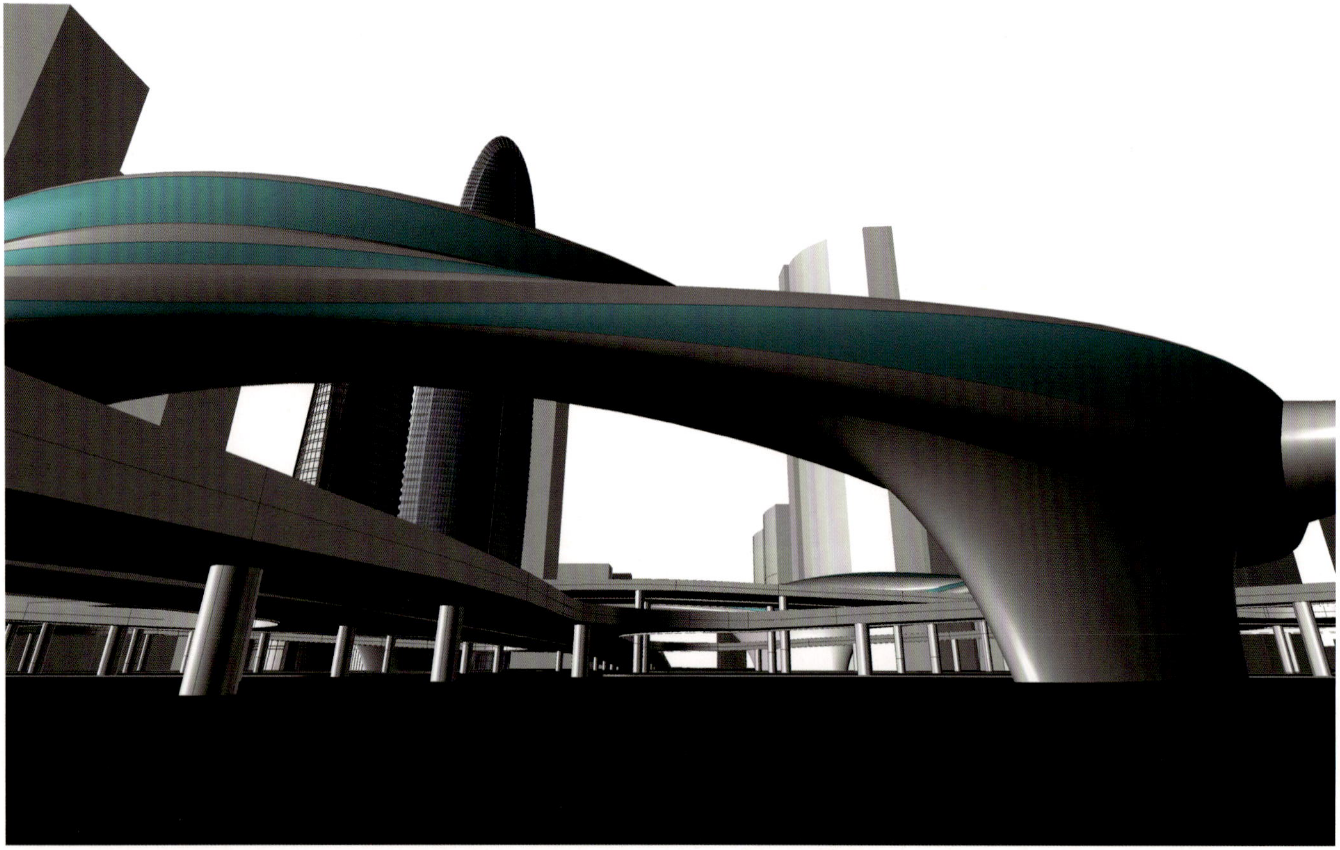

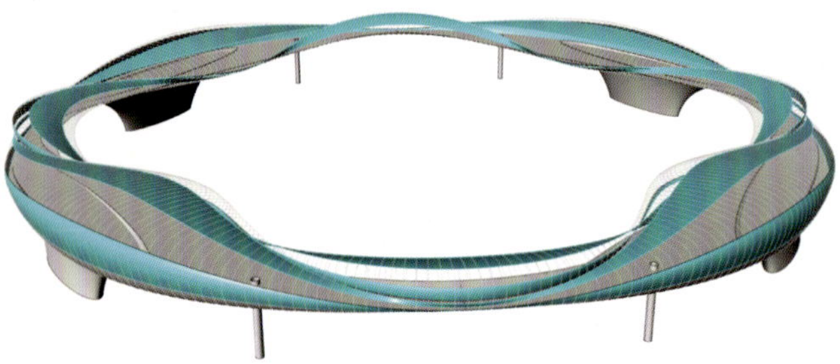

ARCHITECTURAL MASSING

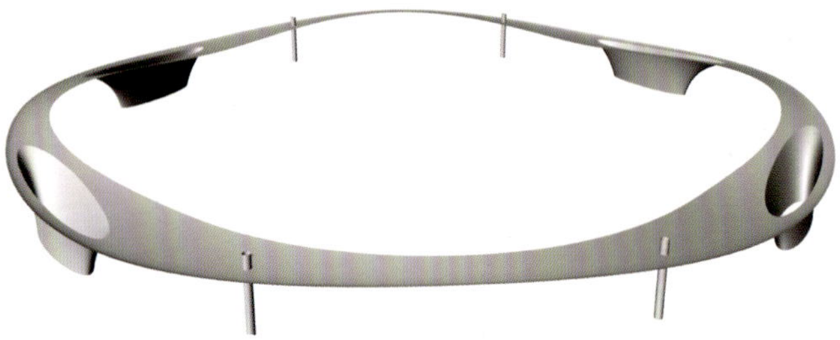

STRUCTURAL MASSING

Eco Bridge

Chicago, Illinois

Chicago Eco-Bridge

Chicago, Illinois

The Chicago Eco-Bridge completes the last major recommendation of the 1909 Burnham Plan of Chicago in a thoroughly modern way that celebrates the city's future as well as its past.

SERVICES
Master Planning
Urban Design

CLIENT
City of Chicago, Department of Environment

FUNCTION
Cultural
Infrastructure

FACTS
2 mile circumference

The two-mile bridge, a breakwater in the Monroe Harbor, celebrates Chicago's position as the greenest city in the United States. The bridge creates a grand new civic space, providing recreational opportunities and offering unparalleled views of the skyline from a central observation tower.

A central Eco-Tower harvests wind and solar power and functions as a public observatory that includes food service and other amenities. A plaza at the tower site is a temporary or permanent performance space. At either end of the bridge, interactive exhibit spaces house a Great Lakes Museum or other cultural facility to complement the nearby Museum Campus.

Vertical-axis wind turbines along the bridge add economic value through the production of clean, renewable energy and showcase Chicago's dedication to sustainability. The turbines double as pieces of sculpture, offering an opportunity for collaboration with visual artists and engineers and the creation of a lively public art walk. The turbines also are outfitted with LED lights, creating a soft necklace of light surrounding the harbor in the evening.

The park is easily accessible from Grant Park and the downtown area. Pedestrian walkways and dedicated bicycle paths encourage healthful and sustainable modes of transit. An electric or solar trolley system further augments the bridge's accessibility, providing transportation from the neighboring downtown areas. The Eco-Bridge also showcases the ecology of the Great Lakes and provides a haven for fish and water plants.

SECTION

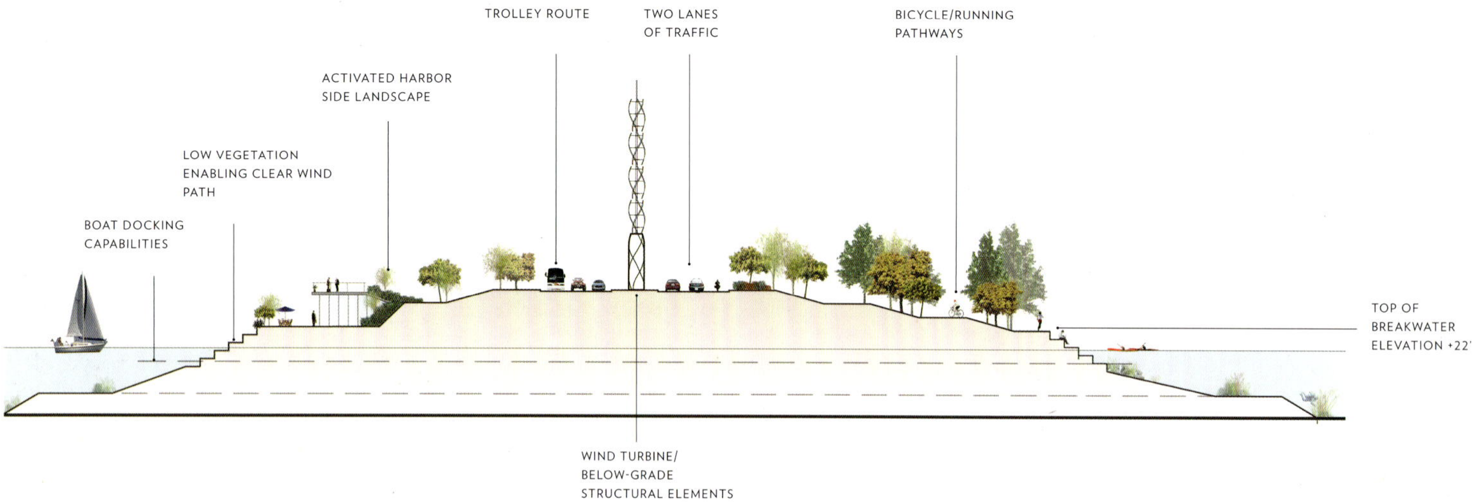
TROLLEY ROUTE
TWO LANES OF TRAFFIC
BICYCLE/RUNNING PATHWAYS
ACTIVATED HARBOR SIDE LANDSCAPE
LOW VEGETATION ENABLING CLEAR WIND PATH
BOAT DOCKING CAPABILITIES
TOP OF BREAKWATER ELEVATION +22'
WIND TURBINE/ BELOW-GRADE STRUCTURAL ELEMENTS

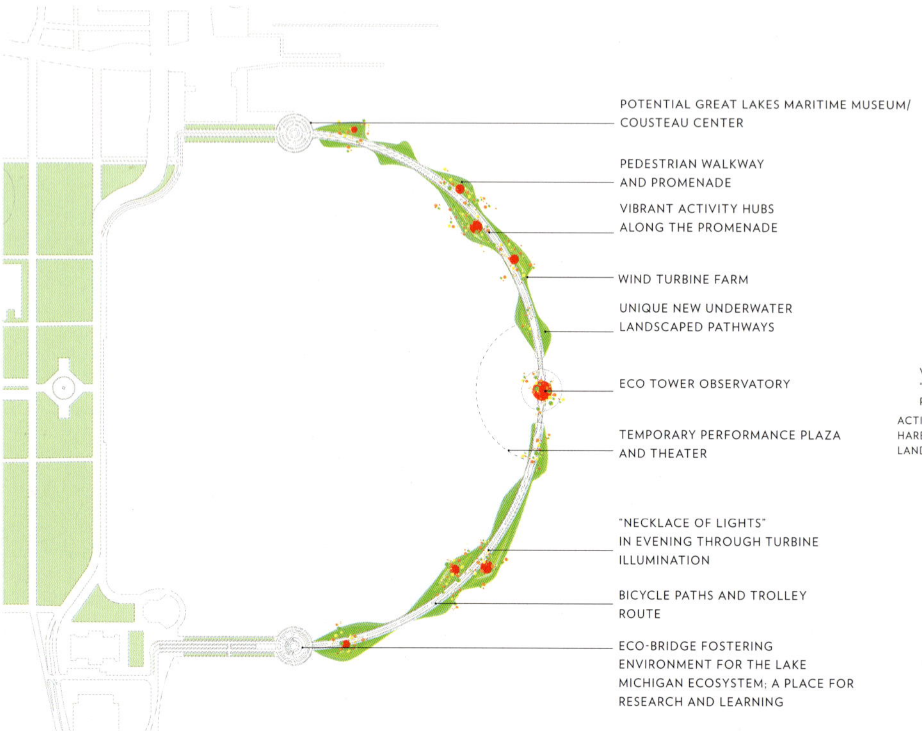
POTENTIAL GREAT LAKES MARITIME MUSEUM/ COUSTEAU CENTER
PEDESTRIAN WALKWAY AND PROMENADE
VIBRANT ACTIVITY HUBS ALONG THE PROMENADE
WIND TURBINE FARM
UNIQUE NEW UNDERWATER LANDSCAPED PATHWAYS
ECO TOWER OBSERVATORY
TEMPORARY PERFORMANCE PLAZA AND THEATER
"NECKLACE OF LIGHTS" IN EVENING THROUGH TURBINE ILLUMINATION
BICYCLE PATHS AND TROLLEY ROUTE
ECO-BRIDGE FOSTERING ENVIRONMENT FOR THE LAKE MICHIGAN ECOSYSTEM; A PLACE FOR RESEARCH AND LEARNING

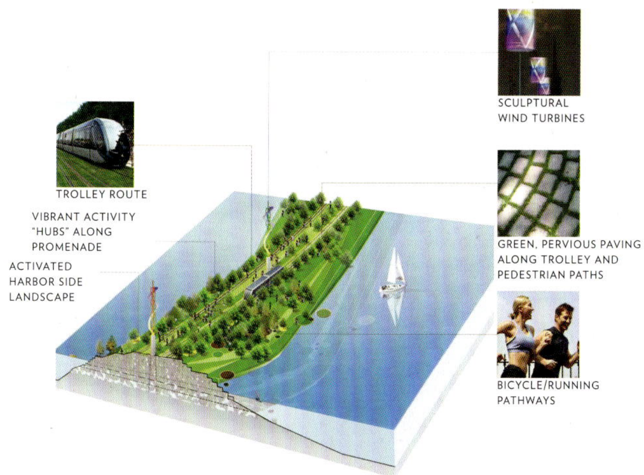
TROLLEY ROUTE
SCULPTURAL WIND TURBINES
VIBRANT ACTIVITY "HUBS" ALONG PROMENADE
ACTIVATED HARBOR SIDE LANDSCAPE
GREEN, PERVIOUS PAVING ALONG TROLLEY AND PEDESTRIAN PATHS
BICYCLE/RUNNING PATHWAYS

EXPO-2017

Astana, Kazakhstan

Astana Expo City 2017

Astana, Kazakhstan

The design of the Astana Expo City 2017 master plan embraces the designated concept of "Future Energy," which is aimed at finding ways to achieve qualitative changes in the energy sector, primarily for the development of alternative sources of energy and transportation.

SERVICES
Architecture
Urban Design
Sustainability Planning

CLIENT
Expo 2017

FUNCTION
Cultural

FACTS
430 acres

AWARDS
The Chicago Athenaeum, American Architecture Award, Kazakhstan Pavilion: Nur Alem

AIA Tap/CCA Innovation Awards, Stellar Design, 2016

The Chicago Athenaeum, Green Good Design Awards, Green Urban Planning, 2016

Re-thinking The Future 2015 Award, Urban Design Concept, Second Award, 2015

The master plan and urban design for Astana Expo City is determined by site specific indicators such as weather conditions, cultural context, and land accessibility. The design team executed a series of studies with the goal of minimizing the site's energy use, while maximizing its energy harvesting potential and comfort levels. The resulting analysis offers the most efficient orientation in order to optimize solar radiation to reduce energy usage for heating. This strategy improves user comfort and maximizes the potential energy that can be generated from building mounted photovolatics.

A significant part of the energy consumed by the expo community is provided from renewable sources. Buildings are designed as generators of power and their energyis used or stored using innovative technologies while being distributed by a smart grid. The forms and language of the buildings are designed to reduce their energy needs and operate as "power plants" that harness energy from the sun and/or wind. The buildings use this power directly or supply it to the district-wide smart grid for storage or use. The expo community also provides the infrastructure to encourage and support the use of vehicles that use renewable fuels.

Split into two phases, the 430-acre project features exhibition and cultural pavilions, a residential development, service areas including shopping, socio-cultural, educational and civic facilities, parks, and parking. Phase I or the "Expo Mode," includes se the design and construction of the exposition buildings including the central Kazakhstan Pavilion; Theme, Corporate, and International Pavilions; as well as hotel, retail, art and performance spaces. Phase I was completed in June 2017 and served the Expo and its visitors. During the now under construction Phase II, or the "Post Expo Mode," expo buildings are being converted into an office and research park to attract international companies and entrepreneurs. Expo parking and service zones are being transformed into thriving, first-class integrated neighborhoods.

The crucial difference of this project from other sustainable master plans is that it is not a demonstration. Because the sustainable aspects of the project continue after the expo is finished, Astana Expo City 2017 forms the basis of a truly sustainable community that serves as a legacy for Astana and Kazakhstan. The design is a catalyst for scientific and academic research and development, which creates new industries, unique skill sets, and new job opportunities.

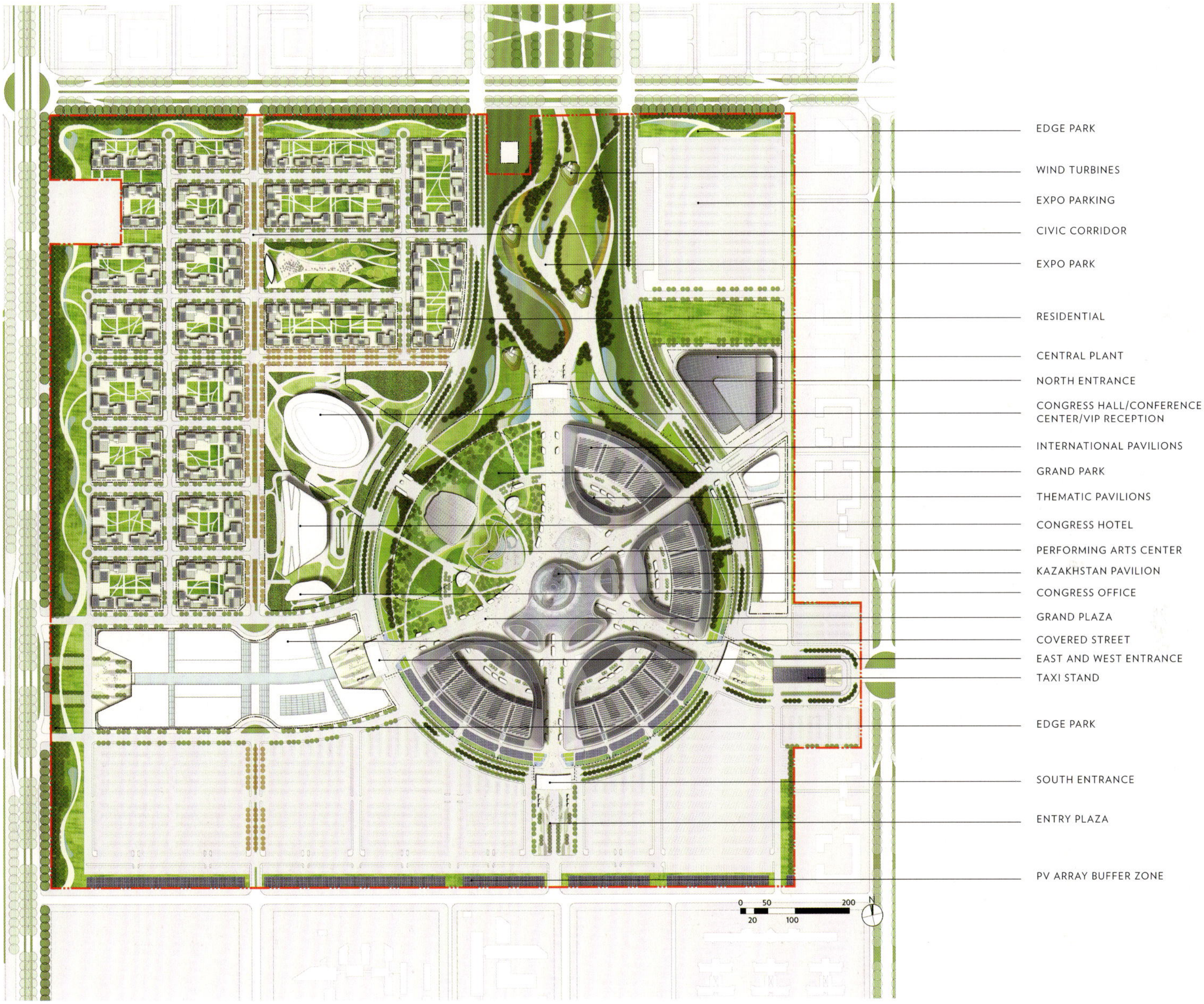
EDGE PARK
WIND TURBINES
EXPO PARKING
CIVIC CORRIDOR
EXPO PARK
RESIDENTIAL
CENTRAL PLANT
NORTH ENTRANCE
CONGRESS HALL/CONFERENCE CENTER/VIP RECEPTION
INTERNATIONAL PAVILIONS
GRAND PARK
THEMATIC PAVILIONS
CONGRESS HOTEL
PERFORMING ARTS CENTER
KAZAKHSTAN PAVILION
CONGRESS OFFICE
GRAND PLAZA
COVERED STREET
EAST AND WEST ENTRANCE
TAXI STAND
EDGE PARK
SOUTH ENTRANCE
ENTRY PLAZA
PV ARRAY BUFFER ZONE
0 50 200
20 100
N

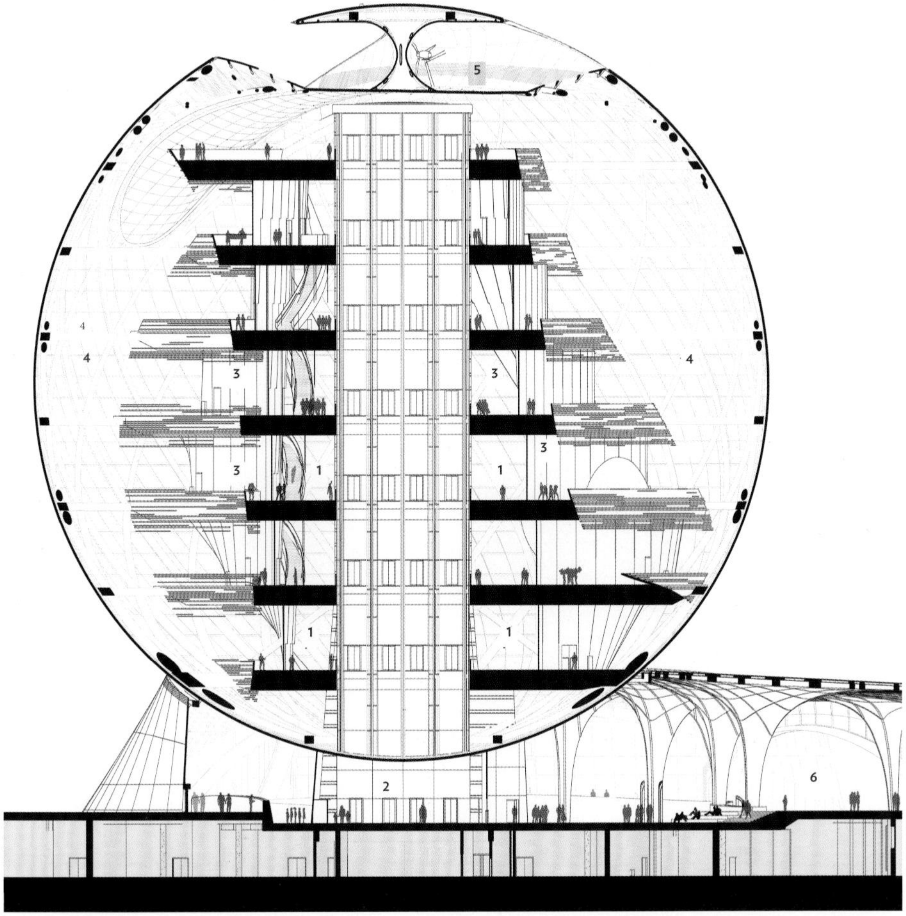

SECTION

1 Exhibit Space

2 Special Exhibit

3 Balcony

4 Atrium

5 Wind Scoop Turbine

6 Covered Street

0m 5m 10m 15m

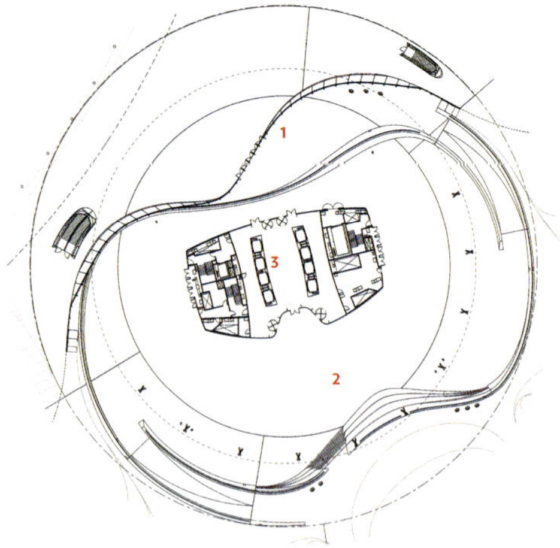

LEVEL 1

1 Entry

2 Exhibit Space

3 Elevator Lobby

MID LEVELS

1 Exhibit Space

2 Special Exhibit

3 Balcony

4 Atrium

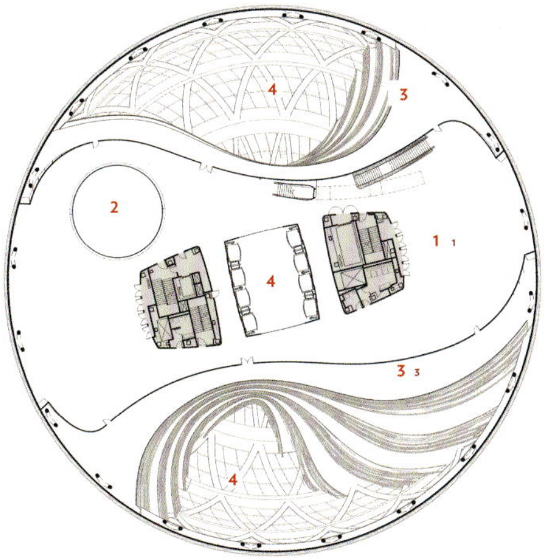

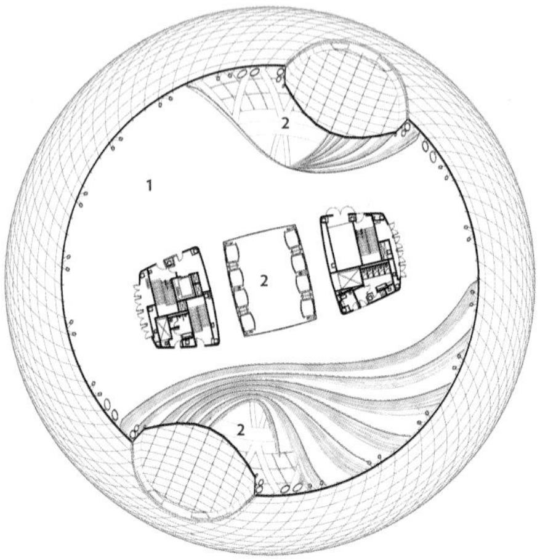

LEVEL 8

1 Observation + Event Space

2 Atrium

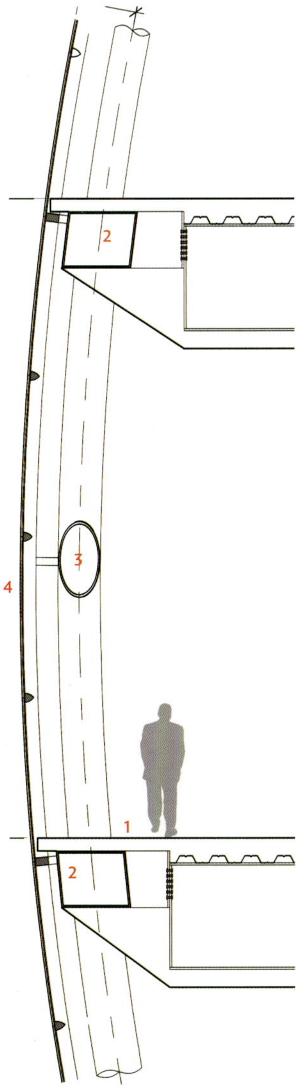

EXTERIOR WALL DIAGRAMS

1 Stainless-Steel Grating

2 Primary Structural Ring Beam

3 Primary Diagonal Structural Member

4 Double Curved IGU With Laminated Low-Iron Glass

EXTERIOR WALL CURVED GLASS PANELS

A detailed design analysis was conducted using Rhino/Grasshopper to refine the spherical form and maximize the sun exposure for the Building Integrated Photo Voltaic cells (BIPV). Many investigations were completed and tested to integrate the solar panels, while balancing the requirements of other critical building components such as MEP surface area requirements, collision with other architectural elements, maximizing wind swept area for the turbines, and the rationalization of the double-curved minimal surface geometry.

Ultimately, Monocrystalline Semi-Transparent BIPV was installed and integrated into the glazing of the scoop that is situated at the top of the sphere. During the testing phase, the energy model predicted 81,056 kWh/yr of electricity or 2.21 percent of total energy demand. The PV percentage integration into glazing panels ranged from 40 percent to 80 percent density. The architectural specification for the BIPV was monocrystalline wafer spaced to allow a percentage of natural daylight to pass through. The light transmittance varied depending on location.

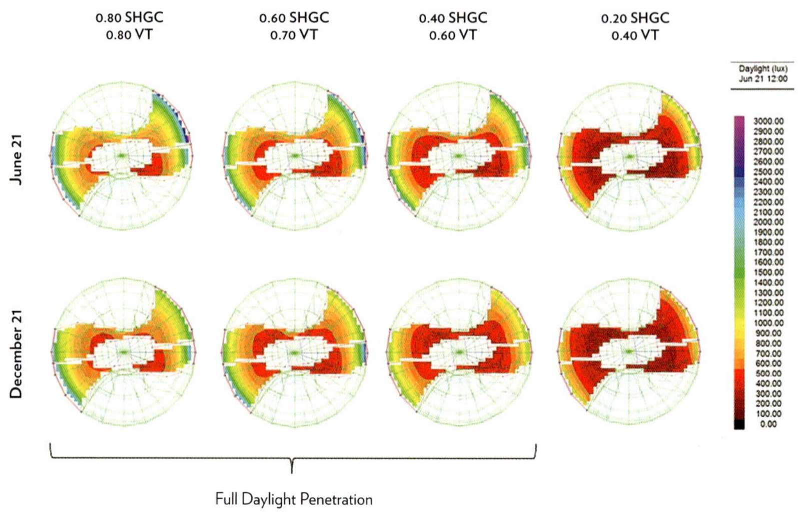

SOLAR STUDIES

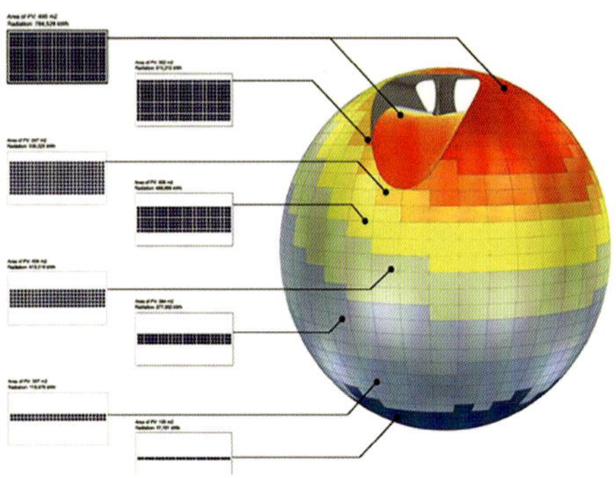

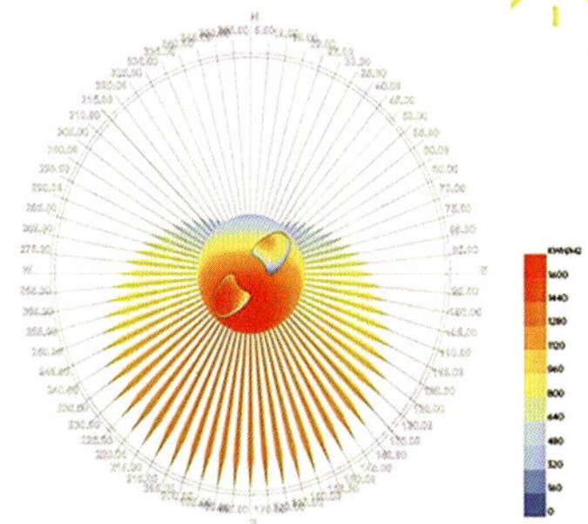

Total Radiation (kWh/m2)
UACC Astana
1 Jan - 31 Dec

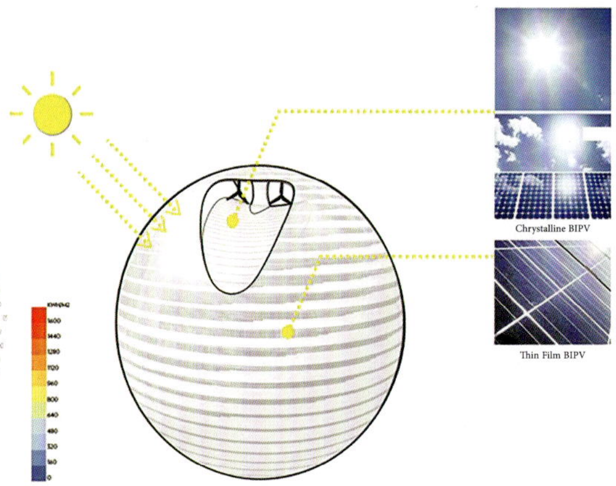

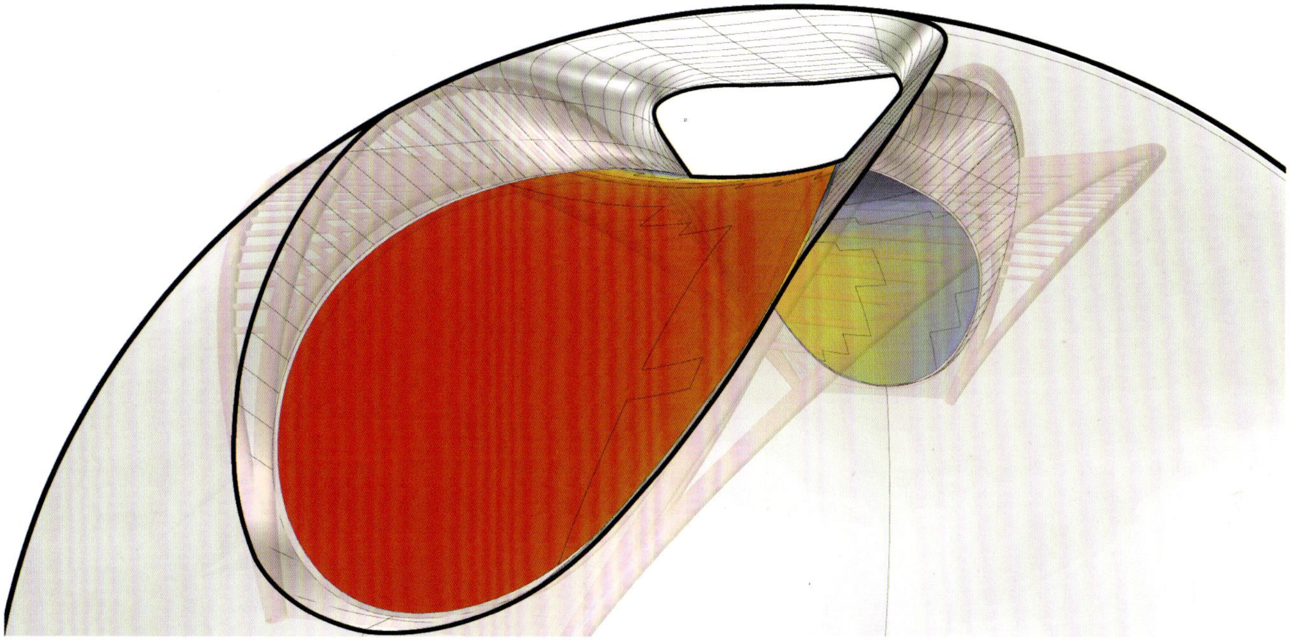

PANELIZATION RHINO MODEL

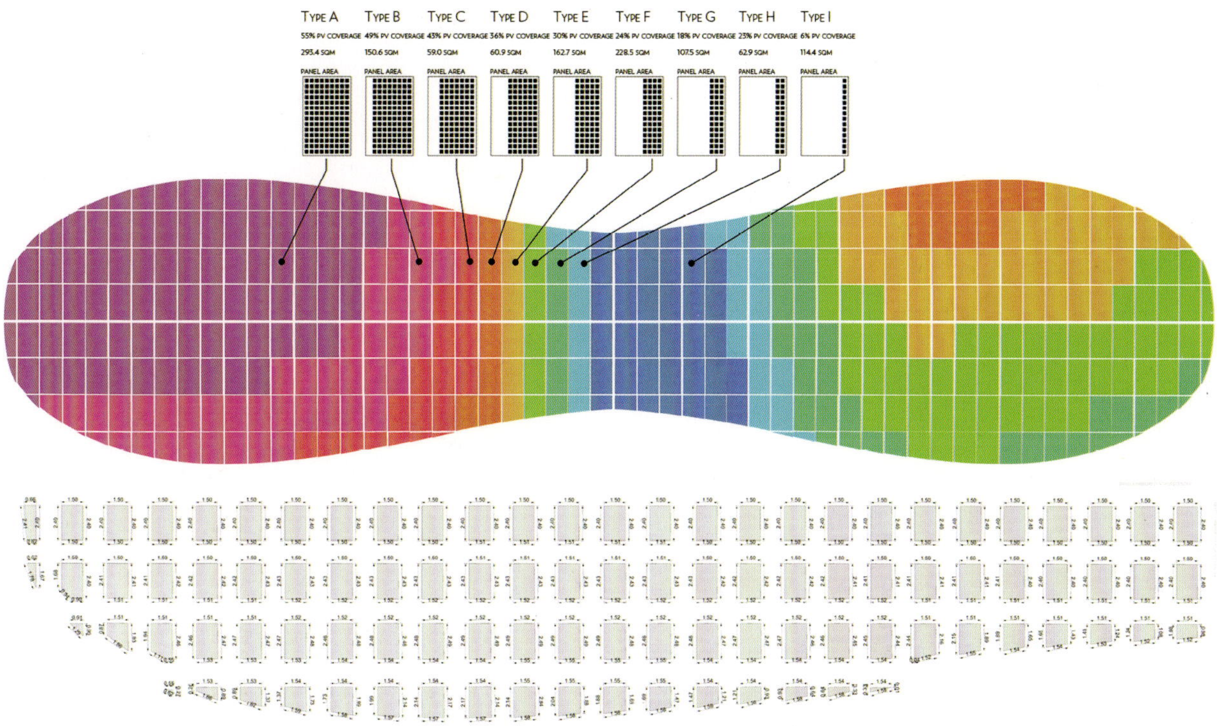

To improve energy generation, several designs were modeled and tested to find an appropriate form that responded to the programmatic requirements and optimized the amount of energy generation that can occur. A final analysis determined that energy can be produced with building integrated wind turbines set within an inlet carved from the top of the structure.

The design team worked closely with wind engineers to design and test multiple overall building forms and eventually the shape of the inlet on the surface of the building. Predominant southwest winds are channeled to activate the turbines that were designed specifically for the harsh winter conditions of Astana. The turbines produce a total of 52,700 kwh/yr of electricity or the equivalent of 1.6 percent of the building's total electricity demand or 0.9 percent of total energy demand.

WIND TURBINE INSTALLATION, 2017

WIND FLOW DIAGRAM

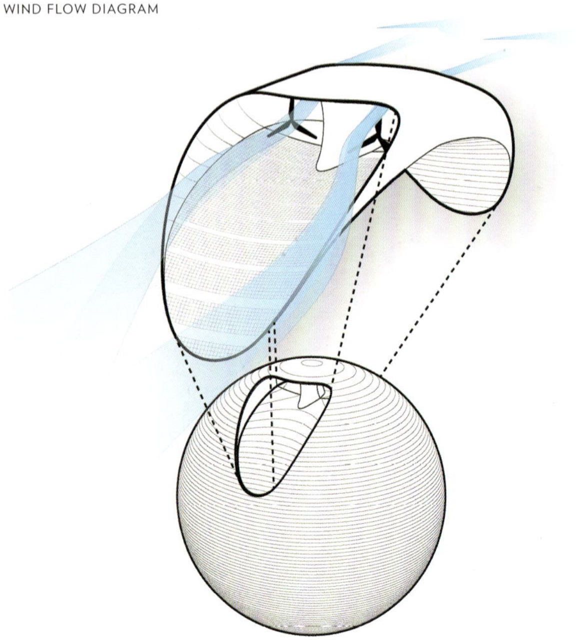

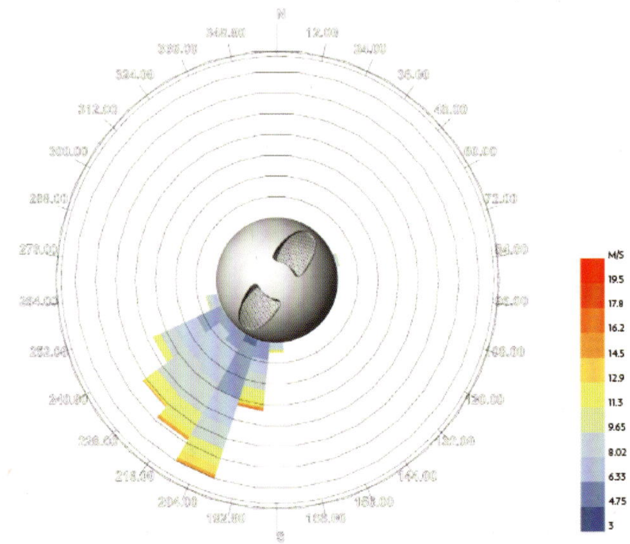

Wind Rose
1 Jan - 31 Dec
Wind Speed > 3m/s - 74% of Total Hours

PHASE 2 SITE PLAN

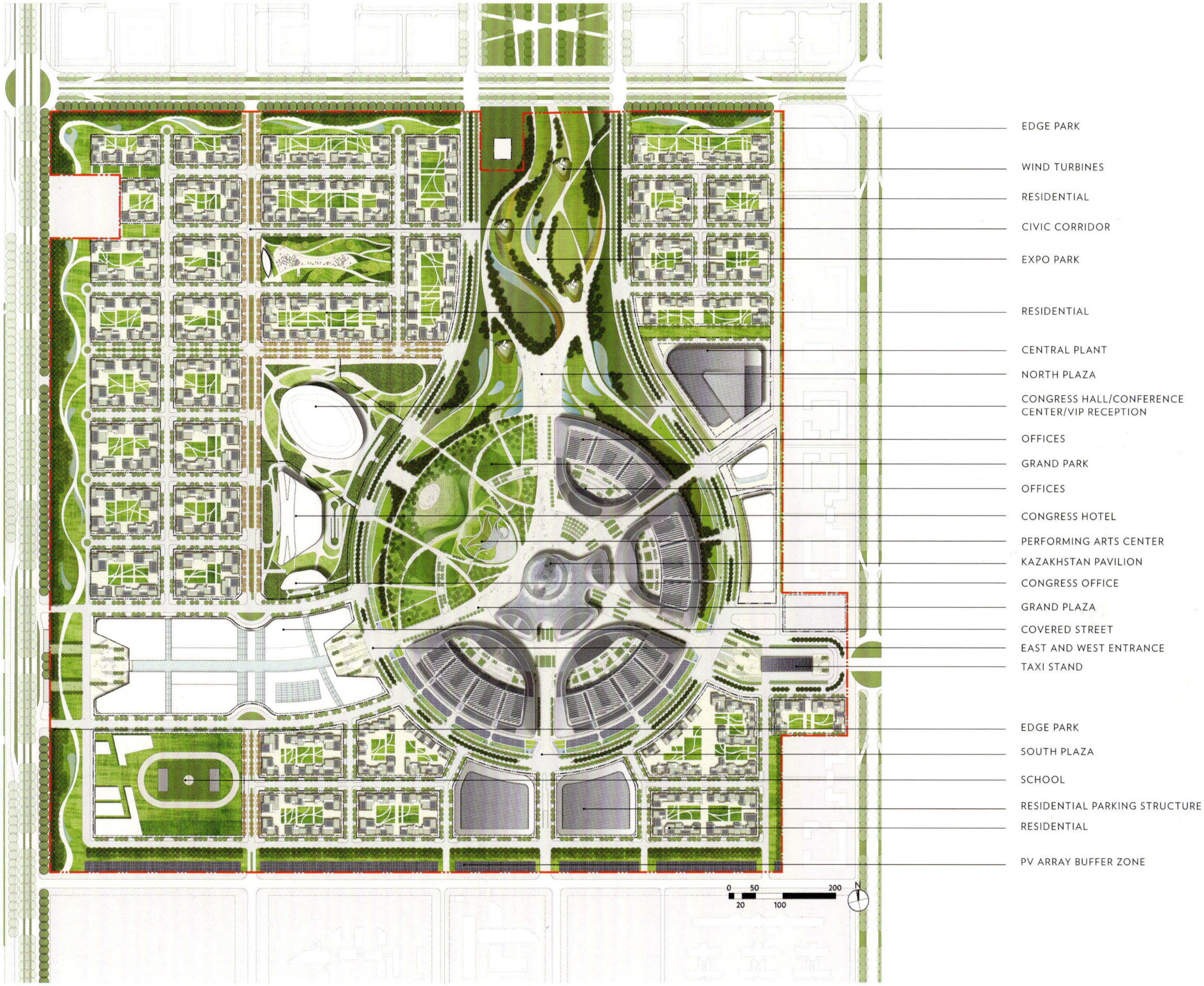

OPENING NIGHT, JUNE 2017

EXPO-2020

Dubai, United Arab Emirates

World Expo 2020

Dubai, United Arab Emirates

AS+GG's City Design studio completed the master planning, urban design, and architectural design for World Expo 2020, which was held in Dubai from October 2021-March 2022. The master plan addressed city-growth goals for Expo investments in infrastructure and buildings advance long-term UAE objectives for economic and social advancement.

SERVICES
Architecture
Urban Design
Sustainability Planning
Interior Design

CLIENT
Expo 2020

FUNCTION
Cultural

AWARDS
The Chicago Athenaeum, International Architecture Award, Al Wasl Plaza, 2021

The Chicago Athenaeum, Green Good Design Award, Al Wasl Plaza, 2021

AIA Chicago, Urban Design, 2019

The 500-acre site is accessible via regional expressways and Dubai Metro commuter rail is under construction. Approximately 5.4 million sf of permanent buildings are being constructed for the Expo that will be converted into office, residential, and educational facilities organized around small-scale blocks and neighborhood parks.

At its center, is Al Wasl Plaza, also designed by AS+GG. Al Wasl is a four-acre garden and performance venue framed by five office and hotel buildings. By day, the plaza is shaded by a 425-foot-wide by 220-foot-tall trellis. By night, the trellis transforms into a dynamic 360-degree projection screen that will be the largest spherical media platform in the world. The trellis enables immersive group experiences, while also creating iconic identity for District 2020.

Following the Expo, the entire site will transform into a mixed-use technology hub focused on global logistics to leverage its adjacency to new international airport and deep-sea port assets. Rebranded District 2020, this urban innovation lab will contain 32 million sf of mixed work-live-learn development with public transit, exhibition facilities, and regional attractions.

ROVE
Centre 9

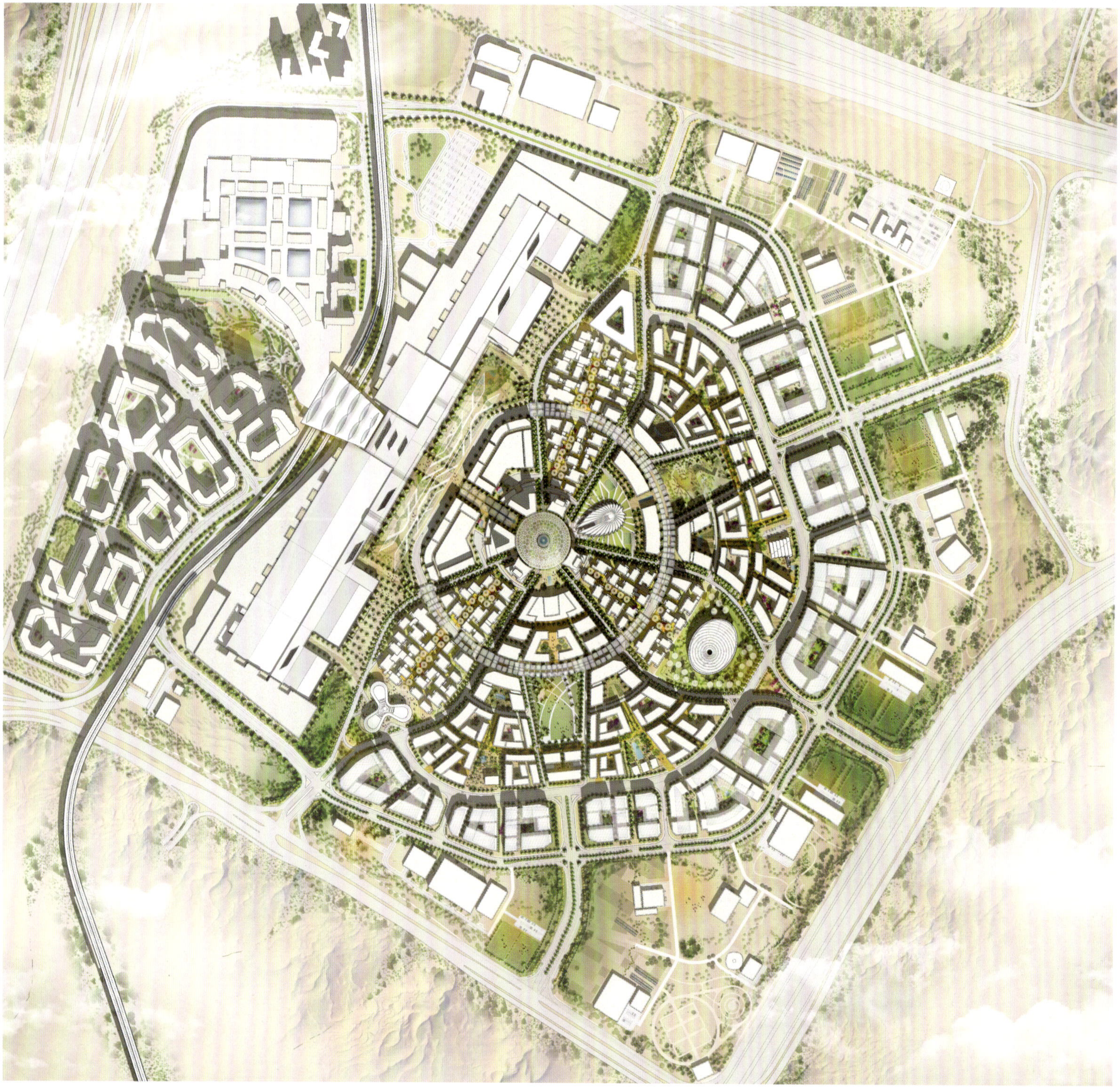

POST EXPO LEGACY DISTRICT

GREAT City

Chengdu, China

GREAT City

Chengdu, China

AS+GG's master plan for Great City Chengdu is the vision for a self-sustaining, environmentally sensitive 1.3-square-kilometer satellite city outside Chengdu, China.

SERVICES
Architecture
Master Planning
Urban Design

CLIENT
Beijing Vantone Citylogic Investment Corp.

FUNCTION
Mixed-use

FACTS
3.65 sq km

AWARDS
The Chicago Athenaeum, Green Good Design Award, Green Urban Planning/Landscape Architecture, 2014

The Chicago Athenaeum, International Architecture Award, Great City Master Plan, 2013

One of the first projects of its kind to be proposed or completed in China, Great City is envisioned as a prototype, or model city, to be replicated in other locations throughout the country. The development is intended to respond to the problem of overburdened infrastructure in many of China's major urban centers without contributing to the high energy consumption and carbon emissions associated with suburban sprawl.

Great City was designed for approximately 30,000 families, or around 80,000 people, many of whom can work within the site. The distance from any location in the city to any other location is walkable within 15 minutes, all but eliminating the need for most automobiles. The city is also be connected to Chengdu and surrounding areas via mass transit to be accessed at a regional transit hub at the Great City center.

The project is designed to achieve a remarkable series of sustainable benchmarks. Great City uses 48% less energy and 58% less water than a conventional development of similar population and produces 89% less landfill waste and generates 60% less carbon dioxide.

The project is also designed to conserve existing farmland, with more than 60% of the 800-acre site area preserved for agriculture and open space. The 320-acre urbanized area is surrounded by a 480-acre buffer landscape, whose natural topography—including valleys and bodies of water—is integrated into the city. 15% of the site's land is devoted to parks and landscaped space, while 60% is parcelized for construction. The remaining 25% is devoted to infrastructure, roads, and pedestrian streets.

As a fully contained development, Great City's functions include commercial, residential, office, light manufacturing, and a medical campus that provides health services to residents as well as a larger regional and even national constituency. The city's medical campus is intended to address the needs of the growing Chinese demographic of young married couples who live in combined households with extended families that may include two sets of grandparents.

In addition to improved efficiencies within buildings, the city is designed to use seasonal energy storage so summer waste heat can be used to provide winter heating. A power generation plant utilizes the latest co-generation technology to provide both electricity and hot water. AS+GG worked with the infrastructure consultant Mott MacDonald on plans for an Eco-Park located on the northwest edge of the city that integrates wastewater treatment, solid waste treatment, and power generation.

AS+GG's master plan additionally includes architectural design guidelines for massing and placement of buildings.

SITE PLAN

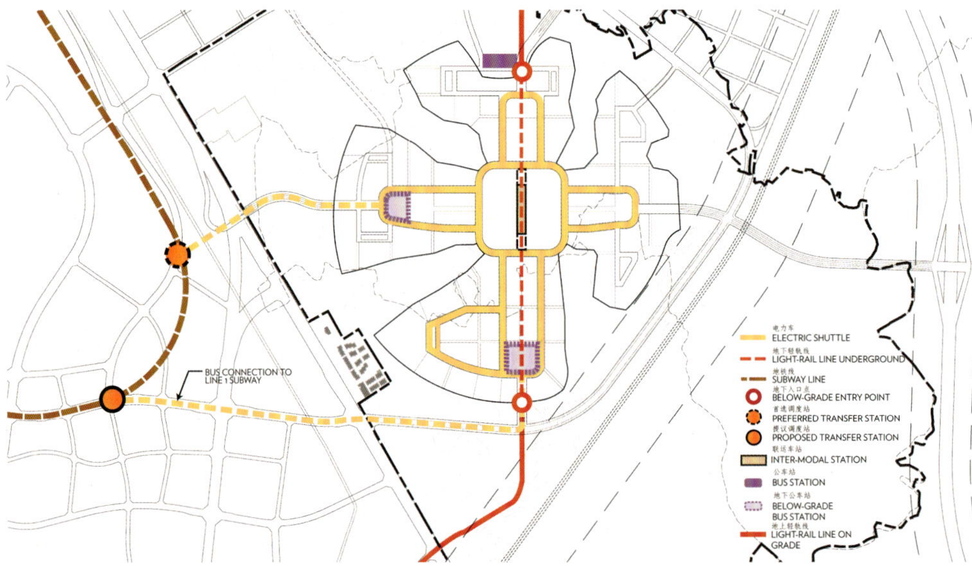

Great City's public realm is composed of two distinct parts: The urban landscape and the buffer landscape. Each part responds to different conditions and allows for different uses, complementing each other and creating a unified and pleasing public realm for the city.

The two parts also create spaces with a wide range of scales, levels, textures, and programs, providing Great City's inhabitants with many opportunities for leisure, work, entertainment, art, and recreation.

立体城市花市

时尚春熙
凤祥楼

凤祥楼

ANTA

SITE CONCEPT + LAND USE PLANS

1- PRESERVE THE VALLEYS

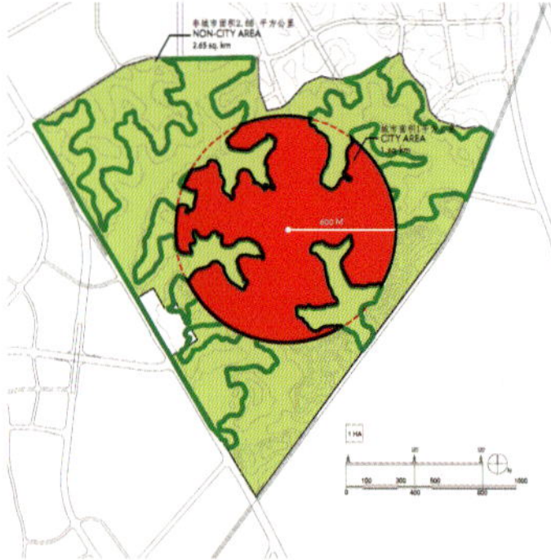

2- DEFINE A CLEAR CITY IDENTITY

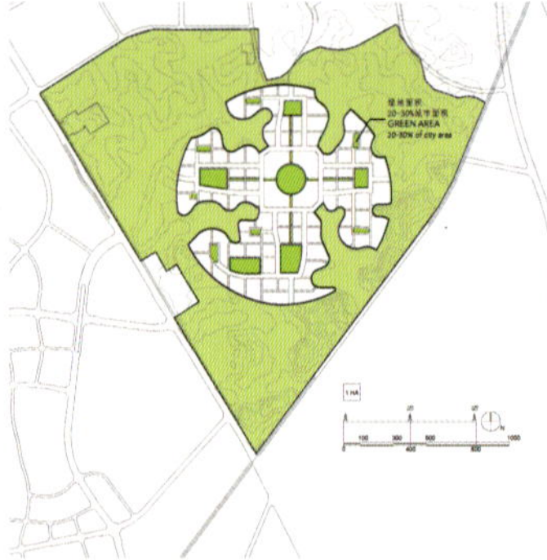

3- CREATE INTERNAL AND EXTERNAL OPEN SPACE

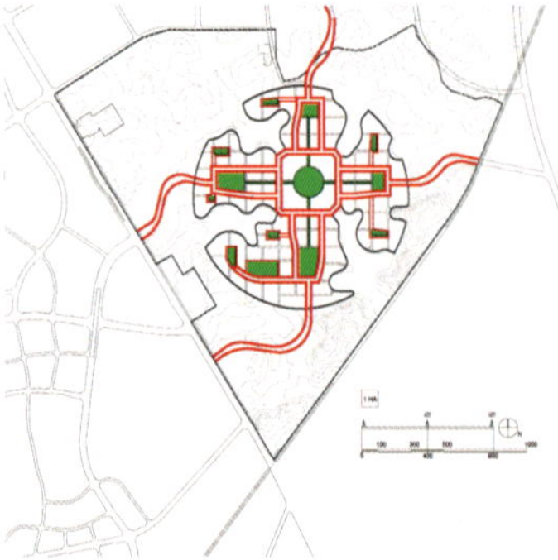

4- IMPLEMENT A LEGIBLE ROAD NETWORK

5- DEFINE BUILDABLE DEVELOPMENT PARCELS

6- ESTABLISH A COMPREHENSIVE GREEN NETWORK

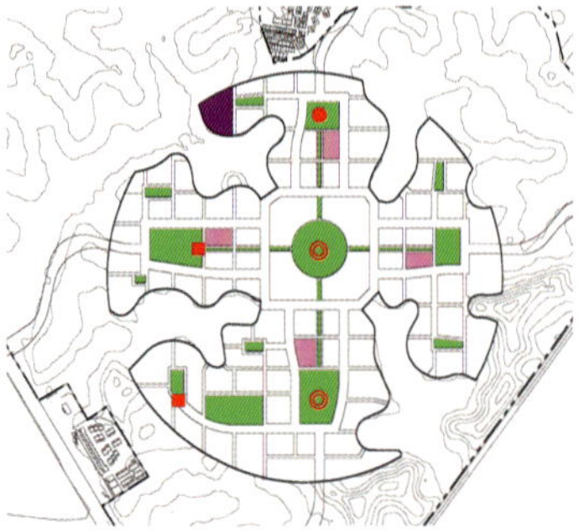

CIVIC / INSTITUTIONAL / PARKS

CIVIC FACILITY · ECO-PARK · PARKS · SUBWAY STATION · LIGHT-RAIL STATION · INTER-MODAL STATION

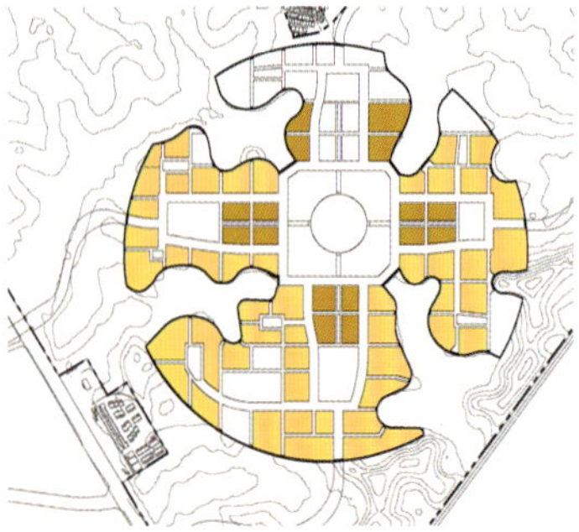

RESIDENTIAL

LOW DENSITY RESIDENTIAL · HIGH DENSITY RESIDENTIAL

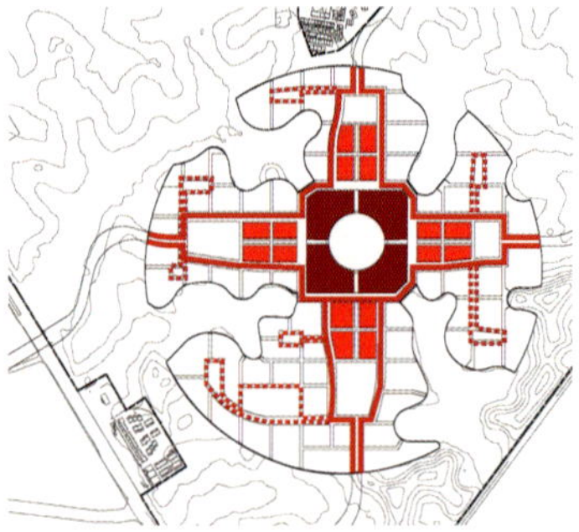

RETAIL

PRIMARY RETAIL (CITY) · SECONDARY RETAIL (DISTRICT) · TERTIARY RETAIL (NEIGHBORHOOD)

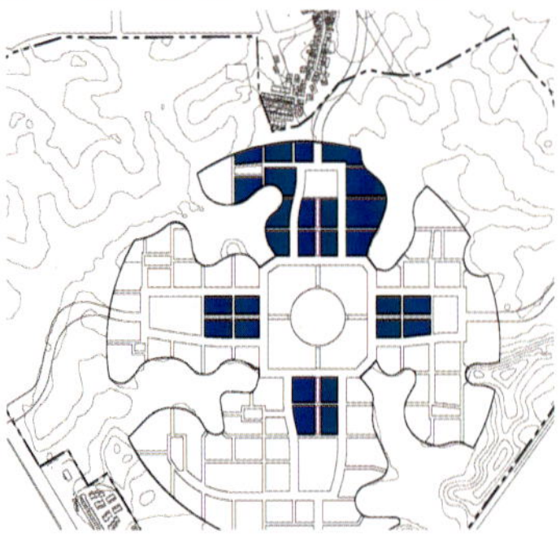

OFFICE

OFFICE

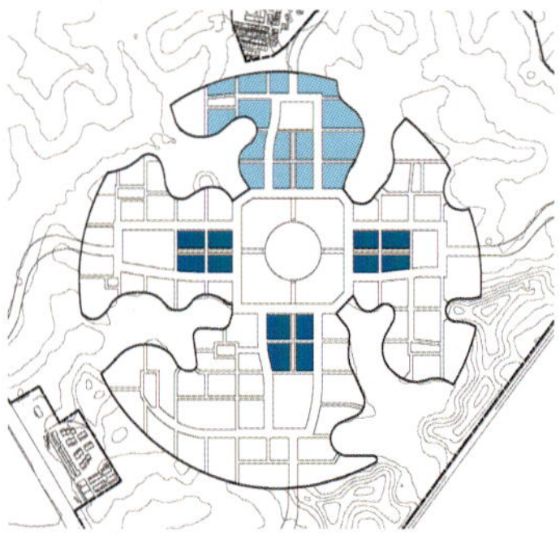

MEDICAL / MANUFACTURING / VERTICAL FARMING

TYPE 1 · TYPE 2

EDUCATIONAL

HIGH SCHOOL · PRIMARY SCHOOL

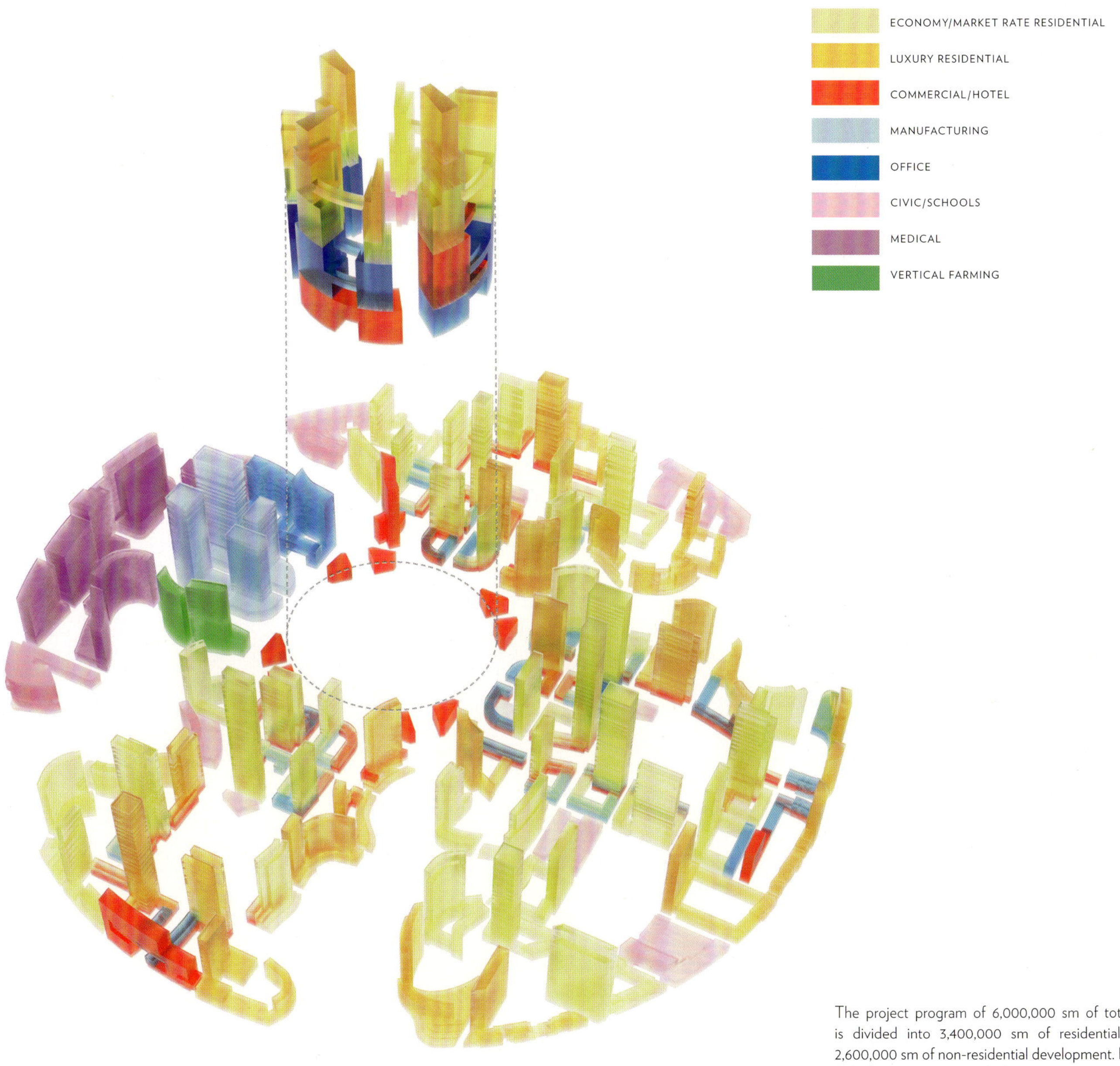

The project program of 6,000,000 sm of total constructed area is divided into 3,400,000 sm of residential development and 2,600,000 sm of non-residential development. Non-residential uses include 600,000 sm medical, 200,000 sm commercial, 525,000 sm agricultural, 600,000 sm office, 525,000 sm manufacturing, 300,000 sm civic and 150,000 sm transportation. Civic uses include 200,000 sm required by Chinese code plus an additional 100,000 sm assigned to higher education or training facilities.

Great City parks are a fundamental component of the public realm, because they synthesize major public spaces and functions within district centers. The parks are conceived not only as open areas around which commerce and central uses are arranged, but also as civic centers with special buildings for public uses such as museums, temples, government buildings, and public institutions. The parks also form a fundamental piece of the storm water management system, and because of their scale and strategic location within the city they assure proper solar access to buildings.

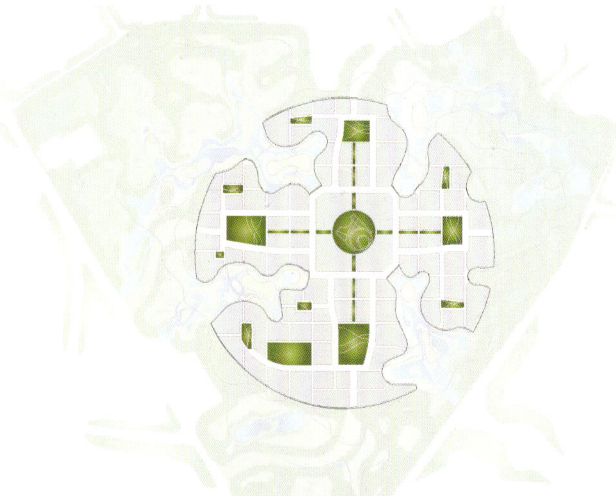

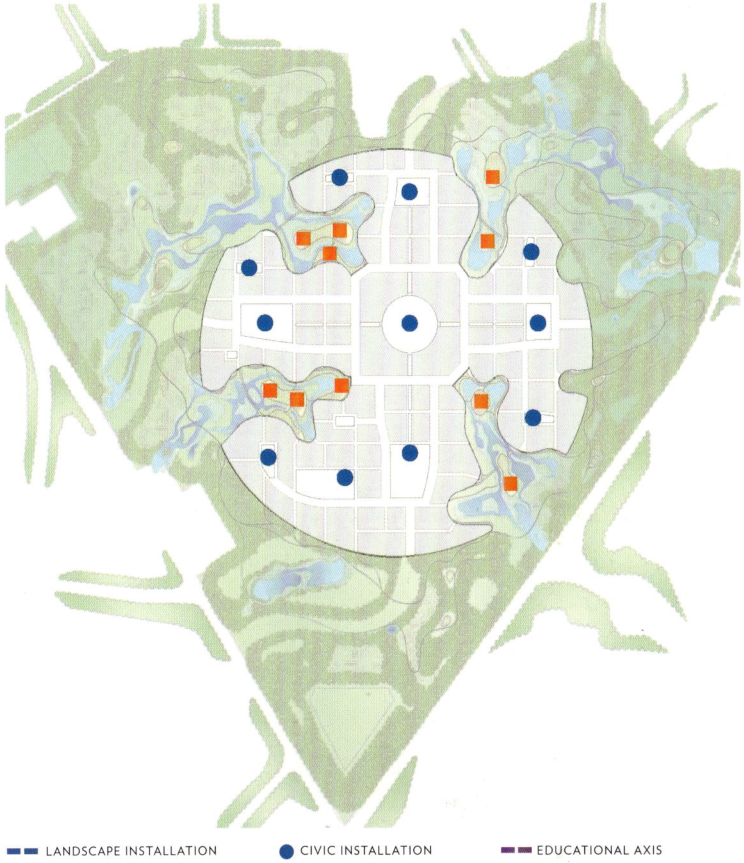

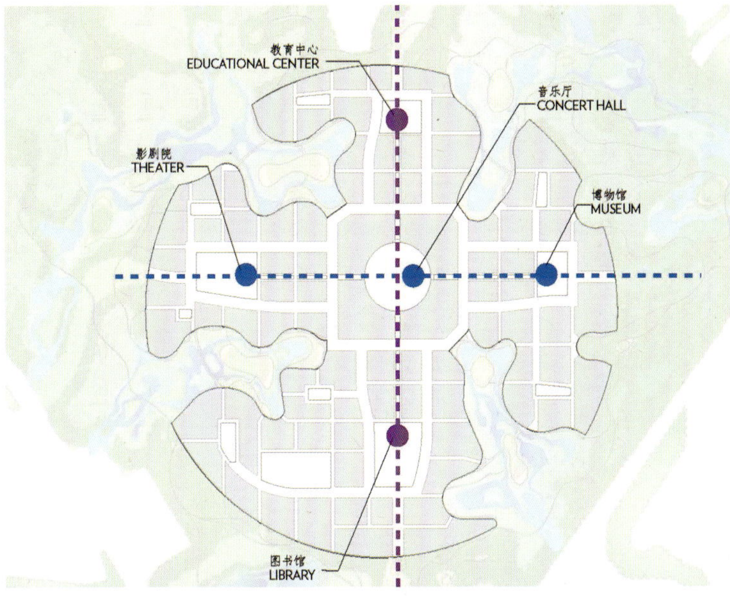

Great City's public realm offers many art opportunities for local, regional, and international artists to create site-specific works unique to the city. Great City's art projects approach environmental responsibilities with a vision for the immediate and long-term future. Ecological sustainability, social responsibility and environmental protection are critical components.

In addition to artwork, the major public spaces of the city are opportunities to create unique, special-use buildings that contain that civic and cultural uses. Within the city, a north-south "educational axis" includes a library and an environmental education center. Complementing this is an east-west "cultural axis" that includes a theater and an art museum. At the center of the city, within the Central Business District, is a multi-purpose indoor/outdoor concert venue, providing a gathering space for all residents and visitors that is connected to the Chengdu transportation network.

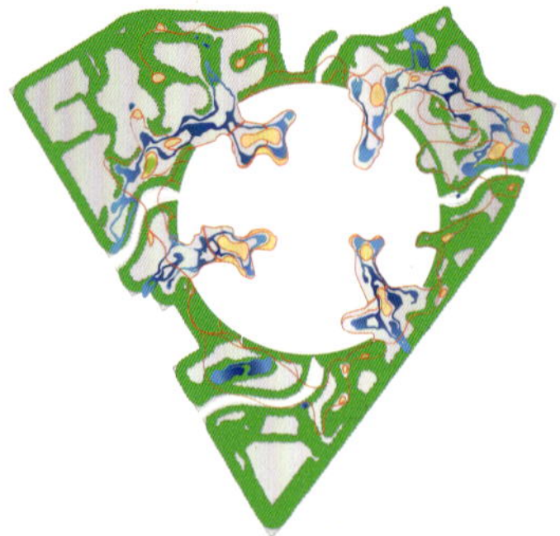

PROGRAMED LANDSCAPE

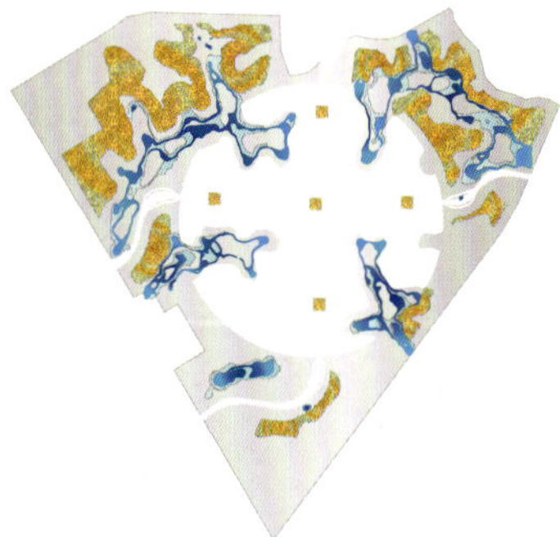

PRODUCTIVE LANDSCAPE

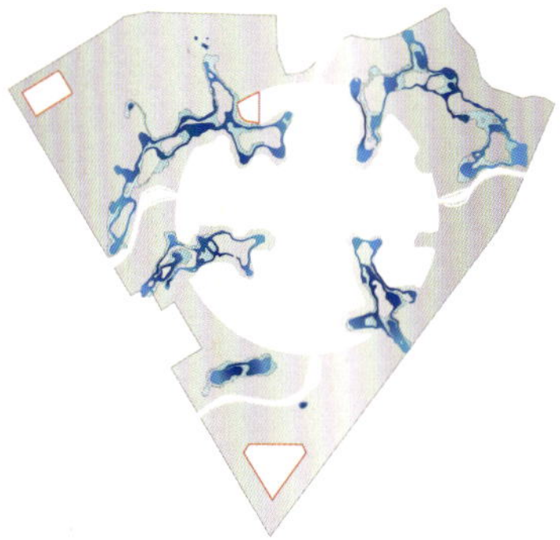

FUNCTIONAL LANDSCAPE

The natural landscape includes all public areas outside of the city's urbanized area (one sq km). The natural landscape is intrinsically engaged with the topography of the site. Interventions within this area maintain and improve the existing conditions of the site by taking advantage of the topography and local climate. The components of this natural system are designed to support and complement the city's various needs that include:

- Recreation: fishing, picnic area, trails, and forest preserves
- Production: agriculture and fish farming
- Operations: utilities, energy generation, and water treatment

The buffer landscape includes the public areas outside of the city's urbanized area and is intrinsically engaged with the topography of the site to be devoted to recreation, wildlife habitat, and agriculture. Interventions within this area maintain and improve the existing conditions of the site by taking advantage of the topography and local climate.

Within the landscape, the forest/biomass component proposes a dense bamboo forest and other local species to provide a buffer for the city from surrounding communities and transit corridors and to produce biomass for energy production and construction materials. Farmlands are located between the bottom of the valleys and the top of the ridges and are fully integrated with other systems for irrigation and recreation. Sustainable and efficient vertical farming facilities within the city also offer modern agricultural solutions.

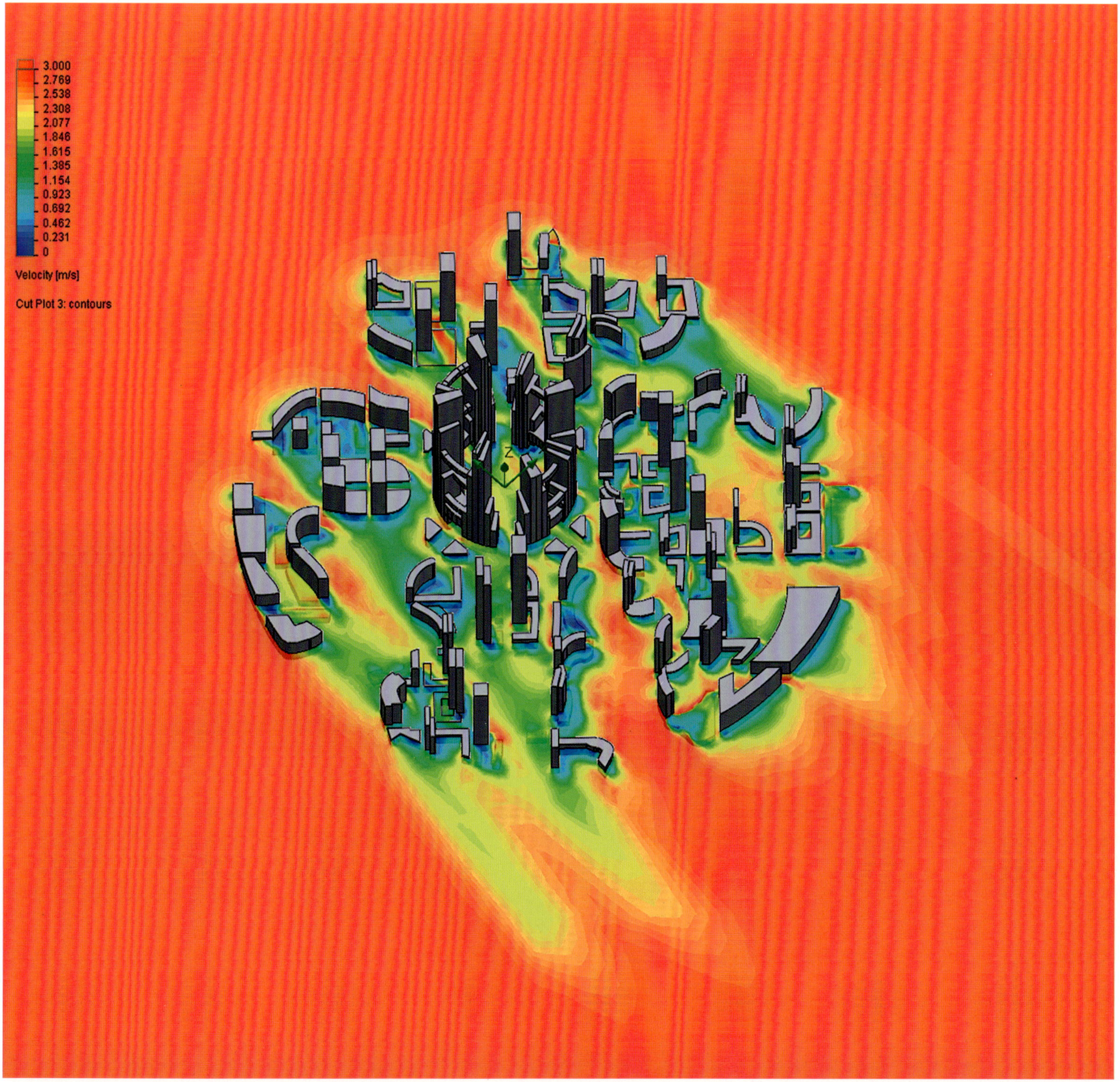
3.000
2.769
2.538
2.308
2.077
1.846
1.615
1.385
1.154
0.923
0.692
0.462
0.231
0
Velocity [m/s]
Cut Plot 3: contours

Xixian GREAT City

Xian, China

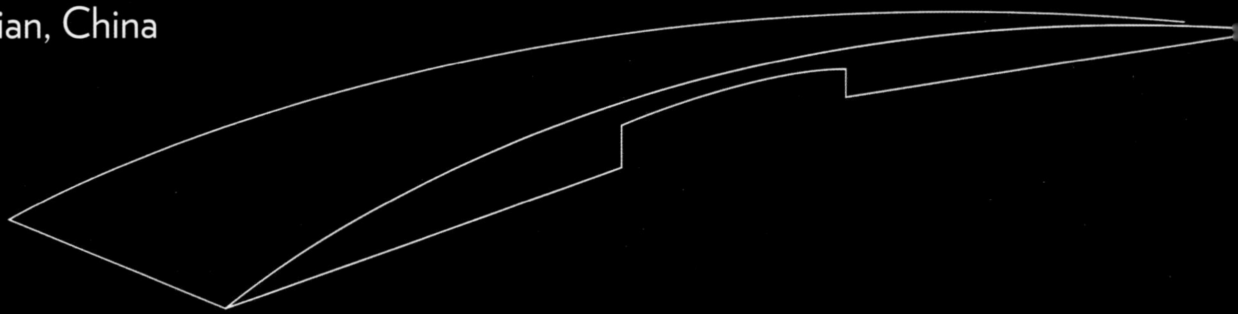

Xixian GREAT City

Xian, China

The master plan for Xixian Great City in Xian, China has an overall project area of 3,817,000 sm. Approximately 47 percent of the land is devoted to farmland conservation, 5 percent to wetland conservation and restoration, 10 percent to roads and infrastructure, and the remaining 38 percent dedicated to urbanized areas.

SERVICES
Architecture
Master Planning
Urban Design

CLIENT
Beijing Vantone Citylogic
Investment Corp.

FUNCTION
Mixed-use

FACTS
382 hectares

AWARDS
WAN Urban Design Award,
Future Projects, Finalist, 2014

The Chicago Athenaeum,
Green Good Design Award,
Green Urban Planning/
Landscape Architecture, 2014

The Chicago Athenaeum,
American Architecture Award,
Xixian Great City, 2013

Within this urbanized area, 56.3 percent of the land is devoted to development parcels, 20.9 percent to public green areas, and 22.8 percent to infrastructure and roads and is comprised of 96 parcels averaging 8,450 square meters. Four of these parcels are designated as district parks and another four are assigned to development that is currently under construction. The remaining 88 parcels are for the development of the Xixian Great City's buildings.

The plan proposes a perimeter building concept for the design of individual parcels, with above-grade parking screened from view by innovative architecture. The concept not only creates strong urban streets but also allows for multiple building configurations on each plot depending on the desired program. The perimeter concept can be applied on both high-density parcels and lower-density parcels, except on civic buildings, as it is desired that these be special buildings with unique architecture.

In the city center, a major "Green Bridge" is proposed over the existing train line. The cost of this significant infrastructure investment is offset by the higher density developments on adjacent parcels. Further, because this structure is elevated above the ground, these higher-density parcels use the space under the bridge for the required additional parking.

Perhaps the most important aspect of the master plan is the extensive sustainable framework that is comprehensively integrated into the physical planning of the city. Eight sustainable themes are presented in the plan, which covers all aspects of life in Xixian and includes Sustainable Economics, Sustainable Transportation, Climate and Energy, Sustainable Community, Ecology and Biodiversity, Waste and Water, Sustainable Agriculture, and Sustainable Construction. Contained in these eight themes are 30 specific sustainable goals for achieving a world-class level of environmental performance.

SITE PLAN

BUFFER AREA
FARM FIELDS
ECO PARK
EDGE PARK
DEVELOPMENT PARCEL
MANUFACTURING DISTRICT
DISTRICT PARK
SCHOOL
MEDICAL DISTRICT
WATER STREET
CITY CENTER
CENTRAL PARK
TRANSIT STA-TION
TUNNEL
EDGE PARK
TERRACOTTA STREET
DISTRICT PARK
SPORTS CENTER
STONE STREET
BRONZE STREET
EDGE PARK
WATER EDUCATION CENTER
WETLAND AREA

Tianfu New District

Chengdu, China

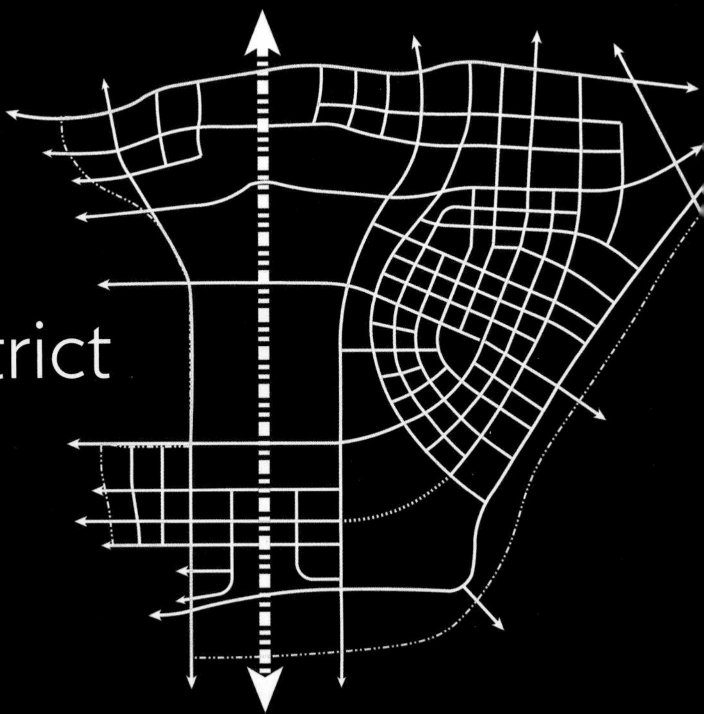

Tianfu New District

Chengdu, China

Tianfu New District is located approximately 30 kilometers south of Chengdu. The city layout considers the unique features in the landscape such as existing valleys, ridges, and slopes and reinterprets them as parks, plazas, pedestrian streets, and retail corridors.

SERVICES
Architecture
Master Planning
Urban Design

CLIENT
Beijing Vantone Citylogic Investment Corp.

FUNCTION
Mixed-use

AWARDS
The Chicago Athenaeum, Green Good Design Award, Green Urban Planning, 2015

The new city perpetuates the character and identity of the region by recreating local traditional design elements like narrow bamboo-lined roads and pedestrian-oriented walkways. The city includes commercial, residential, office, cultural, medical, among other functions typically found in a city.

The master plan concept proposes to integrate sustainable principles into the city through adopting an integrated approach toward meeting the overall objectives of environmental, economic and social sustainability. Several goals are met to achieve the master plan's sustainable vision including drastic carbon dioxide, waste, water-use, and energy use reductions compared to other cities of similar size; natural environment conservation; stormwater management; and public open spaces and transit.

The plan calls for the city to develop a clear roadway framework that is integrated with the natural systems; a network of functional urban spaces that connects to the public realm, to public transportation and infrastructure. It requires inclusion of parcel courtyards, pedestrian streets, and parks, as well as comprehensive green network, that connects the residents to the open space framework and allows them easy and convenient access to green areas and city services.

The proposed architectural design is characterized by sustainability measures such as wind conditions and daylight available. The master plan outlines the design for buildings with landscaped terraces, balconies and sky-gardens to bring outdoor space to each city resident. Buildings range from five-story "podium" buildings that define the public realm and create private courtyards and entry plazas, up to signature towers of over 300 meters. Most buildings will be less than 100 meters tall, or approximately 25 levels, and will be oriented to maximize daylight and ventilation.

Tianfu New District is currently under construction.

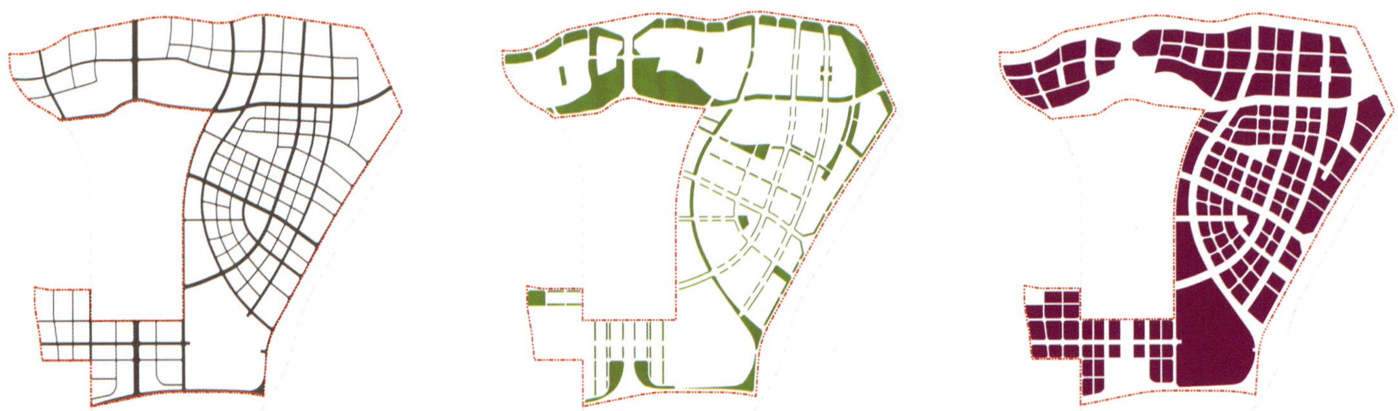

25%

ROAD AND INFRASTRUCTURE
2,380,133 m^2

37%

PUBLIC GREEN AREA
3,372,060 m^2

38%

DEVELOPMENT PARCEL AREA
3,550,965 m^2

TIANFU AVENUE
PARKWAY
CULTURAL DISTRICT
TIANFU PARK
ADMINISTRATIVE AXIS
CONVENTION CENTER
BOULEVARD
MULTIMODAL HUB
BUFFER ZONE
DISTRICT PARK
PRESERVATION AREA
MEDICAL DISTRICT
VANTONE PARK
VANTONE TOWER 300M
PEDESTRIAN ORIENTED STREET
RESIDENTIAL DISTRICT
MULTIMODAL HUB
SIGNATURE TOWER 400M+
CENTRAL DEVELOPMENT PARK
DISTRICT PARK
ICONIC TOWER 300M+
ENTERTAINMENT DISTRICT
EXHIBIT CENTER

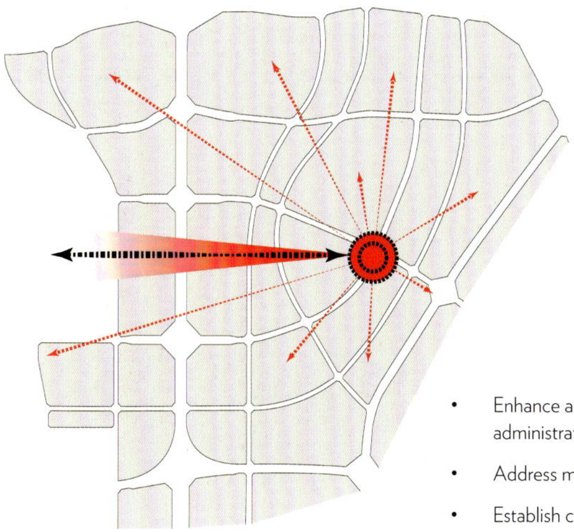

- Enhance axial relationship with administrative district
- Address main high density point
- Establish clear center

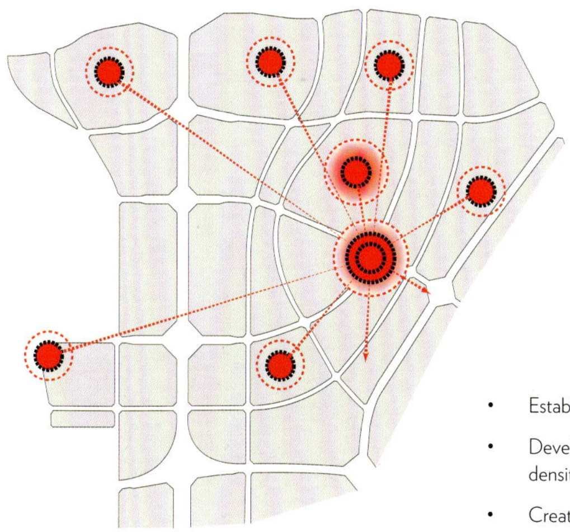

- Establish secondary density points
- Develop and connect this secondary density points around the city center
- Create formal balanced relationships among all the sub centers

- Integrate natural systems with planned road layouts and open space
- Generate a comprehensive network of a variety of open spaces that are interconnected
- Integrate urban open space with Tianfu park and buffer zones.

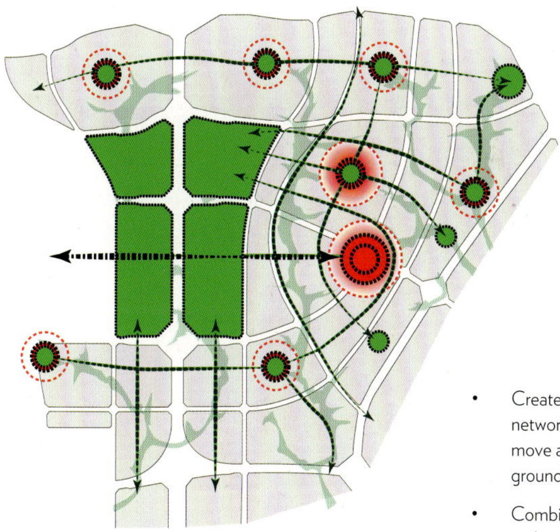

- Create a three-dimensional park network that allows pedestrians to move about the city not only at ground but at multiple levels
- Combine planned components and natural features into the built form that promote connectivity throughout the city
- Create a multilevel park that will become the focus of the CBD district as it receives the administrative district axis

Mumbai Master Plan

Mumbai, India

Mumbai Master Plan

Mumbai, India

The Mumbai Master Plan embodies AS+GG's sustainable design principles by incorporating climatically responsive passive design strategies in conjunction with active clean infrastructure systems to realize a hyper-efficient urban design solution.

SERVICES
Architecture
Master Planning

CLIENT
DB Realty Pvt Ltd.

FUNCTION
Mixed-use

FACTS
590 acres

The new master plan for the region of Mumbai known as Dharavi is dependent on symbiotic relationships between the commercial sector and the residential sector, sharing infrastructure, architectural design solutions, and social/economic dynamics.

Dharavi's rich cultural heritage as well as its robust economy are a direct result of its critical concentration of unique communities. The primary goal of redeveloping the tenement fabric of Dharavi is to reinforce these strong communal relationships through creative and efficient architectural solutions. A sensitive re-imagination of tenement housing results in an enhanced community, one whose infrastructural needs are satisfied and whose communal relationships are reinforced and celebrated. Although the redevelopment of Dharavi necessarily requires an architectural solution, the potential impacts of this redevelopment go far beyond the simple shelter these buildings will provide. For both tenement and commercial buildings, the architecture has been cast as an active participant in the long term economic and ecological health and prosperity of the site.

In addition to providing housing, the tenement architecture filters stormwater, generates food, and creates community space via an extensive network of interconnected rooftop gardens. The buildings enable groups of families to reside in close proximity to one another, thus supporting existing economic, social, religious, and political relationships within Dharavi's resident population.

Market rate office and retail space and commercial buildings also actively works to generate clean power and is responsively shaped to maximize the effectiveness of natural ventilation strategies throughout the site. The massing of the commercial building sectors is tuned to direct cool winds through neighboring residential sectors while preventing strong gusts via integral wind turbine systems that serve to generate power for the offices.

Residential buildings are designed to incorporate water harvesting green roofs that dually serve as urban farms, generating additional revenue and providing visual amenity for the development. Hidden from view is a complex distributed waste-to-power system that provides a substantial portion of the district's power and an enhanced aquifer recharge system. The buildings reinforce strategic relationships—both visually and physically—to adjacent commercial and tenement buildings. Furthermore, each building type responds specifically to its use, maximizing internal efficiencies to provide rich and humane environments for people to live and work.

COMMERCIAL
ICONIC TOWER
RESIDENTIAL LOWRISE
RESIDENTIAL HIGHRISE
EXISTING SRA

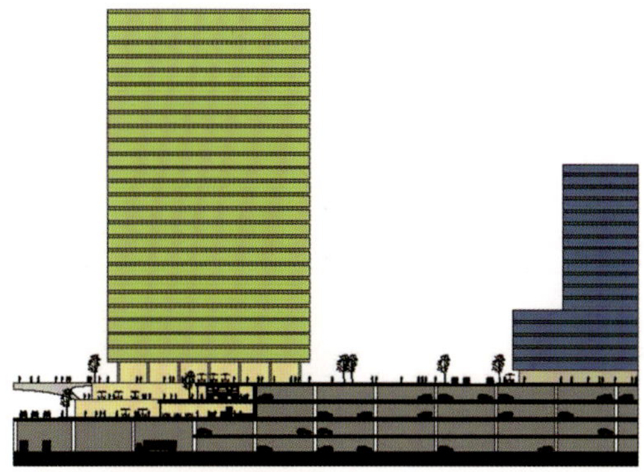

SCENARIO A

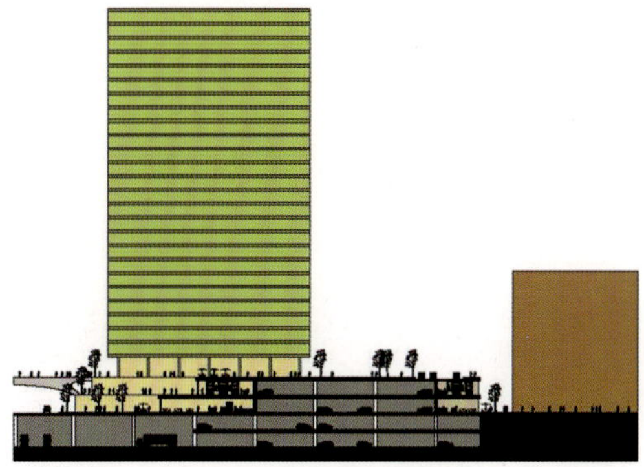

SCENARIO B

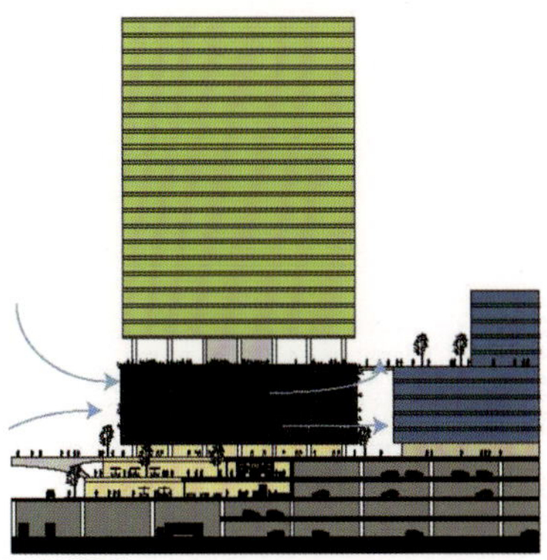

SCENARIO C1

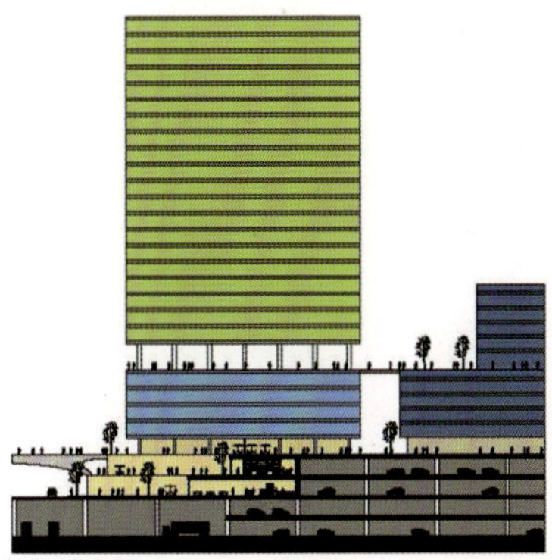

SCENARIO C2

SCENARIO D

PARKING · RETAIL · COMMERCIAL · RESIDENTIAL · EXISTING SRA · HIGHEND RETAIL · RESIDENTIAL PUBLIC

Za'abeel Energy City

Dubai, United Arab Emirates

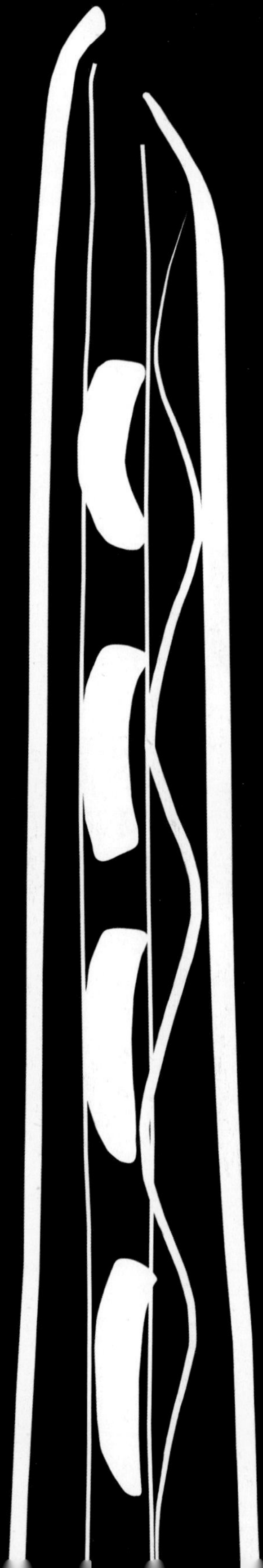

Za'abeel Master Plan

Dubai, United Arab Emirates

The Za'abeel Master Plan is uniquely positioned as a center for both commerce and residential development. The project is designed to embody modern sustainable living, working, and recreation in Dubai.

SERVICES
Architecture
Master Planning
Urban Design

CLIENT
Meraas Development

FUNCTION
Mixed-use

FACTS
4,496,728 sm
building area
918,242 sm
site area

AWARDS
Rethinking the Future, Global Architecture & Design Awards, First Award Commercial, Signature Tower One, 2019

With connections by rail to Jumeirah Gardens and convenient proximity to the Burj Khalifa and downtown, the project is a vibrant mixed-use center. The generative concept behind the Master Plan is the creation of memorable places that define sustainable districts and neighborhoods.

The Master Plan proposes the creation of a major new civic park space. All residents and workers have direct access to the commons through shaded pedestrian passageways. Multi-modal transportation access to the project and opportunities for pedestrian and bicycle use within the development provide all users with a diverse experience . Due to its proximity to transit, the master plan has the opportunity to become a self-contained, mixed-use environment that achieves Dubai's first LEED platinum rating for community design.

Office and hotel functions add interest along the main boulevard and throughout the development, effectively reinforcing this new business center and connection to convention and hospitality functions. Private, luxury residential lofts define the perimeter of the project, providing a unique and intimate living experience.

In addition to creating memorable urban places, the master plan utilizes Islamic patterns and design traditions, reinterpreted for modern materials and lifestyles, to create variation and uniqueness in building designs and landscapes. These patterns—drawn from Islamic textiles, architectural ornament, and traditional village forms—add texture and scale to the project.

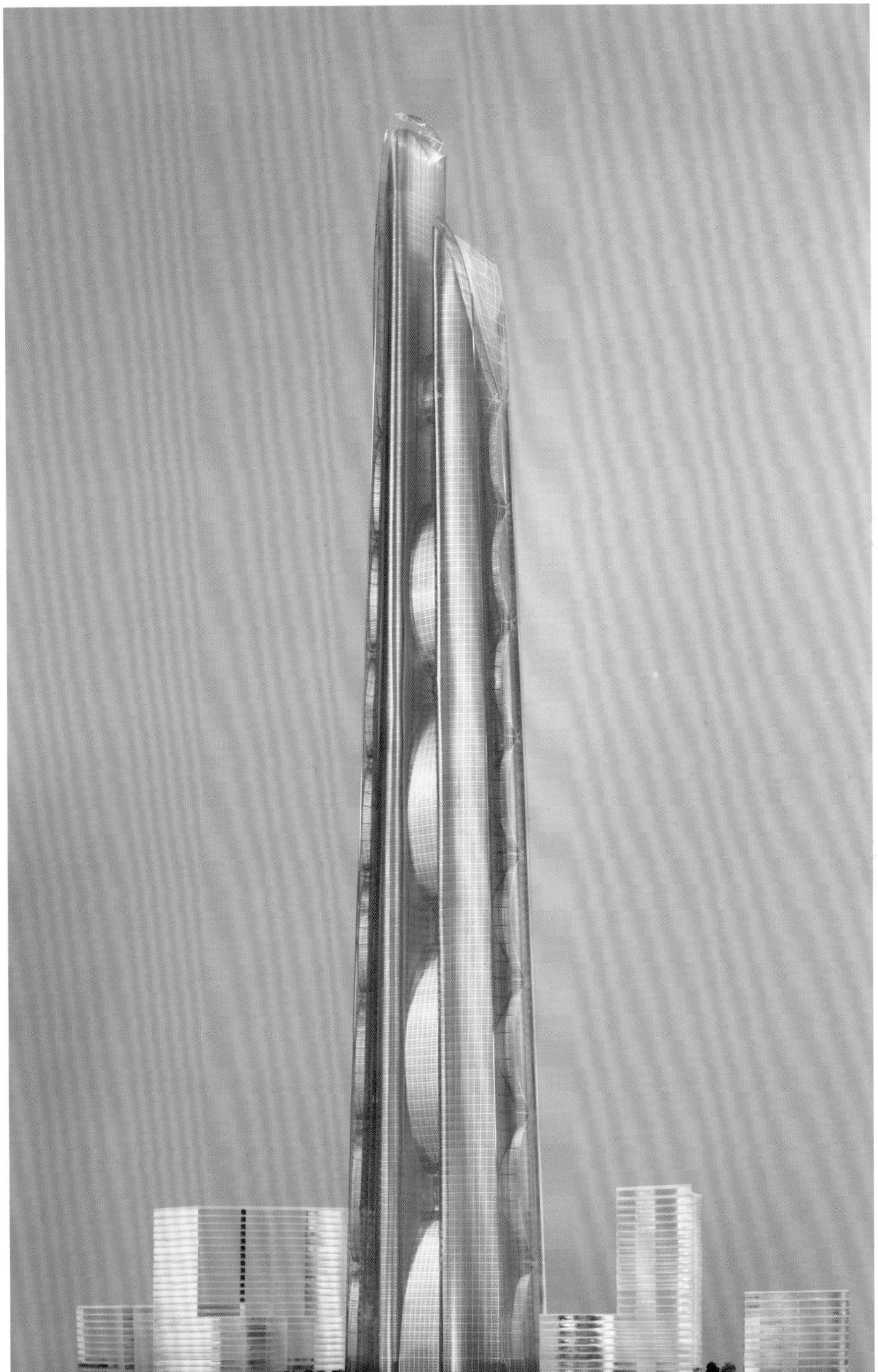

EFFICIENT COOLING SYSTEM:

- Balance demand from commercial and residential users.
- Combined heat and power plant can achieve up to 94% efficiency.
- Increased performance building envelope: design to high-energy efficiency standard.

CO2 EMISSIONS CONTROL:

- Minimize CO2 emissions by using high-performance building design, tri-generation central utility plant, on-site renewable energy systems and potable water conservation.

WATER EFFICIENCY:

- Minimize water consumption; maximize use of reclaimed water for irrigation.
- Graywater use; rain water can penetrate and recharge ground water.
- Reduces volume of storm water run-off and discharge of pollutants.

MAXIMIZE USE OF RENEWABLE ENERGY:

- Wind Turbines
- Photovoltaic Panels
- Thermal Solar Collections
- Fuel Cells/Hydrogen Power

INDOOR ENVIRONMENTAL QUALITY:

- Maximize natural ventilation and daylighting.

ENCOURAGE ALTERNATIVE TRANSPORTATION:

- Maximize uses of existing transit systems
- (RTA + Dubai Metro)
- TRAM / PRT Systems
- PHEV + Premium Charging Services
- Energy Station

HIGH - PERFORMANCE DESIGN ELEMENTS:

- Multi-functional louver
- Photovoltaic Panel at Facade
- Green Roof

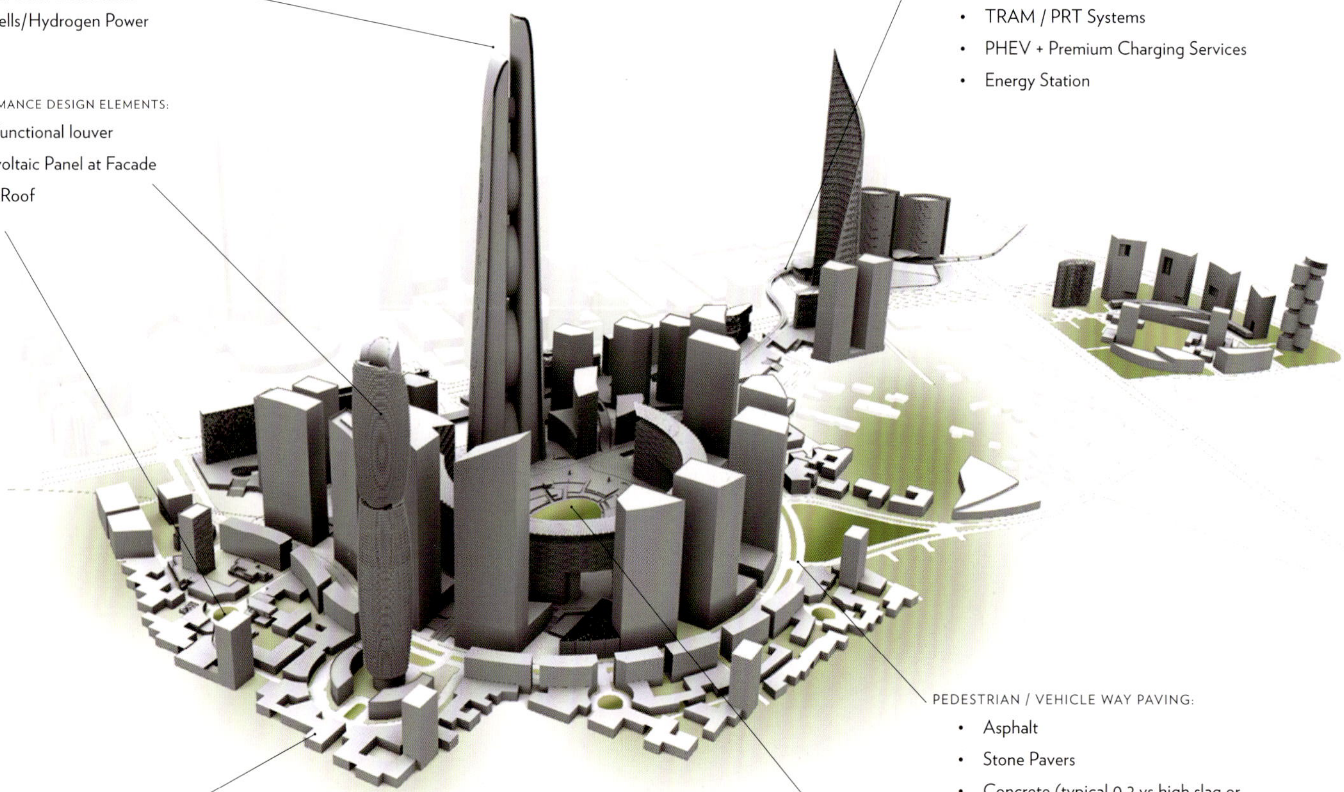

PEDESTRIAN / VEHICLE WAY PAVING:

- Asphalt
- Stone Pavers
- Concrete (typical 0.2 vs high slag or pervious 0.6)
- 7 Lanes Paved vs. 4 Lanes Paved with trees or 4 Lanes Narrowed

WASTE MANAGEMENT:

- Automated Waste Collection System
- Waste-to-Energy Plant

REDUCE HEAT ISLAND EFFECT:

- Maximize the quality and quantity of landscaping.
- Install high-efficiency canopy.
- Offer green spaces.

ENERGY + ATMOSPHERE

Innovative, efficient strategies will decrease energy use and reduce carbon emissions.

WATER

Water will be protected as a valuable resource through intensive conservation and reuse cycles on-site.

CODE COMPLIANT DESIGN

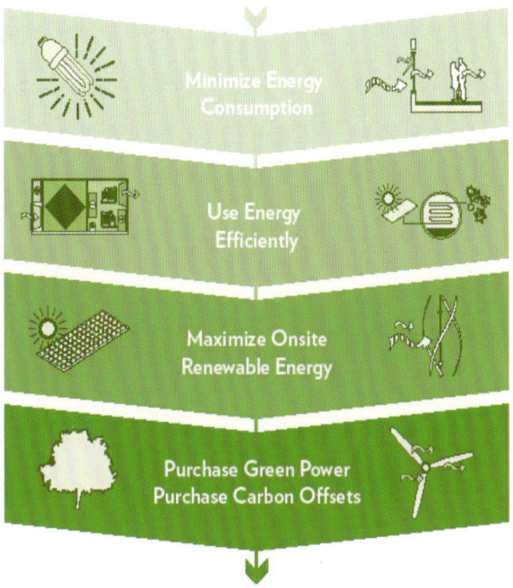

CARBON ZERO

INDOOR ENVIRONMENT

Building occupants will experience healthy, high quality indoor environments that will increase occupant satisfaction and productivity.

CONSTRUCTION PROCESS + MATERIALS

Sustainable material choices and construction practices will reduce the environmental impact of the development on a local and global scale.

CLIMATE RESPONSIVE DESIGN

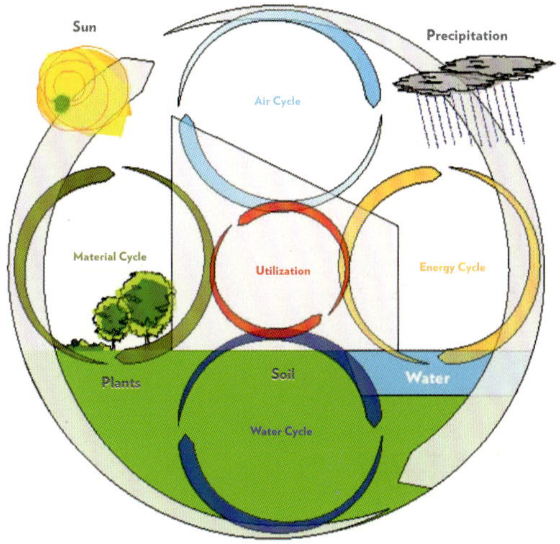

LANDSCAPE + OUTDOOR ENVIRONMENT

Beautiful parks and streetscapes will reduce the urban heat island effect and create comfortable outdoor microclimates.

SHADING DIAGRAM

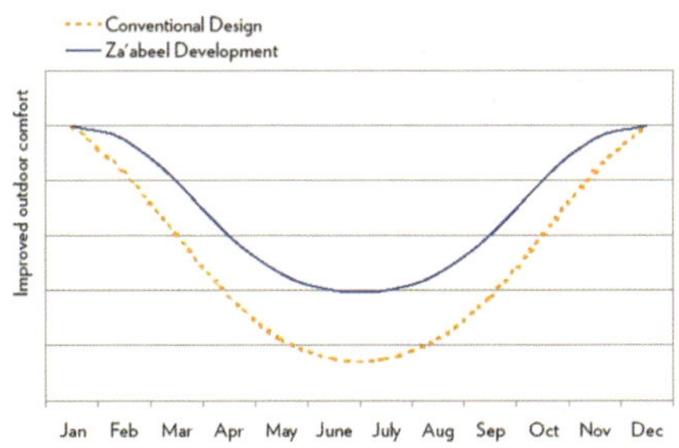

BENCHMARKING + IMPLEMENTATION

Benchmarking with LEED will ensure that the project exceeds current sustainable design standards.

BENCHMARKING

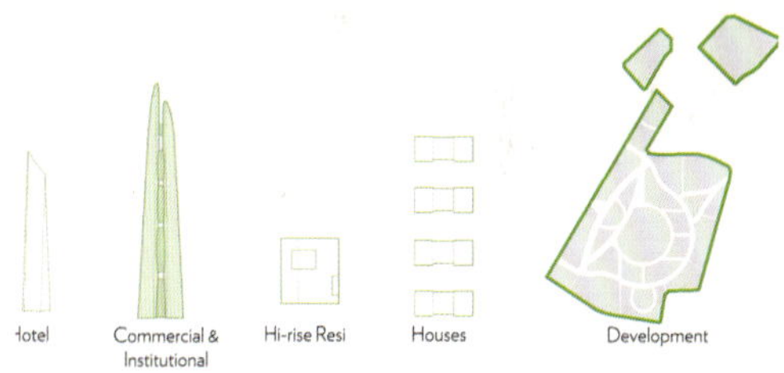

ACCESS + TRANSPORTATION

EFFICIENT TRANSPORTATION

Infrastructure will enable low-carbon and zero-carbon movement throughout the site and encourage pedestrian activity.

WALKING DISTANCE GUIDELINES

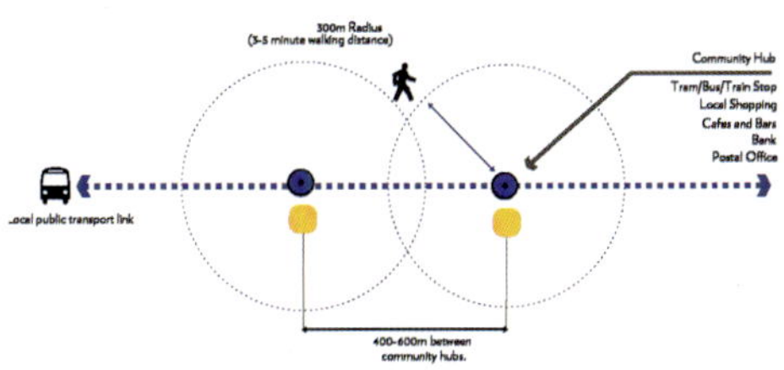

FUTURE OPERATIONS

Continued monitoring and assessment will ensure the ongoing sustainable operation of the buildings and infrastructure within the development.

WASTE REDUCTION STRATEGIES

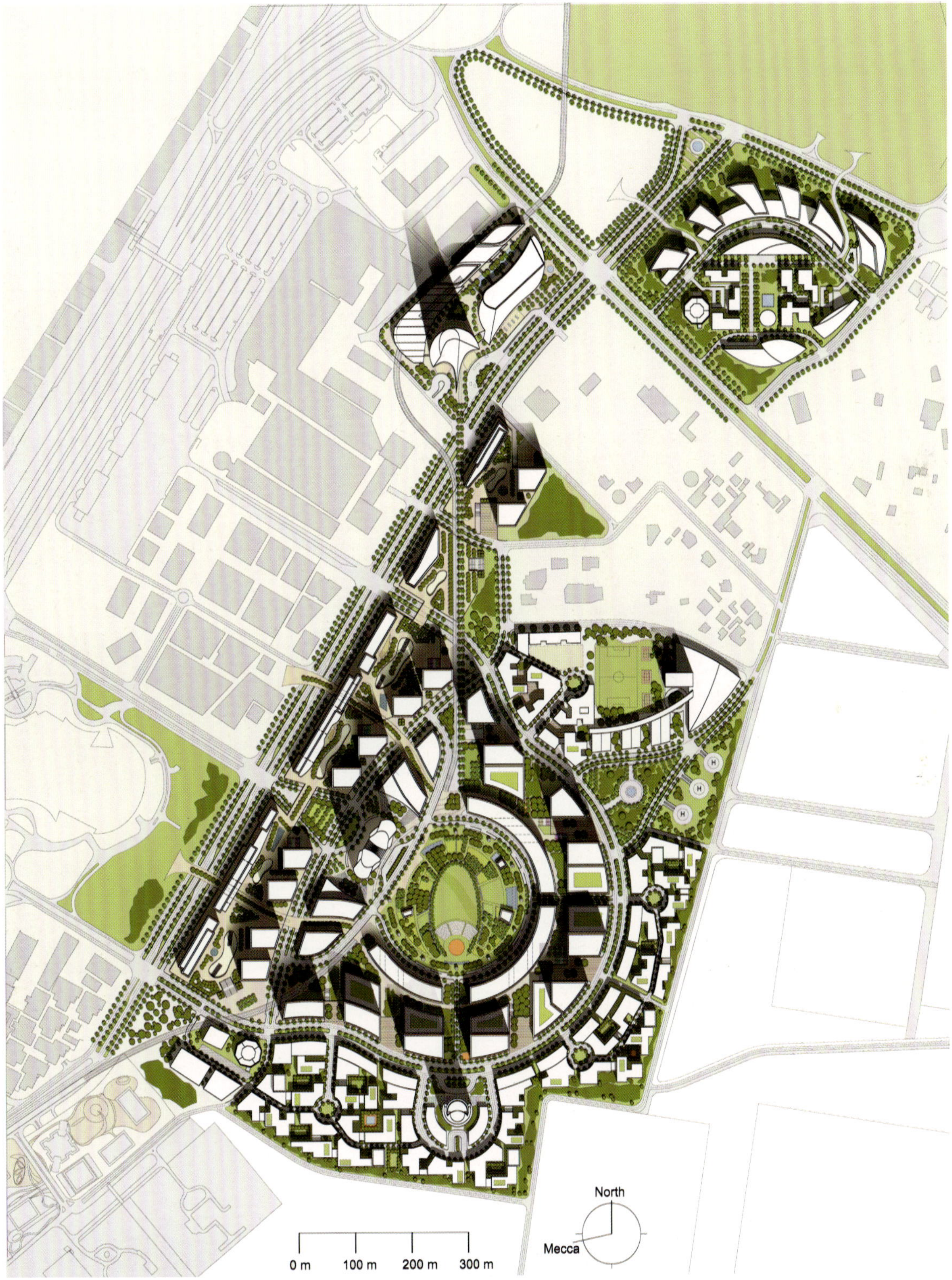
North
Mecca
0 m
100 m
200 m
300 m

Decarb Plan

Chicago, Illinois

Chicago DeCarb Plan

Chicago, Illinois

The Chicago Central Area DeCarbonization Plan aims to reduce the environmental impact and carbon emissions of the downtown and improve the overall quality of life of the city's urban environment.

SERVICES
Master Planning
Urban Design

CLIENT
City of Chicago

FUNCTION
Mixed-use

FACTS
460 acres

AWARDS
Illinois AIA, Daniel Burnham Honor Award, 2013

Chicago AIA, Design Excellence, SustainABILITY Award, 2012

American Architecture Foundation, Sustainable Cities Design Academy Award, 2012

National AIA, Honor Award, Regional and Urban Design, 2011

The Chicago Athenaeum, American Architecture Award, 2011

R+D Award for Sustainability, Architect Magazine, 2010

WAN Awards, Urban Design, Winner, 2010

While the study examines the carbon sources characteristics of the urban condition, the goal is not simply to reach a reduction number that is calculated from an applied set of assumptions. The plan is a beginning process for maintaining the economic and cultural vitality of the downtown urban core, from an energy and carbon perspective. The continued viability of cities and urban living is a core principle in the long-term idea that population growth can continue without its negative impact to the environment becoming detrimental to the planet in the form of global warming.

It is therefore critical that our cities are not only decarbonized, but also continue to develop as great places where people can live happy, healthy lifestyles with a minimized environmental footprint. The DeCarbonization Plan proposes a variety of methods for reducing carbon including aggressive upgrades of the existing building stock and urban fabric.

There are, on the surface, simpler ways to reduce carbon. A wind farm or large scale photovoltaic array can power hundreds of buildings. A single nuclear plant can power an entire region. Why, then, is there a need for a decarbonization plan for a city? If it were a simple matter of replacing greenhouse gas emitting fossil plants with renewable energy resources, urban decarbonization may not be necessary. However, if no urban decarbonization happens and the energy issue is simply solved by the creation of more power plants, many opportunities for the improvement of the urban environment and of social issues are lost, and cities like Chicago may decay over time.

These social issues, which are solved by decarbonization, include all the complexities of carbon production that is bound up in the city. For example, an aging building stock currently consumes much more energy than is necessary, and needs to be upgraded not only for its emissions but for its future economic viability. Commuters currently drive from the suburbs to the city on infrastructure that is costly to maintain, and over-crowded. Stormwater currently pours off of hard surfaces into the water treatment system where it could be recovered, and unshaded surfaces in the city allows high temperatures to occur in a localized area.

The Chicago Central Area DeCarbonization Plan seeks to go beyond the technological fix and advance Chicago's global leadership position not only as a green city but also as a continuing model of architectural and urban innovation.

In addition to buildings, the plan analyzes seven further areas of carbon production and reduction relevant to the urban condition using a parametric model as an analysis tool.

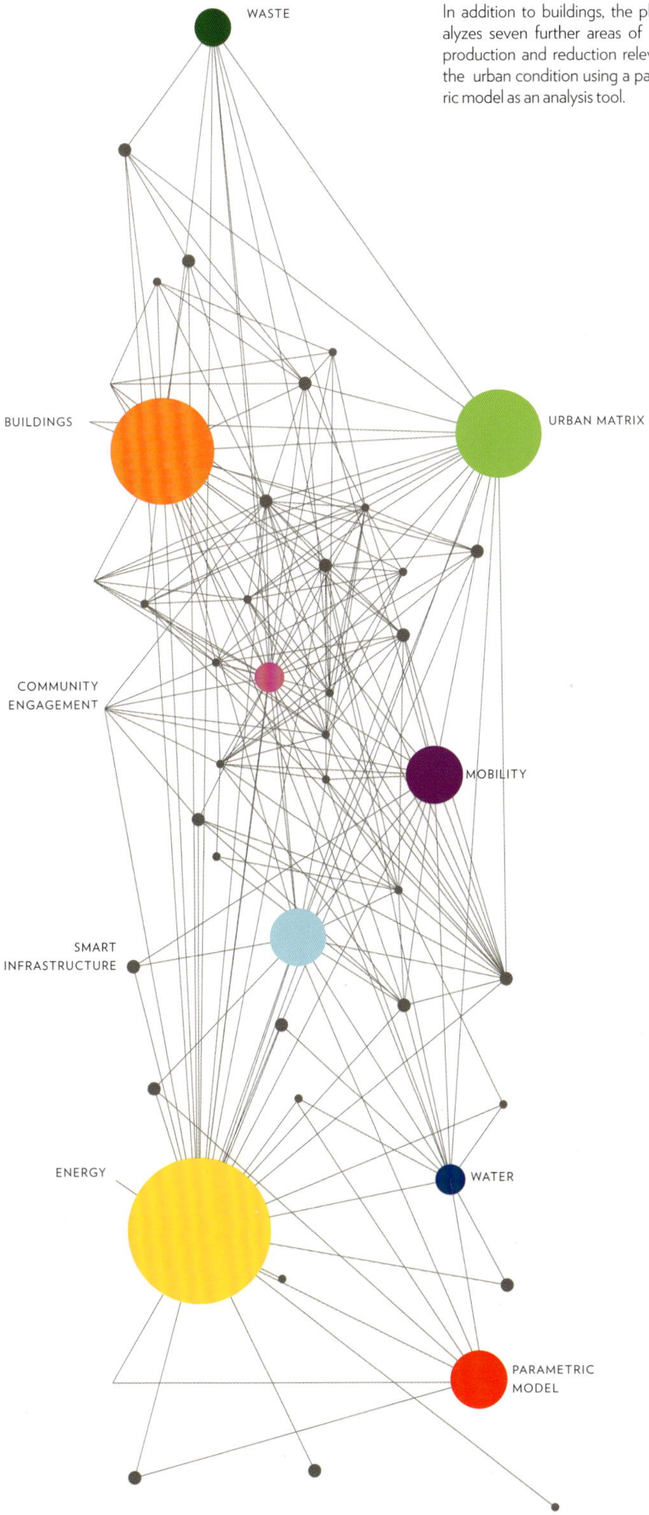

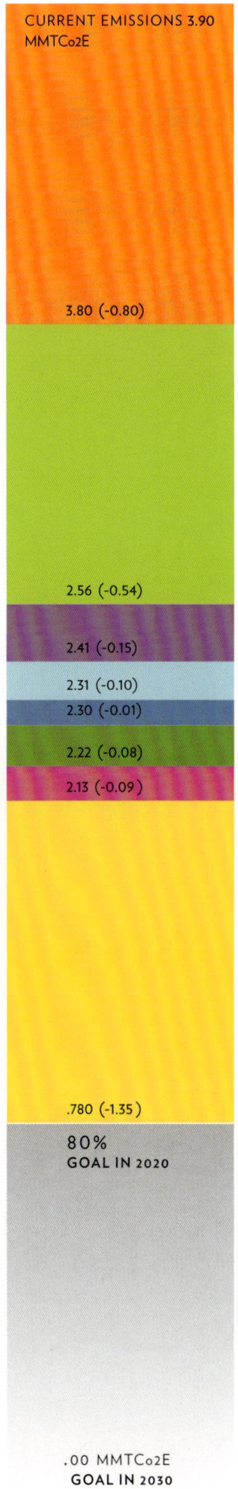

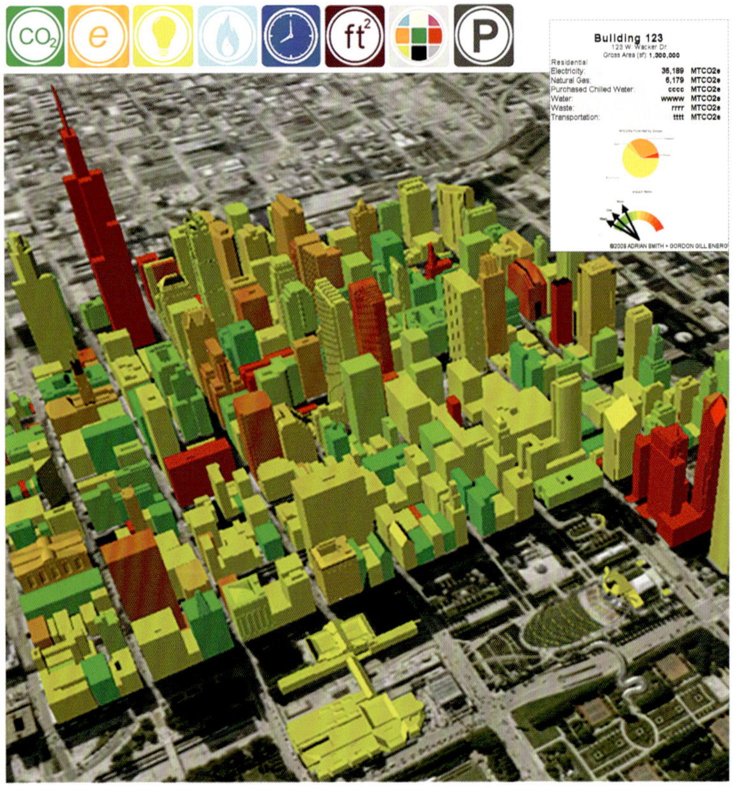

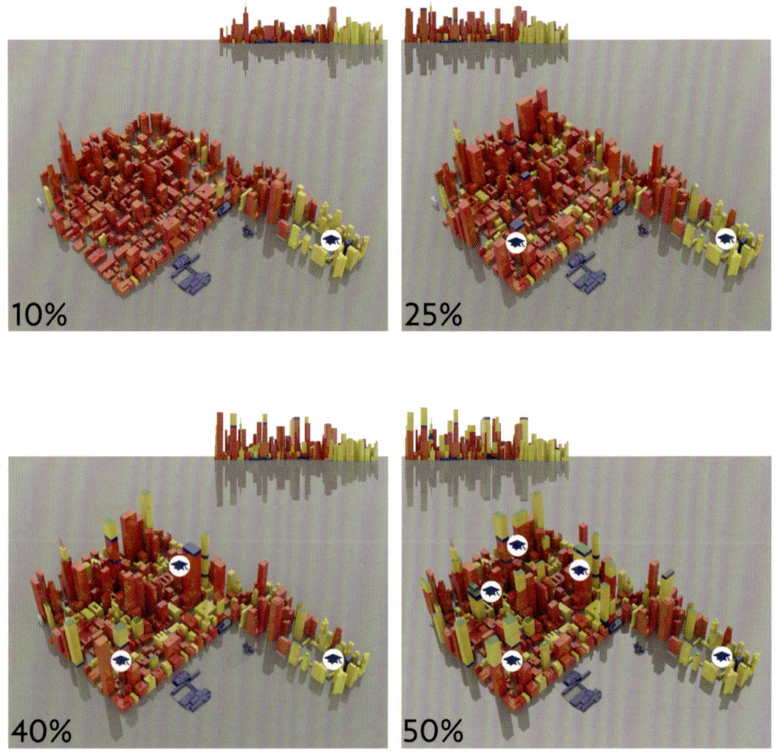

The Data Model is a tool that AS+GG developed to be able to visualize building energy consumption and emissions at a citywide scale. It was developed with the intention of monitoring and communicating all aspects of city buildings that relate to their carbon impact, current and future.

This serves a number of purposes: a method of analysis to inform energy oriented planning decisions including cost data, an advertising platform for companies making efficiency upgrades to their buildings, an educational tool, and a forum to raise awareness about the carbon impact of the built environment and the effectiveness and cost of strategies in place to improve this.

The current occupancy breakdown in the study area is approximately 90 percent commercial and 10 percent residential. This amount of residential area, in addition to the amenities necessary to support that population, such as schools and grocers, falls short of the area that would be needed for even half of the daytime work population.

If the occupancy ratio in the Loop intensified to 50/50 commercial/residential the mix would result in one of the world's most efficient and sustainable live-work communities, creating a new paradigm for cities across the globe.

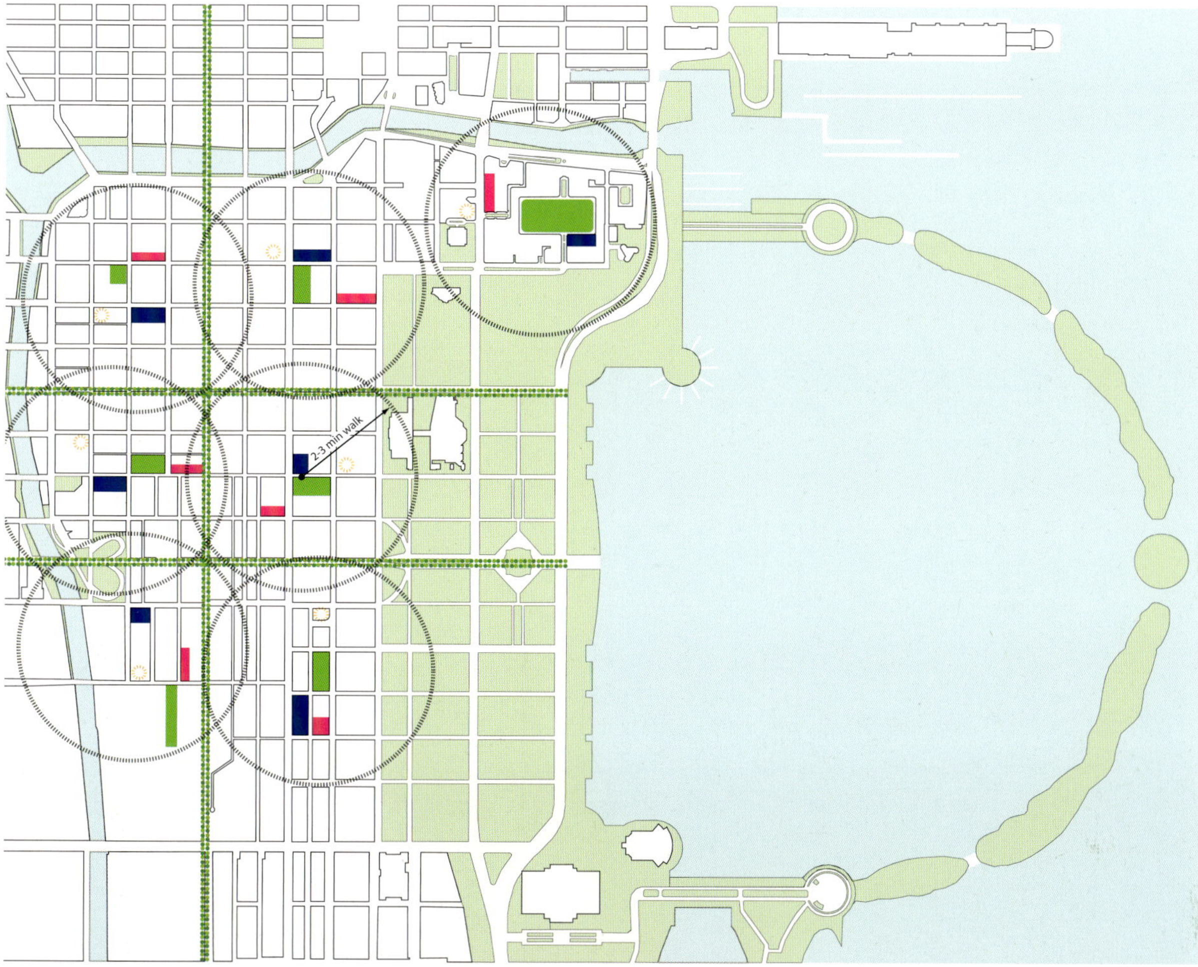

SCHOOLS + DAYCARE CENTERS

DALEY ENVIRONMENTAL SCHOOL

AMENITIES + SERVICES

INTER-MODAL GREENAXIS

URBAN GREEN SPACE

CHICAGO ECO-BRIDGE

The increase in residential real estate in downtown Chicago would lower the area's overall carbon footprint by creating a dense, mixed-use community. Adding significant residential space increases the area's need for amenities that the Loop currently lacks to support residential life: K-12 schools, daycare systems, and grocery stores. The creation of a vibrant urban community relies on the quality of amenities, and the incorporation of these important amenities is a critical step in the Loop's transformation into Chicago's next premier neighborhood for families.

In response to the analysis of the existing transportation options and proposed items in the Chicago Central Area Plan, a series of design strategies evolved as a means to integrate them into a coherent, functional and thriving urban system.

A multi-level East-West Intermodal Axis is created along Monroe Street for a below-grade electric bus route to transport commuters across the Loop. This link also connects to the upgraded underground pedway system with improved retail and amenities.

At grade, Monroe is narrowed to two lanes to allow for a more pedestrian- and bike-friendly experience. The Monroe Street corridor has the potential to be a convenient link for transit and pedestrians, and for retail to thrive. Its central location in the Loop makes it a hub for commuters.

There are currently breaks in the pedway system that can be connected to make one continuous below-grade system. Below grade Monroe East-West Intermodal provides a covered space during inclement weather. This space can be programed to incorporate amenities and services such as schools, shopping, gyms, entertainment, bicycle station, library, spas, grocery stores and restaurants.

Considering the extreme Chicago weather conditions, there is potential for building owners to capitalize on their connection to a thriving pedway system that will encourage potential retail and services to serve increased inhabitants of the Loop. A connection to the proposed East-West Monroe link could aid in optimizing this pedway system. There are locations where the below grade portion erodes and connects with above-grade streetscape. This occurs at open plaza areas such as Chase Plaza. There are also interconnections up and down to the shuttle bus stops.

The green axis is the main spine that links a series of smaller green plazas that support the inhabitants during the day and evening hours. The green connections would improve transportation, livability, reduce heat island effect, reduce storm water treatment requirements, increase air quality and improve amenities.

A superior education system is vital to the evolution and success of the mixed use city. These facilities must be state of the art with advanced programs and a diverse curriculum. Issues in sustainability such as ecology, genomics, biodiversity, and agro-forestry should be introduced to students early in their development. With a diverse student body and holistic approach to early development, institutions like the Daley Environmental School will become the archetype for the Chicago Public Schools.

Burnham's Plan of Chicago was introduced in 1909. The plan developed as a reaction to the effects industrialization of the modern world were having on the quality of the city's inhabitants. Plan commissioner Wacker developed a textbook which taught the major aspects of the Plan to a generation of Chicago schoolchildren. The vision of "The Green City" manual follows in that honorable tradition as a primer of Chicago's vision for a carbon-free future, and should be taught as part of the curriculum at Chicago public schools.

The proposed Chicago Eco-Bridge would complete the last major recommendation of the 1909 Burnham Plan of Chicago in a thoroughly modern way that celebrates the city's future as well as its past. The two-mile bridge, a breakwater in the Monroe Harbor, celebrates Chicago's position as the greenest city in the United States.

The bridge creates a grand new civic space providing educational and recreational opportunities and unparalleled views of the skyline from a central observation tower. This new outdoor space encourages environmental stewardship within its patrons by incorporating a Great lakes Learning Center, Marina Habitat Observatory and other outdoor amenities that celebrate the environment.

Leadership

Adrian Smith FAIA, RIBA, HON D.LITT

Partner

EDUCATION

University of Illinois at Chicago, Bachelor of Architecture, 1969

Texas A & M University, School of Architecture, 1962-66

SELECT PROFESSIONAL REGISTRATIONS + AFFILIATIONS

Licensed architect in IL, FL, MA, NY

American Institute of Architects, Fellow (FAIA)

Ontario Association of Architects (OAA)

Architectural Institute of British Columbia (AIBC)

Registered Architect in the United Kingdom (RIBA)

Royal Institute of British Architects 1973-present

National Council of Architectural Registration Boards (NCARB)

Adrian Smith, FAIA, is an Architect of international renown, having designed many landmark buildings including the two world's tallest structures—Burj Khalifa completed in 2010 in Dubai, and Kingdom Tower, now under construction in Jeddah, Saudi Arabia.

In 2006, he founded Adrian Smith + Gordon Gill Architecture (AS+GG), a firm dedicated to the design of high-performance, energy-efficient and sustainable architecture on an international scale. In 2008, he co-founded the MEP firm of PositivEnergy Practice, which specializes in the environmental engineering of high-performance, energy-efficient architecture. Before he started AS+GG, he was a Design Partner in the Chicago office of Skidmore, Owings & Merrill from 1980 to 2003 and a Consulting Design Partner from 2003 to 2006.

His work has shown an evolving interest in the use of vernacular and indigenous forms and compositions together with state-of-the-art systems and technologies to integrate new buildings Into the regional context. His designs are sensitive to each project's physical environment, taking into consideration conditions such as location, climate, geographical, geological, cultural, and social influences to achieve environmental sustainability.

Over the last several years his work has embraced the principle of "On Site" power generation using the building's design to harvest power from the sun, wind, and geothermal conditions to reduce the buildings reliance on the local infrastructure. In many instances, this has had a dramatic impact on the expression of the architecture and has added an important influence to his philosophy of Global Contextualism.

Throughout his career, Adrian has played an active role in international projects and developments. From 1971 to 1973 he was the resident project architect for the Wills Hartcliffe project near Bristol, England. In 1989, he was selected to participate in the IV Hamburg Bauforum, to lead a team exploring alternative visions for the Speicherstadt district in Hamburg, Germany. In 1990 he participated in a team of 40 international architects and planners in the Zentrum: Berlin symposium, at the Bauhaus in Dessau, to discuss the challenges for the reunification of Berlin. He has also designed buildings in Bahrain, Brazil, China, Dubai, Saudi Arabia, Canada, England, Germany, Guatemala, Indonesia, Korea, Kuwait, Mexico, the United States (Chicago, Boston, Des Moines, St. Louis, Minneapolis, Washington DC, Orlando, and New York City).

National positions include Lifetime Governor of the Urban Land Institute Foundation and member of the Urban Land Institute (1986 to present). He has served on numerous professional juries and committees, including the Chicago Chapter AIA Fellows Committee and the National AIA Large Firm Roundtable. He was Chairman of the National AIA Jury on Institute Honors (1987); the Progressive Architecture Awards Design Jury (1988); the Jury Chairman of the Central States Region AIA Awards Program (1994); the 2000 Advisory Panel to the AIA Board of Directors for the Firm Award and Gold Medal Award recipients 2000); and Chairman of the AIA National Honor Awards for Architecture (2004).

He was keynote speaker at the Council on Tall Buildings and Urban Habitat (CTBUH) Fifth World Congress (1995); CTBUH World Congress Dubai (2009); CTBUH World Congress Chicago (2011); CTBUH World Congress Shanghai (2012); the ABN Amro symposium (1990); the Quaternario conference in Singapore (1991); and has lectured in Amsterdam, London, Buenos Aires, Prague, Frankfurt, Seoul, Shanghai, Hong Kong, Washington DC, Notre Dame, Chicago, New York, and other locations.

He was a Trustee of the Building Experiences Trust Limited, a British organization devoted to furthering architectural education curricula from 1995 to 1998; the Royal Institute of

British Architects British Architectural Library Trust Representative for the British Schools and Universities Foundation from 1994 to present; and has appeared in several documentaries including the BBC *World Service's* film, Chicago Architecture, several episodes of *Chicago Tonight*; and the first two parts of the *Skyline: Chicago* film series. Adrian has been a registered architect in twelve states, the District of Columbia, the United Kingdom, Canada, and the National Council of Architectural Registration Boards, and is also an active member of the College of Fellows of the AIA, the Royal Institute of British Architects, the Ontario Association of Architects and The Architectural Institute of British Columbia.

During his tenure as Design Partner, projects under his leadership and direction have received more than 125 design awards including five international awards, nine National AIA awards, 45 state and Chicago AIA awards and three ULI Awards for Excellence (1989, 2005, 2008); and several Progressive Architecture Design Awards. His work has been exhibited at public museums in Chicago, Europe, South America, and Asia and ten of his projects are in the permanent collection of the Art Institute of Chicago.

Awards, Honors + Important Roles

Marshall Bennett Institute, Lifetime Industry Leadership Award, Adrian Smith, 2018

Honorary Doctorate of Letters Degree, Texas A&M University, 2013

Texas A&M University School of Architecture, Outstanding Alumni Award, 2012

Council on Tall Buildings and Urban Habitat, Lynn S. Beedle Lifetime Achievement Award, 2011

Lake Forest-Lake Bluff Historical Society, Local Legend Award, Adrian Smith, 2011

Texas A&M University, Distinguished Alumni Award, 2011

The Design Futures Council, Senior Fellow, Washington, DC, 2008

University of Illinois at Chicago, Alumni Achievement Award, 1995

Major Projects Throughout Career

UPTOWN TOWER
190,000 sm 72-story mixed-use tower includes office, residential, and hotel functions. The retail podium includes spaces for vehicle parking, MEP rooms, back of house spaces, a ballroom, and conference rooms, as well as separate entrances for the tower's functions. Dubai, United Arab Emirates (AS+GG)

AL WASL PLAZA
Centerpiece for the 4.38-square-kilometer Expo2020 Dubai combines breathtaking design, innovative technology, and a 150-meter diameter domed trellis that incorporates an immersive projection experience. Dubai, United Arab Emirates (AS+GG)

CENTRAL PARK TOWER
Residential tower includes a program with prominent a retail tenant and amenities. New York, New York (AS+GG)

WUHAN GREENLAND CENTER
119-story, 300,000 sm, 606-meter tall, mixed-use tower features 50 office floors, 17 residential floors and 22 hotel floors. Wuhan, China (AS+GG)

GREENLAND TOWER CHENGDU
468-meter-tall, mixed-use tower features a conference center, offices, a hotel, executive residential apartments, and rooftop garden. Chengdu, China (AS+GG)

JEDDAH TOWER
The world's next tallest building features a luxury hotel, office space, serviced apartments, luxury condominiums, and the world's highest observatory. Jeddah, Saudi Arabia (AS+GG)

BURJ KHALIFA
Supertall mixed-use tower comprising residential, commercial, hotel, and retail spaces. Dubai, United Arab Emirates (SOM)

160 FRONT STREET
Office tower in the heart of Toronto's business district features 360-degree views of the city. Designed to meet LEED Platinum certification. Toronto, Ontario (AS+GG)

Adrian Smith FAIA, RIBA, HON D.LITT
Partner

UNA RESIDENCES
47-story luxury residential tower, currently under design, to be located directly on Biscayne Bay. The design takes full advantage of this rare waterfront site and will leverage the features that bring people to Miami, namely expansive views, access to sun, and an indoor-outdoor lifestyle. The 146-residence luxury building recently launched sales. Miami, Florida (AS+GG)

830 BRICKELL
The first new office tower to launch in Miami in nearly a decade. The soaring 57-story, 724-foot-tall tower introduces a premium commercial to the city's booming financial district and seeks to reinvent the workplace lifestyle for the highest-caliber of global workforce. Miami, Florida (AS+GG)

WILLOW CREEK COMMUNITY CHURCH
72,000 sf community church, designed to use natural light and to bring the experience of the surrounding landscape indoors. The new building will feature a center auditorium space, which will act as an anchor for the offices, classrooms, and café spaces, connected by a large circulation area. Glenview, Illinois (AS+GG)

KAZAKHSTAN PAVILION + SCIENCE MUSEUM (NUR ALEM)
Inspired by the EXPO-2017 theme, "Future Energy," this science museum and exhibition pavilion embodies a futuristic design that is optimized to incorporate sustainable philosophies. The building's innovative, double-curved-glass facade features glass panels that gently curve in three dimensions. Building Integrated Photo Voltaic cells (BIPV) installed at the top of the sphere generate renewable energy for the building. Astana, Kazakhstan (AS+GG)

ASTANA EXPO CITY 2017
Master planning and architecture for 174-hectare international exposition site features exhibition and cultural pavilions (118,620 sm); a residential development (686,000 sm); service areas including shopping, socio-cultural, educational and civic facilities; and site-wide parks (72,000 sm). Astana, Kazakhstan (AS+GG)

FKI TOWER
50-story, 240-meter tower features unique exterior wall that features energy-collecting building integrated photovoltaic panels in spandrel areas of the southwest and northwest facades. Seoul, Korea (AS+GG)

BURJ VISTA
Luxury two-tower residential complex with outdoor plaza, a theater and unobstructed views of Burj Khalifa. Dubai, United Arab Emirates (AS+GG)

WALDORF ASTORIA BEIJING
Luxury hotel project located in the heart of downtown Beijing, China. Bronze exterior reflects the character of the site, and the super frame recalls the symmetry and steady character of Chinese traditional architecture. Beijing, China (AS+GG)

ZIFENG TOWER (NANJING GREENLAND FINANCIAL CENTER)
Architectural design for 325,000 sm mixed-use supertall building including office, hotel service apartments, and commercial functions. Nanjing, China (SOM)

TRUMP INTERNATIONAL HOTEL AND TOWER
223,000 sm, 94-story mixed-use tower comprised of luxury residential, hotel, health club, retail, parking, and riverfront park on prominent site along the Chicago River. Chicago, Illinois (SOM)

JIN MAO TOWER
88-story, 279,000 sm multi-use complex including office, hotel, and retail. Shanghai, China (SOM)

PEARL RIVER TOWER
69-story China National Tobacco Corporation headquarters. 303-meter tower designed to harvest wind and solar energy. Every aspect of the 303-meter tower is designed to harvest wind and solar energy. Guangzhou, China (SOM)

TOWER PALACE
73-story, 850,000 sm residential tower for the Samsung Group. Seoul, Korea (SOM)

MASDAR HQ DEVELOPMENT

Architectural design for positive-energy building in zero-carbon, zero-waste city. Program included office, retail, transit, and landscaped green space. Abu Dhabi, United Arab Emirates (AS+GG)

GREAT CITY CHENGDU

One-square-kilometer development will investigate the relationship between high-density urban living and sustainable development. Will accommodate a population of 100,000 people. Chengdu, China (AS+GG)

CHICAGO DECARBONIZATION PLAN

Commission from the City of Chicago that assesses and looks at innovative solutions for the carbon performance of the downtown area Loop using a holistic urban design approach. Chicago, Illinois (AS+GG)

WILLIS TOWER GREENING PROJECT + HOTEL

Integration of sustainable systems to reduce energy consumption and design for highly sustainable, 50-story five-star hotel to be built on the south side of Willis Tower plaza. The hotel will draw net zero energy from the power grid. Chicago, Illinois (AS+GG)

VANCOUVER RESIDENTIAL COMPLEX

Luxury low-rise residential complex with eco-footprint of one. Vancouver, British Columbia, Canada (AS+GG)

LAKESHORE EAST MASTER PLAN

Master plan and architectural design guidelines for mixed-use phased development on 26 acres including residential, office, hotel, school, and parking on a 6-acre neighborhood park. Chicago, Illinois (SOM)

MILLENNIUM PARK

Master planning and architectural design for 16.5-acre performance park, includes multi-modal transit facility. Chicago, Illinois (SOM)

CHEMSUNNY PLAZA

Architecture design services for the new 167,000 sm corporate headquarters for Sinochem. Beijing, China (SOM)

KING ABDULLAH ECONOMIC CITY

Master Plan for new city for 2,000,000 inhabitants, on the Red Sea, north of Jeddah, Saudi Arabia. City will be a modern community comprised of industrial, residential, office, financial, educational, commercial, resort, port facility and governmental agency facilities. Saudi Arabia (SOM)

601 CONGRESS STREET

15-story, 44,000 sm headquarters for Manulife Financial. Boston, Massachusetts (SOM)

201 BISHOPSGATE/THE BROADGATE TOWER

13-story, 680,000 sf office building with two 80,000 sf trading floors and two atriums. London, United Kingdom (SOM)

10 LUDGATE PLACE

Office building, 179,580 sf (16,700 sm), part of a three-building complex master plan, 394,000 sf (36,600 sm), including a new city square, pedestrian routes, public sculpture, shops and restaurants. London, United Kingdom

CANARY WHARF

International banking headquarters buildings: HQ1, DS1, DS3, DS4; FC2. London, United Kingdom (SOM)

JUBILEE PARK PAVILION

Entry pavilion for Jubilee Station. London, United Kingdom

ROWES WHARF

Multi-use complex consisting of office, retail, hotel and condominium space; the project includes piers, a marina and a ferry terminal, 30,000 sf (30,700 sm) office, 12,500 sf (1,200 sm) retail, 230 hotel rooms, 100 residential condominiums and 700 underground parking spaces. Boston, Massachusetts

UNITED GULF BANK

12-story bank and office building with a 10-story interior atrium. Manama, Bahrain (SOM)

BANCO DE OCCIDENTE

Montufar Branch, 400 sm, eight-teller branch banking facility. Guatemala City, Guatemala (SOM)

Gordon Gill FAIA, OAA, AIBC

Partner

EDUCATION

Masters of Architecture, Harvard University, 1993

Masters of Architecture, University of Texas Arlington, 1990

Bachelor of Science in Architecture, Ryerson University, 1987

SELECT PROFESSIONAL REGISTRATIONS + AFFILIATIONS

Licensed Architect in IL, IN

American Institute of Architects, Fellow (FAIA)

Ontario Association of Architects (OAA)

Architectural Institute of British Columbia (AIBC)

National Council of Architectural Registration Boards (NCARB)

Society for College and University Planning (SCUP)

Chicago Architecture Foundation, Board Member

Gordon Gill is one of the world's foremost exponents of performance-based architecture. His work, which ranges from the world's largest buildings to sustainable communities, is driven by his philosophy that there is a purposeful relationship between formal design and performance; and that there is a language of performance, which is the basis of his practice: Form Follows Performance.

A founding partner of award-winning Adrian Smith + Gordon Gill Architecture, Gordon's work includes the design of the world's first net zero-energy skyscraper, the Pearl River Tower (designed at SOM Chicago), the world's first large-scale positive-energy building, Masdar Headquarters, the world's next tallest tower, Jeddah Tower in Jeddah, Saudi Arabia, and most recently the design of Astana Expo City 2017 and its sustainable legacy community for Astana, Kazakhstan.

These landmark projects pursue energy independence by harnessing the power of natural forces on site and striking a balance with their environmental contexts. Gordon's designs also include performing arts centers, museums, strategic carbon planning and urban master plans across the globe.

His work has been published and exhibited widely in the US and internationally and his designs have repeatedly been recognized by the American Institute of Architects.

In 2009, he was selected as Chicago's Best Emerging Architect by the *Chicago Reader* and in 2013 was elected to The College of Fellows at the American Institute of Architects. In 2015 Adrian Smith + Gordon Gill Architecture was ranked the number one firm in the United States of America by Architect magazine.

Prior to founding AS+GG in 2006, Gordon was an Associate Partner at Skidmore, Owings & Merrill and a Director of Design for VOA Associates.

Awards, Honors + Important Roles

UTech, Jamaica, Honorary Degree, Doctor of Technology (Hon DTech), 2019

Marshall Bennett Institute, Lifetime Industry Leadership Award, Gordon Gill, 2018

The Chicago Reader, Chicago's Best Emerging Architect, 2009

Major Projects Throughout Career

UPTOWN TOWER
190,000 sm 72-story mixed-use tower includes office, residential, and hotel functions. The retail podium includes spaces for vehicle parking, MEP rooms, back of house spaces, a ballroom, and conference rooms, as well as separate entrances for the tower's functions. Dubai, United Arab Emirates (AS+GG)

AL WASL PLAZA
Centerpiece for the 4.38-square-kilometer Expo2020 Dubai combines breathtaking design, innovative technology, and a 150-meter diameter domed trellis that incorporates an immersive projection experience. Dubai, United Arab Emirates (AS+GG)

STEPPENWOLF THEATER CAMPUS EXPANSION
Architectural design for major Chicago theater company includes renovations and additions to existing structure. Chicago, Illinois (AS+GG)

CENTRAL PARK TOWER
Residential tower includes a program with prominent a retail tenant and amenities. New York, New York (AS+GG)

160 FRONT STREET
Office tower in the heart of Toronto's business district features 360-degree views of the city. Designed to meet LEED Platinum certification. Toronto, Ontario (AS+GG)

THE YARD AT CHICAGO SHAKESPEARE THEATER
Expansion and renovation of popular theater located on Navy Pier in downtown includes an adaptable, flexible auditorium built from modular towers. Chicago, Illinois (AS+GG)

CHICAGO ARCHITECTURE CENTER
The 20,000-square-foot center at 111 East Wacker Drive is a one-of-a-kind Chicago experience. Visitors can find world-famous river and walking tours, educational programs and new interactive exhibits that reveal the stories behind the city's architectural wonders. Chicago, Illinois (AS+GG)

AVERY FISHER HALL
Programming effort for 1200-seat theater, home of New York Philharmonic. New York, New York (SOM)

RAVINIA FESTIVAL
Master planning and architectural renovation of historic outdoor music venue including outdoor pavilion, indoor theater, and extensive grounds. Highland Park, Illinois (SOM)

TAMPA PERFORMING AND CULTURAL ARTS DISTRICT
Master plan for a large-scale cultural arts district in the central business district. Tampa, Florida (SOM)

UCF SHAKESPEARE THEATER
Renovation of existing Science Center building to include support and rehearsal space, along with a 350-seat thrust stage theater. Orlando, Florida, (VOA)

UNA RESIDENCES
47-story luxury residential tower, currently under design, to be located directly on Biscayne Bay. The design takes full advantage of this rare waterfront site and will leverage the features that bring people to Miami, namely expansive views, access to sun, and an indoor-outdoor lifestyle. The 146-residence luxury building recently launched sales. Miami, Florida (AS+GG)

RENAISSANCE DISTRICT
New campus design of a former 92,903 sm Studebaker manufacturing facility, located in the Renaissance District of South Bend. Redevelopment will provide a platform for data and technology companies. South Bend, Indiana (AS+GG)

830 BRICKELL
The first new office tower to launch in Miami in nearly a decade. The soaring 57-story, 724-foot-tall tower introduces a premium commercial to the city's booming financial district and seeks to reinvent the workplace lifestyle for the highest-caliber of global workforce. Miami, Florida (AS+GG)

TRIBUNE TOWER EAST
Residential mixed-use project includes 200 hotel rooms, 125 condo units, and 439 rental units. Vehicle and pedestrian entries are organized multiple street levels. Chicago, Illinois (AS+GG)

JEDDAH TOWER
The world's next tallest building features a luxury hotel, office space, serviced apartments, luxury condominiums, and the world's highest observatory. Jeddah, Saudi Arabia (AS+GG)

WUHAN GREENLAND CENTER
119-story, 300,000 sm, 606-meter-tall, mixed-use tower features 50 office floors, 17 residential floors and 22 hotel floors. Wuhan, China (AS+GG)

GREENLAND TOWER CHENGDU
468-meter-tall, mixed-use tower features a conference center, offices, a hotel, executive residential apartments, and rooftop garden. Chengdu, China (AS+GG)

FKI TOWER
50-story, 240-meter tower features unique exterior wall that features energy collecting building integrated photovoltaic panels in spandrel areas of the southwest and northwest facades. Seoul, Korea (AS+GG)

Gordon Gill FAIA, OAA, AIBC

Partner

ZIFENG TOWER (NANJING GREENLAND FINANCIAL CENTER)
Architectural design for 325,000 sm mixed-use supertall building including office, hotel service apartments, and commercial functions. Nanjing, China (SOM)

PEARL RIVER TOWER
69-story China National Tobacco Corporation headquarters. 303-meter tower designed to harvest wind and solar energy. Every aspect of the 303-meter tower is designed to harvest wind and solar energy. Guangzhou, China (SOM)

WALDORF ASTORIA BEIJING
Luxury hotel project located in the heart of downtown Beijing, China. Bronze exterior reflects the character of the site, and the super frame recalls the symmetry and steady character of Chinese traditional architecture. Beijing, China (AS+GG)

KAZAKHSTAN PAVILION + SCIENCE MUSEUM (NUR ALEM)
Inspired by the EXPO-2017 theme, "Future Energy," this science museum and exhibition pavilion embodies a futuristic design that is optimized to incorporate sustainable philosophies. The building's innovative, double-curved-glass facade features glass panels that gently curve in three dimensions. Building Integrated Photo Voltaic cells (BIPV) installed at the top of the sphere generate renewable energy for the building. Astana, Kazakhstan (AS+GG)

ASTANA ENERGY HALL
The main performance space for EXPO-2017 Astana, Kazakhstan and the legacy development, post expo. The 6500 sm, 1,000 seat multi-functional theater is a "theater-within-a-theater" that integrates the complex program requirements of a fixed-seat proscenium-type theater along with the need for the otherwise opaque form to respond to and activate the most populated area of the Expo. Astana, Kazakhstan (AS+GG)

ASTANA CONGRESS CENTER
Inspired by the fluid movements of the Golden Eagle or a "bürkit," which is portrayed on the national flag of Kazakhstan, the structure's tapered edges and sleek sweeping form also minimizes the scale and surface area of the building, reducing construction costs. The center's futuristic design features a state-of-the-art 3000 person auditorium, exhibition spaces, sponsor presentation areas, secure VIP and VVIP areas, associated press rooms, supporting offices', and a dedicated parking garage. Astana, Kazakhstan (AS+GG)

ASTANA EXPO CITY 2017
Master planning and architecture for 174-hectare international exposition site features exhibition and cultural pavilions (118,620 sm); a residential development (686,000 sm); service areas including shopping, socio-cultural, educational and civic facilities; and site-wide parks (72,000 sm). Astana, Kazakhstan (AS+GG)

GREAT CITY CHENGDU
One-square-kilometer development will investigate the relationship between high-density urban living and sustainable development. Will accommodate a population of 100,000 people. Chengdu, China (AS+GG)

CHICAGO DECARBONIZATION PLAN
Commission from the City of Chicago that assesses and looks at innovative solutions for the carbon performance of the downtown area Loop using a holistic urban design approach. Chicago, Illinois (AS+GG)

WILLIS TOWER GREENING PROJECT + HOTEL
Integration of sustainable systems to reduce energy consumption and design for highly sustainable, 50-story five-star hotel to be built on the south side of Willis Tower plaza. The hotel will draw net zero energy from the power grid. Chicago, Illinois (AS+GG)

MASDAR HQ DEVELOPMENT
Architectural design for positive-energy building in zero-carbon, zero-waste city. Program included office, retail, transit, and landscaped green space. Abu Dhabi, United Arab Emirates (AS+GG)

VANCOUVER RESIDENTIAL COMPLEX
Luxury low-rise residential complex with eco-footprint of one. Vancouver, British Columbia, Canada (AS+GG)

SHANGHAI GRAND
Design services for office building in Pudong district, 80,000 sm above grade, 20,000 sm below grade. Shanghai, China (SOM)

KING ABDULLAH ECONOMIC CITY
Master plan for new city for 2,000,000 inhabitants, on the Red Sea, north of Jeddah, Saudi Arabia. City will be a modern community comprised of industrial, residential, office and financial, educational, commercial, resort, port facility, and governmental agency facilities. Saudi Arabia (SOM)

VIRGINIA BEACH CONVENTION CENTER
Master planning and architectural design for a 500,000 sf facility which includes a 150,000 sf exhibit hall, a 30,000 sf ballroom and 25,000 sf of meeting space. Virginia Beach, Virginia (SOM)

KOYANG INTERNATIONAL EXHIBITION CENTER
Master plan and architectural design for a 325,000 sm mixed-use complex including 180,000 sm convention space. Seoul, Korea (SOM)

HANGZHOU CONVENTION CENTER
Competition entry for a 62,500 sm state-of-the-art, sustainable convention facility reinforcing the garden city quality of Hangzhou as well as accommodating expansion and modification over time. Hangzhou, China (SOM)

COMPENSAR FAMILY ENTERTAINMENT CENTER
Master planning and design of multi-purpose glass pavilion. The design also incorporates a new plaza area, as well as interactive and contemplative garden spaces. Bogotá, Columbia (VOA)

CURITIBA INTERNATIONAL TRADE CENTER
Architectural design for complex featuring a 66,000 sm exhibition center, a 350-room hotel, 20,000 sm of retail and entertainment, and 12,000 sm office space. Curitiba, Paraná, Brazil (VOA)

RUSH UNIVERSITY MEDICAL CENTER
Large-scale complex, phased urban medical campus redevelopment to address clinical, research, teaching, operational and infrastructure improvements. Chicago, Illinois (SOM)

JESSE BROWN MEDICAL CENTER
200-bed inpatient expansion to the existing VA Westside Medical Center including new Departments for ICU, Surgery and Emergency Medicine. The eight-story, 22,000 sm building with a creative allocation of space, establishing a new entry sequence and clearly articulated wayfinding on the tight, urban site. Chicago, Illinois (SOM)

DENVER MEDICAL CENTER
Department of Veterans Affairs replacement facility includes ambulatory care, surgery, psychiatry, long-term care, and spinal cord injury unit; a research laboratory, structured parking, energy plant, and warehouse facilities. Aurora, Colorado (SOM)

HEALTH AND LIFE SCIENCES BUILDING
Florida International University, University Park, Multi-phased, four-story facility containing laboratories, classrooms and administrative offices for the various disciplines of allied health and biological sciences. Miami, Florida (SOM)

Robert Forest FAIA, OAA, AIBC, LEED AP

Partner

EDUCATION

Bachelor of Architecture, Carleton University, Ottawa, Canada, Dean's List, 1994

SELECT PROFESSIONAL REGISTRATIONS + AFFILIATIONS

Registered Architect in IL, NY, NV, PA

National Council of Architectural Registration Boards (NCARB)

LEED Accredited Professional (LEED AP)

American Institute of Architects, Fellow (FAIA)

Ontario Association of Architects (OAA)

Architectural Institute of British Columbia (AIBC)

Royal Institute of British Architects (RIBA)

Robert Forest has extensive knowledge and experience with the execution of projects on an international scale. Bob's expertise in both project management and technical architecture contribute to his comprehensive understanding of both the built environment and the practice of architecture.

A recognized authority on the economics of sustainable design, Bob has combined his knowledge of local and international policies, funding sources and varied economic models to develop a system of "best practices" for the management of high-performance projects. He has lectured and published his work on a national scale.

Bob is dedicated to the advancement of the management discipline within an architectural context. After over a decade spent practicing abroad, Bob has developed a unique understanding of architectural practices across the globe and has used this knowledge in the management of numerous large-scale, complex projects. He works diligently alongside design teams from all disciplines throughout each project, ensuring that designs are executed with a careful understanding of each client's goals and vision.

Prior to founding Adrian Smith + Gordon Gill Architecture LLP in 2006, Bob was an Associate Partner in the Chicago office of Skidmore, Owings & Merrill LLP, and had previously worked at design firms in Toronto, Hong Kong, and Osaka, Japan.

Prior to beginning his architectural career, Bob played professional football for Canadian teams the Ottawa Rough Riders and Montreal Machine. He utilizes the leadership skills and understanding of team dynamics gained from this experience today in a professional capacity.

Most recently, Bob was elected President of the AIA Chicago in 2019 and was elected a Fellow by the American Institute of Architects in 2014.

Awards, Honors + Important Roles

AIA Chicago, President, 2019

AIA Chicago Board of Directors, 2010-2021

Major Projects Throughout Career

UPTOWN TOWER
190,000 sm 72-story mixed-use tower includes office, residential, and hotel functions. The retail podium includes spaces for vehicle parking, MEP rooms, back of house spaces, a ballroom, and conference rooms, as well as separate entrances for the tower's functions. Dubai, United Arab Emirates (AS+GG)

AL WASL PLAZA
Centerpiece for the 4.38-square-kilometer Expo2020 Dubai combines breathtaking design, innovative technology, and a 150-meter diameter domed trellis that incorporates an immersive projection experience. Dubai, United Arab Emirates (AS+GG)

STEPPENWOLF THEATER CAMPUS EXPANSION
Architectural design for major Chicago theater company includes renovations and additions to existing structure. Chicago, Illinois (AS+GG)

CENTRAL PARK TOWER
Residential tower includes a program with prominent a retail tenant and amenities. New York, New York (AS+GG)

160 FRONT STREET
Office tower in the heart of Toronto's business district features 360-degree views of the city. Designed to meet LEED Platinum certification. Toronto, Ontario (AS+GG)

THE YARD AT CHICAGO SHAKESPEARE THEATER
Expansion and renovation of popular theater located on Navy Pier in downtown includes an adaptable, flexible auditorium built from modular towers. Chicago, Illinois (AS+GG)

CHICAGO ARCHITECTURE CENTER

The 20,000-square-foot center at 111 East Wacker Drive is a one-of-a-kind Chicago experience. Visitors can find world-famous river and walking tours, educational programs and new interactive exhibits that reveal the stories behind the city's architectural wonders. Chicago, Illinois (AS+GG)

UNA RESIDENCES

47-story luxury residential tower, currently under design, to be located directly on Biscayne Bay. The design takes full advantage of this rare waterfront site and will leverage the features that bring people to Miami, namely expansive views, access to sun, and an indoor-outdoor lifestyle. The 146-residence luxury building recently launched sales. Miami, Florida (AS+GG)

830 BRICKELL

The first new office tower to launch in Miami in nearly a decade. The soaring 57-story, 724-foot-tall tower introduces a premium commercial to the city's booming financial district and seeks to reinvent the workplace lifestyle for the highest-caliber of global workforce. Miami, Florida (AS+GG)

JEDDAH TOWER

The world's next tallest building features a luxury hotel, office space, serviced apartments, luxury condominiums, and the world's highest observatory. Jeddah, Saudi Arabia (AS+GG)

WUHAN GREENLAND CENTER

119-story, 300,000 sm, 606-meter-tall, mixed-use tower features 50 office floors, 17 residential floors and 22 hotel floors. Wuhan, China (AS+GG)

GREENLAND TOWER CHENGDU

468-meter-tall, mixed-use tower features a conference center, offices, a hotel, executive residential apartments, and rooftop garden. Chengdu, China (AS+GG)

FKI TOWER

50-story, 240-meter tower features unique exterior wall that features energy collecting building integrated photovoltaic panels in spandrel areas of the southwest and northwest facades. Seoul, Korea (AS+GG)

WALDORF ASTORIA BEIJING

Luxury hotel project located in the heart of downtown Beijing, China. Bronze exterior reflects the character of the site, and the super frame recalls the symmetry and steady character of Chinese traditional architecture. Beijing, China (AS+GG)

BURJ KHALIFA

Supertall mixed-use tower comprising residential, commercial, hotel, and retail spaces. Dubai, United Arab Emirates (SOM)

ZIFENG TOWER (NANJING GREENLAND FINANCIAL CENTER)

Architectural design for 325,000 sm mixed-use supertall building including office, hotel service apartments, and commercial functions. Nanjing, China (SOM)

BURJ VISTA

Luxury two-tower residential complex with outdoor plaza, a theater and unobstructed views of Burj Khalifa. Dubai, United Arab Emirates (AS+GG)

GANG XIA TOWER

198-meter, 43-story tower in Shenzhen's Futian Central District, with views to the adjacent Civic Center Park and a series of high performance solar shades. Shenzhen, China (AS+GG)

VANTONE CENTER TIANJIN

185-meter tower consists of 64,000 square-meters of above-grade Class A office and high-end retail space, along with an additional 30,000-square meters of below-grade retail and parking. Also features a 27-meter-tall private club for building tenants at its top. Tianjin, China (AS+GG)

Robert Forest FAIA, OAA, AIBC, LEED AP

Partner

ZHONGZHOU HOLDINGS FINANCE CENTER
Zhongzhou Holdings Finance Center is a mixed-use complex located in Shenzhen's Nanshan Culture District, consisting of a multi-purpose podium, a 300-meter office and hotel tower, and a related 160-meter residential tower. The design achieve balance and harmony for the building's tenants, inhabitants, and users. Shenzhen, China (AS+GG)

SHANGHAI GRAND
Design services for office building in Pudong district, 80,000 sm above grade, 20,000 sm below grade. Shanghai, China (SOM)

GREAT CITY CHENGDU
One-square-kilometer development will investigate the relationship between high-density urban living and sustainable development. Will accommodate a population of 100,000 people. Chengdu, China (AS+GG)

XIXIAN GREAT CITY
A 1.4-square-kilometer development in China that represents a shift in the approach to providing high density housing and employment in suburban China. The city is designed around a number of key sustainability criteria focusing on a sustainable and healthy urban environment while at the same time being affordable. Xian, China (AS+GG)

TIANFU NEW DISTRICT MASTER PLAN
Located 30 kilometers south of Chengdu, this new city plan considers unique features such as existing valleys, ridges, and slopes and reinterprets them as parks, plazas, pedestrian streets, and retail corridors. Developed guidelines for buildings that range from five-story buildings, up to signature towers of over 300 meters. Chengdu, China (AS+GG)

SOLAR EV DOCK
Prototypical structure harvests solar energy and power electric/hybrid vehicles. Chicago, Illinois (AS+GG)

RENAISSANCE DISTRICT
New campus design of a former 92,903 sm Studebaker manufacturing facility, located in the Renaissance District of South Bend. Redevelopment will provide a platform for data and technology companies. South Bend, Indiana (AS+GG)

CHICAGO DECARBONIZATION PLAN
Commission from the City of Chicago that assesses and looks at innovative solutions for the carbon performance of the downtown area Loop using a holistic urban design approach. Chicago, Illinois (AS+GG)

WILLIS TOWER GREENING PROJECT + HOTEL
Integration of sustainable systems to reduce energy consumption and design for highly sustainable, 50-story five-star hotel to be built on the south side of Willis Tower plaza. The hotel will draw net zero energy from the power grid. Chicago, Illinois (AS+GG)

VANCOUVER RESIDENTIAL COMPLEX
Luxury low-rise residential complex with eco-footprint of one. Vancouver, British Columbia, Canada (AS+GG)

MASDAR HQ DEVELOPMENT
Architectural design for positive-energy building in zero-carbon, zero-waste city. Program included office, retail, transit, and landscaped green space. Abu Dhabi, United Arab Emirates (AS+GG)

KAZAKHSTAN PAVILION + SCIENCE MUSEUM (NUR ALEM)
Inspired by the EXPO-2017 theme, "Future Energy," this science museum and exhibition pavilion embodies a futuristic design that is optimized to incorporate sustainable philosophies. The building's innovative, double-curved-glass facade features glass panels that gently curve in three dimensions. Building Integrated Photo Voltaic cells (BIPV) installed at the top of the sphere generate renewable energy for the building. Astana, Kazakhstan (AS+GG)

ASTANA ENERGY HALL
The main performance space for EXPO-2017 Astana, Kazakhstan and the legacy development, post expo. The 6500 sm, 1,000 seat multi-functional theater is a "theater-within-a-theater" that integrates the complex program requirements of a fixed-seat proscenium-type theater along with the need for the otherwise opaque form to respond to and activate the most populated area of the Expo. Astana, Kazakhstan (AS+GG)

ASTANA CONGRESS CENTER
Inspired by the fluid movements of the Golden Eagle or a "bürkit," which is portrayed on the national flag of Kazakhstan, the structure's tapered edges and sleek sweeping form also minimizes the scale and surface area of the building, reducing construction costs. The center's futuristic design features a state-of-the-art 3000 person auditorium, exhibition spaces, sponsor presentation areas, secure VIP and VVIP areas, associated press rooms, supporting offices', and a dedicated parking garage. Astana, Kazakhstan (AS+GG)

ASTANA EXPO CITY 2017
Master planning and architecture for 174-hectare international exposition site features exhibition and cultural pavilions (118,620 sm); a residential development (686,000 sm); service areas including shopping, socio-cultural, educational and civic facilities; and site-wide parks (72,000 sm). Astana, Kazakhstan (AS+GG)

TRUMP INTERNATIONAL HOTEL AND TOWER
223,000 sm, 94-story mixed-use tower comprised of luxury residential, hotel, health club, retail, parking, and riverfront park on prominent site along the Chicago River. Chicago, Illinois (SOM)

CANARY WHARF HQ1 AND DS3
Architectural design services for corporate headquarters. London, United Kingdom (SOM)

JUBILEE PARK PAVILION
Entry pavilion for Jubilee Park underground retail shopping. London, United Kingdom (SOM)

PEARL RIVER TOWER
69-story China National Tobacco Corporation headquarters. 303-meter tower designed to harvest wind and solar energy. Every aspect of the 303-meter tower is designed to harvest wind and solar energy. Guangzhou, China (SOM)

CHEMSUNNY PLAZA
Architecture design services for the new 167,000 sm corporate headquarters for Sinochem. Beijing, China (SOM)

SUZHOU NANMENLU MASTER PLAN
Master plan for one of the main districts and streets of Suzhou including infrastructure components. Suzhou, China (SOM)

SUZHOU INTERNATIONAL EXPO CENTER
Architectural design for 260,000 sm convention center and exhibition facility. Suzhou, China (SOM)

NINGBO MASTER PLAN
Master plan and architectural design of approximately 300,000 sm of office, residential development for the Ningbo planning authority. Ningbo, China

ZHONGSHAN CONVENTION CENTER
Competition entry for a 62,500 sm state-of-the-art, sustainable convention facility reinforcing the garden city quality of Hangzhou as well as accommodating expansion and modification over time. Zhongshan, China (SOM)

444 NORTH MICHIGAN AVENUE
New entrance lobby and lighting scheme to rebrand Michigan Avenue office building as modern icon of Magnificent Mile. Chicago, Illinois (SOM)

Essays

The Evolution of Contextualism

Adrian Smith FAIA, RIBA, HON D.LITT

For me, a good building and its context have always gone hand in hand, reflecting and commenting on each other. My buildings are what they are, in a fundamental sense, because of where they are.

This feeling for context has remained the same over the past 45 years of my life as an architect. I have always tried to engage the history, art, landscape, climate, vernacular architecture, and indigenous materials of the places where my buildings are located. I have always sought to interpret and honor the cultures that my buildings serve, to forge a unique dialogue between culture and place, and to foster a strong connection to the people who see and use these buildings.

But these ideas about contextualism, which have been the bedrock of my architectural philosophy, also have been elastic enough to change and grow with the times. At Adrian Smith + Gordon Gill Architecture (AS+GG), they are still evolving.

That evolution has had three layers thus far. During the formation of the first layer early in my career, I was influenced by Luis Barragan and Ricardo Legorreta, with whom I collaborated on projects in Mexico at Skidmore, Owings & Merrill (SOM). Ricardo insisted that buildings ought to be informed by the particular character of their locales, which in Central America had primarily to do with the hot climate and the textures and colors of local building materials.

In 1980, I put those ideas into practice in a trio of buildings for Banco de Occidente in Guatemala City. It was my first major as a project as a Design Partner and is still one of my favorites. I designed the exterior walls with a high thermal mass and deep-set fenestration, using virtually all local materials. I emphasized courtyards, indoors and out, and used louvered skylights to provide natural light and natural ventilation. I designed Banco de Occidente (1978-1981) to operate entirely without electricity, as would sometimes be necessary due to the frequent power outages in Guatemala. In retrospect, I was interested in sustainability long before the word came into common usage; I did not use it myself until many years later.

Over the next decade, I did several more projects in this vein, including Rowes Wharf in Boston (1984-1990) and United Gulf Bank in Manama, Bahrain (1986-1993). In both projects, I borrowed the local cultural and physical motifs— the classical details and maritime heritage of Boston and fishing boats and Islamic tapestries in Bahrain—and transformed them with abstraction and transfigurations of scale. It has always been important for me not to quote my sources of inspiration directly but, rather, to reinterpret them in a contemporary and often fairly oblique way. If the viewer doesn't "get" my references immediately, that's fine with me. Over time, they will get them, and the moments of recognition will be an even richer experience.

Particularly in Bahrain, my early exploration of sustainable design began to pick up speed. A decade before the drumbeat of sustainability began to be heard around the world, I designed United Gulf Bank with an exterior wall and daylighting scheme that used deeply recessed windows with heat-absorbing glass fins and light shelves that bring natural light into the interior spaces in a way that is most useful and comfortable to the occupants.

The 1980s were good to me—Banco de Occidente, United Gulf Bank, and Rowes Wharf all won National AIA Honor Awards—but by the early '90s, my contextualism was to take on its second layer: the use of technology to reflect the present moment. I was still committed to cultural and physical referencing, but it was important to express and introduce elements of unique technologies, construction methods and advancements in building methods, and innovative building products and systems, into my work.

In 10 Ludgate Place (1992-1995), for example, I incorporated the 19th century industrial aesthetic, as well as the neo-Gothic character of the site context into the building. I included an interpretation of flying buttresses and the character of the railroad tracks systems running beneath the building into the design of the exterior wall, creating a highly textured metal and stone cladding system that could only have been designed and built in the late 20th century.

In Jin Mao Tower (1993-1999) in Shanghai, I honored the ancient traditions of China in an abstract composition using the ancient Pagoda as my reference. Through a finely tuned lattice of vertical and horizontal stainless steel and aluminum members assembled to form a deep texture for the exterior wall, and composing the tower's mass as a figurative biaxially symmetrical stepping mass, the composition references the ancient pagoda in a completely current and holistic manner. (Gordon Gill's nickname for that exterior wall is "Full Metal Jacket.")

In Burj Khalifa (2003-2010) in the United Arab Emirates, I referenced desert flowers and Islamic onion domes, among other things, but did so in such an oblique and technologically advanced way that one of the most frequently used adjectives to describe the tower is "futuristic." I do not describe it that way myself—I think of the Burj as very much of its time—but I understand why the word occurs to other people who view the tower.

Which brings me to the third layer of my work, which has to do with the contextual absorption and harvesting of a building sites' natural sources of power. I had begun moving in this direction as early as 1995 with my feasibility study for Samsung Togok that featured apertures through which wind could be harvested by turbines and converted to usable energy. In one of our last major projects for SOM, Gordon and I advanced and refined some of the ideas in Togok for Pearl River Tower, completed in 2010 in Guangzhou, China. In this project, designed as the world's first net-zero-energy tall building, we concentrated on the building's orientation, which faces the wind, and the sculpting of the form to harness that wind, funneling and accelerating it into building-integrated turbines.

When Gordon, Bob Forest, and I left SOM in late 2006 to form AS+GG, we knew we wanted to continue to build on what we had accomplished with Pearl River Tower. We did just that, I think, with a prototype we developed early on, Clean Technology Tower (2006-2007), and even more with Masdar Headquarters designed for a site just outside Abu Dhabi in the United Arab Emirates, which uses a combination of passive strategies and energy generation technologies to produce more power than the building needs to operate. The surplus energy was designed to be donated to the Masdar City grid, suggesting possibilities for the sharing of energy between buildings and city blocks around the world.

At AS+GG, my cultural and physical contextualism has evolved into the concept of *Global Environmental Contextualism*. While the influence of local culture continues to play an important role in our designs, they now respond first to extensive environmental analysis, which takes into full account solar orientation, wind conditions, geothermal properties and other factors at the buildings' site.

Examples include the Masdar Headquarters cones, whose bell-like shape helps draw warm air up and out of the building, and Clean Technology Tower and the Willis Tower hotel, which use softly molded exteriors to channel the wind into strategically positioned building-integrated turbines. Building form also aids energy generation via photovoltaics in Masdar Headquarters, whose vast flat roof features the world's largest solar panel array, and Park Gate, whose curving towers and canopies are ideal for building-integrated photovoltaics. Our design for the head office sof the Federation of Korean Industries, FKI Tower, showcases a high-performance exterior wall system which incorporates building-integrated photovoltaics on spandrel panels that are angled outward 15 degrees to maximize solar collection.

In Jeddah Tower in Jeddah, Saudi Arabia—designed to be the world's tallest building at more than 1,000 meters—we developed a high-performance exterior wall that reduces solar heat gain while maintaining the breathtaking views that building occupants will expect. As with Burj Khalifa, the form of Jeddah Tower is shaped to disrupt the buildup of wind vortex action. The shape is also culturally contextual, with the building's three wings resolving and splitting off at different heights in a manner that evokes young desert plant growth—a concept that is also symbolically important for Saudi Arabia at this point in its history on the world stage.

Using a holistic approach that engages all disciplines, our projects—which Gordon and I typically design in collaboration together, supported by our amazingly talented design teams and consultants—meet the challenges with integrated systems and strategies that facilitate energy efficiency and on-site energy generation from renewable sources. As always, we apply this approach to various typologies, from low- and mid-rise buildings to supertall and megatall towers.

We are especially interested in advancing the ideas embodied in the phrase *Form Follows Performance*, which we refer to as the relationship of an architectural form that is informed by conditions that are taken into consideration that together effect and advance the performance of a building.

I had been developing aspects of that concept at SOM with the design of 7 South Dearborn, an unbuilt supertall tower for Chicago, and Burj Khalifa, in which we manipulated the forms of the towers to mitigate the negative forces of the wind. The idea was to shape the exterior in such a way as to "confuse the wind," allowing the tower to shed the vortices that build up around it. On 7 South Dearborn, we accomplished this with a series of deep notches and on Burj Khalifa with the asymmetric shifting of setbacks that spiral around the central core and culminate with a spire at the top.

Increasingly, too, we are expanding the idea of *Global Environmental Contextualism* to adapt itself more fully to urban design projects. As a profession, we need to be smarter about how we plan large-scale developments, especially in terms of transit. In too many instances, urban planning around the world is still making the same mistakes of the last half-century, emphasizing cars and highways rather than public transit and features that encourage people, including families, to live near their places of work. For an example of our thinking on this topic, see the section in this book on the Chicago Central Area DeCarbonization Plan, which lays out a comprehensive vision for helping Chicago's central area to reach its carbon reduction goals in the downtown Loop by 2030.

And so the idea of context in my work is still evolving and will continue to do so, no doubt in unexpected ways at times. In our first 15 years as a firm, we have made real progress toward a new approach and a new architecture, both of which respond to shifting conditions in a changing world. For me personally, it has been the latest chapter in a remarkable story that is still unfolding. I can't wait to see what happens next.

The Language of Performance

Gordon Gill FAIA, OAA, AIBC

Buildings, like people, should seek to be of a purpose that is greater than themselves. The Language of Performance is the implementation of the Form Follows Performance philosophy where form is purposeful and an expression of performance. In short, there is a co-dependent relationship between the design of all buildings and the performance criteria placed upon them. This language is visual, of course, and its essence is revealed in the course of the performance itself.

In the design of cars and aircraft, for example, the inspiration of the aesthetic is often imbedded in the performance which results in the expression. Timelessness and beauty are the realization of the best combination of performance and functionality through physical expression. The process, we endeavor to pursue, is to optimize the relationship between purposeful form and outstanding performance in buildings where the building as a whole performs as one; where interior and envelope together, structure and space are woven meticulously, and technology is introduced to improve the aspects of the building and ultimately the human experience.

To optimize performance with high efficiency, expressed through beauty, is the apex of performative design. The marriage of form and function is performance; where beauty, well-being, elegance, and function are all realized.

Performance, in this process, is an expansion beyond function. Defined by Webster, function is the natural or proper action of anything; special purpose duty or the like; to operate; or to work. Performance is defined as the doing of one's particular duty. The better one performs that duty, the greater the performance.

In these two examples, performance expands the function or how something works to the measure of the effectiveness related to its contribution. When something performs, it contributes to its surroundings beyond just it's function.

High performance suggests that it functions at a very high level that is quantifiable or measurable. The ability to quantify a systems' performance has always been an integrated aspect of design. Structural performance, floor plate efficiencies, thermal performance and of course, energy and carbon performance are such examples. Today, more and more, the expectations placed on the built environment require that they need to perform and perform well and in a symbiotic manner.

Performance may also be defined as the measurable efficiencies of systems designed in harmony with their environment to maximize output and consequently define purpose. High performance systems have output, and the measure of output is one of the key determinants of the level of performance. The higher the quantifiable positive output from the system, the more performative it is.

Understanding that form can contribute to a building's performance is a step forward in giving architectural expression genuine purpose. If buildings are expressive, even exuberant at times as they inspire a place and a culture, it is important to work toward their expression as a means of the efficient integration of form. From a performance perspective, it is no longer enough to be only formal in terms of the expression of the building. While pure form can contribute aesthetically, and sometimes beautifully, the singular aesthetic mission is simply not enough anymore.

A harmonious relationship between form, performance, and beauty is the goal. There is beauty in utility. The idea of utility is constantly evolving. Today we can determine the thermal properties of the building's skin as it relates to the interior configurations, palettes, and materials and we can understand the behavioral characteristics of comfort as they apply to individual dress or where one sits within a floor plate. How specific do we get? As far as science and common sense can take us.

Performance + Form

Performance gives form purpose. It opens a new world of investigation into designing buildings as they specifically relate to the organization, ventilation, access, comfort, and experience. From cities to supertall to the single-family home, performance can eliminate or at least serve as a filter to identify and challenge the quality of design. Through the lens of performance as criteria, clients, developers, and designers can pursue the genuine performance of their work where form can have great meaning. This gives the design purpose and value, resulting in more meaningful architecture.

Performance + Efficiency

The efficiency of a building can mean many things to different people. Here, we speak of the energy use and carbon content of an occupied building. Is it possible to improve the way a building functions as well as reduce its embodied energy through a process that integrates systems in a measurable way? Yes, it is. At one level performance is efficiency. It expands the meaning to include qualities of space and comfort that may not have originally been measures of efficiency. Today we are challenging the value system of buildings and what efficiency really means.

Performance + Comfort

A well-performing building increases comfort for its users through understanding thermal characteristics, cultural and social characteristics, and use. The psychology of comfort is also important as systems are designed. Views of nature, for example, are considerations for comfort and healing in medical facilities, supporting quantifiable reduced lengths of stay for recovering patients. The performance characteristics for buildings varies with their functionality and use.

Performance + Carbon Footprint

The Language of Performance recognizes and accepts that energy and carbon are valuable aspects of performance. If we agree that efficiency is good, then a high-performance building will decrease the carbon footprint and be a genuine contributor to its environment beyond its use and aesthetics. As we mature as a practice, the depth of investigation that we reach for our clients and our society, will only serve to make buildings better.

Performance + Economics

Economics is one of the metrics by which we measure performance. Not restricted to first costs but defined through life cycle analysis that measures the economic performance of a building over the duration of its use.

Performance + Culture

To be truly performative, a building must be deeply rooted in its locale and ultimately therefore, its culture. It demands the understanding of place. The performance of culture also ties into the primitive and vernacular systems. Relationships constructed between indigenous cultures and their architecture in the absence of high technology are meaningful. As technology has advanced, what has it removed from the architecture? If the answer is that it has removed cultural adjacencies, decor, and relationships, then how can this be infused with advanced technology into a performative architecture with a highly curated sense of place?

Understanding the principles of indigenous architecture is critical to expressing how culture has transformed and how it, meets the future. It is not about copying a form or an expression but instead expanding principles that still apply and introducing new principles that are environmentally and culturally appropriate.

Over the centuries, architecture has evolved, through technologies, in the name of progress. The pursuit of improving standards through technology can arrive at the point where, as slaves to some technologies, we have abandoned and unlearned the basic aspects of sustainable design and consequently truly sustainable living. This unlearning stems from a slow and steady process of uncritical, blind acceptance of technology, which can result in the replacement of purposeful design with the sensational and trite. Instead of applying technology and unlearning environmental principles, we can embrace our environment and utilize technology as a means of improving the balance between nature and the built environment. The goal is to improve our environment through the buildings.

I would suggest that the essence of what is now referred to as sustainable design, is rooted in the most basic of structures found in indigenous architecture or any buildings of early civilizations. Sadly, abandonment of these principles as well as the reproduction or replication of these typologies, has transferred through technology without understanding the principles that tied those buildings to a place has become a dangerous substitute for sustainability today.

Performance + Beauty

Performance can define, test, and defend aesthetics. Given a deeper understanding of how a building specifically needs to perform, the design may demand certain massing solutions and accept apertures for light or wind that liberate form and define aesthetic. In practice, the solutions are rarely the same since climate orientation and site characteristics change from project to project. Indeed, given that, relocation of a specific project from one site to another, the aesthetics would by definition, change. This has allowed us to utilize single systems as frameworks that change dramatically across multiple buildings individually oriented on a single site.

The role of landscape in the context of beauty is often ignored in its relationship to the built environment yet when asked to close their eyes and envision their favorite places, most people see landscapes, not buildings. Landscape plays a critical role in visible beauty. Not as an applied layer but as an integrated member of design, working with the built form to create spaces and qualities that are both performance-enhanced and beautiful.

Beauty is an attribute that gives deep pleasure to the mind arising from sensory manifestations: shape, smell, color; a meaningful pattern in which ephemeral qualities manifest. All of which are enhanced through a deeper understanding of place, environment, and performance.

The Language

Like all expandable systems, the performance of any single network of systems is at its best as it propagates itself and finds its balance in an ecosystem. For buildings, these are our cities and our countries. As a philosophy, the architecture of performance can be both singular and multiple; expanded to work together as a built environment that seeks harmony with nature. This is not an ideal. This is not a utopia, but a working method of constant development and adjustment with an understanding that both nature and technology are vital aspects of our lives.

We have built for ourselves enormous environments for living. Our cities are our ecosystems and through a truly integrated understanding of performance, we will need to resolve what we have built, with a future that exports ideas and corrects weaknesses in the systems. It is these weaknesses in the systems of our cities which will lead to ultimate decay and obsolescence. The complexity of the City: its economics, infrastructure, physical presence, capacity for growth, and quality of life describes the integration of systems that must be designed to create performative environments.

The global context plays a strong role in the Language of Performance since it recognizes not only the specifics of a place and a region in order to absorb and interpret it, but it also endeavors to understand the far-reaching issues associated with development, urban densities, and technologies as they apply to nature and consequently sustainable design and its global impact. This extension of what can be determined as a Global Environmental Contextualism is at the basis of understanding that results in a global scope of performance.

True sustainable design for tomorrow needs to accept its natural environment and merge it in a purposeful way through technology to result in an architecture that contributes to a deeper meaning of form, quality of life and beauty.

The Language of Performance is specific. It's not anonymous and demands analysis. It demands purposeful reason behind form for the purposes of improving the built environment.

The architecture of performance understands the purposeful and deliberate result of form—like a violin, an aircraft, a high-performance vehicle, or even a well-designed utensil—molded and designed to perform at their highest level with more than a mere aesthetic purpose.

The language occupies that space between craft and science and has at its core: sustainability or the ability to maintain itself over time as current and useful in a balanced and efficient manner. In this way, sustainability is design. It has never been and should never be a layered or additive approach to problem-solving.

Those who see sustainability – efficiency in design – as a separate or independent process are destined to produce products that are less than comprehensive and ultimately obsolete. While perhaps acceptable in the moment, they cannot withstand the future. The demand for quantifiable quality in architecture is here, and here to stay.

The Economics of Sustainability

Robert Forest FAIA, OAA, AIBC, LEED AP

Prologue

This essay was written in 2009 as a culmination of a series of lectures that I gave to the AIA, Northwestern University, and the CTBUH Dubai Conference. It is as relevant today as it was then and gives insight into our approach to design when we started Adrian Smith + Gordon Gill Architecture (AS+GG). As one of the original architecture firm signatories to the UN Global Compact it was important to us to state our position regarding sustainable design and its economics. I would argue that today, globally, people are much more aware of the need for sustainable design but are now facing much different challenges, such as how to approach design in a Post-COVID world. AS+GG's philosophy does not need to be redefined for today—it remains strong as is.

The Economics of Sustainability

The phrase "sustainable architecture" embodies a spirit of optimism about the future, but for some clients, developers, and existing building owners, considering green retrofits, can also conjure a certain unease. Doing our part to combat climate change is obviously a worthy goal and the right approach, but how much is it going to cost? The question is not trivial. If the business community is not convinced that investment in high-performance architecture makes economic sense, in both the near and long terms, our designs will not be realized because they will not be commissioned or built. Sustainability is the goal. But to reach that goal, the economics need to work.

When approaching the economics, we need to take a holistic look at the equation and challenge the math. Sustainable design is not only about reduced energy use, but is also based in efficiency, longevity, and competitiveness.

Fortunately, there are persuasive arguments to be made that sustainable architecture and sound economics are far from mutually exclusive. In fact, they go hand in hand. Whatever their positions on global warming, real estate owners and managers are discovering that sustainably designed properties give them a competitive advantage in the marketplace. Sustainable architecture produces buildings that are more energy-efficient and therefore significantly less expensive to operate—a savings that increases over time as energy costs escalate; hard to argue with that.

At AS+GG, w are focused on creating sustainable designs that have quantifiable performance metrics that demonstrate the inherent efficiency of the design.

And whatever their personal views, no building owner can fail to recognize that with respect to sustainability, the culture has shifted. After years of discussion and sometimes fractious debate, the imperative of sustainability is now a matter of wide consensus. In particular, the public is now far more aware of the impact of buildings on the environment in terms of land use, energy consumption, and carbon emissions. Even corporate executives who remain skeptical about global warming are recognizing that for their current and prospective employees, the issue is becoming a higher priority with every passing year.

In response, building tenants are demanding that their workplaces be more eco-friendly. In a 2008 global real estate survey by CoreNet/Jones Lang LaSalle, 70% of companies identified sustainability as a critical business issue, up from 47% in 2007. In the same survey, 76% of the companies polled named energy and sustainability as significant factors influencing their decisions about where to locate. Only 10% of the companies said these factors did not matter.

For many companies, in fact, sustainability has become a key part of their brand management, employee retention, liability and insurance cost reduction, and public relations strategies. Dozens of major corporations, including Hewlett-Packard, JPMorgan Chase, Coca-Cola, Intel, UPS, Sun Microsystems, and Pfizer, have proudly announced ambitious carbon reduction goals, with more following suit every year. In today's world, being a good corporate citizen—or a good city, state, university, or medical campus—means demonstrating a genuine commitment to sustainability.

There is also increasing recognition among corporate executives (as well as other entities with extensive real estate holdings, such as governments, universities, and hospitals) that high-performance buildings make for high-performance workers. Studies have shown that worker turnover and absenteeism typically drop between 10% and 18% when companies relocate from older structures to newer office space with better lighting and better air quality; productivity increases correspondingly. That helps explain the fact that when tenants are frustrated by the sustainable performance of their current buildings, they are increasing willing to go in search of that performance elsewhere.

In contrast to the relative murkiness of such searches in the past, tenants now have at their disposal an increasing amount of comparative information from LEED, BREEAM, Energy Star, and other sustainability metrics and financial modeling tools. In this competitive marketplace, new buildings need to perform at the highest levels, while existing buildings need to upgrade to avoid obsolescence.

Even companies still uninterested in sustainability per se are finding themselves impressed by the energy cost savings associated with green buildings, which can reduce operating expenses by 10% to 40%. With the most advanced sustainable design practices in place, energy cost reductions can reach 70% or higher compared to conventional buildings of the same size. Net-zero-energy and even positive-energy buildings, such as AS+GG's Masdar Headquarters, which was designed to generate 103% of the energy it consumes, are no longer a matter of speculative fiction. They are becoming a reality. In our lifetime, I believe, projects such as Masdar HQ and AS+GG's Vancouver Residential Complex, which was designed to achieve a 90% reduction in energy and an 80% reduction in GHG emissions relative to typical homes in the neighborhood, will become the norm, as building owners are increasingly willing to invest to provide added value for greater and greater cost savings and reduced carbon emissions in the future.

Increasingly, too, developers, existing building owners, and their tenants are being enticed to save more energy by incentives (including tax-increment funding and other financial vehicles) from utility companies, municipalities, states, and the federal government. Our client the Federation of Korean Industries' new headquarters, FKI Tower, for example, was able to take advantage of a renewable energy generation incentive offered by the City of Seoul, South Korea. The building-integrated photovoltaics (BIPV) on FKI's exterior wall generates about 3% of the building's energy needs, but that energy will be sold to the Seoul power grid at about 10 times the price (about 50 cents per kWh) of the energy that FKI buys from the grid (about 5 cents per kWh, in 2008 dollars).

At the same time, the FKI BIPV has zero environmental impact in terms of land use, as opposed to building a PV solar field. In this way, the FKI exterior wall system achieves a win-win scenario for all parties. As our research as part of the Chicago Central Area DeCarbonization Plan showed, existing building owners can qualify for similar incentives by improving, maintaining, and operating their base buildings more sustainably through initiatives such as mechanical system and exterior wall upgrades, green cleaning practices, and recycling programs.

At some point in the foreseeable future, the carrot of government incentives could well be supplemented by the stick of regulation. In many parts of Europe, cap-and-trade policies are gaining favor; the United States may not be far behind. Corporations, developers, and existing building owners who voluntarily self-monitor, self-report, and self-regulate their carbon emissions will be ahead of the curve.

And as the larger culture has shifted regarding sustainability, so have significant portions of the real estate community. New sustainable design and green retrofits can require some additional capital outlay, but not as much as some people believe. Davis Langdon's groundbreaking 2004 national study, revisited in 2006, showed no major difference in average costs for green buildings vs. their conventional counterparts. Smaller studies, including one released in 2009 by the Urban Green Council in New York City, confirmed the absence of a major gap between construction costs of residential towers and commercial interiors that meet LEED standards and those that do not.

As sustainable design gets smarter, it also becomes more affordable. As we look at sustainable design solutions, more holistic, mutually beneficial efficiencies arise. New sustainable solutions in exterior wall systems, natural and artificial lighting, air quality, materials, and finishes are appearing almost every day. Energy generation technologies—especially photovoltaics and wind turbines, as well as fuel cells and systems to harness building sites' geothermal properties—have also come a long way in recent years, in both quality and price.

To the extent that developers and building owners are laying out more money for sustainable design, they are also getting more for that investment, and are beginning to reap the benefits as payback periods get shorter and shorter. They are also realizing a range of additional benefits, including lower maintenance costs, higher rental rates, reduced tenant vacancy, and increased satisfaction by building occupants.

The average cost (in 2009 dollars) for constructing a LEED compliant high rise residential tower in New York City is about $440 per square foot, according to the 2009 Urban Green Council study, compared to $437 per square foot for conventional projects. The average cost for LEED compliant commercial interiors is less expensive than conventional interiors—$191 per square foot vs. to $204 per square foot for conventional interiors. Other studies, including a recent one (2009) by the University of San Diego and CoStar Group, have confirmed that sustainably designed commercial buildings outperform non-green buildings in occupancy, sale price, and rental rates. In short, sustainable design is beginning to pay for itself.

Just as important, developers and building owners are beginning to think more holistically about the economics of sustainability. They are recognizing that it is more than a matter of short-term costs; it is also about the long-term life-cycle costs of a building. A sustainably designed building will cost far less to operate over time, and the rate of savings will accelerate in relation to the rising cost of energy over the same period. The same is true of an existing building which has undertaken a green retrofit. In both cases, the value of the asset will obviously be increased.

There are, of course, degrees of excellence in sustainable design, and corresponding variations in the associated premiums. There is a significant difference in cost between the average LEED-compliant building and the high-performance, often high-tech buildings we are designing at AS+GG. But if the financial challenges are higher in high-performance buildings, so are the potential rewards.

Our ultimate goal is to work with clients to pursue the highest levels of sustainability within the established budget. Yes, we want to do our part to pursue the best performing design and make our world a better place, and we also want to save our clients' money while adding value to their project. There is no reason these goals cannot work together.

It is all about efficiency, looking at the sustainable economic equation holistically, and how our design philosophy *Form Follow Performance* can help create better, higher performing buildings.

Epilogue

In 2022, we are also now focusing on Embodied Carbon Emissions, or the carbon emissions of the building's manufacturing and construction process. This is a more holistic approach to evaluating carbon emissions and efficiency in the materials used in our projects. More efficient material use equals lower costs and additional savings for our clients. We have found that investing in sustainable design in a holistic manner reaps significant rewards in the long term. We are actively doing R&D on one of the most significant construction materials – concrete – with respect to embodied carbon. We are testing negative-carbon-emission concrete, which we believe will be a game changer in the construction industry. We are also actively looking at what effects a Post-COVID world has on architectural design, as it has permanently changed the way the public looks at enclosed spaces and has increased the awareness and demand for healthy spaces.

Honors + Media

Awards

2022
-National AIA, Interior Architecture Award, Chicago Architecture Center
-Re-Thinking the Future Awards, First Award, Cultural Built, Al Wasl Plaza
-Re-Thinking the Future, First Award, Mixed-Use Concept, Golden Leaf Gardens

2021
-The Chicago Athenaeum, International Architecture Award, Al Wasl Plaza
-AIA Chicago, Citation of Merit, Burj Vista Self-Shading Balconies
-The Chicago Athenaeum, American Architecture Award, Central Park Tower
-CTBUH Awards, Best Tall Building 400 meters and above Award of Excellence, Central Park Tower
-The Chicago Athenaeum, Green Good Design, LinkedIn Middlefield Campus Carbon Action Plan
-The Chicago Athenaeum, Green Good Design Award, Al Wasl Plaza

2020
-AIA Chicago, Interior Architecture Award, Citation of Merit, Chicago Architecture Center
-World Travel Awards, China's Leading Hotel 2020, Waldorf Astoria Beijing
-World Travel Awards, Beijing's Leading Luxury Hotel, Waldorf Astoria Beijing
-AIA Chicago, Interior Architecture Award, Citation of Merit, Chicago Architecture Center

2019
-ENR Midwest's 2019 Best Projects, Merit Award, Chicago Architecture Center
-AIA Chicago, Honor Award, Urban Design, Dubai World Expo Legacy Master Plan
-Chicago Athenaeum, Good Design Awards, Graphic Design, Resi-Density
-Chicago Athenaeum, American Architecture Award, Kazakhstan Pavilion: Nur Alem
-Chicago Athenaeum, International Architecture Awards, Astana Arts Center
-GCFD Special Achievement Real Estate Award, Chicago Architecture Center
-Rethinking the Future, Global Architecture & Design Awards, First Award, Commercial, Signature Tower One
-Rethinking the Future, Global Architecture & Design Awards, First Award, Cultural, Astana Arts Center
Architect's Newspaper, Best of Design, Editor's Choice, Beaubien Woods Action Plan

2018
-AIA Chicago, Unbuilt FORWARD Award, Astana Arts Center
-AIA Chicago, Unbuilt FORWARD Award, Istanbul Cultural Center
-WAN Awards, Future Projects, Urban Design, Shortlist, New Baishizhou Shenzhen
-Architect's Newspaper Best of Design Awards, Urban Design, Honorable Mention, North Branch Framework Plan
-Structural Engineers Association of Illinois (SEAOI), Excellence in Structural Engineering Awards, Best Project, $10-$50 million, The Yard at Chicago Shakespeare Theater
-ENR Midwest, Best Project, The Yard at Chicago Shakespeare Theater
-Re-thinking the Future, Global Architecture & Design, Second Award, Awards Kazakhstan Pavilion: Nur Alem
-Architizer A+ Awards, Cultural-Hall-Theater, Finalist, The Yard at Chicago Shakespeare Theater
-Architizer A+ Awards, Residential-Unbuilt - Multi-Unit Housing, Finalist, Lakeside Residential Towers
-The Chicago Athenaeum, Green Good Design, Green Architecture, South Bend Renaissance District
-The Chicago Athenaeum, Green Good Design, Green Architecture, Zhongzhou Holdings Finance Center

2017
-AIA Innovation Awards, Stellar Architecture, Honorable Mention, The Yard at Chicago Shakespeare Theater
-WAN Awards, Future Projects Commercial Award, Winner, Hotel Atlantic
-WAN Awards, Facade Award, Finalist, Waldorf Astoria Beijing
-Bavarian Association for the Promotion of Solar Energy Building Integrated Solar Technology, Architectural Award, Shortlist, FKI Tower
-The Chicago Athenaeum, Green Good Design, Green Architecture, South Bend Renaissance District
-The Chicago Athenaeum, Green Good Design, Green Architecture, Zhongzhou Holdings Finance Center
-AIA Chicago, Divine Detail Award, Waldorf Astoria Beijing's Bronze Facade
-The American Architecture Prize, Architectural Design, Tall Buildings, Winner, FKI Tower
-The American Architecture Prize, Cultural Buildings, Honorable Mention, The Yard at Chicago Shakespeare
-The Chicago Athenaeum, International Architecture Awards, Yangtze Tower
-ASLA Award, Analysis and Planning, Honor Award, Positioning Pullman
-The American Architecture Prize, Firm of the Year, Multidisciplinary Architecture, Shortlist, AS+GG
-The Chicago Athenaeum, American Architecture Awards, Willow Creek North Shore
-The Chicago Athenaeum, American Architecture Awards, Confidential Residential Development
-The Chicago Athenaeum, Green Good Design Award, Green Urban Planning, Wuhan Bridgehead CBD
-The Chicago Athenaeum, Green Good Design Award, Green Architecture, Wuhan Greenland Center

2016
-Re-Thinking the Future, Sustainability Award, First Award, Mixed-Use, Wuhan Greenland Center
-Re-Thinking the Future, Sustainability Award, First Award, Commercial, FKI Tower
-AIA Chicago, Divine Detail Award, FKI Tower BIPV
-AIA Chicago, Regional and Urban Design Awards, Citation of Merit, Positioning Pullman
-AIA National Tap/CCA Innovation Awards, Stellar Design, Astana Expo City
-LEAF Awards, Hospitality Building of the Year, Waldorf Astoria Beijing
-The Chicago Athenaeum, American Prize for Architecture: Louis H. Sullivan Award, AS+GG
-Architect's Newspaper, Best of Design Awards, Urban Design, Honorable Mention, Positioning Pullman
-AIA Illinois, 2016 Daniel Burnham Award, Positioning Pullman
-APA-IL Chapter Awards, Strategic Plan, Positioning Pullman
-The Chicago Athenaeum, International Architecture Award, Waldorf Astoria Beijing
-The Chicago Athenaeum, International Architecture Award, FKI Tower
-The Chicago Athenaeum, International Architecture Award, Istanbul Cultural Center
-The Chicago Athenaeum, International Architecture Award, Golden Horn Shipyard
-The Chicago Athenaeum, International Architecture Award, Greenland Tower Chengdu
-AIA Illinois, 2016 Daniel Burnham Award, Positioning Pullman
-The Chicago Athenaeum, Green Good Design Award, Green Urban Planning, Positioning Pullman
-The Chicago Athenaeum, Green Good Design Award, Green Urban Planning, Astana Expo City 2017
-The Chicago Athenaeum, Green Good Design Award, Green Urban Planning, Lincoln Park Sustainability Roadmap

-Architizer A+ Awards, Plus Categories, Details: Architecture +Metal, Finalist, Waldorf Astoria Beijing
-Architizer A+ Awards, Typology Categories, Cultural: Unbuilt Cultural, Special Mention, Istanbul Cultural Center
-Architectural Review, MIPIM Future Project Award, Cultural Regeneration, Commendation, Istanbul Cultural Center
-Architectural Review, MIPIM Future Project Award, Tall Buildings, Commendation, Biophilic Tower

2015
-WAN Future Projects, Civic Award, Winner, Istanbul Cultural Center
-WAN Future Projects, Urban Design Award, Shortlist, Golden Horn Shipyard
-Re-Thinking The Future 2015 Award, Urban Design Concept, First Award, Great City Chengdu
-Re-Thinking The Future 2015 Award, Urban Design Concept, Second Award, Astana Expo City
-AIA Chicago, Distinguished Building Award, Citation of Merit, Waldorf Astoria Beijing
-IIDA Red Awards, Product Design, Winner, Fracture Dining Table
-The Chicago Athenaeum, American Architecture Award, Waldorf Astoria Beijing
-The Chicago Athenaeum, International Architecture Award, Hotel Atlantic
-The Chicago Athenaeum, Green Good Design Award, Green Architecture, FKI Tower
-The Chicago Athenaeum, Green Good Design Award, Green Architecture, Kellogg School of Management
-The Chicago Athenaeum, Green Good Design Award, Green Architecture, Dancing Dragons
-The Chicago Athenaeum, Green Good Design Award, Green Urban Planning, Tianfu New District Master Plan
-HD Awards, Winner, Hotel Luxury/Upscale, Waldorf Astoria Beijing
-Civic Trust Awards, Civic Trust Award, FKI Tower
-Civic Trust Awards, Civic Trust Award, Waldorf Astoria Beijing

2014
-Korean Architecture Award, Excellence Award, FKI Tower
-Korea Presidential Commission on Architecture Policy, Korea Green Building Award, FKI Tower
-Re-Thinking the Future, Sustainability Award, Honorable Mention, FKI Tower
-WAN Urban Design Award, Future Projects, Finalist, Xixian Great City Master Plan
-AIA Middle East, Non-Built Category, Merit Award, Jeddah Tower (as Kingdom Tower)
-AIA Chicago, Distinguished Building Award, Citation of Merit, FKI Tower
-The Chicago Athenaeum, International Architecture Award, Dancing Dragons
-CTBUH, Best Tall Building Asia and Australasia, Finalist, FKI Tower (as Federation of Korean Industries)
-The Chicago Athenaeum, Green Good Design Award, Green Urban Planning, Xixian Great City Master Plan
-The Chicago Athenaeum, Green Good Design Award, Green Urban Planning, Great City Chengdu Master Plan
-The Chicago Athenaeum, Green Good Design Award, Green Architecture, Solar EV Canopy
-The Chicago Athenaeum, Green Good Design Award, Green Research / Technology, the Density Study: A Carbon Analysis of Residential Typologies
-OPP, Making a Difference in Asia Award, Firm Award
American Institute of Steel Construction, IDEAS2 Awards,
-Excellence in Steel-Frame Building, Solar EV Canopy
Structural Engineers Association of Illinois, Excellence in Structural Engineering, Winner, Best Project $150 million and over, FKI Tower (as Federation of Korean Industries)
-IIDA RED Award, Furniture Design, GG Table
-Architizer A+ Award, Office Building High Rise, Finalist, FKI Tower (as Federation of Korean Industries)
-Architizer A+ Award, Unbuilt Category, Architecture + Technology, Finalist, Chengdu Greenland Tower

2013
-The Chicago Athenaeum, American Architecture Award, Dancing Dragons
-The Chicago Athenaeum, American Architecture Award, Xixian Great City
-The Chicago Athenaeum, American Architecture Award, Biophilic Tower
-The Chicago Athenaeum, American Architecture Award, Wave Tower (Scheme 1 Dancing Dragons)
-The Chicago Athenaeum, International Architecture Award, Great City Master Plan (as Tianfu Ecological City)
-AIA Illinois, Daniel Burnham Honor Award, Chicago Central Area DeCarbonization Plan

2012
-AIA Chicago, Design Excellence, SustainABILITY Award, Chicago Central Area Decarbonization Plan
-The Chicago Athenaeum, American Architecture Award, KAPSARC
-Ace Mentor Program, Green Visionary Award, Firm Award
-The Chicago Athenaeum, International Architecture Award, Burj Khalifa Gatehouses
The Chicago Athenaeum, International Architecture Award, Solar EV Dock

2011
-CTBUH, Lynn S. Beedle Lifetime Achievement Award, Adrian Smith
-National AIA, Honor Award, Regional and Urban Design, Chicago Central Area DeCarbonization Plan
-AIA Chicago, Unbuilt Design, Honor Award, KAPSARC
-AIA Chicago, Unbuilt Design, Citation of Merit, Dubai Bridge
-The Chicago Athenaeum, International Architecture Award, Gold Cross Sky Ring

2010
-AIA Chicago, Design Excellence, Unbuilt Design, Matrix Gateway Complex
-WAN Awards, Urban Design, Chicago Central Area DeCarbonization Plan
-International Property Awards, Arabian Property Award for Architecture, Middle East Region, Masdar Headquarters
-R+D Award for Sustainability, Architect Magazine, Chicago DeCarbonization Plan
-The Chicago Athenaeum, International Architecture Award, Vancouver Residential Complex
-P/A Award, Architect Magazine, Matrix Gateway Complex

2009
-The Chicago Athenaeum, American Architecture Award, Matrix Gateway Complex
-The Chicago Athenaeum, International Architecture Award, Matrix Gateway Complex
-SOAR, Vision into Reality Award, Firm Award
-The Chicago Reader, Chicago's Best Emerging Architect, Gordon Gill

2008
-Construction Week Awards, Sustainable Design Award, Masdar Headquarters
-International Property Awards, Arabian Property Award for Architecture, Middle East Region, Verde Residences
-Middle East Architect Awards, Green Project of the Year, Masdar Headquarters
-Cityscape Architectural Awards, Environmental Award, Masdar Headquarters

Media

2022

The Architect's Newspaper, "Adrian Smith + Gordon Gill Architecture's expansion of the Steppenwolf Theatre brings the backstage to the house," Anjulie Rao, January 12, 2022

The National News, "Dubai's latest skyscraper Uptown Tower peaks at 329 metres," January 22, 2022

World-Architects, "US Building of the Week: Steppenwolf Theatre Campus Expansion," John Hill, January 24, 2022

The National News," Dubai's latest skyscraper Uptown Tower peaks at 329 metres," January 25, 2022

Global Construction Review, "Besix's Dubai Uptown Tower tops out at 329m," Robd Sweet, January 26, 2022

Prestige, "These Are Expo 2020 Dubai's Most Breathtaking Pavilions," January 28, 2022

Arabian Business, "Uptown Tower, Dubai's new supertall skyscraper set for Q3 completion," January 29, 2022

Daily Commercial News, "Tarp Covered Tower: 160 Front Street West," William Conway, February 16, 2022

Clairn, "Un Jardin urbano y un domo traslucido, el corazon de Dubai," Graciela Baduel, February 22, 2022

Forbes, "Inside A $65.8 Million Residence In The World's Tallest Residential Building," Emma Reyolds, March 1, 2022

The National, "Ten attractions to continue at Expo 2020 Dubai, from UAE pavilion to famous water illusion," Ramola Talwar Badam, March 1, 2022

2021 Domus, "The world's most Googled buildings," March 3, 2022

The Chicago Crusader, "Chicagoland Youth Artists create original works for Steppenwolf," Bonnie DeShong, March 4, 2022

2021

Boston Business Journal, "Boston's first net-zero-carbon building could tower over Downtown Crossing," Catherine Carlock, February 11, 2021

Construction Week, "'Digitalisation' accelerates construction on Dubai's Uptown Tower," Ranju Warrier, March 9, 2021

ArchDaily, "Chicago-London International Dialogue: Tall Buildings & the Zero-Carbon Agenda," March 27, 2021

Wonderful Engineering, "Skyscraper of the Day: Meet the Tallest Residential Tower In The World," March 29, 2021

Gulf News, "Al Wasl Plaza: Dubai Expo 2020 is home to the world's largest 360-degree projection dome," Sahar Ejaz, April 29, 2021

Block Club Chicago, "Steppenwolf to Open New Theater Building, Education Center During 2021 Comeback Season," Jake Wittich, May 4, 2021

Dezeen, "Photos show supertall skyscraper Central Park Tower nearing completion in New York," May 25, 2021

The New York Times, "Buildings with Sections That Seem to Hover in Midair," Tim McKeough, June 4, 2021

The New York Times, "Building a Cantilever," Tim McKeough, June 4, 2021

Designboom, "World's Tallest Residential Building 'Central Park Tower' Nears Completion in New York City," June 7, 2021

New York Magazine, "A Slide of the Sky: The Supertall 111 West 57th is what the ruling class buildings for itself," Justin Davidson, June 9, 2021

ArchDaily, "Expo 2020 Dubai "Connects Minds and Creates the Future," Christele Harrouk, July 13, 2021

Dezeen, "Six new supertall skyscrapers changing New York's skyline," India Block, July 19, 2021

Third Coast Review, "Dialogs: Architecture Collides with Theater in Steppenwolf Podcast, "Collision," Featuring AS+GG's Gordon Gill," Nancy S. Bishop, August 5, 2021

Surface Magazine, "Inside Central Park Tower, the World's Tallest Residential Building," Ryan Waddoups, August 16, 2021

Architectural Digest, "Exclusive Look Inside the World's Tallest Residential Skyscraper," Nadja Sayej, August 12, 2021

Islander News, "What's it like living in the World's Tallest Luxury Residential Skyscraper?" August 15, 2021

Architect Magazine, "Why R+D Matters," September 1, 2021

Dezeen, "9/11 led to "a renaissance of tall building design" say skyscraper designers," Lizzie Crook, September 7, 2021

Newcity Stage, "Collision Course: Steppenwolf Emerges from the Pandemic with New Leadership and a New Theater," September 9, 2021

ArchDaily, "Expo Dubai 2020 Reveals New Images," Christele Harrouk, September 13, 2021

Crain's Chicago Business, "Supertall and sustainable: The future of skyscrapers," Dennis Rodkin, September 23, 2021

Arquitectura Viva, "The tallest residential building in the world," September 23, 2021

Architectural Record, "Dubai's World Expo, Lavish but Late," September 24, 2021

The American Bazaar, "'Jamaica Makes it Move' with food, music and sports," October 9, 2021

Broadway World, "Steppenwolf Names its New In-The-Round Theater and Education Center," Stephi Wild, October 21, 2021

The New York Times, "A World-Class World Expo," Sam Lubell, October 24, 2021

Khaleej Times, "Expo 2020 Dubai: Al Wasl Plaza is my best work ever, says designer," SM Ayaz Zakir, October 28, 2021

Architectural Record, "Dubai Expo's Fantastical National Pavilions," Ilana Herzig, October 29, 2021

Chicago Sun-Times, "Steppenwolf Theatre's new Arts and Education Center is a 'love letter to Chicago,'" Clare Spaulding, October 31, 2021

Ahram Online, "Expo 2020 Dubai: Connecting the world," Nora Koloyan-Keuhnelian, November 2, 2021

WTTW, "Steppenwolf Theatre Returns After 20-Month Intermission, Dedicates New Wing," Marc Vitali, November 2, 2021

Newcity, "Steppenwolf Debuts Lefkofsky Center," November 3, 2021

Architectural Record, "Smith + Gill Architecture Expands the Steppenwolf Theater Campus in Chicago, James Gauer, November 4, 2021

BBC News, "Does the skyscraper still have a future?" Judith Dupre, November 4, 2021

Chicago Now, "The Wolf Strikes again with Steppenwolf Theatre Company Liz and Eric Lefkofsky Arts and Education Center expansion," November 6, 2021

ArchDaily, "Residensity A carbon Analysis of Residential Typologies," November 12, 2021

The Chicago Crusader, "Expanded Steppenwolf campus a cultural nexus for Chicago New state-of-the-art theater and dedicated education center," Elaine Hegwood Bowen, November 15, 2021

Urban Toronto, "160 Front West Starts to Show Its Curves," Teana Graziani, November 26, 2021

The Telegraph, "Building goals: the architecture of Dubai's ambition," Sarah Hedley Hymers, December 1, 2021

blogTO, "Toronto's new leaning office tower is now joining the city skyline," December 6, 2021

2020

Architectural Digest, "The 11 Most Anticipated Buildings of 2020," January 14, 2020

Architect Magazine, "With Housing's Carbon Footprint, Density Matters," January 16, 2020

Arabian Business, "Kingdom building: Sixteen of the top projects currently shaping Saudi Arabia," January 23, 2020

Architectural Record, "On the Boards: A Museum, Towers, and New Urban Waterfronts," Josephine Minutillo, January 27, 2020

Architect Magazine, "The Pathway to Net Zero Carbon Buildings," Dr. Christopher Drew, PhD. January 28, 2020

The Next Miami, "830 Brickell Marks The Start Of Vertical Construction & Releases New Renderings, On Track To Become Miami's Second Tallest Office Tower In 2021," February 4, 2020

Vancouver is Awesome, "Revamped design for controversial Waterfront Station tower just released," Naoibh O'Conner, February 5, 2020

Chicago Tribune, "5 years later, Pullman Monument poised to fulfill potential," February 20, 2020

Trains, "Plans for Pullman site include rebuilding of manufacturing facilities," February 24, 2020

Dezeen, "Ten upcoming supertall skyscrapers from the world's best-known architects," India Block, March 1, 2020

AV Magazine, "Creating a cultural icon," Zoe Mutter, March 30, 2020

The Nanjinger, "500 Metres High! Tallest Building in Nanjing set for Change," Frank Hossack, April 1, 2020

American Theatre, "If You Build It, Will They Come?" Kate Mazade, April 27, 2020

Curbed Chicago, "A look at the new skyscrapers that will forever change Chicago's skyline," Jay Kozlarz, April 30, 2020

Chicago Sun-Times, "City planners OK tall neighbor for Tribune Tower," David Roeder, May 8, 2020

Forbes, "A First Look at Four Big City Hot Properties With Spectacular Views," Keith Flamer, July 31, 2020

Dezeen, "Nine examples of spherical architecture from around the globe," Tom Ravenscroft, August 29, 2020

Big Think, "Is it possible to build a mile-high skyscraper," Mike Colagrossi, September 14, 2020

Dezeen, "Dubai Expo reveals main pavilions ahead of rescheduled event," Tom Ravenscroft, October 1, 2020

Bureau International des Expositions (BIE), "Al Wasl Plaza: the heart and soul of Expo 2020 Dubai," October 1, 2020

The Architect's Newspaper, "Expo 2020 Dubai teases blossoming pavilions ahead of rescheduled festival," Matt Hickman, October 14, 2020

Architect Magazine, "Una Residences," October 19, 2020

For Construction Pros, "It's Only Just Begun: Miami's $25 Million Underground Parking Garage," November 6, 2020

Chicago Tribune, "Rising in a pandemic: Steppenwolf's new theater campus is a $54 million bet on returning to normalcy," Chris Jones, November 12, 2020

Greentech Media, "Getting Building Height Right for the Climate," Ingrid Lobet, November 30, 2020

2019

News Atlas, "There's a new contender for the World's Second Tallest Skyscraper," Adam Williams, January 9, 2019

Archinect, "Adrian Smith + Gordon Gill to design Shimao Shenzhen Longgang Master Plan and 700m anthropomorphic tower," January 9, 2019

ArchDaily, "Adrian Smith + Gordon Gill to Design China's Tallest Skyscraper," January 11, 2019

Dezeen, "Adrian Smith + Gordon Gill reveals design for China's next skyscraper," Lizzie Crook, January 14, 2018

The Architect's Newspaper, "Adrian Smith + Gordon Gill Designs Tallest Building in China," January 16, 2019

Building Design + Construction, "AS+GG Designed Tower will be the tallest in China," January 16, 2019

Wall Street Journal, "The man Behind Billionaire's Row Battles to Sell the World's Tallest Condo," Katherine Clarke and Candace Taylor, January 17, 2019

New York Post, "The super-tall towers transforming NYC's skyline," Emily Nonko, January 23, 2019

USA News Hub, "China's tallest building: AS+GG Reveals plans for 700m skyscraper," January 24, 2019

Designboom, "China's Tallest Building: AS+GG reveals plans for 700m skyscraper," January 24, 2019

Architect Magazine, "Shenzhen-Hong Kong International Center," February 5, 2019

Offsite, "Chicago's Architecture Center Shines While Houston's Waits to be Rebuilt after Harvey Flooding," February 19, 2019

Curbed New York, "Central Park Tower architect calls building 'respectful' of NYC skyline," Zoe Rosenberg, February 25, 2019

Egypt Independent, "Dubai and Saudi Arabia towers in time war to be world's tallest," March 4, 2019

Curbed Chicago, "Steppenwolf expands theater with dramatic, geometric design from Smith + Gill," Jay Koziarz, March 5, 2019

Re Journal, "Iconic Chicago institution Steppenwolf Theatre breaks ground on extensive expansion," March 5, 2019

Chicago Tribune, "Steppenwolf Theatre, known for bold moves, plans a new $54M theater-in-the-round project on Halsted Street," March 5, 2019

Glass on Web, "Guardian Glass Project: Astana Expo," April 17, 2019

Construction Week, "Expo 2020 Dubai's 130m Al Wasl Plaza set for Christie's visuals shows," Ranju Warrier, May 2, 2019

Curbed Chicago, "Willis Tower loses claim to highest roof in the Western Hemisphere to NY skyscraper," Jay Koziarz, July 30, 2019

World Architecture News, "Future designs benefit local communities globally," Emilia Nuzzaci, August 29, 2019

Architectural Digest, "An Architecture Lover's Guide to Manhattan's 57th Street," Katherine McGrath, August 29, 2019

Redbook, "10 New Skyscrapers That Are Changing City Skylines," Heath Owens, August 30, 2019

Construction Business News, "Expo 2020 Dubai lifts final piece of Al Wasl Plaza's dome into place," Kasun Illankoon, September 9, 2019

The Next Miami, "New Details of 830 Brickell Released, set to begin Vertical Construction Now and Become Miami's Most Modern Office Tower," September 10, 2019

New York Magazine, "The Challenges of Constructing New York's Tallest Apartment Building," September 16, 2019

The Architect's Newspaper, "Central Park Tower tops out to become the world's tallest residential building," Sydney Franklin, September 18, 2019

MEED, "Al-Wasl Plaza dome adorned with steel crown," September 18, 2019

Construction Week Online, "Expo 2020 Dubai video features HE Reem Al Hashimy praising Al Wasl Plaza; says 'she carries the original name of Dubai," Neha Bhatia, September 19, 2019

The Architect's Newspaper, "Central Park Tower out to become the world's tallest residential building," September 19, 2019

Dezeen, "This week, the world's tallest residential skyscraper topped out," Lizzie Crook, September 28, 2019

Global Construction Review, "Adrian Smith, Gordon Gill win 700m tower in China," November 1, 2019

Architect Magazine, "South HeXi Yuzui Financial District and Tower," November 6, 2019

Media

News Atlas, "Sculpted supertall skyscraper will boast energy-efficient design," Adam Williams, November 13, 2019

ArchDaily, "AS+GG Releases Design for New Financial District in China," Christele Harrouk, November 13, 2019

Architect Magazine, "This Week in Tech: A Tower in China that Repurposes Rainwater," Katharine Keane, November 15, 2019

Engineering News Record, "Chicago Architecture Center Completed in Tight Timeline," November 20, 2019

ReJournals, "Fresh look at new supertall project next to Tribune Tower," Matt Baker, November 20, 2019

Block Club Chicago, "$56 million Pullman National Monument Overhaul Has 'Turned The Lights Back On' In Historic South Side Neighborhood," Jamie Nesbitt Golden, November 26, 2019

Stir World, "Adrian Smith and Gordon Gill on skyscraper architecture and energy-efficient buildings," Vladimir Belogolovsky, December 19, 2019

2018

Mansion Global, "World's Tallest Residential Building is One Step Closer to Completion," Beckie Strum, January 2, 2018

Wallpaper, "Letter from Chicago: keeping up with construction in the Windy City," January 2, 2018

The Gulf Today, "Expo 2020 Dubai awards two major construction contracts to Laing O'Rourke," January 23, 2018

The Architect's Newspaper, "Chicago's Tribune Tower is gutted for condos as a supertall is proposed next door," January 26, 2018

The Wall Street Journal, "House Call: How the Designer of the World's Tallest Tower Got His Career Off the Ground," February 13, 2018

The Architect's Newspaper, "Construction on world's tallest tower moves forward," February 14, 2018

Thrillist, "Here's What the New World's Tallest Skyscraper Will Look Like," James Chrisman, February 22, 2018

Glass on Web, "Guardian Glass Project: Astana Expo," February 26, 2018

Curbed Miami, "47-story Una condo tower will rise on Brickell Waterfront," Adele Chapin, March 7, 2018

Dezeen, "Construction of world's tallest tower moves forward after delays," Tom Ravenscroft, March 12, 2018

Mansion Global, "Miami Area Gets Newest Crop of Condos," Bill Cary, March 29, 2018

Tall Buildings Russia, "Future Energy," pp. 86-95; 132-133, April 2018

Building Design + Construction, "Developers reveal plans for 1,422-foot-tall skyscraper in Chicago," David Malone, April 17, 2018

Chicago Magazine, "Developers Plan Chicago's Second-Tallest Tower at Tribune Site," AJ LaTrace, April 17, 2018

Crain's Chicago Business, "See what Tribune Tower owners want to build next door," Danny Ecker, April 17, 2018

Curbed Chicago, "1,422-foot Tribune Tower addition would be Chicago's second tallest building," Jay Koziarz, April 17, 2018

Chicago Sun-Times, "Developers pitch skyscraper near Tribune Tower that would be city's 2nd tallest," Sam Charles, April 17, 2018

Building Design + Construction, "Adrian Smith + Gordon Gill Architecture designs 47-story condo tower in Miami," David Malone, April 24, 2018

Dezeen, "Chicago's second-tallest skyscraper planned beside Tribune Tower," Bridget Cogley, April 27, 2018

Arch Daily, "AS+GG Architecture to Design Yacht-Inspired Tower in Miami," Niall Patrick Walsh, April 30, 2018

Curbed New York, "Construction on Extell's Central Park Tower hits supertall status," April 30, 2018

Courier International, "Chicago Architect," May 10, 2018

Daily Hive, "New design for 'origami' tower at Waterfront Station to be revealed next week," Kenneth Chan, May 11, 2018

Dezeen, "Work begins on world's second-tallest skyscraper in Shenzhen," India Block, May 16, 2018

Chicago Tribune, "Five decades after Chicago's greatest skyscraper boom, city aims high again," Ryan Ori, May 19, 2018

World Architecture News, "AS+GG head for the heights in Miami," May 24, 2018

Chicago Business Journal, "Chicago Architecture Foundation's new home debuts soon," Lewis Lazare, June 12, 2018

Curbed Chicago, "A first look inside the Chicago Architecture Foundation's new riverfront space," Jay Koziarz, June 13, 2018

Canadian Architect, "AS+GG and B+H's 160 Front Street to break ground in 2019," June 13, 2018

The Architect's Newspaper, "Chicago Architecture Foundation reveals its new home," Elizabeth Blasius, June 14, 2018

Michigan Avenue Magazine, "These two buzzed-about design projects are must-visits this season," AJ LaTrace, June 21, 2018

The Architect's Newspaper, "Saudi Arabia is building a future for its millennial population," Antonio Pacheco, June 25, 2018

The Architect's Newspaper, "AN tracks the largest projects in Saudi Arabia," Antonio Pacheco, June 26, 2018

Architect Magazine, "Chicago Architecture Center Debuts in August," Sara Johnson, June 27, 2018

New Atlas, "Sustainable skyscraper is sculpted for the wind," Adam Williams, July 11, 2018

Dezeen, "Adrian Smith + Gordon Gill reveals skyscraper for 160 Front Street in Toronto," Bridget Cogley, July 12, 2018

Architect Magazine, "160 Front Street," July 13, 2018

Forbes, "7 Supertall Buildings in the Works Around the Globe," Kristin Tablang, July 22, 2018

Chicago Magazine, "The Chicago Skyline in 2023," AJ LaTrace, August 16, 2018

Artsy, "The Incomparable, Futuristic Architecture of Kazakhstan's Young Capital," August 16, 2018

Crain's Chicago Business, "Check out the Chicago Architecture Foundation's new digs," Lisa Bertagnoli, August 24, 2018

Architectural Digest, "The New Chicago Architecture Center Debuts in a Riverside Mies van der Rohe Building," Laura Itzkowitz, August 28, 2018

Chicago Tribune, "The Chicago Architecture Foundation has a new name and home. Skyscraper models are the stars of its engaging riverfront exhibition space," Blair Kamin August 29, 2018

The Chicago Reader, "The Chicago Architecture Foundation is now the Chicago Architecture Center," Deanna Isaacs, August 29, 2018

Re Journal, "First look at the new Chicago Architecture Center," August 29, 2018

The Chicago Sun-Times, "Chicago Architecture Center takes its place as 'must-see' cultural destination," Fran Spielman, August 29, 2018

My Modern Met, "20,000-Square-Foot Chicago Architecture Center Opens Its Doors to the Public," Jessica Stewart, August 29, 2018

Chicago Magazine, "The Chicago Architecture Center Opens Tomorrow: Here's What to See," AJ LaTrace, August 30, 2018

Architect Magazine, "Look Inside the New Chicago Architecture Center," August 31, 2018

Curbed Chicago, "Chicago Architecture Center debuts new riverfront location to the public," Jay Koziarz, August 31, 2018

The Architect's Newspaper, "The new Chicago Architecture Center offers informative, tangible experiences," Elizabeth Blasius, September 6, 2018

Re Journal, "Adrian Smith and Gordon Gill to be honored at Marshall Bennett Institute gala," September 7, 2018

Jamaica Gleamer, "New Parliament building could be country's most edifice, says architect Gordon Gill," Paul Clarke, October 12, 2018

Hypebeast, "New York's Central Park Tower Will Be Recognized as the Tallest Residential Building in the World," October 16, 2018

Metropolis Magazine, "Take a Closer Look at the Design of the World's Tallest Residential Tower," Anna Fixsen, October 18, 2018

Jamaica Observer, "Gordon Gill speaks on architecture's common sense at Utech," October 21, 2018

Chicago Magazine, "Pullman's Renaissance," October 26, 2018

Dezeen, "Eight mega-scale architecture projects underway in Saudi Arabia as the desert kingdom modernizes," November 9, 2018

Chicago Tribune, "Best architecture for 2018: It was a vital year, just not in the usual places," Blair Kamin, December 10, 2018

2017

CLADGlobal, "Green Developments: Gordon Gill, Adrian Smith + Gordon Gill," January 2017

Crain's Chicago Business, "The Takeaway: Architect Adrian Smith's view from on high," January 6, 2017

Chicago Tribune, "Plan calls for replacing Thompson Center with new tower," January 20, 2017

The Chicago Reader, "How would plans to replace the Thompson Center impact service at Clark/Lake?" February 1, 2017

South Bend Tribune, "Chicago architect preps Studebaker building for 21st-century tech economy," Margaret Fosmoe, February 6, 2017

Daily Herald, "Chicago architect preps Studebaker building for 21st century," Margaret Fosmoe, February 11, 2017

The Architect's Newspaper, "Adrian Smith + Gordon Gill will transform former Studebaker factory in South Bend, Indiana into tech hub," Matthew Messner, February 14, 2017

Curbed, "10 tallest buildings under construction or in development around the world," Patrick Sisson, February 21, 2017

Architectural Record, "Adrian Smith + Gordon Gill's Massive Astana Expo City Nears Completion," Anna Fixsen, March 2017

The National, "Huge dome planned for Dubai's Expo 2020 site," Ramola Talwar Badam, April 3, 2017

Emirates 24/7, "Expo 2020 Dubai unveils new design space with Al Wasl Plaza," April 3, 2017

Construction Week, "Design of Expo 2020 Dubai's Al Wasl Plaza revealed," Jochebed Menon April 4, 2017

Forbes Middle East, "A New Breathtaking Hall is in the Making for Expo 2020 Dubai," Amro Elserty, April 5, 2017

Chicago Tribune, "Chicago Shakes announces 2017-18 season, opening of The Yard," Chris Jones, April 13, 2017

Gulf News, "Al Wasl Plaza at Expo 2020 site to offer a variety of experiences," April 17, 2017

Departures Magazine, "Expo 2017: Astana Unveiled," Nathan Turner, April 20, 2017

Architectural Record, Tall Buildings Issue, "Jeddah Tower," p. 124, May 2017

Architect's Newspaper, "Bauer Latoza Studio and Adrian Smith + Gordon Gill tapped for Pullman National Monument Visitor Center," Matthew Messner, May 24, 2017

Dezeen, "Architects unveil energy-themed pavilions at Astana Expo 2017," Jessica Mairs, June 20, 2017

American Theater, "The Yard Beyond the Bard," Kerry Reid, July-August 2017

Chicago Architect, "The slings and arrows of outrageous innovation," pp. 18-19, July-August 2017

Chicagoly, "From Up on High," pp. 20-22, Alan P. Henry, Summer 2017

The Possible, "Interview with Gordon Gill: Searching for Better Answers," Katie Puckett, July 2017

The Economist, "Kazakhstan: the crossroads of the new Silk Road," July 1, 2017

South Bend Tribune, "South Bend Studebaker plant ready for massive facelift," Erin Blasko, July 3, 2017

The Architect's Newspaper, "Clear Vision: Kazakhstan Pavilion," Heather Corcoran, July 26, 2017

Chicago Architect, "The Slings and Arrows of Outrageous Innovation: Chicago's New Shakespeare Theater by Adrian Smith + Gordon Gill Architecture Readies to Open," July/August 2017

The Astana Times, "Astana to be featured in National Geographic's Megastructures television series," Yerbolat Uatkhanov, August 5, 2017

Architect's Newspaper, "Adrian Smith + Gordon Gill's ambitious glass sphere pavilion," August 11, 2017

Dezeen, "Central Park Tower to become world's tallest residential skyscraper," Dan Howarth, August 16, 2017

Crain's Chicago Business, "The Yard at Navy Pier: Game-changer," Catey Sullivan, August 28, 2017

CladMag, "The Yard at Chicago Shakespeare," p. 75; "Reflections on Astana Expo," p. 75, Issue 4 2017

Curbed Chicago, "Chicago Architecture Foundation announces new architecture center," Jay Koziarz, September 7, 2017

Chicago Tribune, "Architecture Foundation moving to the riverfront," Blair Kamin, September 7, 2017

Arch Daily, "New Chicago Architecture Center to Open in 2018," Patrick Lynch, September 7, 2017

Building Design + Construction, CAF announces plans for 20,000-sf Chicago Architecture Center to be built on East Wacker Drive," David Malone, September 8, 2017

Dezeen, "Chicago Architecture Foundation plans move to Mies van der Rohe-designed tower," Bridget Cogley, September 8, 2017

Broadway World, "The Yard at Chicago Shakespeare Opens on Navy Pier," September 11, 2017

Architect's Newspaper, "Chicago Architecture Foundation announces new Chicago Architecture Center," Matthew Messner, September 12, 2017

Chicago Sun-Times, with the Yard, Chicago Shakespeare sets engineering poetry in motion," Hedy Weiss, September 13, 2017

Crain's Chicago Business, "First look: The Yard, Navy Pier's new mind-blowing theater," Catey Sullivan, September 13, 2017

Chicago Magazine, "Chicago Shakes' New Venue Will Literally Let People Reshape the Theater Experience," Brian Golden, September 15, 2017

Daily Herald, "Chicago Shakespeare Theater's The Yard emerges on Navy Pier," Barbara Vitello, September 19, 2017

ENRMidwest, "Chicago's Flexible, Transforming Theater Space," pp. 28-32, Jeff Yoders, September 19, 2017

Chicago Tribune, "Flexible, intimate and innovative, The Yard at Chicago Shakespeare Theater," Blair Kamin, September 20, 2017

Media

Construction Week, "Construction begins on new mixed-use district near Dubai's JLT," September 25, 2017

Architect Magazine, "Education and the Performance Imperative," Katie Green, October 5, 2017

Architect Magazine, "AIA Announces Winners of 2017 Innovation Awards," October 30, 2017

Curbed New York, "Extell's Midtown supertall, Central Park Tower, is getting its façade," Tanay Warerkar, November 8, 2017

Curbed Chicago, "New Chicago Architecture Center working toward 2018 opening," Jay Koziarz, November 17, 2017

Architectural Digest Mexico, "Diseño bajo el Reflector," Lilia Ceballos, November 28, 2017

Chicago Tribune, "Best architecture of 2017: An innovative new theater at Navy Pier," Blair Kamin December 15, 2017

2016

Inventions, "Seit wann kratzen Hochhäuser an den Wolken?" pp. 36-37, January 2016

Architect's Newspaper, "AIA Chicago outlines Pullman's future as a national monument," Matthew Messner, January 4, 2016

Azernews, "Green building to rise over Baku," Amina Nazarli, January 13, 2016

Architect Magazine, "Worldwide Total of Supertall Buildings Reaches 100," Caroline Massie, January 14, 2016

Chicago Tribune, "Cities defined by more than tall buildings," Blair Kamin, January 15, 2016

Building Design + Construction, "How to make a 'pure' glass sphere," pp. 43-44, February 2016

The Wall Street Journal, "Jeddah Aiming for Towering Height," pp. C1; C8, February 3, 2016

Building Design + Construction, "How to make a 'pure' glass sphere," pp. 42-44, Robert Cassidy, February 18, 2016

Architect and Culture, "FKI Tower," pp. 100-109, March 2016

Newton, "Kingdom Tower (Chinese)," pp. 31-37, March 2016

Chicago Sun-Times, "Shakespeare Theater announces $35 million expansion on Navy Pier," Fran Spielman, March 2, 2016

Chicago Tribune, "New Chicago Shakespeare stage will transform Navy Pier," Chris Jones, March 2, 2016

TimeOut Chicago, "Chicago Shakespeare announces Navy Pier expansion," Kris Vire, March 2, 2016

Daily Herald, "Chicago Shakespeare Theater announces expansion plans," Barbara Vitello, March 3, 2016

Arq, "Ciudad Verde Y Futurista," pp. 18-25, March 5, 2016

Building Design + Construction, "Adrian Smith + Gordon Gill Architecture incorporates Biblical parable into church design," Mike Chamernik, March 24, 2016

Tall Buildings Russia, "AXMAT TAY3P" pp. 36-45, April 2016

Building Design + Construction, "Adrian Smith + Gordon Gill Architecture's The Yard at Chicago Shakespeare to begin construction this spring at Navy Pier," April 1, 2016

Boston Globe, "New Downtown Crossing skyscraper to rival Millennium Tower," Tim Logan, April 4, 2016

World Architecture News, "Wuhan's supertall tower heads for the top," April 6, 2016

Curbed, "Supertalls and Sustainable Skyscrapers: Architect Adrian Smith on the Mile-High Building," Patrick Sisson, April 12, 2016

Curbed, "A More Detailed Look at the Chicago Shakespeare Theater Expansion," AJ LaTrace, April 13, 2016

Engineering News-Record, "Proposal Made for 683-ft Downtown Boston Tower," Johanna Knapschaefer, April 13, 2016

World Architecture News, "Gordon Gill to design new Chicago theatre," April 14, 2016

Boston Herald, "Tower to house all its affordable units on-site," April 30, 2016

Design Diffusion, "Playing with Angles," pp. 104-107, Manuela Di Mari, May 2016

Architect's Newspaper, "Adrian Smith + Gordon Gill Architecture design 72,000-square-foot Church in Glenview, Illinois," May 9, 2016

Newcity, "Pullman's Past, Present, and Future," Tim Joyce, May 17, 2016

Structure Magazine, "Rising to the clouds with confidence," pp. 37-40, Jon Galsworthy, June 2016

Chicago Magazine, "The man with his head in the clouds," pp. 97-99; 144, Tom Chiarella, June 2016

SkyriseCities, "Tackling 'Humankind's Greatest Challenge' at Expo 2017," June 17, 2016

Gizmag, "Six-hundred-meter-tall aerodynamic eco-tower being built in China," Darren Quick, June 22, 2016

Time Magazine, "Big Idea: Buildings that power themselves" Julie Shapiro, July 2016

Civil Engineering Magazine, "Iconic Glass Globe Anchors Expo Community," Kevin Wilcox, July 19, 2016

Engineering News-Record, "Kazakhstan Seeks Attention with Multi-Billion-Dollar Expo Build," Neelam Mathews, July 19, 2016

Southeast Asia Building, "Astana Expo City 2017, designed by AS+GG, is now under construction," p. 38, September-October 2016

Civil Engineering Surveyor, "Learnings from the Jeddah Tower," pp. 22-23, Paul Daynes, September 2016

Miami Herald, "Doronin names architect for second Miami project," Jane Wooldridge, October 13, 2016

Business Insider, "A multi-billion-dollar futuristic city will host the 2017 World's Expo," Leanna Garfield, October 18, 2016

Concrete International, "Engineering Jeddah Tower," pp. 23-29, Robert C. Sinn, November 2016

Civil Engineering, "Church Building Design Features Sweeping Curves and Connection to Nature," pp. 24-27, Robert Reid, November 2016

World Architecture News, "Jin Mao Tower, Shanghai, China: A towering achievement," November 7, 2016

Chicago Tribune, "World renowned architect designs North Shore church," Manya Brachear Pashman, November 28, 2016

Building Design + Construction, 'Pure Sphere' for Kazakhstan World's Fair nearing completion," Robert Cassidy, December 29, 2016

2015

New York Magazine, "The Rise of the Mile-High Building," Justin Davidson, March 24, 2015

Visual, "City of the Future: Great City by Adrian Smith + Gordon Gill Architecture," March 29, 2015

Architect Magazine, "Up and Running: Words of Advice for Young Firms," Nate Berg with essay from Gordon Gill, March 31, 2015

Tengri News, "Nazarbayev tours EXPO-2017 construction site," Assel Satubaldina, April 7, 2015

International Journal of High-Rise Buildings, "The Environmental Impact of Tall vs. Small: A Comparative Study," Christopher Drew, Katrina Fernandez Nova, Keara Fanning, June 2015

The Guardian, "Jeddah's Kingdom Tower: how much higher can skyscrapers go?" Herbert Wright, June 4, 2015

Construction Week, "Adrian Smith + Gordon Gill to design Burj 2020," Nick Ames, June 16, 2015

Time Magazine, "When it comes to new ultra-tall towers, the sky is the limit," Vivienne Walt, July 20, 2015

Nonstop Gulfstream, "The Sky is not the limit," Lesley Conn, Summer 2015

Popular Science, "Where does the glass for the new supertall skyscapers come from?" Clay Risen, August 3, 2015

The National, "Burj 2020: Architectural duo set their sights on Dubai," James Langton, September 8, 2015

Design MENA, "Burj 2020 by Adrian Smith and Gordon Gill will be 'Diamond of Dubai,'" Nick Ames, September 8, 2015

The Gulf Today, "World's leading real estate players converge on Dubai," p. 5, September 9, 2015

Khaleej Times, "Architects of Dubai's Burj 2020 swear by sustainability," Deepthi Nair, September 10, 2015

Architect Magazine, "Architect 50: Adrian Smith + Gordon Gill takes top honors," September 11, 2015

Manderin Quarterly, "Net-Zero Energy Buildings," Winter 2015

Engineering News-Record, "Jeddah Tower's 'Climb' to One Kilometer Picks Up Speed," Nadine M. Post, November 11, 2015

The Telegraph, "Jeddah's Kingdom Tower a step closer to becoming world's tallest building," Natalie Paris, November 30, 2015

The Huffington Post, "Saudi Arabia's Jeddah Tower Will Be the World's Tallest Building," Nina Golgowski, November 30, 2015

Architect Magazine, "How to Heat and Cool a Supertall," Clay Risen, December 1, 2015

Chicago Tribune, "Saudi Arabia plans to build the world's tallest skyscraper," Anna White, December 2, 2015

The Telegraph, "Onwards and upwards for the skyscraper," December 6, 2015

Building Design + Construction, "Saudi Arabia secures funding for world's first kilometer-tall skyscraper: Jeddah Tower," Mike Chamernik, December 8, 2015

The New Age, "Saudi Arabia to build world's tallest tower at one kilometer high," December 19, 2015

2014

HOPSCA III, "Wuhan Greenland Center," 188-197, January 2014

The Skycourt and Skygarden: Greening the Urban Habitat, "Dancing Dragons," pp. 188-191, January 2014

Tall and Supertall Buildings: Planning and Design, "Kingdom Tower," p. 189, January 2014

Architect Magazine, "Architecture and the 3rd Industrial Revolution," pp. 100-103, Thomas Fisher, January 2014

Greater Middle East, "Thought Leaders: Adrian Smith, AS+GG Architecture," January 8, 2014

Chicago Tribune, "The Global City: Designed in Chicago, Made in China," pp. 23-27, Blair Kamin, February 2014

Architectural Record, "Big Bigger Biggest," pp. 114-115, Anna Fixen, March 2014

Kohkoku, "Higher than Higher," p. 138, March 2014

Bloomberg BusinessWeek, "Shedding the Vortex," pp. 92-95, Bryan Urstadt, March 24, 2014

Southeast Asia Building, "Adrian Smith + Gordon Gill Architecture wins international design competition for Expo-2017 in Astana, Kazakhstan," p. 22, March-April 2014

cci Zeitung, "Wie kommt Flussigbeton 700 m hoch?" p. 4, May 23, 2014

Chicago Architect, "High Riser," p. 74, Zurich Esposito, May-June 2014

International New Landscape, "Chicago DeCarbonization Plan," pp. 38-43, May-June 2014

Architectural Record, "Gordon Gill Recommends," June 19, 2014

Wealth Magazine, "Touch the Sky," pp. 58-64, Joni Wedderburn, Summer 2014

Four, "Kingdom Tower, Jeddah," p. 16, Summer 2014

CTBUH Journal, "High Performance Design Shapes Sustainable Supertall Building," pp. 12-17, Issue II 2014

Aura, "Reach for the Sky," pp. 48-52, Catherine Slessor, Volume Two, 2014

Mandarin Quarterly, "Sustainable Architecture," pp. 34-37, Suyu Li, Winter 2014

OC Magazine, "The Sultan of Skyscrapers," pp. 66-69, David M. Winter, December 2014

2013

Perspectives, "A Solution for All," January 2013

Evolo Magazine Asian Edition, January, "Chengdu Tianfu District Great City," January 2013

Wuhan, China"PM Network, "Closing Credits," January 2013

World Architecture News, "A slice of life in Chengdu," January 7, 2013

Southeast Asia Building, "Adrian Smith + Gordon Gill Architecture wins competition to design Qintai Center, new corporate headquarters," January/February 2013

U Magazine, "Never Ends: Dancing Dragons," February 2013

ArchOne, "Alumnus who designed world's tallest building to receive honorary doctorate degree," February 11, 2013

Popular Science, "Rise of Supertall," Clay Risen, February 15, 2013

Daily Telegraph, "World's best architects vie to make their mark on Sydney," February 15, 2013

Icon, "Towering Ambition," pp. 62-67, March 2013

Tall Buildings (Russia), "1 Dubai," pp. 46-47 "FKI Tower," 49-53, March 2013

CTBUH Journal, "Kingdom: Creating a One-Kilometer-High Tower," March 2013

High-Rise Apartment, "Dancing Dragons : Breathing Skin," pp. 41-53, May 2013

Jetset and Lifestyle, "Adrian Smith + Gordon Gill architecture designs Kingdom Tower, to be the world´s tallest building," pp. 138-143, May 2013

Wall Street Journal, "Barangaroo bidders go with the flow," Bridget Carter, May 4, 2013

ArchDaily, "Adrian Smith and Gordon Gill Architecture Unveils Proposal for Mumbai's Tallest Tower," Karissa Rosenfield, May 7, 2013

Trends Magazine, "Head for Heights," p. 14, June 2013

Chicago Architect, "Get Smart," pp. 24-27, Ben Schulman, August 2013

Evolo, "Dancing Dragons for Yongsan International Business District in Seoul," Marija Bojovic, August 1, 2013

The Architect's Newspaper, "Unveiled: 505 Church St." p. 3, August 7, 22013

Chicago Grid, "To Build the World's Tallest Building, It Takes an Office Fit for Big Ideas," Meg Graham, August 21, 2013

MGS Architecture, "AS+GG's Holistic Approach for Creating High Performance, Sustainable Architecture," pp. 2-6, September 2013

Green Source, "Growing Pains," Katharine Logan, September 2013

Voir Vert, "Le prototype de la Clean Technology Tower," Marie-Eve Sirois, September 17, 2013

Chicago Tribune, "Pick of the week: Adrian Smith," September 26, 2013

B1 Magazine, "Expo 2017 Pavilion," pp. 38-39, October 2013

Arquitectura Viva, "Adrian Smith + Gordon Gill to design Expo 2017 site in Astana," October 29, 2013

Media

Bustler, "Adrian Smith + Gordon Gill wins Kazakhstan Astana World Expo 2017 competition," November 1, 2013

ArchDaily, "AS+GG Wins Competition for Astana World EXPO 2017," Karissa Rosenfield, November 1, 2013

Crain's Chicago Business, "Northwestern unveils finalists' designs for ex-Prentice site," November 7, 2013

Gizmodo, "What Does a City of the "Third Industrial Revolution" Look Like?" Kelsey Campbell-Dollaghan, November 12, 2013

Businessweek, "A Mile-High Skyscraper Isn't a Fantasy. At Least Outside the US," Eric Chemi, November 14, 2013

Green Buildings, "Expo-2017," pp. 16-21, December 2013

B1, "Expo 2017 Pavilion: Astana, Kazakhstan," pp. 38-39, December 2013

Urbanland, "Expo Astana 2017," December 9, 2013

2012

The Epoch Times, "China's Risky Skyscraper Extravaganza," Jin Jing, January 31, 2012

Mein Eigen Heim, "Hallo Zuknft: Okostadt Masdar," pp. 14-17 February 2012

Bloomberg News, "Chinese Tower May Add Floors to Become World's Tallest after Burj Khalifa," February 27, 2012

China Daily, "Wuhan Greenland Center to be China's tallest building," February 27, 2012

CRI English, "Wuhan Mulls Tallest Building in China," February 27, 2012

The Construction Index, "Challenger emerges for China's tallest tower record," February 28, 2012

China Daily, "Bigger is better, developer decides midway," Guo Rui, February 28, 2012

Nox, "Dualidad Geometrica," Winter-Spring 2012

Chicago Sun-Times, "Development buzz at Reese site," David Roeder, March 14, 2012

Building Capacity, "A Taste of Living Future 2012," May 2012

World Architecture News, "Enter the Dragons: Architects unveil twin Korean towers with lizard-like 'scales' of glass that let the buildings 'breathe,'" May 11, 2012

B1, "Dancing Dragons Towers," June 2012

Green Architecture Now 2, "Adrian Smith + Gordon Gill Architecture: Head Offices of the Federation of Korean Industries," June 2012

Southeast Asia Building, "Adrian Smith + Gordon Gill Architecture designs Dancing Dragons, a two-tower complex for Seoul's Yongsan International Business District," July/August 2012

Perspective, "Dancing in the dragon hills," p. 20, August 2012

Building Design + Construction, "Mixed-Use Towers in Seoul Awake the Dancing Dragons," August 2012

idesign travel, "Wuhan Greenland Center," pp. 59-65, August 2012

IDT, "Wuhan Greenland Center," August 2012

Beyond Magazine, "Dragon Dancing Twin Towers," August 2012

Architect Magazine, "Dancing Dragons," August 22, 2012

Northwest Tourism, "Dimensional Life - Delicate Space," pp. 27-33, September 2012

Civil Engineering, "Ancient Architecture Inspires Contemporary Tower Complex," September 2012

MADE, "Yongsan International Business District: Dancing Dragons," September 2012

Wall Street Journal, "Designing Towers to Catch the Sky," James R. Hagerty, September 22, 2012

Zenith Business Report, "Starship to Riyadh," pp. 10-12, September-October 2012

Chicago Architect, "Built to Scale," pp. 28-32, Dennis Rodkin, September-October 2012

Ideat, "Special Architecture: Kingdom Tower," p. 24, October 2012

World Architecture News, "AS+GG strikes the right note," October 3, 2012

New York Magazine, "9 Experiments in Large: Jeddah, World's Tallest Building," October 15, 2012

Wired, "From AT&ATs to iPhones: Early Sketches of 10 Iconic Objects," October 30, 2012

Men's Book Chicago, "The Visionaries: Hitting the Heights," pp. 90-91, Fall 2012

Men's Book Chicago, "On Top of the World," pp. 42-44, Thomas Conners, Fall 2012

Concept Magazine, "Yongsan International Business District: Dancing Dragons," pp. 48-59, Special Issue 2012,

Arab Construction World, "The Kingdom Tower: Middle East's New Landmark," Dina Fawaz, November 2012

Surface Asia, "Seoul Searching: The Dancing Dragons in YIBD," November 2012

Design Boom, "Adrian Smith + Gordon Gill: Qintai International Tower, Wuhan," November 6, 2012

Crain's Chicago Business, "Overseas planning gigs: A closer look," November 16, 2012

Areas Globales, "Reduccion de las emisiones de carbono en el area central de Chicago," November 27, 2012

Chicago Architect, "2012 SustainABILITY Awards: Citation of Merit, Chicago Loop Decarbonization Plan," November/December 2012

Net Zero Energy, "A Guide for Commercial Architecture," December 2012

Beyond Magazine, "Efficient Streamlined Design," December 18, 2012

Beyond Magazine, "A Shining Example of the Urban Future," "Form Follows Performance: Qintai Center," December 26, 2012

2011

Hospitality Style, "Q+A: Adrian Smith," p. 56, Winter 2011

That's Shanghai, "The architect's architect," pp. 28-29, January 2011

Architect's Newspaper, "Smart Grid City," Ann Lok Lui, January 17, 2011

The Battalion, "Aggie reaches for the sky," pp. 1,5, April Baltensperger, February 25, 2011

Archone, "Adrian Smith visits students, presents Rowlett Lecture," March 4, 2011

Crain's Chicago Business, "Crain's 2011 Coolest Chicago Offices: Adrian Smith + Gordon Gill Architecture," March 7, 2011

Nissan Technology Magazine, "2025: The future of mobility and our future cities," Gordon Gill, April 28, 2011

Archone, "College of Architecture names eight 2011 Outstanding Alumni: Adrian Smith," May 17, 2011

One, "(Re)Conceiving Cities," pp. 13-15, Spring/Summer 2011

Inhabitat, "AS+GG Aerodynamic Wuhan Greenland Center to be World's 4th Tallest Building," June 21, 2011

e-architect, "Wuhan Greenland Center Tower," June 21, 2011

World Architecture News, "Adrian Smith + Gordon Gill, Thornton Tomasetti and PositivEnergy Practice to design world's fourth tallest building," June 21, 2011

Construction Week, "Burj architect gets lifetime achievement award," June 23, 2011

World Architecture News, "Adrian Smith Wins 2011 Lynn S. Beedle Lifetime Achievement Award from the CTBUH," June 24, 2011

World Architecture News, "Gordon Gill on Chicago's changing climate," Sharon McHugh, June 28, 2011

The Wall Street Journal, "Architect Q&A: The State of Super-Tall Towers," Maura Webber Sadovi, July 8, 2011

Identity, "High Life," p. 68, August 2011

Civil Engineering, "Wuhan Greenland Center," p. 29, August 2011

Architectural Record, "On the Boards: Wuhan Greenland Center," August 2011

Huffington Post, "Kingdom Tower: Adrian Smith talks designing world's tallest building," Paul Needham, August 2, 2011

msnbc, "World's tallest building coming to Saudi Arabia," August 2, 2011

Popular Science, "Saudi's set to build Kingdom Tower, soon to be the world's tallest building," Clay Dillow, August 2, 2011

Chicago Sun-Times, "Chicago firm designing new tallest building," August 2, 2011

The Telegraph, "Saudi Arabia takes step to build world's tallest tower," August 2, 2011

Emirates 24/7, "Kingdom Tower to top reigning champ Burj Khalifa by 173m," August 2, 2011

World Architecture News, "AS+GG Confirmed to design world's tallest tower," August 2, 2011

Chicago Tribune, "Chicago architecture firm to design world's tallest tower," August 2, 2011

Globe and Mail, "Saudi thrusts forward with plan for world's tallest tower," August 2, 2011

Baltimore Sun, "Chicago architecture firm to design world's tallest tower," August 2, 2011

Washington Post, "Saudi presses forward with plans to build world's tallest tower, outdoing neighbor Dubai," Adam Schreck, August 2, 2011

The Times of India, "At 1000m, Jeddah to have world's tallest tower," August 3, 2011

Wall Street Journal, "Saudi's plan world's tallest tower," Summer Said, pp. C8-12, August 3, 2011

Red Eye, "3,280" August 3, 2011

NPR, "World's tallest building to be built in Saudi Arabia," August 8, 2011

The Gulf Today, "A Bird? A Plan? It's Kingdom Tower!" August 11, 2011

The Sun, "King of towers hits the heights," August 12, 2011

Construction Week, "King of Skyscrapers," Oliver Ephgrave, August 13, 2011

New York Magazine, "Higher," Justin Davidson, August 14, 2011

Metropolis, "Move Over, Burj Khalifa," Martin C. Pedersen, August 16, 2011

Bloomberg, "Kingdom Tower architect grapples the wind at 3,000 ft," Zainab Fattah, August 30, 2011

Perspective, "Higher up in the wind," p. 106, September 2011

B1, "Kingdom Tower," September 2011

DFUN Magazine, "World of Great Towers: Kingdom Tower," September 2011

Chicago Architect, "People + Places: Kingdom Tower," September 2011

Los Angeles Times, "Skyscrapers remain powerful symbols, post 9/11," Christopher Hawthorn, September 4, 2011

World Architecture News, "Why the big firms are reaching out to find new work," Sian Disson, September 5, 2011

Wall Street Journal, "The skyscraper as a pillar of confidence," Julie Iovine, September 8, 2011

Huffington Post, "A Call for Urban Doctors," Gordon Gill, September 28, 2011

Southeast Asia Building, "Adrian Smith + Gordon Gill Architecture wins competition to design Wuhan Greenland Center," September/October 2011

Perspective, "Reigning over the sky," October 2011

Sphere, "Arabian Heights," Autumn 2011

Homes & Lifestyle, "Dubai's Comeback," pp. 13-17; "IM Interview: Adrian Smith," pp. 18-21, Helmut Melzer, Autumn 2011

Sciences et Avenir, "En Image: Plu pres du ciel," p. 33, October 2011

Lake Forester, "Tall order," October 27, 2011

Nashville Post, "Giarrantana unveils trio of proposed skyscrapers," November 3, 2011

Tall Buildings (Russia),"Kingdom Tower," November 2011

2010

NZZ am Sonntag, "Strom und Hehr an der Aussenhulle produziert," January 2010

Vertical Density, "Torre Meraas," pp. 212-213 January 2010

Architecture Now! Vol. 7, "Skidmore, Owings & Merrill: Burj Khalifa," pp. 432-437, January 2010

The Los Angeles Times, "The Burj Dubai and architecture's vacant stare," January 1, 2010

The Chicago Tribune, "The tallest building ever (brought to you by Chicago)," January 3, 2010

The Chicago Tribune, "The Burj Dubai: New world's tallest building shows that nothing succeeds like excess," January 4, 2010

The New York Times, "Dubai opens a tower to beat all," January 4, 2010

Emirates Business, "The impossible transformed into reality," January 5, 2010

Khaleej Times, "Meet the architect of the world's tallest tower," January 5, 2010

The Providence Journal, "Superman, meet Dubai's superscraper," January 7, 2010

The Lake Forester, "Sky-high: Lake Forest's Adrian Smith designs world's tallest building in Dubai," January 7, 2010

Spiked, "What's wrong with towering ambition?" January 7, 2010

The National, "Ancient practice of feng shui underpins soaring achievement," January 9, 2010

The National, "Sky is still the limit for architect," January 9, 2010

e-architect, "Chicago architect Adrian Smith's Burj Khalifa, world's tallest building, opens in Dubai," January 11, 2010

The Orange County Register, "San Clemente gave architect of world's tallest building a foundation," January 18, 2010

Architect, "What if an entire city could be housed under one roof?" pp. 60-63, January 20, 2010

Chicago Sun-Times, "Architect defends his stature," January 20, 2010

Brownbook, "Building Big," p. 71, January/February 2010

Archone, "Former student Adrian Smith '66 designs world's tallest building," February 1, 2010

The New Yorker, "Castle in the Air," pp.62-64, February 8, 2010

The Architects Newspaper, "Unveiled: Federation of Korean Industries," February 11, 2010

World World Architecture News, "AS+GG completes first phase of Chicago DeCarbonization Plan," February 18, 2010

inhabitat.com, "Adrian Smith + Gordon Gill hatch massive plan to decarbonize Chicago," February 22, 2010

Fortune, "World's greenest skyscraper," February 23, 2010

Media

Eco-Structure, "Adrian Smith + Gordon Gill Architecture Offers a Low-Carb Plan for Chicago," February 25, 2010

Crain's, "In going green average isn't good enough for Willis Tower" March 1, 2010

RICS Buisness, "Power tower," p. 7 March, 2010

Architect, " Burj Khalifa curtain wall," pp. 23-24, March 2010

Perspectives, "Building for change," pp. 84-87, April 2010

The National, "Masdar showcased at a Smithsonian Institution's Museum," May 26, 2010

B1 Magazine, "Sustainable Excellence: Masdar," pp. 36-41, June 2010

Metropolis, "Skyline: Willis Tower," p. 83, June 2010

Ecolibrium, "Desert Star," p. 7, July 2010

Architect Magazine, "2010 Award for Sustainability: Chicago Central Area Decarbonization Plan," August 2010

The New York Times, "Planning a Sustainable City in the Desert," September 25, 2010

inhabitat.com, "Korean Tower Boasts One of World's Most Efficient Solar Facades," October 29, 2010

GreenSource, "The rise of retrofit," pp. 106-113, December

2009

Space, "Clean Technology Building," pp. 86-90, January 2009

Engineering News-Record, "Green-retrofit work thrives in uncertain economic times", p. 22, January 19, 2009

Medill Reports, "Local architects plan an eco-bridge to complete Burnham's plan," January 29, 2009

Riscaldamento Climatizzazione Idronica, "Biomimetica per edifici," pp. 68-74, February 2009

Midwest Construction, "In a Stalled Economy," p. 23, February 1, 2009

Blueprint Magazine, "Reject the Dubai Clichés," February 11,

Science Illustrated, "Building Towards the Clouds", pp. 36-43, March/April 2009

Architectural Record, "Is the Green-Building Market Recession-Proof?" March 4, 2009

ABC News, "Burj Dubai: Architectural miracle in the desert," March 9, 2009

Urban Land Middle East, "Burj Dubai", pp. 54-55, Spring 2009

Crain's, "Sears Tower owners propose 5-star hotel" June 24, 2009

New York Times, "Sears Tower to be revamped to produce most of its own power," June 24, 2009

Chicago Tribune, "Sears Tower plans hotel, self-greening," June 25, 2009

Chicago Sun-Times, "Lofty 'green' renovation for Sears Tower," June 25, 2009

Wall Street Journal, "Big hotel planned next to Sears Tower," June 25, 2009

Architecture + Urbanism, "Relationship between design and construction", pp. 30-33, August 2009

RIBA Journal, "The color of money," pp. 44-50, August/September 2009

Business, "Green giant," p. 9, September 2009

Chicago Tribune, "Adrian Smith: building to the stars like never before," September 11, 2009

cnn.com, "Sexy architecture alive and well in the Middle East" October 8, 2009

The Toronto Star, "Towering Example," October 10, 2009

The Architect's Newspaper, "They might be giants: Willis Tower," p. 15, October 14, 2009

The New York Times, "New agency to lead global energy push," October 20, 2009

The Plan, "Abu Dhabi: A new metropolitan city emerges from the desert," p. 53, December 2009

Engineering News-Record, "Design team held to competition promises," December 9, 2009

2008

Shanghai: The Architecture of China's Great Urban Center, p. 66-67, January 2008

Chicago Public Radio, "Architects Float Idea for Bridge," January 2008

Articolo Architecttura, "Le Nuove Frontiere del Biomimetismo," January 2008

The Big Project, "Geometrics of the Desert Flower," Issue 10 2008

Enjeux Les Echos, "Adrain Smith; Paris-La Defense a Besoin d'une tour de 500 m de haut," January 2008

Building, "The Middle East green building challenge" February, Issue 8 2008

Chicago Public Radio, "Radio Interview," February 22, 2008

Chicago Tribune, "'Green' Light for Chicago Design" February 22, 2008

Chicago Tribune, "Sweet New Start for Chicago Architect," Section 5, p. 3, February 24, 2008

Financial Times, "Walkable, Pleasant, Urbane, Hot," February 27, 2008

Skyscrapers, "Post-Modernism and the Rise of the Middle East," p. 108-109, March 2008

Emirates Business 24/7, "Giving Shape to Big Ambitions and Tall Buildings Around the World," March 7, 2008

Regina Leader Post, "Architects Building New Cities," March 12, 2008

Engineering News-Record, "Building sector needs reeducation," p. 10, March 17, 2008

Middle East Architect, "Sprawl to Tall," pp. 14-15, April 2008

AIArchitect, "Beyond Zero: Adrian Smith + Gordon Gill Architecture's Desert Experiment," April 4, 2008

Real Estate Forum Magazine, "Abu Dhabi Sustainable Project Moves Forward," p. 8, April 8, 2008

Al Bawaba, "ETA Star Launches VERDE Towers in Dubai Maritime City" April 28, 2008

Khaleej Times, "Man of Many Storeys" April 28, 2008

Modern Design, "The 11 Hour and the Carbon Conflict: Smooth Operator," p. 75, May 2008

Gulf Life, "Head in the Clouds," May 1, 2008

Gulf News, "Dubai: City of Supertowers," May 4, 2008

Arabian Business, "ETA Star Launches Adrian Smith and Gordon Gill Designed Towers," May 5, 2008

Architectural Record, "Smith + Gill Tapped for Ultra-Green Abu Dhabi Project," p. 29, May 7, 2008

Gulf News, "Dubai Gives the Necessary Freedom Designers Need," May 9, 2008

The Sunday Times, "Dinosaurs bite the dust," p. 10, May 11, 2008

Al Bawaba, "ETA Star's 'Green' Campaign on Channel 4 is an Instant Hit Among Listeners," May 15, 2008

Trading Markets, "Building Slows Along with Economy," May 25, 2008

Aktuellt, "Positive Energiatgang," p. 4 June 2008

Focus, "The Rise and Rise of the Superscraper," pp. 34-42, June 2008

Chicago Architect, "The Next Big Thing," pp. 32-35, June 2008

Crain's, "Smith & Gill Wins Dubai Deal," p. 21, June 2, 2008

AIArchitect, "Adrian Smith, FAIA, RIBA," June 6, 2008

Architect, "Positive Energy," p. 74-79, June 8, 2008

The Chicago Tribune, "Smith and Gill's 'Eco-Bridge': Coming to Chicago's Lakefront?" June 12, 2008

Grist, "The Daley Show; Hot Plans Rile the Chicago Waterfront," June 13, 2008

The New York Times, "Scraping the sky and then some," p. 20, June 15, 2008

The Chicago Tribune, "Chicago Architect Walter A. Netsch Dies at 88," June 15, 2008

Living Design, "Den Gronne Skyskraber,' pp. 34-36, Winter 2008

BPM "Masdar," p. 12, Issue 91, Summer 2008

Limited Edition, "Adrian Smith; The Master of Skyscrapers," pp. 18-22, Summer 2008

Residence, "Renast i varlden," p. 72, Number 7, 2008

Chicago Tribune (online), "Why do the Olympics start on 8-08 at 8:08 pm? For the same reason that many Chinese skyscrapers are 88 stories tall," August 5, 2008

New York Times, "Reaching for the clouds in Dubai," p. 24, August 10, 2008

International Herald Tribune, "Rising in Dubai: Adrian Smith's Vision of Green: taller and getting taller," August 12, 2008

The Wall Street Journal, "Skyline Gets Facelift Ahead of Asian Games," August 20, 2008

The Chicago Tribune, "Getting the inside story on the Pearl River Tower, billed as the world's greenest skyscraper," August 28, 2008

Metropolis, "Innovation from the Innovators," October 2008

Building, "Burj Dubai: Top of the world," p. 18 October 3, 2008

Crain's Chicago Business, "Who's Who: Chicago's Power," September 1, 2008

The National, "Dubai sees no reason to stop scraping skies" October 6, 2008

The National, "Meraas tower to join Dubai's buildings in the sky," October 6, 2008

Khaleej Times, "Cityscape $1 trillion showcase," p. 1, October 7, 2008

Khaleej Times, "Dubai Launches Dh350b Jumeirah Gardens," p. 1 Business, October 7, 2008

The Chicago Tribune, "Chicago architects plan more towers in Dubai," October 7, 2008

The National, "Tall Buildings put us on the map, says Burj Dubai architect," October 8, 2008

Building, "Sears tower set for L85m green makeover," October 8, 2008

The Chicago Sun-Times, "Developers turn to rentals in downturn," October 8, 2008

World Architecture News, "Meraas Development taps Adrian Smith + Gordon Gill for megaproject," October 9, 2008

Building, "The tallest building in the world: the contenders," October 14, 2008

Business Week, "Undaunted, skyscrapers reach higher," October 15, 2008

Globe and Mail, "Market panic? Bring it on," October 18, 2008

The National, "Architectural 'exuberance' could slow," October 30, 2008

identity, "The future is now", pp. 106-110; "Green giants," pp. 112-113, November, 2008

Solares Bauen, "Masdar-Hauptquartier Bei Abu Ahabi Von AS+GG Architecture: Ultra Green," pp.80-81, November 2008

Cityscape Magazine, November, "Cityscape Dubai: the regional reality", pp. 30-33; "New look for old", pp. 40-42

GEO, "Masdar City: Die Null-Emmissions-Stadt in der Wuste," November 2008

Travel + Leisure, "New American Landmarks," p.221-230, November 2008

The Chicago Tribune, "Skyline on pause: Credit crunch leaves Spire, other towers short," November 3, 2008

Globe and Mail, "A building with an energy all its own," November 11, 2008

The New York Times, "A new wind is blowing in Chicago" November 19, 2008

The Columbus Dispatch, "Tall tales: ever-higher buildings reflect solutions for the future," November 30, 2008

Green Source, "Urban Harvest", pp. 108-113, November/December 2008

Millionaire, "Yearning to soar," pp. 36-43 December Issue 11 2008

2007

Urban Land, "Managing Risk Before and During Construction," p. 142, January 2007

Metropolis, "Parting Company," pp. 30, 32, January 2007

The Big Project, "King Abdullah Economic City: Honored for Service to Comm. Cancer Center," Issue 2, 2007

Id+, "Saudi's single largest private sector investment," pp. 34-43, January 2007

Business Times, "Burj Dubai is 100 Stories High," p. 1, January 17, 2007

The American Magazine, "Lust for Height," p. 16, January/February 2007

Chicago Magazine, "A New Order," pp. 62-65, 98-104, February 2007

GULF Life, "High, Higher, Highest," pp. 34-38, 40,42, May 2007

CNN Traveller, "World of Tomorrow," May/June 2007

JAM: Art, Architecture & Design, "Interview: large-scale mixed-use and supertall; The American architect Adrian Smith," pp. 31-35, Spring/Summer 2007

Chicago Sun-Times, " Chicago Architect Says World's Tallest Building Still Growing," July 24, 2007

El Tiempo, "En flores se inspiró Adrian Smith para diseñar la torre más alta del mundo: el Burj Dubai," July 28, 2007

UIC Alumni Magazine, "Unfinished Business," p. 14, July/August,

The Big Project, Issue 7, "Viewpoint: Sustainability has deep roots," pp. 74-77

Chicago Sun-Times, "Sears Tower hires green architects," Business Briefs, August 16, 2007

Architectural Record, "The Skyscraper: Still Soaring," August 17, 2007

Chicago Tribune, "How to build today's supertalls," August 19, 2007

GQ, "Green Giants," pp. 221-222, September 2007

Chicago Magazine, "Chicago Architecture in 2020," p. 94, September 2007

The Architect's Newspaper, "Imitation of Life," September 2007

Bund Pictorial, "The Work of Adrian Smith," October 2007

Blueprint, "A New Practice with a Zero Energy Approach", p. 47, October 2007

Chicago Sun-Times, "Tall order for tower," p. 57, October 12, 2007

Gulf News, "Ground Breaking," September 5, 2007

The Sunday Times, "City Salvation" November 4, 2007

The Chicago Tribune, "Developers embracing 'green' to gain an edge," p. 3, November 7, 2007

Metropolis, "Beyond the Spectacle," November 8, 2007

Credits

Team

Jeddah Tower

Design Partners	Adrian Smith and Gordon Gill
Management Partner	Robert Forest
Project Manager	Brian M. Jack | Ben Johnson
Senior Designer	Alejandro Stochetti
Senior Technical	Peter Weismantle | Sara Beardsley
Interiors Director	John Burcher | Marc Cerone
Interiors Technical	Rebecca Cryder
Sustainability Director	Christopher Drew

Project Team: Miguel Alvarez, Mohamad Araji, George Baciu, Ryan Bakke, Rachel Banach, Frederik Berte, Juan Betancur, Jillian Blakey, Ana Blomeier, Gail Borthwick, Nathan Bowman, Brett Bridgeland, Hayes Brister, Sydney Brown, Alexis Burson, Jessica Butler, Ashley Byers, Sally Cathcart, Raymond Coleman, Charles Collett, Colin Craig, Rebecca Cryder, Katherine Dailey, Ryan Dalgaard, Thomas Demetrion, Michelle Dumont, Elliot Eakin, Kyle Faulkner, Sobieslaw Fedyk, Robert Finigan, Patrick Fitzpatrick, Joshua Frank, Natalya Ganyukova, Krystian Gardula, Dimitra Gelagoti, Danielle Gharst, Brendan Gibbons, Gordon Gill, Gail Goldstead, Felix Griggs, Christopher Harvey, Zachary Heaps, Jessica Hogue, Travis Howe, Stephen Hsueh, Brian Hubbard, London Huenefeld, Christopher Hurst, Brooke Ingram, Brian Jack, DongSoo Jang, Matthias Janikowski, Robert Jillson, Laura Jimenez, Tamara Jimshitashvili, Changhoon Kim, Lin Kim, Soo Hye Kim, Peter Kindel, Alexander Knowles, Hans Koesters, So Young Lee, Soeun Lee, David LeFevre, Rebecca Lemaster, Randi Lesniewski, Todd Mackinson, John Maher, Takuya Mamada, Jaclyn Marcus, Tashio Martinez, Rucha Mehendale, Olia Miho, Christopher Miller, Michael Newton, Vanessa Newton, Tyler Noblin, Matthew Nyweide, David Osmond, Luis Palacio, Griffin Pemberton, Michael Perez, Robert Perry, Benjamin Raines, David Rariden, Katie Rariden, Dennis Rehill, Yi Ren, Albert Rhee, Beumhyeung Rhee, Catherine Rogg, Mostapha Roudsari, Sean Satterfield, Thomas Schneider, David Schweim, Rachel Sears, Myongki Seong, Mohamed Sheriff, Matthew Simpson, Jason Smith, Donald Stark, Andrew Suszko, Michelle Swanson, Afaq Syed, Anthony Trifiletti, Chen-Han Tu, Les Ventsch, Anthony Viola, Michael Waldo, Christopher Walker, Brent Watanabe, Kirsten Weismantle, Preston Welker, Marc Woodcock, Margaret Yo

Central Park Tower

Design Partners	Adrian Smith and Gordon Gill
Management Partner	Robert Forest
Project Manager	Brian M. Jack
Senior Designer	David Schweim
Senior Technical	Donald Stark

Project Team: Miguel Alvarez, George Baciu, Nicholas Berchtold, Frederik Berte, Jae Yun Cho, Allison Conley, Nathan Diestelkamp, Patrick Fitzpatrick, Marshall Ford, Brendan Gibbons, Richard Gnat, Gail Goldstead, Heng Gu, Charles Harris, Kira Ho, Robert Jillson, Changhoon Kim, Hyungwoo Kim, Paul Kim, Todd Mackinson, Jennie Matusova, Michelle Pak, Viorica Pisau, David Rariden, Yi Ren, Jonathan Reyes, Thomas Schneider, Myongki Seong, Jeff Snodgrass, Alex Valverde, Les Ventsch, Timothy Winstanley, Jing Zhang

Chengdu Greenland Tower

Design Partners	Adrian Smith and Gordon Gill
Management Partner	Robert Forest
Project Manager	Ben Johnson
Senior Designer	Fei Xu
Senior Technical	Peter Weismantle | Iris Gan
Interiors Director	Marc Cerone
China Director	Weiwei Luo

Project Team: Tyler Austin, Rustem Baishev, Mariela Bayer, Sara Beardsley, Rachael Bennett, Nicholas Berchtold, John Burcher, Jessica Butler, Ashley Byers, Sally Cathcart, Daniel Caven, Rebecca Cryder, Katherine Dailey, Michelle Dumont, Elliot Eakin, David Emmons, Keara Fanning, Sobieslaw Fedyk, Dian Feng, Patrick Fitzpatrick, Joshua Frank, Natalya Ganyukova, Dimitra Gelagoti, Brendan Gibbons, Gail Goldstead, Felix Griggs, Kira Ho, DongSoo Jang, Tamara Jimshitashvili, Joel Kerner, Angela Khermouch, Changhoon Kim, Hyungwoo Kim, Alexander Knowles, Alison Lampier, Rebecca LeMaster, Randi Lesniewski, Mengxi Li, Yuchen Liu, Jaclyn Marcus, Tashio Martinez, Christopher Miller, Jongpil Park, Benjamin Raines, Daniel Ramos, Yi Ren, Catherine Rogg, Matthew Simpson, Chad Smith, Jeff Snodgrass, Jiatuo Song, James Struthers, Anthony Trifiletti, Luis Villafane, Anthony Viola, Brent Watanabe

Wuhan Greenland Center

Design Partners	Adrian Smith and Gordon Gill
Management Partner	Robert Forest
Project Manager	Ben Johnson
Senior Designer	Juan Betancur
Senior Technical	Peter Weismantle
Interiors Director	John Burcher | Marc Cerone
China Director	Weiwei Luo

Project Team: Rachael Bennett, Jillian Blakey, Ana Blomeier, Nathan Bowman, Sally Cathcart, Raymond Coleman, Colin Craig, Rebecca Cryder, Emily Dones, Patrick Fitzpatrick, Joshua Frank, Iris Gan, Brendan Gibbons, Felix Griggs, Kira Ho, Brian Hubbard, Brooke Ingram, DongSoo Jang, Qi Jia, Robert Jillson, Laura Jimenez, Tamara Jimshitashvili, Trudie Kahler, Joshua Kuffner, Ryan Kukuraitis, Soeun Lee, David LeFevre, Rebecca Lemaster, Randi Lesniewski, Miaoqi Liu, Takuya Mamada, Christopher Miller, Suncica Milosevic, Luis Palacio, Robert Perry, James Reisinger, Yi Ren, Catherine Rogg, Mario Romero, Rachel Sears, Daniel Segraves, Mohamed Sheriff, Matthew Simpson, Jason Smith, Joshua Smith, Matt Snoap, Jorge Soler, Michelle Swanson, Corey Thomas, Anthony Trifiletti, Chen-Han Tu, Anthony Viola, Perry Wreaks, Si Wu, Dong Yan, Margaret Yoo, Andrew Zell, Jing Zhang, Yueming Zhou

Shenzhen-Hong Kong International Center

Design Partners	Adrian Smith and Gordon Gill
Management Partner	Robert Forest
Project Manager	Ben Johnson
Senior Designer	Fei Xu
Senior Technical	Iris Gan
China Director	Weiwei Luo

Project Team: Alexander Bahr, Bintou Coulbaly, Sobieslaw Fedyk, Liyuan Ge, Yongsan Huang, Soeun Lee, Yuchen Liu Luis Palacio, Jonathan Reyes, Jeff Snodgrass, Maria Sturchio, Zilong Tan, Jing Zhang, Richard Wilson, Yuxin Zheng, Ruoqi Zhong

South Hexi Yuzui Financial District

Design Partners	Adrian Smith and Gordon Gill
Management Partner	Robert Forest
Project Manager	Ben Johnson
Senior Designer	Fei Xu
Senior Technical	Iris Gan
China Director	Weiwei Luo

Project Team: Nora Ames, Tyler Austin, Alexander Bahr, Nicholas Berchtold, Jennifer Cooper, Rebecca Cryder, Caitlin Dashiell, Sobieslaw Fedyk, Iris Gan, Rebecca Greenberg, Wilson Harkhono, Yongsan Huang, Ryan Kukuraitis, Miaoqi Liu, Yuchen Liu, Luis Palacio, Jonathan Reyes, Thomas Schneider, Zilong Tan, Perry Wreaks, Tianyu Xu, Dong Yan, Jing Zhang, Ruoqi Zhong

1 Dubai

Design Partners	Adrian Smith and Gordon Gill
Management Partner	Robert Forest
Project Manager	Brian M. Jack
Senior Designer	Jeff Stafford
Senior Technical	Peter Weismantle

Project Team: Nicholas Addison, Miguel Alvarez, Gabriel Ball, John Burcher, Marc Cerone, Anthony Cissell, Charles Collett, Joshua Cooper, Reinaldo Correa, Thomas Denney, Robert Finigan, Christina Halatsis, Christopher Harvey, Gregg Herman, Travis Howe, Brian Hubbard, Boyka Ivanova, Jeffrey Knapke, Phat Nguyen, Andrew Osvalds, Julia Robertson, Karen Rutherford, Kshitij Sawant, Mordecai Scheckter, Daniel Segraves, Siddant Sinha, Eric Snow, Brett Sterly, Rebecca Stewart, Anthony Trifiletti, Brent Watanabe

The Biophilic Tower

Design Partners	Adrian Smith and Gordon Gill
Management Partner	Robert Forest
Project Manager	Ben Johnson
Senior Designer	Juan Betancur

Project Team: Rachael Bennett, Charles Harris, Travis Howe, Brooke Ingram, Hyungwoo Kim, Michelle Pak, Jongpil Park, Robert Perry, James Reisinger, Yi Ren, Anthony Viola

Dancing Dragons

Design Partners	Adrian Smith and Gordon Gill
Management Partner	Robert Forest
Project Manager	Brian M. Jack
Senior Designer	Sara Beardsley
Senior Technical	Sae Hwang Oh
Interiors Director	John Burcher | Marc Cerone
Sustainability Director	Christopher Drew

Project Team; Miguel Alvarez, James Bayless, Frederik Berte, Brett Bridgeland, Ashley Byers, Sally Cathcart, Raymond Coleman, Rebecca Cryder, Sobieslaw Fedyk, Katrina Fernandez Nova, Patrick Fitzpatrick, Masumeh Geranpayeh, Brendan Gibbons, Felix Griggs, Kira Ho, Brooke Ingram, Qi Jia, Laura Jimenez, Tamara Jimshitashvili, Hyungwoo Kim, Lin Kim, Soo Hye Kim, Hans Koesters, June Hae Lee, Soeun Lee, Randi Lesniewski, Takuya Mamada, Jonathan Orlove, Michelle Pak, Jongpil Park, Catherine Rogg, Mostapha Roudsari, David Schweim, Chen-Han Tu, Brent Watanabe, Margaret Yoo

1 Park Avenue

Design Partners	Adrian Smith and Gordon Gill
Management Partner	Robert Forest
Project Manager	Ben Johnson
Senior Designer	Jeff Stafford and Fei Xu
Senior Technical	Peter Weismantle
Senior Technical	Donald Stark

Project Team: Leslie Baluga, Charles Collett, Joshua Cooper, Richard Cosgrove, Patrick Fitzpatrick, Brendan Gibbons, Simon Gore, Christopher Harvey, Jessica Hogue, Darren Hoppa, Zhya Jacobs, Matthew Nyweide, David Rariden, Bradley Riemann, Siddant Sinha, Teddy Slowik, Rebecca Stewart, Abhijit Thenge, Bradley Wilkins

Team

Zhongzhou Holdings Financial Center

Design Partners Adrian Smith and Gordon Gill
Management Partner Robert Forest
Project Manager Brian M. Jack
Senior Designer Jeff Stafford
Senior Technical Peter Weismantle | Iris Gan
China Director Weiwei Luo

Project Team: Fred Afshari, Mohamad Araji, Gabriel Bunea, April Chen, Gregg Herman, Travis Howe, Ben Johnson, Xiang Li, Matthew Nyweide, Luis Palacio, Jason Smith, Joshua Smith, Renato Tonelli, Anthony Trifiletti, Anthony Viola, Brent Watanabe

Mile High Prototype

Design Partners Adrian Smith and Gordon Gill
Management Partner Robert Forest
Senior Designer Dennis Rehill and Anthony Viola

Project Team: Miguel Alvarez, Chris Harvey, Alejandro Stochetti, Matthew Nyweide, Brent Watanabe, Ashley Satterfield

FKI Tower

Design Partners Adrian Smith and Gordon Gill
Management Partner Robert Forest
Project Manager Brian M. Jack | Ben Johnson
Senior Designer Juan Betancur
Senior Technical Sae Hwang Oh
Interiors Director John Burcher

Project Team: Elyse Agnello, Miguel Alvarez, Olga Anaya, Sara Beardsley, Rachael Bennett, Alexis Burson, Marc Cerone, April Chen, Colin Craig, Rebecca Cryder, Michelle Dumont, Patrick Fitzpatrick, Danielle Gharst, Brendan Gibbons, Felix Griggs, Ryan Hayes, Gregg Herman, Kira Ho, Jessica Hogue, Brian Hubbard, Jeffrey Knapke, So Young Lee, Soeun Lee, David LeFevre, Michael Newton, Vanessa Newton, Tyler Noblin, Steven Pantazis, David Rariden, Dennis Rehill, Daniel Retzner, Beumhyeung Rhee, Sean Satterfield, Martin Salas, Corey Schnobrich, Daniel Seagraves, Joshua Smith, Eric Snow, Anthony Viola, Michael Waldo, Brent Watanabe, Peter Weismantle, Bradley Wilkins, Marc Woodcock

Meraas Tower

Design Partners Adrian Smith and Gordon Gill
Management Partner Robert Forest
Senior Designer Fei Xu

Project Team: Olga Anaya, Megan Beidler, Gail Borthwick, Jeffrey Boyer, Brendan Gibbons, Kira Ho, Tyler Noblin, Brent Schuettpeltz, Les Ventsch, Nathan Woods

Clean Technology Tower

Design Partners Adrian Smith and Gordon Gill
Management Partner Robert Forest
Senior Designer Les Ventsch

Project Team: Ann Buckman, Jorge Soler, Brad Wilkins

Gang Xia Tower

Design Partners Adrian Smith and Gordon Gill
Management Partner Robert Forest
Project Manager Ben Johnson
Senior Designer Jeff Stafford
Senior Technical Peter Weismantle | Iris Gan
China Director Weiwei Luo

Project Team: Olga Anaya, Rachel Banach, Brett Bridgeland, Gabriel Bunea, John Burcher, Sarah Cathcart, Marc Cerone, April Chen, Raymond Coleman, Rebecca Cryder, Sobieslaw Fedyk, Felix Griggs, Jessica Hogue, Travis Howe, Brian Hubbard, Robert Jillson, Laura Jimenez, Bethany Johnson, Randi Lesniewski, Xiang Li, Liu Liu, Emily McGuire, Luis Palacio, Daniel Ramos, Katie Rariden, Daniel Retzner, Beumhyeung Rhee, Mostapha Sadeghipour Roudsari, Rachel Sears, Daniel Segraves, Matthew Simpson, Jason Smith, Joshua Smith, Afaq Syed, Renato Tonelli, Anthony Trifiletti, Anthony Viola, Michael Waldo, Brent Watanabe, Siyuan Zhang

Zhongzhou Holdings Financial Center

Design Partners	Adrian Smith and Gordon Gill
Management Partner	Robert Forest
Project Manager	Brian M. Jack
Senior Designer	Jeff Stafford
Senior Technical	Peter Weismantle | Iris Gan
China Director	Weiwei Luo

Project Team: Fred Afshari, Mohamad Araji, Gabriel Bunea, April Chen, Gregg Herman, Travis Howe, Ben Johnson, Xiang Li, Matthew Nyweide, Luis Palacio, Jason Smith, Joshua Smith, Renato Tonelli, Anthony Trifiletti, Anthony Viola, Brent Watanabe

160 Front Street

Design Partners	Adrian Smith and Gordon Gill
Management Partner	Robert Forest
Project Manager	Jonathan Orlove
Senior Designer	Laura Jimenez
China Technical	Sae Hwang Oh
Sustainability Director	Christopher Drew

Project Team: Ethan Alspaugh, Nora Ames, Tyler Austin, Rachael Bennett, Nicholas Berchtold, Aaron Berman, Frederik Berte, John Burcher, Sarah Cathcart, Marc Cerone, Alexis Crates, Rebecca Cryder, Nathan Diestelkamp, Stephen Dinnen, Michelle Dumont, Elliot Eakin, Kiel Fahnstrom, Keara Fanning, Kyle Faulkner, Katrina Fernandez Nova, Patrick Fitzpatrick, Brendan Gibbons, Gail Goldstead, Rebecca Greenberg, Felix Griggs, Heng Gu, Kira Ho, Jessica Hogue, Travis Howe, Tamara Jimshitashivili, Nishtha Kandoi, Joel Kerner, Hyungwoo Kim, Ryan Kukuraitis, Rebecca Lemaster, Xiang Li, Alvaro Luna, Jose Marti, Tashio Martinez, Christopher Miller, Loran Newman, Levy Nguyen, Heidi Nickel, Sae Hwang Oh, Michelle Pak, Jongpil Park, Griffin Pemberton, Shawn Phillips, Natalia Quintanilla, Benjamin Raines, Daniel Ramos, Daniel Retzner, Catherine Rogg, Leslie Sadkowski, Michael Sandrzyk, Alondra Santos, David Schweim, Holden Scully, Arham Siddiqui, Michaela Singson, Chad Smith, Jeff Snodgrass, Donald Stark, Milica Stojsavljevic, James Struthers, Nikita Troufanov, Pablo Velazquez, Christopher Walker, Ning Wang, Alexis Wilson, Fei Xu, Meng Zhang, Siyuan Zhang

Vantone Center Tianjin

Design Partners	Adrian Smith and Gordon Gill
Management Partner	Robert Forest
Project Manager	Jonathan Orlove
Senior Designer	Fei Xu
Senior Technical	Iris Gan
China Director	Weiwei Luo

Project Team: John Burcher, Eric Cheng, Marc Cerone, Raymond Coleman, Colin Craig, Michelle Dumont, Iris Gan, Felix Griggs, Kira Ho, Jessica Hogue, Brooke Ingram, Tamara Jimshitashvili, Ben Johnson, Hyungwoo Kim, Lin Kim, Soeun Lee, Rebecca Lemaster, Christopher Miller, Tyler Noblin, Sae Hwang Oh, Carlo Parente, Jongpil Park, James Reisinger, Daniel Retzner, Catherine Rogg, Rachel Sears, Jason Smith, Joshua Smith, Jorge Soler, Anthony Trifiletti, Chen-Han Tu, Anthony Viola

Ahlamana + Hilal Tower

Design Partners	Adrian Smith and Gordon Gill
Management Partner	Robert Forest
Project Manager	Ben Johnson | Jonathan Orlove
Senior Designer	Bradely Wilkins | Christopher Hurst
Senior Technical	Donald Stark

Project Team: Fred Afshari, Miguel Alvarez, George Baciu, Rachel Banach, Rachel Bennett, Brett Bridgeland, Hayes Brister, Gabriel Bunea, John Burcher, Ashley Byers, Marc Cerone, Raymond Coleman, Colin Craig, Rebecca Cryder, Thomas Demetrion, Michelle Dumont, Keara Fanning, Robert Finigan, Patrick Fitzpatrick, Iris Gan, Danielle Gharst, Felix Griggs, Christopher Harvey, Kira Ho, Jessica Hogue, Brian Hubbard, Shahed Hydari, Brendan Gibbons, Bethany Johnson, Brian M. Jack, Trudie Kahler, Lin Kim, Peter Kindel, So Young Lee, Soeun Lee, Ying Liu, Michael Newton, Matthew Nyweide, Robert Perry, Benjamin Raines, David Rariden, Beumhyeung Rhee, James Reisinger, Daniel Retzner, Alyson Reuter, Catherine Rogg, Daniel Ruberg, Martin Salas, Sean Satterfield, Corey Schnobrich, David Schweim, Rachel Sears, Matt Snoap, Jorge Soler, Amy Sonbuchner, Corey Thomas, Anthony Trifiletti, Angel Valtierra, Brent Watanabe

Team

830 Brickell

Design Partners	Adrian Smith and Gordon Gill
Management Partner	Robert Forest
Project Manager	Jonathan Orlove
Senior Designer	Sobieslaw Fedyk
Senior Technical	Sara Beardsley
Interiors Director	Marc Cerone
Sustainability Director	Christopher Drew

Project Team: Nicholas Berchtold, Jennifer Cooper, Bintou Coulibaly, Alexis Crates, Rebecca Cryder, Kiel Fahnstrom, Gail Goldstead, Rebecca Greenberg, Felix Griggs, Taylor Hess, Miaoqi Liu, Luis Palacio, Griffin Pemberton, Natalia Quintanilla, Mario Romero, Matthew Schneider, Arham Siddiqui, Chad Smith, Jeff Snodgrass, Michelle Swanson, Jennie Tolfa, Perry Wreaks

Renaissance District

Design Partners	Adrian Smith and Gordon Gill
Management Partner	Robert Forest
Project Manager	Ben Johson
Senior Designer	Luis Palacio
Sustainability Director	Christopher Drew

Project Team: Nora Ames, George Baciu, Sara Beardsley, Nicholas Berchtold, Frederik Berte, John Burcher, Ashley Byers, Sarah Cathcart, Marc Cerone, Rebecca Cryder, Michelle Dumont, Keara Fanning, Sobieslaw Fedyk, Katrina Fernandez Nova, Patrick Fitzpatrick, Joshua Frank, Iris Gan, Brendan Gibbons, Felix Griggs, Kira Ho, Jessica Hogue, Travis Howe, Dongsoo Jang, Qi Jia, Tamara Jimshitashivili, Angela Khermouch, Changhoon Kim, Hyungwoo Kim, Soeun Lee, Rebecca Lemaster, Randi Lesniewski, Melissa Marrero, Jose Marti, Tashio Martinez, Christopher Miller, Suncica Milosevic, Michelle Pak, Jongpil Park, Natalia Quintanilla, Benjamin Raines, Daniel Ramos, Hiram Rodriguez, Catherine Rogg, Rachel Sears, Matthew Simpson, Chad Smith, Jeff Snodgrass, Jorge Soler, Donald Stark, Milica Stojsavljevic, Zilong Tan, Jennie Tolfa, Nikita Troufanov, Chen-Han Tu, Luis Villafane, Anthony Viola, Brent Watanabe, Peter Weismantle, Matthew Wild, Jonathan Wilkinson, Richard Wilson, Fei Xu, Tianyu Xu, Jing Zhang, Yueming Zhou

Xiamen Oceanfront Center

Design Partners	Adrian Smith and Gordon Gill
Management Partner	Robert Forest
Project Manager	Ben Johson
Senior Designer	Alejandro Stochetti | Juan Betancur
City Design Director	Richard Wilson
China Director	Weiwei Luo
Sustainability Director	Christopher Drew

Project Team: Tyler Austin, Alexander Bahr, Sara Beardsley, Nicholas Berchtold, Marc Cerone, Allison Conley, Sobieslaw Fedyk, Iris Gan, Yongsan Huang, Brandon Kroger, Yifei Li, Miaoqi Liu, Natalia Quintanilla, Mario Romero, Michael Sandrzyk, Thomas Schneider, Jeff Snodgrass, Michelle Swanson, Zilong Tan, Amber Watkins, Peter Weismantle, Fei Xu, Dong Yan, Jing Zhang, Meng Zhang, Yuxin Zheng, Ruoqi Zhong, Yueming Zhou

High Tech Park

Design Partners	Adrian Smith and Gordon Gill
Management Partner	Robert Forest
Project Manager	Ben Johnson
Senior Designer	Jeff Stafford
Senior Technical	Iris Gan
China Director	Weiwei Luo

Project Team: Rachael Bennett, John Burcher, Marc Cerone, Katrina Fernandez Nova, Patrick Fitzpatrick, Krystian Gardula, Travis Howe, Brian Hubbard, Laura Jimenez, Lin Kim, Joshua Kuffner, Soeun Lee, David Lefevre, Liu Liu, Weiwei Luo, Matthew Nyweide, David Schweim, Rachel Sears, Jason Smith, Anthony Viola, Michael Waldo, Si Wu, Siyuan Zhang

Masdar Headquarters

Design Partners	Adrian Smith and Gordon Gill
Management Partner	Robert Forest
Project Manager	Jonathan Orlove
Senior Designer	Les Ventsch | Ying Liu
Senior Technical	Jorge Soler
Interiors Director	John Burcher | Marc Cerone
Sustainability Director	Christopher Drew

Project Team: Ahmed Abdeltam, Fred Afshari, Elyse Agnello, Fernando Alessandrini, Olga Anaya, Mohamad Araji, Gabriel Ball, Rachel Banach, Rachel Bennett, Emily Bernstein, Juan Betancur, Gail Borthwick, Nathan Bowman, Jeffrey Boyer, Hayes Brister, John Burcher, Alexis Burson, Ashley Byers, Marc Cerone, April Chen, Raymond Coleman, Charles Collett, Colin Craig, Rebecca Cryder, Sergio De Los Reyes, Thomas Dementrion, Christopher Drew, Michelle Dumont, Mark Farmer, Robert Finigan, Patrick Fitzpatrick, Iris Gan, Danielle Gharst, Brendan Gibbons, Autumn Godwin, Felix Griggs, Christina Halatsis, Jon Hiatt, Kira Ho, Travis Howe, Christopher Hurst, Shahed Hydari, Laura Jimenez, Bethany Johnson, So Young Lee, David LeFevre, Thomas Loveless, Michael Newton, Tyler Noblin, Matthew Nyweide, Andrew Osvalds, Luis Palacio, Carlo Parente, Robert Perry, Silviu Petrea, James Pint, Darren Poon, James Reisinger, Daniel Retzner, Beumhyeung Rhee, Bradley Riemann, Mario Romero, Martin Salas, Corey Schnobrich, Brent Schuettpelz, David Schweim, Daniel Segraves, Siddant Sinha, Teddy Slowik, Jason Smith, Joshua Smith, Amy Sonbuchner, Quentin Stanton, Donald Stark, Afaq Syed, Renato Tonelli, Tuan Tran, Anthony Trifiletti, Anthony Viola, Michael Waldo, Brent Watanabe, Eylul Wintermeyer, Julianna Wokurka, Marc Woodcock, Fei Xu

Incheon International Airport

Design Partners Adrian Smith and Gordon Gill
Management Partner Robert Forest
Project Manager Jonathan Orlove
Senior Designer Sara Beardsley
Senior Technical Sae Hwang Oh
Sustainability Director Christopher Drew

Project Team: Andrew Akins, George Baciu, Ali Bacon, James Bayless, Rachael Bennett, John Burcher, Sarah Cathcart, Marc Cerone, Colin Craig, Lin Kim, Peter Kindel, Joshua Kuffner, Matias La Serna, Vanessa Newton, Maria Palencia, Benjamin Raines, Katie Rariden, Dennis Rehill, Daniel Retzner, Mario Romero, David Schweim, Donald Stark, Leslie Ventsch, Andrew Zell

Kuwait University Master Plan

Design Partners Adrian Smith and Gordon Gill
Management Partner Robert Forest
Project Manager Brian M. Jack
Senior Designer Fei Xu

Project Team: Miguel Alvarez, Rebecca Cryder, Christopher Hurst, Brendan Gibbons, Michael Newton, Matthew Nyweide, David Rariden, Dennis Rehill, Bradley Riemann, Sean Satterfield, David Schweim, David Siegel, Siddant Sinha, Tuan Tran, Michael Waldo, Marc Woodcock

The Yard at Chicago Shakespeare Theater

Design Partners Adrian Smith and Gordon Gill
Management Partner Robert Forest
Project Manager Ben Johnson
Senior Designer Juan Betancur
Senior Technical Jorge Soler | Chad Smith
Interiors Director Marc Cerone

Project Team: Nora Ames, Nicholas Berchtold, Rebecca Cryder, Stephen Dinnen, Felix Griggs, Gail Goldstead, Travis Howe, Joel Kerner, Robert Jillson, Rebecca LeMaster, Jennie Matusova, Christopher Miller, Katrina Fernandez Nova, Darcy Osting, Andy Park, Natalia Quintanilla, Thomas Schneider, Matthew Snoap, Melissa Marrero, Jeff Snodgrass, Donald Stark, Milica Stojsavljevic, James Struthers, Maria Sturchio, Michelle Swanson, Jennie Tolfa, Alex Valverde, Zhaochen Wang

Chicago Architecture Center

Design Partners Adrian Smith and Gordon Gill
Management Partner Robert Forest
Project Manager Jonathan Orlove
Senior Technical Chad Smith
Interiors Director Marc Cerone

Project Team: Julie Bartocci, Rebecca Cryder, Ryan Dalgaard, Kiel Fahnstrom, Gail Goldstead, Felix Griggs, Griffin Pemberton, Mario Romero, Jeff Snodgrass, Michelle Swanson

Kellogg School of Management

Design Partners Adrian Smith and Gordon Gill
Management Partner Robert Forest
Project Manager Brian M. Jack
Senior Designer Carlo Parente
Interiors Director Marc Cerone
Sustainability Director Christopher Drew

Project Team: Miguel Alvarez, Ali Bacon, Sara Beardsley, Nathan Bowman, John Burcher, Ashley Byers, Sarah Cathcart, Colin Craig, Rebecca Cryder, Patrick Fitzpatrick, Brendan Gibbons, Felix Griggs, Jessica Hogue, Travis Howe, Brooke Ingram, Jocelyn Moriarty, Caroline Neill, Luis Palacio, Mario Romero, Sean Satterfield, Rachel Sears, Michelle Smearman, Jason Smith, Afaq Syed, Chen-Han Tu, Andrew Zell

KAPSARC

Design Partners Adrian Smith and Gordon Gill
Management Partner Robert Forest
Project Manager Brian M. Jack
Senior Designer Jeff Stafford
Senior Technical Peter Weismantle

Project Team: Miguel Alvarez, Gabriel Ball, Rachel Banach, Juan Betancur, Jeff Boyer, Brett Bridgeland, Gabriel Bunea, John Burcher, Alexis Burson, Ashley Byers, Rebecca Cryder, Thomas Denney, Danielle Gharst, Brendan Gibbons, Gregg Herman, Jessica Hogue, Travis Howe, Christopher Hurst, Ben Johnson, David LeFevre, Vanessa Newton, Michael Newton, Matthew Nyweide, Benjamin Raines, David Rariden, Dennis Rehill, Sean Satterfield, David Schweim, Daniel Segraves, Jason Smith, Joshua Smith, Michael Waldo, Brent Watanabe, Marc Woodcock, Fei Xu

Steppenwolf Theater Campus Expansion

Design Partners Adrian Smith and Gordon Gill
Management Partner Robert Forest
Project Manager Jonathan Orlove
Senior Designer Laura Jimenez
Senior Technical Sara Beardsley | Donald Stark
Interiors Director Marc Cerone

Project Team: Nora Ames, George Baciu, Jade Boudreaux, Marc Cerone, Allison Conley, Jennifer Cooper, Rebecca Cryder, Kiel Fahnstrom, Kyle Faulkner, Sobieslaw Fedyk, Felix Griggs, Gail Goldstead, Brandon Kroger, Yuchen Liu, Melissa Marrero, Jose Marti, Heidi Nickel, Luis Palacio, Griffin Pemberton, Michael Sandrzyk, Arham Siddiqui, Chad Smith, Alyson Hurd Sternquist, Christopher Strasser, James Struthers, Zilong Tan, Jennie Tolfa, Pablo Velazquez, Timothy Winstanley

Team

Willow Creek Community Church

Design Partners Adrian Smith and Gordon Gill
Management Partner Robert Forest
Project Manager Jonathan Orlove
Senior Designer Sara Beardsley
Technical Director Sae Huang Oh
Sustainability Director Christopher Drew

Project Team: George Baciu, Connor Borchardt, John Burcher, John Campbell, Marc Cerone, Sally Cathcart, Rebecca Cryder, Nathan Diestelkamp, Elliot Eakin, Rezvan Farahany, Kyle Faulkner, Joshua Frank, Gail Goldstead, Felix Griggs, Patrick Keeney, Ryan Kukuraitis, Rebecca LeMaster, Mateusz Nosek, Sae Hwang Oh, Darcy Osting, Michelle Pak, Natalia Quintanilla, Catherine Rogg, Christopher Strasser, Paul Thong, Luis Villafane, Jiajing Xie, Wie Yu

Willis Tower Greening Project + Hotel

Design Partners Adrian Smith and Gordon Gill
Management Partner Robert Forest
Project Manager Ben Johnson
Senior Designer Sara Beardsley

Project Team: Olga Anaya, Juan Betancur, Gail Borthwick, Alexis Burson, Ann Buckman, Ashley Byers, April Chen, Joshua Cooper, Ahmed Constable, Cara Ellis, Patrick Fitzpatrick, Iris Gan, Brendan Gibbons, Travis Howe, Brian Hubbard, Joshua Hutchison, Brian Kneesel, Soeun Lee, David LeFevre, Alex Martinez, Jason Minor, Kevin Nance, Michael Newton, Tyler Noblin, Jonathan Orlove, Luis Palacio, Mario Romero, Chung Rhee, Sean Satterfield, Kshitij Sawant, Brent Schuettpelz, Teddy Slowik, Jason Smith, Joshua Smith, Jorge Soler, Amy Sonbuchner, Anthony Viola, Alison Weeks, Peter Weismantle, Fei Xu

Sanya Haitang Bay Resort

Design Partners Adrian Smith and Gordon Gill
Management Partner Robert Forest
Project Manager Jonathan Orlove
Senior Designer Jeff Stafford
China Director Weiwei Luo
Sustainability Director Christopher Drew
Interiors Director John Burcher | Marc Cerone

Project Team: Ana Blomeier, Ian Bulling, Sarah Cathcart, Daniel Caven, Rebecca Cryder, Sobieslaw Fedyk, Katrina Fernandez Nova, Patrick Fitzpatrick, Iris Gan, Krystian Gardula, Brendan Gibbons, Felix Griggs, Kira Ho, Jessica Hogue, Travis Howe, Christopher Hurst, Brooke Ingram, Dongsoo Jang, Laura Jimenez, Tamara Jimshitashivili, Peter Kindel, June Hae Lee, Soeun Lee, Randi Lesniewski, Haoyu Li, Xiang Li, Andres Lopez Montoya, Luis Palacio, Catherine Rogg, Myongki Seong, Mohamed Sheriff, Matthew Simpson, Jason Smith, Leslie Ventsch, Michael Waldo, Brent Watanabe, Si Wu, Siyuan Zhang

Matrix Gateway, Wings Museum, and Crystal Center

Design Partners Adrian Smith and Gordon Gill
Management Partner Robert Forest
Design Director Leslie Ventsch
Project Manager Ben Johnson
Senior Designer Dennis Rehill

Project Team: Jeff Boyer, Brett Bridgeland, Brendan Gibbon, Andy Leitz, Ben Loeffler, Benjamin Raines, Alejandro Stochetti

Waldorf Astoria Beijing

Design Partners Adrian Smith and Gordon Gill
Management Partner Robert Forest
Project Manager Ben Johnson | Weiwei Luo
Senior Designer Fei Xu
Senior Technical Donald Stark

Project Team: Mohamad Araji, Rustem Baishev, Raymond Coleman, Michelle Dumont, Patrick Fitzpatrick, Joshua Frank, Brendan Gibbons, Shahed Hydari, Hyungwoo Kim, Michael Newton, Mengxi Li, Silviu Petrea, Sean Satterfield, Brent Schuettpelz, David Schweim, Afaq Syed, Michael Waldo

Hotel Atlantic

Design Partners Adrian Smith and Gordon Gill
Management Partner Robert Forest
Project Manager Jonathan Orlove
Senior Designer Sara Beardsley
Interiors Director John Burcher | Marc Cerone
Sustainability Director Christopher Drew

Project Team: Miguel Alvarez, Frederik Berte, Connor Borchardt, Sarah Cathcart, Nathan Diestelkamp, Elliot Eakin, Rezvan Farahany, Sobieslaw Fedyk, Katrina Fernandez Nova, Joshua Frank, Felix Griggs, Zachary Heaps, Lin Kim, Yong Jae Kim, Hans Koesters, Yu Kono, Rebecca Lemaster, Tashio Martinez, Lauren Mcclellan, Rucha Mehendale, Christopher Miller, Mateusz Nosek, Daniel Ramos, Dennis Rehill, Yi Ren, Catherine Rogg, Mostapha Sadeghipour Roudsari, Thomas Schneider, Mohamed Sheriff, Matthew Simpson, Nikita Troufanov

Lakeside Residential Towers

Design Partners Adrian Smith and Gordon Gill
Management Partner Robert Forest
Project Manager Matthew Dumich
City Design Director Richard Wilson
Senior Designer Alejandro Stochetti | David Schweim
Senior Technical Peter Weismantle

Project Team: Tyler Austin, Nicholas Berchtold, Allison Conley, Nathan Diestelkamp, Joel Kerner, Hyungwoo Kim, Soeun Lee, Jennie Matusova, Andy Park, Jonathan Reyes, Jay Schairbaum, Jeff Snodgrass, Alejandro Stochetti, Michelle Swanson, Zilong Tan, Alex Valverde, Timothy Winstanley

Una Residences

Design Partners Adrian Smith and Gordon Gill
Management Partner Robert Forest
Project Manager Jonathan Orlove
Senior Designer Alejandro Stochetti | David Schweim
Interiors Director Marc Cerone
Sustainability Director Christopher Drew

Project Team: Julie Bartocci, Sara Beardsley, Nicholas Berchtold, Juan Betancur, Marc Cerone, Rebecca Cryder, Ryan Dalgaard, Nathan Diestelkamp, Kiel Fahnstrom, Kyle Faulkner, Katrina Fernandez Nova, Gail Goldstead, Felix Griggs, Robert Jillson, Laura Jimenez, Changhoon Kim, Rebecca Lemaster, Mengxi Li, Weiwei Luo, Melissa Marrero, Sae Hwang Oh, Griffin Pemberton, Natalia Quintanilla, Seychelle Reed, Jonathan Reyes, Thomas Schneider, Alexander Semochkin, Myongki Seong, Arham Siddiqui, Chad Smith, Jeff Snodgrass, Jorge Soler, Alejandro Stochetti, Bailey Stultz, Maria Sturchio, Anthony Viola, Jonathan Wilkinson

The Mansion

Design Partners Adrian Smith and Gordon Gill
Management Partner Robert Forest
Senior Designer Carlo Parente

Project Team: Fred Afshari,Olga Anaya, Thomas Denney, Krystian Gardula, Autumn Godwin, Brian Kneesel, Hrishikesh Madane, Sae Hwang Oh, Luis Palacio, James Pint, Jorge Soler, Brent Schuettpelz, Alejandro Stochetti

Beijing Franshion Development

Design Partners Adrian Smith and Gordon Gill
Management Partner Robert Forest
Project Manager Ben Johnson
Senior Designer Carlo Parente

Project Team: Miguel Alvarez, Olga Anaya, Mohammad Araji, Nathan Bowman, Jeffrey Boyer, Brett Bridgeland, John Burcher, Ashley Byers, Marc Cerone, Thomas Demetrion, Michelle Dumont, Patrick Fitzpatrick, Krystian Gardula, Danielle Gharst, Brendan Gibbons, Felix Griggs, Christopher Harvey, Kira Ho, Travis Howe, Matthias Janikowski, Ying Liu, Weiwei Luo, Michael Newton, Tyler Noblin, Luis Palacio, Silviu Petrea, Benjamin Raines, James Reisinger, Albert Rhee, Rachel Sears, Renato Tonelli, Leslie Ventsch, Brent Watanabe, Marc Woodcock, Fei Xu

Imperial Tower

Design Partners Adrian Smith and Gordon Gill
Management Partner Robert Forest
Project Manager Jonathan Orlove
Senior Designer Carlo Parente
Sustainability Director Christopher Drew

Project Team: Rachel Bennett, Marc Cerone, Michelle Dumont, Patrick Fitzpatrick, Krystian Gardula, Brendan Gibbons, Matthias Janikowski, Michael Newton, Vanessa Newton, Tyler Noblin, Beumhyeung Rhee, Marc Woodcock

Burj Vista

Design Partners Adrian Smith and Gordon Gill
Management Partner Robert Forest
Project Manager Brian M. Jack | Ben Johnson
Senior Designer Alejandro Stochetti
Senior Technical Sae Hwang Oh

Project Team: Fernando Alessandrini, Olga Anaya, Nathan Bowman, Brett Bridgeland, Ann Buckman, Joshua Cooper, Colin Craig, Rebecca Cryder, Barbara Di Gregorio, David Ellis, Patrick Fitzpatrick, Brendan Gibbons, Simon Gore, Ryan Hanlon, Ryan Hayes, Jessica Hogue, Matthew Kidd, David LeFevre, Hrishikesh Madane, Ian Mills, Vanessa Newton, Matthew Nyweide, Steven Pantazis, Carlo Parente, Jean Reibel, Mario Romero, Sean Satterfield, Brent Schuettpelz, Siddant Sinha, Jorge Soler, Jeff Stafford, Matthew Stewart, Les Ventsch, Bradley Wilkins

Vancouver Residences

Design Partners Adrian Smith and Gordon Gill
Management Partner Robert Forest
Senior Designer Gail Borthwick

Project Team: Fred Afshari, Olga Anaya, Megan Beidler, Gail Borthwick, Brett Bridgeland, Hayes Brister, John Burcher, Ashley Byers, Joshua Cooper, Sergio De Los Reyes, David Ellis, Patrick Fitzpatrick, Jeff Gibbon, Brendan Gibbons, Gregg Herman, Darren Hoppa, Brian Hubbard, Bethany Johnson, Matthew Kidd, Alex Martinez, Michael Newton, Tyler Noblin, Luis Palacio, James Pint, Mario Romero, Brent Schuettpelz, Teddy Slowik, Jorge Soler, Jeff Stafford, Bradley Wilkins, Nathaniel Woods

Yixing Dongju Far East Development

Design Partners Adrian Smith and Gordon Gill
Management Partner Robert Forest
Project Manager Brian M. Jack
Senior Designer Fei Xu
China Director Weiwei Luo

Project Team: Juan Betancur, John Burcher, Ashley Byers, Patrick Fitzpatrick, Brendan Gibbons, Brian Hubbard, Christopher Hurst, Michael Newton, Tyler Noblin, Matthew Nyweide, David Rariden, Sean Satterfield, David Schweim, Daniel Segraves, Jason Smith, Brent Watanabe

Elphinstone + Jupiter Mills

Design Partners Adrian Smith and Gordon Gill
Management Partner Robert Forest
Senior Designer Les Ventch

Project Team: Olga Anaya, Gail Borthwick, Nathan Bowman, April Chen, Joshua Cooper, Cara Ellis, David Ellis, Ryan Hayes, Jessica Hogue, Jeff Gibbon, Brendan Gibbons, Luis Palacio, Hrishikesh Madane, Alex Martinez, Carlo Parente, Nalin Ramkumar, Mario Romero, Kshitij Sawant, Teddy Slowik, Jorge Soler, Matthew Stewart, Les Ventsch

Team

Burj Khalifa Gatehouses

Design Partners	Adrian Smith and Gordon Gill
Management Partner	Robert Forest
Project Manager	Brian M. Jack | Ben Johnson
Senior Designer	Alejandro Stochetti

Project Team: Fred Afshari, Leslie Baluga, Brett Bridgeland, Gabriel Bunea, Anthony Cissell, Charles Collett, Autumn Godwin, Benjamin Harber, Kira Ho, Joshua Hutchinson, Thomas Loveless, Michael Newton, Luis Palacio, Carlo Parente, Bradley Riemann, Jorge Soler, Donald Stark, Alejandro Stochetti, Abhijit Thenge, Anthony Trifiletti, Peter Weismantle, Nathaniel Woods

Dubai Bridge

Design Partners	Adrian Smith and Gordon Gill
Management Partner	Robert Forest
Project Manager	Brian M. Jack
Designer	Brett Bridgeland

Project Team: Kaaren Rutherford

Chicago Eco-Bridge

Design Partners	Adrian Smith and Gordon Gill
Management Partner	Robert Forest
Master Planning	Peter Kindel
Senior Designer	Jeff Stafford

Project Team: Gail Borthwick, Ann Buckman, Patrick Fitzpatrick, Brendan Gibbons, Brian Hubbard, Peter Kindel, Michael Newton, Brent Schuettpelz, Daniel Segraves, Jason Smith, Michael Waldo, Brent Watanabe

Golden Cross Sky Ring

Design Partners	Adrian Smith and Gordon Gill
Management Partner	Robert Forest
Project Manager	Ben Johnson
Senior Designer	Fei Xu
China Director	Weiwei Luo
Sustainability Director	Christopher Drew

Project Team: Olga Anaya, Rachael Bennett, Jeffrey Boyer, John Burcher, Marc Cerone, Colin Craig, Michelle Dumont, Patrick Fitzpatrick, Danielle Gharst, Brendan Gibbons, Felix Griggs, Soeun Lee, Michael Newton, Silviu Petrea, Dennis Rehill, Sean Satterfield, David Schweim, Rachel Sears, Daniel Segraves, Joshua Smith, Brent Watanabe

Solar Canopy/EV Dock

Design Partners	Adrian Smith and Gordon Gill
Management Partner	Robert Forest
Project Manager	Brian M. Jack
Senior Designer	Carol Parente

Project Team: Jeffrey Boyer, Thomas Loveless, Luis Palacio

Astana Expo City 2017

Design Partners	Adrian Smith and Gordon Gill
Management Partner	Robert Forest
Project Manager	Brian M. Jack | Matthew Dumich
Design Director	Alejandro Stochetti
Senior Technical	Jorge Soler | Sara Beardsley | Sae Hwang Oh
City Design Director	Richard Wilson
Interiors Director	John Burcher | Marc Cerone
Sustainability Director	Christopher Drew

Project Team: Miguel Alvarez, Nora Ames, Regine Antenor, Brian Apple, Tyler Austin, George Baciu, Rustem Baishev, Ross Battoclette, Nicholas Berchtold, Frederik Berte, Olga Block, John Burcher, Jessica Butler, Daniel Caven, Marc Cerone, Jae Yun Cho, Sung Jin Cho, Dan Coleman, Allison Conley, Rebecca Cryder, Katherine Dailey, Seth Davis, James Deane, Nathan Diestelkamp, Stephen Dinnen, Emily Doom, Iliana Doytcheva, Elliot Eakin, Mihael Efremov, Peter Eichberger, Keara Fanning, Rezvan Farahany, Kyle Faulkner, Sobieslaw Fedyk, Dian Feng, Katrina Fernandez Nova, Marshall Ford, Natalya Ganyukova, Dimitra Gelagoti, Richard Gnat, Gail Goldstead, Thomas Gonzalez, Zachary Grajewski, Felix Griggs, Heng Gu, Victoria Gueglio Saccone, Brian Havener, Kira Ho, Theodore Hogan, Chuen-huei Huang, Richard Huizenga, Robert Jillson, Don Kalant Jr, Patrick Keeney, Joel Kerner, Hyungwoo Kim, Lin Kim, Paul Kim, Yong Jae Kim, Peter Kindel, Alexander Knowles, Sunghak Ko, Hans Koesters, Yu Kono, Ryan Kukuraitis, Soeun Lee, Rebecca LeMaster, Haoyu Li, Mengxi Li, Xiang Li, Yuchen Liu, Liam Lowry, Weiwei Luo, Jaclyn Marcus, Melissa Marrero, Tashio Martinez, Jennie Matusova, Christopher Miller, Dean Mueller, Miriam Neet, Mateusz Nosek, David Osmond, Darcy Osting, Michelle Pak, Luis Palacio, Jongpil Park, Sarah Park, Youngmi Park, Shawn Phillips, Viorica Pisau, Trevor Ponder, Natalia Quintanilla, Kaleb Quirin, Benjamin Raines, Daniel Ramos, Michael Reinersman, Yi Ren, Alyson Reuter, Jonathan Reyes, Catherine Rogg, Mario Romero, Mostapha Sadeghipour Roudsari, Thomas Schneider, Paul Schroeckenstein, Katherine Seaver, Myongki Seong, Mohamed Sheriff, Matthew Simpson, Chad Smith, Matt Snoap, Jeff Snodgrass, Yaroslav Soltys, Jiatuo Song, Youngin Song, Donald Stark, Christopher Strasser, Maria Sturchio, Michelle Swanson, Zilong Tan, Jennie Tolfa, Anthony Trifiletti, Nikita Troufanov, Alex Valverde, Luis Villafane, Anthony Viola, Zhaochen Wang, Kirsten Weismantle, Preston Welker, Matthew Wild, Jonathan Wilkinson, Timothy Winstanley, Fei Xie, Jiajing Xie, Fei Xu, Shuonan Yang

World Expo 2020 Dubai

Design Partners Adrian Smith and Gordon Gill
Management Partner Robert Forest
Project Manager Matthew Dumich
Design Director Alejandro Stochetti
City Design Director Richard Wilson
Senior Technical Peter Weismantle
Interiors Director Marc Cerone
Sustainability Director Christopher Drew

Project Team: Narjes Abbasabadi, Tyler Austin, Alexander Bahr, Gregory Barber, Sara Beardsley, Nicholas Berchtold, Aaron Berman, Alison Conley, Jennifer Cooper, Rebecca Cryder, Stephen Dinnen, Tobias Dold, Kiel Fahnstrom, Kyle Faulkner, Sobieslaw Fedyk, Katrina Fernandez Nova, Gail Goldstead, Felix Griggs, Victoriano Hernandez, Theodore Hogan, Brian Jack, Lizhi Jiang, Joel Kerner, Changhoon Kim, Sunghak Ko, Ryan Kukuraitis, Inyong Lee, Soeun Lee, Yifei Li, Miaoqi Liu, Yuchen Liu, Yue Liu, Alvaro Luna, Melissa Marrero, Jose Marti, Cory Mollet, Dilip Muralidharan, Christian Newman, Loran Newman, Sae Hwang Oh, Hazem Owais, Luis Palacio, Griffin Pemberton, Jessica Pfeiffer, Natalia Quintanilla, Daniel Ramos, Hiram Rodriguez, Mario Romero, Michael Sandrzyk, Thomas Schneider, Michaela Singson, Jeff Snodgrass, Donald Stark, Alyson Hurd Sternquist, James Struthers, Michelle Swanson, Jennie Tolfa, Eric Tomich, Pablo Velazquez, Ning Wang, Amber Watkins, Timothy Winstanley, Xi Yi, Yuxin Zheng, Ruoqi Zhong

Xixian Great City

Design Partners Adrian Smith and Gordon Gill
Management Partner Robert Forest
Project Manager Brian M. Jack | Ben Johnson
Master Planning Peter Kindel
China Director Weiwei Luo
Sustainability Director Christopher Drew

Project Team: Miguel Alvarez, Sara Beardsley, Yu Chen, Katherine Dailey, Keara Fanning, Katrina Fernandez Nova, Patrick Fitzpatrick, Joshua Frank, Iris Gan, Brendan Gibbons, London Huenefeld, Soeun Lee, Xiang Li, Lauren Mcclellan, Olia Miho, Luis Palacio, Benjamin Raines, Daniel Ramos, Yi Ren, Daniel Retzner, James Rosen, Mostapha Sadeghipour Roudsari, Christopher Walker, Si Wu, Xi Yi, Jing Zhang

Mumbai Master Plan

Design Partners Adrian Smith and Gordon Gill
Management Partner Robert Forest
Project Manager Jonathan Orlove

Project Team: Elyse Agnello, Jeffrey Boyer, Brett Bridgeland, Ahmed Constable, Matthew Hall, Zhya Jacobs, Soeun Lee, Daniel Segraves, Quentin Stanton, Bradley Wilkins, Marc Woodcock

Za'abeel Master Plan

Design Partners Adrian Smith and Gordon Gill
Management Partner Robert Forest
Senior Designer Juan Betancur | Sara Beardsley

Project Team: Elyse Agnello, Alexis Burson, Ahmed Constable, Josh Hutchinson, Brian Kneesel, Michael Newton, Chung Rhee, Josh Smith, Anthony Viola

Great City Chengdu

Design Partners Adrian Smith and Gordon Gill
Management Partner Robert Forest
Project Manager Brian M. Jack | Ben Johnson
Master Planning Peter Kindel
China Director Weiwei Luo
Sustainability Director Christopher Drew

Project Team: Kirsten Bladh, Ana Blomeier, Nathan Bowman, Jeffrey Boyer, Brett Bridgeland, Hayes Brister, David Erven, Patrick Fitzpatrick, Masumeh Geranpayeh, Brendan Gibbons, Russell Gilchrist, Christopher Harvey, Travis Howe, Brian Hubbard, Qi Jia, Laura Jimenez, David Lefevre, Ying Liu, Suncica Milosevic, Luis Palacio, Carlo Parente, Robert Perry, Benjamin Raines, Katie Rariden, Dennis Rehill, Yi Ren, Daniel Ruberg, Mostapha Sadeghipour Roudsari, Sean Satterfield, David Schweim, Daniel Segraves, Michelle Smearman, Jeff Stafford, Donald Stark, Afaq Syed, Brent Watanabe, Si Wu, Fei Xu

Tianfu New District

Design Partners Adrian Smith and Gordon Gill
Management Partner Robert Forest
Project Manager Brian M. Jack | Ben Johnson
Master Planning Peter Kindel
China Director Weiwei Luo
Sustainability Director Christopher Drew

Project Team: Mariela Bayer, Rachael Bennett, Frederik Berte, Juan Betancur, Ana Blomeier, Daniel Caven, Katherine Dailey, Keara Fanning, Kyle Faulkner, Katrina Fernandez Nova, Brian Havener, Joel Kerner, Angela Khermouch, Hyungwoo Kim, Soeun Lee, Haoyu Li, Xiang Li, Luis Palacio, Jongpil Park, Yi Ren, Mario Romero, Mostapha Sadeghipour Roudsari, Paul Schroeckenstein, Myongki Seong, Shuonan Yang, Xi Yi, Jing Zhang

Chicago Central Area DeCarbonization Plan

Design Partners Adrian Smith and Gordon Gill
Management Partner Robert Forest
Senior Designer Sara Beardsley | Gail Borthwick
Master Planning Peter J. Kindel
Engineer Jeffrey Boyer
Sustainability Director Christopher Drew

Project Team: Miguel Alvarez, Rachael Bennett, Nathan Bowman, Gabriel Bunea, Hayes Brister, Ashley Byers, Michelle Dumont, Iris Gan, Gregg Herman, Brian Hubbard, Christopher Hurst, Brian Jack, Jocelyn Moriarty, Kevin Nance, Carrie Neill, Tyler Noblin, Matthew Nyweide, Jonathan Orlove, Luis Palacio, Robert Perry, Silviu Petrea, David Rariden, Dennis Rehill, Sean Satterfield, David Schweim, Daniel Segraves, Jeffrey Stafford, Katherine Smith, Jason Smith, Leslie Ventsch, Michael Waldo, Brent Watanabe, Brad Wilkins, Marc Woodcock

Photography

Jeddah Tower
All images © Adrian Smith + Gordon Gill Architecture

Central Park Tower
Photography © Extell Development pp. 25, 30; © Michael Young p. 26
All other images © Adrian Smith + Gordon Gill Architecture

Chengdu Greenland Tower
Photography © Greenland Group pp. 38-40
All other images © Adrian Smith + Gordon Gill Architecture

Wuhan Greenland Tower
Photography © Huang Shiyong pp. 49-50
All other images © Adrian Smith + Gordon Gill Architecture

Shenzhen-Hong Kong International Center
All images © Adrian Smith + Gordon Gill Architecture

South Hexi Yuzui Financial District
All images © Adrian Smith + Gordon Gill Architecture

Dancing Dragons
All images © Adrian Smith + Gordon Gill Architecture

The Biophilic Tower
All images © Adrian Smith + Gordon Gill Architecture

1 Dubai
All images © Adrian Smith + Gordon Gill Architecture

1 Park Avenue
All images © Adrian Smith + Gordon Gill Architecture

Park Gate
All images © Adrian Smith + Gordon Gill Architecture

Meraas Tower
All images © Adrian Smith + Gordon Gill Architecture

Mile High Prototype
All images © Adrian Smith + Gordon Gill Architecture

Clean Technology Tower
All images © Adrian Smith + Gordon Gill Architecture

FKI Tower
Photography © Namgoong Sun pp. 135-137, 140-144
All other images © Adrian Smith + Gordon Gill Architecture

Gang Xia Tower
All images © Adrian Smith + Gordon Gill Architecture

Zhongzhou Holdings Financial Center
Photography © ShuHe Architectural Photography Studio pp. 153, 155-156
All other images © Adrian Smith + Gordon Gill Architecture

Vantone Center Tianjin
All images © Adrian Smith + Gordon Gill Architecture

160 Front Street
All images © Adrian Smith + Gordon Gill Architecture

Ahlamana
All images © Adrian Smith + Gordon Gill Architecture

Hilal Tower
All images © Adrian Smith + Gordon Gill Architecture

830 Brickell
All images © Adrian Smith + Gordon Gill Architecture

High Tech Park
All images © Adrian Smith + Gordon Gill Architecture

Renaissance District
Photography © Renaissance District p. 188
All other images © Adrian Smith + Gordon Gill Architecture

Masdar Headquarters
All images © Adrian Smith + Gordon Gill Architecture

Xiamen Oceanfront Center
All images © Adrian Smith + Gordon Gill Architecture

Incheon International Airport
All images © Adrian Smith + Gordon Gill Architecture

Kellogg School of Management
All images © Adrian Smith + Gordon Gill Architecture

Kuwait University Master Plan
All images © Adrian Smith + Gordon Gill Architecture

KAPSARC
All images © Adrian Smith + Gordon Gill Architecture

The Yard at Chicago Shakespeare Theater
Photography © James Steinkamp pp. 237, 242; Chuck Osgood p. 240; Vito Palmisano p. 241
All other images © Adrian Smith + Gordon Gill Architecture

Chicago Architecture Center
Photography © James Steinkamp pp. 245-250

Steppenwolf Theatre Campus Expansion
Photography © James Steinkamp pp. 253-258

Willow Creek Community Church
Photography © Tom Rossiter pp. 261, 266-270
All other images © Adrian Smith + Gordon Gill Architecture

Matrix Gateway Complex
All images © Adrian Smith + Gordon Gill Architecture

Wings Museum
All images © Adrian Smith + Gordon Gill Architecture

Crystal Center
All images © Adrian Smith + Gordon Gill Architecture

Willis Tower Greening Project + Hotel
All images © Adrian Smith + Gordon Gill Architecture

Waldorf Astoria Beijing
Photography © ShuHe Architectural Photography Studio pp. 299-306

Hotel Atlantic
All images © Adrian Smith + Gordon Gill Architecture

Sanya Haitang Bay Resort
All images © Adrian Smith + Gordon Gill Architecture

Lakeside Residential Towers
All images © Adrian Smith + Gordon Gill Architecture

Una Residences
All images © Adrian Smith + Gordon Gill Architecture

Burj Visa
Photography © Ales Vyslouzil pp. 337, 340
All other images © Adrian Smith + Gordon Gill Architecture

The Mansion
All images © Adrian Smith + Gordon Gill Architecture

Vancouver Residences
All images © Adrian Smith + Gordon Gill Architecture

Beijing Franshion Development
All images © Adrian Smith + Gordon Gill Architecture

Yixing Dongju Far East Development
All images © Adrian Smith + Gordon Gill Architecture

Imperial Tower
All images © Adrian Smith + Gordon Gill Architecture

Elphinstone + Jupiter Mills
All images © Adrian Smith + Gordon Gill Architecture

Burj Khalifa Gatehouses
Photography © James Steinkamp pp. 381-382
All other images © Adrian Smith + Gordon Gill Architecture

Solar Canopy/EV Dock
Photography © Connor Steinkamp pp. 385, 387-388
All other images © Adrian Smith + Gordon Gill Architecture

Dubai Bridge
All images © Adrian Smith + Gordon Gill Architecture

Golden Cross Sky Ring
All images © Adrian Smith + Gordon Gill Architecture

Chicago Eco-Bridge
All images © Adrian Smith + Gordon Gill Architecture

Astana Expo City 2017
Photography © Leyla Kabdi pp. 405, 421; Nick Melnichenko pp. 406, 417; Mapache p. 419; Diego Fiore p. 424; Shutterstock_713671489 p. 426
All other images © Adrian Smith + Gordon Gill Architecture

World Expo 2020 Dubai
Photography © Expo 2020 Dubai LLC pp. 429, 432-433
All other images © Adrian Smith + Gordon Gill Architecture

Great City Chengdu
All images © Adrian Smith + Gordon Gill Architecture

Xixian Great City
All images © Adrian Smith + Gordon Gill Architecture

Tianfu New District
All images © Adrian Smith + Gordon Gill Architecture

Mumbai Master Plan
All images © Adrian Smith + Gordon Gill Architecture

Za'abeel Master Plan
All images © Adrian Smith + Gordon Gill Architecture

Chicago Central Area DeCarbonization Plan
All images © Adrian Smith + Gordon Gill Architecture